MAINE BIOGRAPHIES

HARRIE B. COE

Reprinted in Two Volumes

Volume II

CLEARFIELD

Originally published as *Maine Resources, Attractions, and Its People:*
A History, 4 volumes, ed. Harrie B. Coe
New York, 1928

Volume IV [Biographies] reprinted for Clearfield Company, Inc. by
Genealogical Publishing Co , Inc.
Baltimore, Maryland, 2002

International Standard Book Number: 0-8063-5126-8
Set Number 0-8063-5124-1
Made in the United States of America

NOTE: The numerous illustrations originally included in this volume of
Maine Resources, Attractions, and Its People: A History were
not reproduced in the Clarfield Company reprint.

JUDGE CHARLES PUTNAM BARNES— Consideration of the essential support given by the American judicial system by the maintenance of political institutions throughout the history of this country points to the importance of individual judges. A community looks at its own judges, not at the system as a whole. The public feels assured of justice with juries of experience, of integrity, and of ability. These high officials must perform arduous and manifold duties, but they must above all uphold and enhance the dignity and weight of the judiciary. The Supreme Court of Maine has notably lived up to such a high ideal, individually and collectively. To reach a place there as Associate Justice, Charles Putnam Barnes, of Houlton, Maine, has served his fellow citizens long and ably as a lawyer, as an inspiring political leader, as a public-spirited citizen. He has proved his fitness.

Charles Putnam Barnes was born in Houlton, October 12, 1869, son of Francis and Isa A. (Putnam) Barnes, and descendant of a Revolutionary hero. He was educated in the local public schools and Ricker Classical Institute in preparation for college, and at Colby College, receiving the degree of Bachelor of Arts in 1892, that of Master of Arts in 1893, and Doctor of Laws in 1927. In 1923 the University of Michigan conferred on Judge Barnes the degree of Master of Arts. The first eight years of his maturity were spent in teaching. At the same time he was preparing for the legal profession by reading in the office of Judge Joseph W. Symonds at Portland. He was principal of the Norway and Lisbon, Maine, high schools, and later of the Attleboro, Massachusetts, High School, passing from that activity to the executive post of superintendent of the Norway Schools. His interest in education has continued unabated, and Judge Barnes has been a member of the school boards of Norway and Houlton.

Since his admission to the bar in 1900, and until his appointment to the bench, in 1924, he has been primarily concerned with his practice of the law. His early office was in Norway, and his growing reputation led to his selection for the office of attorney of Oxford County, in 1905. In 1909 he resigned to take up the duties of Assistant Attorney General of Maine. When he resigned in 1911, he made his headquarters at Houlton, where for twelve years he managed a growing practice and shared actively in all civic affairs. He is a trustee of the Houlton Public Library, the Ricker Classical Institute, Colby College, and the Houlton Savings Bank. He served Aroostook County as Food Administrator during the World War period. During this period his name came into wider prominence in connection with State politics, for he was Commissioner for Maine on the National Commission on Uniform State Laws from 1913 to 1921, and member of the Maine House of Representatives from 1917 to 1921, serving as Speaker the last term. It was in 1924 that this active and proven lawyer and citizen was appointed Associate Justice of the Supreme Judicial Court of Maine by Governor Baxter. He believes in the independence of the judiciary, the need of better legal education, the simplification of practice, and the necessity for putting a check on waste of time in the trial of cases. He has the confidence and respect alike of litigants and the general public.

In fraternal and social circles Judge Barnes is popular. He is a member of the Delta Kappa Epsilon fraternity and the Free and Accepted Masons, and of the Medunxkeag Club. He belongs also to the American Bar Association and to the Sons of the Maine Bar Association, and to the American Revolution. His political allegiance is given to the Republican party. Judge Barnes is a communicant of the Baptist church.

August 19, 1896, Charles Putnam Barnes married, at Norway, Maine, Annie Maud Richardson, a native of that town, daughter of Albert and Louise (Larkin) Richardson. Mrs. Barnes is also prominent in local progress, a member of the Woman's Christian Temperance Union, the Daughters of the American Revolution, the Order of the Eastern Star, the American Legion Auxiliary, the Sigma Kappa, the Houlton Woman's

Club, the Houlton Music Club, and the American Association of University Women. She is a Guardian of the Camp Fire Girls and a communicant of the First Baptist Church. Children: Phineas P., John A., George B., Margaret L., and Francis Barnes.

RAY R. STEVENS—In the comparatively short time in which he has been in Island Falls as manager of the Island Falls branch of the Katahdin Trust Company, of Patten, Maine, Ray R. Stevens has proved himself to be a man of keen judgment and sound business ability. Before he came to Island Falls, he was employed in Ashland, where he was also engaged in banking. Previous to his banking experience, Mr. Stevens was interested in several other types of work, and was, among other things, in the Naval Reserve, in which he served for two and one-half years.

He was born in Ashland, Maine, on March 3, 1894, the son of David B. and Esther (Robinson) Stevens, both of Ashland, where they were farmers. As a boy he attended the public schools of Ashland, his native town, and was graduated from the high school there in the class of 1912. Thereupon he became a student in the University of Maine, in which he was a member of the class of 1917. At length he left the University to enter the service of his country, enlisted in Portland in the Naval Reserve, and served two and one-half years as ship cook. Finally he was discharged in New York City with the rank of junior lieutenant. After he received his discharge, he became employed in the offices of the Fish River Lumber Company, where he remained for two years, at the end of which time he became manager of the potato house, at Ashland, for C. C. Brewer, of Presque Isle. He left this position to go with the Ashland Trust Company, in Ashland, for which institution he was assistant treasurer. When he had been with the Ashland Trust Company for four years, he left that position to come to Island Falls where, since November 1, 1926, he has been manager of the Island Falls branch of the Katahdin Trust Company, of Patten. Although Mr. Stevens is kept busy with his business activity, he has time to participate actively in the fraternal life of his community, being a member of the Free and Accepted Masons, in which order he is affiliated with the Blue Lodge, in Ashland, and with the Chapter, in Houlton.

Ray R. Stevens married Agnes Warman, who was born in Ludlow, Maine, the daughter of Fred and Jane (Green) Warman. Ray R. and Agnes (Warman) Stevens are the parents of one child, Marian Virginia. The Stevens family's religious affiliation is with the Congregational church.

HON. PETER CHARLES KEEGAN—Few members of the legal profession are better known in the beautiful St. John Valley section of Maine than is Hon. Peter Charles Keegan, successful attorney, judge of the municipal court of Van Buren, and for many years a member of the State Legislature. Mr. Keegan has persistently and effectively worked for the good of this section of the State, and his vigorous, wholesome personality, his "genius for work" and his genuine ability have enabled him to achieve in one not-yet-finished life time more than three or four ordinary men usually have to their credit at the close of a long life span. His parents were pioneers in northern Aroostook County, and he has all the initiative and energy usually associated with those who tame the forest and reduce a wilderness to the law and order of civilization.

James Keegan, father of Mr. Keegan, was born in Slone, County Meath, Ireland, in 1803, and settled in Van Buren, northern Aroostook County, Maine, October 16, 1826, when he was twenty-two years of age. This section of the State was then a wilderness, and it was to the life of the pioneer that James Keegan had come from his native land. He was able and a hard worker and cleared many acres of ground in this section, remaining here to the time of his death, which occurred in 1892, when he was eighty-nine years of age. He was one of the very active members of the community, and was serving as constable in June, 1837, when Ebenezer Greeley, of Dover, Maine, who had been appointed census taker, by Governor Dunlap, of Maine, was arrested, during the dispute over the northeastern boundary of Maine. He married Lucy Parent, who was born in St. Mary, County

Beauce, Province of Quebec, Canada, and they became the parents of a family of children, among whom was Peter Charles.

Hon. Peter Charles Keegan was born in Aroostook County, Maine, May 13, 1850. As his parents were pioneers in this unsettled section of the State, there were only such schools as could be maintained by a few scattered people of a community uniting to hire a teacher, the term running as long as the money held out. To such a school Peter Charles Keegan was sent when he was four years of age. His teacher, it is recorded, was the typical schoolmaster of sixty years ago, with blue coat, brass buttons, stock, and beaver hat, also with a rod, which he used freely when occasion demanded, but he knew the subjects he was expected to teach, and he saw to it that his "scholars" learned them too. When young Peter Charles was nine years of age the only school within reach of the Keegan home was situated across the St. John River, in New Brunswick. There were no ferries, and the lad tramped to the river with his dinner pail in the morning, paddled across in a dug-out, and walked two miles to the schoolhouse, returning the same way at night. Three years later the nearest school was three and a half miles away, and he walked the distance twice a day. He finished his preparation for college at Grand Falls, New Brunswick, and then entered the University of New Brunswick, from which he was graduated in 1868. In the entrance examinations he won the second highest place, and at graduation he was one of the honor men in a class which included among its members several who have since become eminent in Canadian government affairs. After the completion of his college course he read law in the office of William A. Evans, at Fort Fairfield, Maine, and he was admitted to the bar September 20, 1869. He was also elected to the State Legislature in September, 1869. He had noted that certain concessions were needed for the development of the valley and that these could be obtained only through the State Legislature. He therefore decided to go to the Legislature, and though he was told that it would be impossible to secure the election on a Democratic ticket, in a section which was overwhelmingly Republican, he persisted and secured the election. For seven consecutive terms he served, and on several occasions since he has been chosen to serve for a term or two.

He has always taken an active interest in the St. John section of Maine, and he has always made his influence felt when he advocated any measure. He was a personal friend of President Roosevelt, and was appointed by him to serve as a member of the International Commission dealing with Great Britain and the Dominion of Canada. He is now (1928) in addition to his various other legal activities, serving as judge of the municipal court of Van Buren and Fort Kent, in Maine, having been appointed to that office by Governor Brewster, and he is well known as one of the most notable and resourceful members of the bench in this section of Maine. He is president of the Van Buren Trust Company, and is still a very hard worker. The habit of long-continued activity, formed in the stress and struggle of his early life, has become a somewhat fixed one, a part of his character. He lives on a big farm, a hundred acres of which is a part of the home place where he was born. The comfortable farmstead crowns one of the rolling hills which swell upward from the river, and from the pine-shadowed veranda a superb view of the beautiful St. John Valley opens northward. Neighbors were wont to say that his alarm clock was the big rooster in the hen house, and his quitting time anywhere from midnight to morning, according to when the last task of the day was finished. He works at politics as skillfully as he practices law, and farms for recreation, making good at all three by "keeping everlastingly at it." Wholesome, genial, friendly, he is acquainted with practically everybody in the valley, and it is said of him that he knows most of the children of the valley by name, no small achievement, considering the size of the families in that land. That he is as much at home with the big tasks as with the every-day amenities of life is evidenced by the following statement made in Sprague's Journal of Maine History, published May, 1915, concerning his service as a member of the International Commission in 1910: "He rendered with distinguished honor an important service to the State and Nation."

Hon. Charles Peter Keegan was married to Mary Sharkey, who was born in Frederickton, New Brunswick, and they have reared one foster-son, Harold Burchell Keegan, who married Lillian Keegan. The family are members of the Roman Catholic Church.

OSCAR S. SMITH—To the all-important cause of public education, Oscar S. Smith has given many years, and today he is superintendent of schools of the Island Falls district, comprising Island Falls, Sherman, Crystal, and Silver Ridge, Maine. He came to public school work from other forms of public service which followed his years of faithful ministerial work.

Oscar S. Smith was born at Marion, Washington County, Maine, in 1876, son of Samuel and Elizabeth (Reed) Smith. His father was a lumberman and farmer. The son rounded out his education by four years of study at Boston University and graduated in 1908, in the theological course. Meantime he had received practical experience by supplying several small churches. He then filled the pulpit of the Methodist Episcopal church at Bangor for six years; the First Methodist at Orono for two years, and that at Vinal Haven for three years. He spent a year also in Texas and a year and a half in the transport service. From this occupation he passed to that of secretary for the Young Men's Christian Association, a position he filled for two and a half years. It was at the end of this period of varied activities that Mr. Smith entered the educational field as principal of the Brownville Junction schools. He then accepted that same office in the high school at Caribou, and a year later at Island Falls. After three years of such able leadership in the Island Falls schools that the whole community came to have utmost confidence in his ability and devotion, Mr. Smith was chosen superintendent of schools for the four towns above designated. In the two years in which he has thus officiated, he has administered the schools well and accomplished much that was progressive in general and in particular. Mr. Smith is a Republican in politics and a member of the Free and Accepted Masons, with the third degree. Although a Methodist in religious faith, while his wife is a Baptist, he attends the Congregational church with her.

Oscar S. Smith married, at Vinal Haven, Hazel Parker, born at Patten, Maine, daughter of Edward and Adriana (Stafford) Parker. Children: 1. Verna, wife of William Fragle, newspaperman of Detroit, by whom she has two children: Jane and William Fragle, Jr. 2. Irving, a student at Boston University. 3. Ruth. 4. Frances. 5. Oscar Samuel Smith, Jr.

THOMAS PUTNAM PACKARD, Superintendent of schools for the 118th School District of Maine, and one of the prominent and highly respected citizens of Houlton, Maine, was born on February 13, 1888, at Orient, in this same State. Mr. Packard is a son of Corbett L. and Sarah L. (May) Packard, both of whom were native-born to Maine. Corbett L. Packard, the father, was for some time identified with the oil business in Pennsylvania, and during the latter years of his life he returned to Maine and purchased a farm. He was a veteran of the Civil War, and a man respected by all with whom he came in contact.

His son, Thomas Putnam Packard, received his early education in the public schools of the community in which he was born, and he later attended the Ricker Classical Institute. He then pursued a course of studies at Colby, graduating from there with the class of 1911. Immediately after the completion of these courses of study he at once branched out for himself, obtaining his first real contact with the world as a sub-master at the Ellsworth (Maine) High School, an office which he filled for some two years. He then removed to Houlton, where he was appointed principal of the Houlton High School. After serving in this capacity for four years, he was appointed school superintendent for School District No. 118, of Maine, comprising the three towns of Houlton, Littleton and Hammond. He has now filled this important post for eleven consecutive years, making a total service in this one district of more than fifteen years' duration.

During the period of the emergency created by the entry of the United States into the conflict of the World War, Mr. Packard served as a captain in Headquarters Company, Combat Train, 1st Battery, 1st Battalion, 152d Field Artillery of the Maine State National Guard. Despite the break caused by this service and by the many and exacting duties of the civilian work in which he is and has been engaged, Mr. Packard has nevertheless found time in which to take a keen interest in the civic and general affairs of his community. In his political views, he is a staunch supporter of the Republican party, and as such he is noted for the fine manner in which he stands behind any movement designed for the welfare or advancement of Houlton and its immediate vicinity. He has been almost equally active in his club and social life, for he is fraternally affiliated with the Houlton Lodge,

Free and Accepted Masons, of which he is a Past Master; and he also holds membership in the Meduxnekeag Club.

Thomas Putnam Packard married Annie E. Houdlett, who was born at Dresden Mills, Maine, a daughter of Joseph L. and Frances (Cate) Houdlett. Mr. and Mrs. Packard have become the parents of five children: 1. Joseph L., who was born in 1916. 2. Patricia, who was born in 1918. 3. Priscilla, who was born in 1921. 4. Sarah Frances, who was born during the year 1923. 5. Thomas Putnam, Jr., born August 6, 1927. Mr. Packard and his family maintain their residence in Houlton, Maine, in which community they attend the Congregational church.

GEORGE P. HAMILTON—One of the prosperous business men in Limestone, Maine, is George P. Hamilton, owner and manager of a first-class hardware business which he established in 1913. He is also president of the Limestone Trust Company, with which he has been associated for a period of seven years. He is a member of the Masonic Order, and has a host of friends in this locality.

Samuel Hamilton, father of Mr. Hamilton, was for many years engaged in business as a lumber man and farmer, and was active in the public affairs of Washington County, but for the past eight years he has been a resident of Limestone, where he is now (1928) living retired. Both he and his wife are natives of New Brunswick, Canada, and came to the States in 1887. He married Louise Spinney.

George P. Hamilton, son of Samuel and Louise (Spinney) Hamilton, was born in Washington County, Maine, January 16, 1887, and received his early education in the public schools of Topsfield, Maine, later attending Lee Academy for two terms and taking a business course in Bangor. When his commercial training was completed he accepted a position as bookkeeper in a potato house, where he remained for four years. He then began his connection with the hardware business by serving as clerk in a hardware house. At the end of two years he established, in 1913, a hardware business of his own carrying a general hardware stock, farm machinery, and farmers'

supplies. From the beginning the enterprise has prospered, and Mr. Hamilton has become one of the active and successful business men of the place. In 1925 he was elected president of the Limestone Trust Company, having been associated with the bank for five years previous to that time, totaling now seven years, and his ability and sound judgment are important factors in the standing which the bank has attained. In his political affiliations Mr. Hamilton is a Republican. He is a member of the Limestone Lodge, Free and Accepted Masons, of which he is a charter member, and he is also identified with Caribou Chapter, Royal Arch Masons. His religious affiliation is with the Methodist church.

George P. Hamilton is married to Elsie E. Thompson, who was born in Limestone, Maine, daughter of Arthur H. and Madelia (Noyes) Thompson. Mr. and Mrs. Hamilton are the parents of five children: Eveline E., Lena, Dorothy, Laversa, and Shirley.

GEORGE H. COLLINS—Forty years of continuous experience in the newspaper publishing and editing business have made George H. Collins a veteran in this field, and as editor of the "Presque Isle Star-Herald," he has become an intimate part of the life of the residents of this section of Aroostook County. Mr. Collins is a Republican, and prior to engaging in the newspaper business was reporter of debates in the Pennsylvania Legislature. He conducts a sheet which meets the needs of the subscription list most adequately, and his long experience in this section has made him thoroughly familiar with the tastes and needs of those whom he serves.

George H. Collins was born in Ripley, Somerset County, Maine, September 18, 1851, son of George W. and Elizabeth (Green) Collins. After attending the local public schools he continued study in Bucksport Seminary, and then, having early decided that he would eventually enter the newspaper business, gained valuable experience by serving as a reporter of debates in the Pennsylvania Legislature, serving in that capacity from 1879 to 1885. In 1887 he achieved his goal by engaging in newspaper work. As editor of the Presque Isle "Star-Herald," he has been an important factor in the life of this part of Aroostook County, and has achieved financial success as the result of excellence of service. He is widely and favorably known in this locality, and is a loyal supporter of the principles and the candidates of the Republican party, but he is progressive and discerning, and believes in giving his readers the benefit of close observation, keen discrimination, and unbiased judgment. Fraternally, he is identified with the Masonic Order, and his religious membership is with the Unitarian church.

George H. Collins was married at Harrisburg, Pennsylvania, and has two children: 1. Charlotte H., the wife of Charles F. West. 2. Mrs. George P. Larrabee. The family make their home in Presque Isle.

LYMAN F. GETCHELL—Spring Brook Farm, on the State road from Limestone, Van Buren, Maine, is owned by Lyman F. Getchell, who has the distinction of having served thirty years on the school committee, also has served as a selectman for seven years, and represents the third generation of the first of pioneer settlers in this region.

In 1870, the land about Limestone was a lumber region, and Dennis Getchell, who settled there in that year, was not only a lumberman, but speedily became a mill owner, and then acquired a tract of State land. This he added to by purchase from Eastman and Morse estate. Lyman F. Getchell was his grandson, and the son of Daniel and Susan (Bridges) Getchell. Born July 28, 1868, one of the first children born in Limestone, he was educated in the common schools, and was associated in business with his father until he was twenty-five years of age. He then bought Spring Brook Farm from his father, and developed it for diversified crops, with a large acreage in potatoes, although not specializing. His rule, in fact, has been to obtain good results by careful selection of seed. He is also a director in the Limestone Trust Company. Besides his thirty years on the school committee, Mr. Getchell was a selectman for seven years, and has always taken an interest in Republican politics. He is a member of the Free and Accepted Ma-

sons, Limestone Chapter, and Caribou Council, of Presque Isle. He is also a member of the Modern Woodmen of America, and of the Knights of Pythias. The family are communicants of the Protestant Episcopal Church, of which Mr. Getchell is treasurer.

Lyman F. Getchell married (first) Mary Bolier, daughter of Thomas and Tansie Bolier; their children being: 1. Hope, who was educated in the Limestone schools, and the Presque Isle Normal School, and is now a teacher in Oregon. 2. Emery, who married Tinna Finnemore, a farmer of Limestone. Mr. Getchell married (second) Rachel Weatherhead, daughter of Frank and Barbara Weatherhead.

ERNEST E. GETCHELL—Like his elder brother, Lyman F. Getchell (see accompanying sketch), Ernest E. Getchell, of Limestone, is among the most prosperous and successful farmers of this region, where his family were pioneers; and on his three hundred and seventy-acre farm on the old Noyes Mill Road, helps to maintain Maine's reputation for fine produce of kinds, and excellent potatoes in particular.

Grandson of Dennis Getchell, the first settler in Limestone, and son of Daniel and Susan (Bridges) Getchell, he was born March 15, 1882, and was educated in the local schools. Until he was thirty years of age he continued on the farm as his father's assistant, and then bought the property on which he now lives, from his father, and has greatly developed and improved it. For nine years he has been a member of the Board of Selectmen, and is now first selectman. He is a director in the Limestone Trust Company, and a trustee of the Methodist Episcopal Church. He is a member of the Free and Accepted Masons, and of Limestone Chapter, Royal Arch Masons, and Caribou Council, Royal and Select Masters. He is also a member of the Patrons of Husbandry, and of the Knights of Pythias.

Ernest E. Getchell married Melinda Gray, born in New Brunswick, Canada, daughter of William and Ethel (Kelley) Gray, both life-long residents of New Brunswick, where they are buried. Of this union were born: 1. Daniel W., who married Katie Sullivan, their children being Joyce and Leslie. 2. Wallace I., who married Velma Libby. 3. Harry E., who married Pauline Lewis, their daughter being June Elizabeth. 4. Winnifred Laura. 5. Maria Susan. 6. Albert.

home place with his brother Waldo. 6. Amy Pearl, who married Orrin Russell, and lives in Fort Fairfield, their children being Fred Forrest and Garthe Lavere. 7. Donald Clair Spear.

FRED F. SPEAR—Now living in retirement in Limestone, Maine, Fred F. Spear was for many years one of the most enterprising and successful of the prosperous class he typifies, but he was also a keen business man, and a useful public servant, filling a number of important local offices.

Born in Limestone, May 13, 1867, he was the son of Joseph Everett and Mary (Grant) Spear, both descended from good farming stock in Gardiner, Maine, and the grandson of Edmund Spear, of Gardiner. After completing the course in the local schools and high school, Fred F. Spear acquired possession of one hundred and fifty acres of unimproved land on the Caribou and Limestone Road. He cleared it, erected the necessary farm buildings, and while growing the crops then customary, specialized in potatoes. He also dealt in farm machinery and fertilizers, and bought and shipped potatoes to the city markets. He was also one of the organizers, and the first president of the Limestone Trust Company. Always a Republican, he was for many years a member of the school board, was selectman for twelve years, trial justice for six years, and in 1921-22, was a member of the lower house in the Maine Legislature.

Mr. Spear is a member of the Free and Accepted Masons, of the Knights of Pythias, and of the Patrons of Husbandry. He attends the Baptist church with his family. Since 1919, when he purchased a home in Limestone, and sold his farm to his two sons, he has given even more freely of his time to community affairs.

He married Helen T. Noyes, daughter of Josiah M. and Sybil (Conant) Noyes, who died May 1, 1914. Their children were: 1. Forest L., a merchant in Fort Fairfield; married Fern Lundy, their daughter being Helen May. 2. Willia, deceased. 3. Waldo G., who lives on the home place, married Rilla Ramsey, and has two children, Shirley May and Ellwood Everett. 4. Ruby, who lives with her father. 5. William McKinley, who works on the

VERNUM ELLSWORTH WILDER—Few men pass from this sphere of their labors and successes more deeply mourned than was that leading agriculturist, Christian gentleman and first citizen of his community, the late Vernum E. Wilder, of Washburn, Aroostook County. Mr. Wilder had touched life at so many points, it is impossible to measure his loss by mere words. What he accomplished so efficiently, generously and joyfully speaks a record of a remarkable career of love and service in many and important interests.

Vernum Ellsworth Wilder had the good advantage of descending from sound, vigorous and desirable stock. His birth occurred and he died on the very place whereon five generations of the Wilder family have lived, and where five generations today have their home—on the beautiful, well-kept farmstead in the village of Washburn. He was born December 31, 1874, the son of Robert Wilder, a pioneer citizen of Washburn, who with his good wife bore a most honorable part in laying well the foundations of his community and in helping in its upbuilding along sound lines. Other children of the immediate family surviving are: Lewis Wilder, of Gardiner; Mrs. Alice (Wilder) Huston, of Portland, and Mrs. William (Wilder) Farnham, of Thomaston.

The education of Vernum E. Wilder was received in the common schools of his native district, and when he left his textbooks to face the world on his own resources, he had been well grounded in the fundamentals of the local school system's curriculum. To this he added an abundant common sense plus a natural ability, with which he was blessed beyond many of his fellows. He remained on the homestead, carrying out a fine family tradition, by becoming one of the most finished farmers of Aroostook County. He did more—he rose in the esteem, affections and favor of the community and the countryside. Progressive in his own affairs and trustworthy in every particular, he soon took a commanding place as a leader in county agriculture and as one of the foremost citizens. He made a specialty of raising seed potatoes and developing pure-bred Jersey cattle, in both of which lines he attained eminent success. Dealing in fertilizer also constituted a large part of his business enterprise.

Mr. Wilder's public spirit took him far afield from the pursuit of a farmer. He was one of the original promoters of the Bangor & Aroostook Railway, and of him it was afterward said by so high an authority as Senator Gould and other officials of the road that it was Mr. Wilder's strong influence which was one of the important factors that made the building of the road a success. His financial acumen won recognition through election to the executive board of the Merchants Trust Company, of Presque Isle. For many years he was a director and moving spirit of the Northern Maine Fair, and vice-president at the time of his death. He was one of the organizers and a charter member of the Washburn Volunteer Fire Department, in whose work and service he was always keenly interested.

In municipal affairs he was esteemed a most useful citizen of the town of Washburn. He held at different times the offices of first, second and third selectman, and was actively associated with the forward movement in education, having served for fifteen years as a member of the School Board. In fraternal circles he was also actively engaged and highly stationed—a Royal Arch Mason, member of the Order of the Eastern Star, the Independent Order of Odd Fellows, the Daughters of Rebekah, and the Patrons of Husbandry, having served as Master of the Pomona Grange, and being an influential patron in the councils of that order.

In religious matters, Mr. Wilder was not less ardent than in those other circles in which he was such a happy and helpful figure. For twenty years he was treasurer of the Washburn Baptist Church, for a quarter of a century he was secretary of the organized Men's Bible Class of that church, and at the time of his passing was an honored member of the board of deacons. He was an enthusiastic and liberal supporter of all departments of church work, and his catholic spirit embraced all communions of the evangelical faith.

Vernum Ellsworth Wilder married, January 1, 1897, at Castle Hill, Maine, Victoria P. Smith, who survives him as do their two children: 1. Carrol D. (q. v.). 2. Arline, married Laurel Thompson, assistant treasurer of the Washburn Trust Company, and they have a daughter, Laurine.

The death of Mr. Wilder occurred with shocking suddenness, on August 23, 1926, following an operation at the Presque Isle Hospital. The entire community and its environs were stricken by a deep and poignant grief at the loss of so good and able a man. A contemporary, who had been a minister over the church Mr. Wilder attended, said among other things in tribute to his memory: "Vernum Wilder was without exception the most faithful man—to God and the cause of the church—that I have ever met in my ministry of forty-three years. He is absent from his dear family . . ., but he is with God. It was the plan of the Great Father to take him home. How mysterious is that plan! In my ears there echoes this message: 'And God shall wipe away all tears.'" The Men's Bible Class of the Baptist Church also voiced its tribute to its departed secretary, concluding with these eloquent words: "We have lost a man who lived his religion, cheerfully and well." Still another contemporary gave his pen to this appreciation of Mr. Wilder's sterling worth and his invaluable service to the community: "The sudden and untimely death of Mr. Wilder is a great shock to his family, to a very large circle of friends, and is a distinct loss to the community where he was born and where he had lived his life so cleanly, usefully and worthily. It is not only a loss to his immediate community, but to the county as a whole, whose strength is in the citizenship of such men and which is made the poorer by the loss of such useful and high-minded lives."

———

JOHN E. WEBB—The progress and prosperity of Island Falls in every civic and business department of the growth of the community have upon all occasions concerned the public-spirited interest of John E. Webb, leading merchant in this section of the State, prominent in the ice business and general store activities, and one who in town office has discerned and sponsored the needs of the townspeople.

John E. Webb was born March 26, 1858, at Ludlow, a son of James Webb, native of Merrimashee, New Brunswick, and Ella (Bell) Webb, who was born in the north of Ireland, both of Protestant Irish families. Mr. Webb attended the common schools in Houlton, and for twenty-two years afterwards he was in the employ of F. W. Tilcomb, fifteen years of that time in charge of the mill at New Limerick. For four years he was foreman for the Mattawamkeag Lumber Company, and he then purchased the Exchange Hotel, which he conducted for nine years. In 1917, Mr. Webb established himself in his present ice business, supplying Island Falls and Oakfield; and besides he carries the mail from the station, and has a taxi-cab business, with his stable at the hotel. With his nephew, Vinal E. Webb, he also owns and operates a general store. In the political field a Republican, Mr. Webb served three years as a member of the Island Falls Board of Selectmen, and he has always been active in town affairs, not from the standpoint of financial or merely political matters, but invariably in behalf of those matters that are for the betterment of the town. He is a member of the foremost group of agitators for waterworks for the town, and he was very active in having sidewalks laid. With his family he attends the Baptist church.

John E. Webb married, at Sangerville, Mary E. Snow, daughter of John Snow, of Parkman, Maine, and they were the parents of Donald E. Webb, who died when he was two and a half years old. Mr. and Mrs. Webb adopted Donald McLeod, and gave him the name Walter D. Webb. Walter D. Webb, who resides in Waterville, married Arline Murray.

JAMES A. STONE—Fifteen years ago James A. Stone purchased a farm of one hundred and fifteen acres along the North Road in the town of Littleton, Maine. Though hardly twenty years old at the time he had had considerable farming experience, and he began the raising of potatoes and other general farm produce. His energy and genuine ability have made him very successful in this field. He is also a member of the firm of Titcomb and Stone, potato shippers, who own two warehouses on the Bangor and Aroostook Railway, and he has taken an active part in the civic and fraternal life of Littleton. His father, James Stone, a mason, was born in the Province of New Brunswick, Canada, but he came to the United States while still young and lives at present at Houlton, Maine. He married Minnie Yerxa, and James is their son.

James A. Stone was born on March 31, 1892, at Littleton, Maine. He attended the local public schools, and when he completed his education, began work on a farm. For a number of years he was employed by various local farmers, and for a time he worked with his father, but he soon went into the farming business for himself. About fifteen years ago he bought his present farm from W. C. Adams, and since that time he has lived there, supervising the raising of his potato crops and other farm produce. He is also part owner of two potato warehouses on the Bangor and Aroostook Railway, being a member of the firm of Titcomb and Stone, potato shippers.

Politically, Mr. Stone is a member of the Republican party, and for three years he served as a member of the Board of Selectmen of the town of Littleton. He is affiliated fraternally with the Ancient Free and Accepted Masons, in which organization he is a Master Mason. He is also a member of the Grange and for a time he served as Overseer and Gate Keeper of that order. He supports the local Baptist church.

James A. Stone married Ada Lowry, the daughter of Alexander Lowry, a farmer, and of Mary (Smith) Lowry, both of Maine, and both now deceased. Mr. and Mrs. Stone are the parents of one child, Arline Ruth, who is six years old.

HERBERT C. PETTENGILL—The Island Falls section of the State has no more enterprising business man than Herbert C. Pettengill, whose varied activities are all accompanied with a most satisfactory degree of success, whether in partnership or on his own individual account. The communities in which his interests are centered benefit, also, by the thoroughgoing business plans of Mr. Pettengill, who is favorably known as merchant, lumber dealer, theater owner and financier.

Herbert C. Pettengill was born November 23,

1872, at St. Stephen, New Brunswick, son of
Columbus L. Pettengill and Mary (Bradbury)
Pettengill. His parents were both natives of this
State, but had temporarily removed to New
Brunswick, where their son, Herbert C., was
born, his father having been a lumber dealer.
After attending the public schools, Mr. Pettengill went to work in a lumber mill at Vanceboro,
and he removed to Island Falls in 1893, and here
he established a general store in 1894, which he
continued in connection with his lumber business,
his father being associated with him to the time
of his death in 1920.

Mr. Pettengill continues to conduct his general
store at Island Falls, and in partnership with
Herb Donnell, of Houlton, is one of the proprietors of the Fashion Store at Island Falls, an establishment that makes a specialty of women's
wear. Mr. Pettengill is also owner of the moving
picture theater at Island Falls, and of a lumber
mill at Crystal Station; and he is a member of the
board of directors of the Katahdin Trust Company.

In civic matters, Mr. Pettengill holds a foremost place at Island Falls, and he was selectman
for two years. Fraternally, he is affiliated with
the Free and Accepted Masons, the Royal Arch
Chapter of Masonry, Commandery of the Knights
Templar, Ancient Arabic Order Nobles of the
Mystic Shrine, the Order of the Eastern Star,
and the 306 Foresters. It is of interest to note
that his father, Columbus S. Pettengill, established the Portage Mill Company, at Portage
Mill, that was sold to the firm of Blanchard and
Sharp, and is now conducted by Mr. Blanchard.

Herbert C. Pettengill married Alice W. Donham, who was born at Island Falls, daughter of
George H. and Sarah (Martin) Donham. Their
children: 1. Carl M., who is in charge of the mill
at Crystal Station. 2. Theodore, who is also engaged in the activities of the mill. 3. Herbert,
a graduate of the University of Maine. 4. Waldo,
a student at Island Falls. The family attend the
Congregational church.

J. SAUNDERS WOLVERTON—As an energetic young agriculturist in the new progress
of the State of Maine, J. Saunders Wolverton is
prominent in the communities of Littleton and

Houlton where he is associated with his father
in the business of farming. His father owns the
well-known Deep Lawn Farm of one hundred
and twenty acres, and Mr. J. Saunders Wolverton
owns and operates a farm of one hundred acres.
Both these farms are on the North Road. J.
Saunders Wolverton is the son of Joseph and
Myrtle (Sweet) Wolverton, who were natives and
residents of New Brunswick until 1903 when they
came to live in the State of Maine and have continued to reside here ever since.

J. Saunders Wolverton was born at Knoxford,
New Brunswick, on July 21, 1899, and lived there
until he was four years of age when he came
with his parents to Maine. He was educated in
the schools of Littleton and was graduated from
the Ricker Classical Institute in 1918. He has
never had any other business than that of farming
on which he concentrates all of his energies with
good success. The crops of both his father's and
his farm are about equally divided between general farm crops and potatoes. He is a Republican
in politics and has been town selectman. He is a
member of the Grange and also of the Baptist
church.

J. Saunders Wolverton married Carrie Graham,
daughter of Isaac and Annie (Parks) Graham, of
Monticello, Maine. They have one child: Joyce.

BENJAMIN C. WALKER—For twenty-six
years active in the business life of Island Falls,
and now retired from commercial affairs, Benjamin C. Walker, in association with George A.
Palmer (q. v.), is engaged in the cultivation of a
farm near Island City, composed of one hundred
and sixty acres on Harding Street; and three hundred acres on Lake Mattawamkeag, which is given
over mainly to timber. In addition to these properties, which he owns jointly with Mr. Palmer, Mr.
Walker maintains the interest and personal concern
that he always has felt in affairs of the community, and is a member of the board of directors of
the Katahdin Trust Company.

Benjamin C. Walker was born at Searsport,
Maine, on August 22, 1868, son of Benjamin R.
and Geneva (Merrithew) Walker. Benjamin R.,
the father, was born at Thorndike, the mother at
Monroe, Maine; and after their establishment of

residence in Island Falls, in 1870, they remained here during the remainder of their lives, and were the parents of seven children, four sons and three daughters. Benjamin C. Walker received his education in the public schools of Island Falls, then occupied himself at various positions in commercial endeavor until he reached his majority, when, with an uncle, J. C. Walker, he opened a shop for commerce in groceries and meats under the style of J. C. and B. C. Walker. This was in 1894; in 1920 he disposed of his control to J. E. Webb and V. L. Webb. Mr. Walker is a member of the Republican party, and throughout his career in business took an active share in the civic life of Island Falls. For thirteen years he was town treasurer; for a number of terms he was on the Board of Selectmen; and for six years he was deputy sheriff. In these public capacities he constantly strove for the betterment of conditions in Island Falls. His influence, always considerable, has done much toward the maintenance of sound principles of economics in the conduct of the town treasury, the support of law and order, and the wise selection of methods for the purpose of successfully completing works started, as well as in the formulation of campaigns for works about to be commenced. He is a member of the Free and Accepted Masons, Blue Lodge, Island Falls; Royal Arch Masons, at Island Falls; St. Aldemar Commandery, Knights Templar, at Houlton; and the Ancient Arabic Order Nobles of the Mystic Shrine, at Lewiston. He is a member of the Congregational church.

Benjamin C. Walker married Jennie V. Morrison, daughter of Alphonso J. Morrison, of Sherman. Mr. and Mrs. Walker are the parents of three children: 1. Vaughan A., educated in the Island Falls public schools, one year at Bowdoin College, now (1927) in the United States Navy on board the battleship "Tennessee," married Ruth McLaughlin. 2. Geneva L., graduate of the Island Falls High School and the Presque Isle Normal School. 3. Kathlyn M., student in high school.

BERT HANNING—For many years Bert Hanning has been prominent in the life of the town of Littleton, Maine. He is the owner of two

farms situated along the North Road, one of two hundred and thirty acres, on which he lives, and the other one hundred and thirty acres in extent, which is operated by his son Waldo. Mr. Hanning is thoroughly familiar with the best farming methods and is very successful in raising potatoes and other general farm produce for sale to local buyers. He is highly esteemed in his community as a public-spirited citizen, and is active in local church work. His father, Charles Hanning, born in Maine, was a farmer, and he engaged in this work until his death. His mother, Augusta Hanning, was also born in Maine. Charles and Augusta Hanning were the parents of five children: 1. Alvah. 2. Trissie, who married James Jamieson. 3. Annie, the wife of Ernest Mitchell. 4. Charles. 5. Bert.

Bert Hanning was born at Houlton, Maine, on May 27, 1873. He attended the local public schools and at the age of fourteen began work on the farm with his father. This arrangement continued until his father's death, at which time Mr. Hanning took over the operation of the home farm, continuing it for about fifteen years. In 1917 he bought from Isaac Gerow the farm where he now lives. He has devoted himself since that time to improving the property and raising his crops, handling chiefly potatoes. Politically, Mr. Hanning supports the principles and candidates of the Republican party. He attends the local Baptist church, in which both he and his wife have been very active.

He married Eva Lorom, born in Maine, the daughter of Randolph and Louise (Elliott) Lorom. Mr. and Mrs. Hanning are the parents of three children: 1. Lorom, who married Mary Crane, and is now engaged in farming. 2. Waldo, also a farmer. He married Bula Crouse and they have one child. 3. Gilchrist, who was married to Roy Ingraham, a farmer of the town of Littleton.

HAROLD E. HILLMAN—For many years Harold E. Hillman has been prominent in the life of the town of Littleton, Maine. He is the owner of two farms, one of seventy-five acres along the North Road, where he lives, and the other of one hundred and four acres situated in the same township, behind the home farm. Mr. Hillman has been very successful in his chosen occupation, raising fine crops of potatoes and other general farm produce, and he is also connected with the potato shipping business, being part owner of a warehouse on the Wiley Road siding. He has always occupied a high place in the esteem of his community.

Mr. Hillman was born in the province of New Brunswick, Canada, on May 2, 1872, the son of George and Margaret (Stewart) Hillman, both of New Brunswick. George Hillman came to the United States when his son was only six years old, and found work near Houlton, Maine, as a laborer. Later he bought the farm along the North Road, where he remained for the rest of his life.

Harold E. Hillman attended the public schools of the town of Littleton, and when he completed his education began work with his father on the farm. This arrangement he continued until his father's death, when he inherited the property, and has carried on the business for himself since that time. He is also associated with Louis Carson and D. L. Woodworth in the potato shipping business, being part owner of a potato warehouse on the Wiley Road siding. Politically, Mr. Hillman is a member of the Republican party. He is affiliated fraternally with the Modern Woodmen of America. He and his family attend the local Baptist church.

He married Kathlyn M. Watson, the daughter of William and Rebecca (Henderson) Watson. Mr. and Mrs. Hillman are the parents of two children: 1. George A., who is now twenty-six years old, associated with his father on the farm, and who married Marion Nason; they have one child, John. 2. Eloise, who is six years old.

DAVID E. HAMMOND—Owner of two farms near Houlton, David E. Hammond maintains both of them, on which he does general farming, cultivating potatoes and grain for his own use. One of the farms consists of one hundred acres on the North Road out of Houlton, and the other is the Hammond homestead on the Lowrey Road. Keenly interested in the public affairs of Houlton

and vicinity, Mr. Hammond is active in the life and the development of the town, in which he has won a favorable reputation for splendid citizenry.

He was born on the Hammond homestead farm on the Lowrey Road, on February 12, 1875, the son of William and Jemima (Parks) Hammond. His father was born on the Forcraft Road, while his mother, who went to New Brunswick for a time when she was three years old but soon after returned to Maine, was born in the White settlement. Both of the parents spent the greater part of their lives on the Hammond farm in this section, where they were well known and highly respected citizens and reared a family of nine children. David E. Hammond, one of this family, received his education in the public schools of Houlton; worked later on the farm of his father, who died when David E. Hammond was seventeen years old; then continued on the home farm until 1920. In that year he bought the North Road farm from Frank Ketchum. Always keenly interested in the affairs of his town, Mr. Hammond has been active in the political life of the community, being affiliated with the Republican party, whose opinions he holds. He and his family are members of the Baptist church, which they attend, and are active in church affairs.

David E. Hammond married Nora Ackerson, who was born in Easton, Maine, a daughter of Joseph Ackerson. David E. and Nora (Ackerson) Hammond are the parents of the following children: 1. Shirley, who was born in 1908, was educated in the public schools of Houlton, and is a student at business college. 2. Merlin, who has just entered high school.

WILLIAM H. ANDERSON—Prominent as a farmer and esteemed throughout this section for his public spirit in taking an active part in civic affairs, William H. Anderson is one of the most industrious men in the community. He is the son of Charles and Elizabeth (Foster) Anderson of New Brunswick who moved to Littleton in the early days and brought up a large family of children, all of whom are now deceased except William H. Anderson and his two sisters, Anna and Lottie.

William H. Anderson was born in New Brunswick on July 25, 1876. He came to this country with his parents when a lad of sixteen years. He received his education in the public schools and has spent the rest of his life principally in farming, with kindred interests. He owns a four hundred acre farm out from Littleton on the Framingham Road, where he raises chiefly a crop of potatoes, although he does some general farming. He has a large warehouse at the Littleton Station from which he ships quantities of potatoes. He has constantly improved his farm by erecting buildings and installing equipment and now has one of the most notable farms in this section. He is a member of the Grange and an Orangeman and in politics a staunch Republican, working actively for the party at all times, although he has never held office.

William H. Anderson married Sadie Stithan, of Winn, Maine, daughter of Thaddeus and Lillian (White) Stithan. They have six children: 1. Linwood, educated in Littleton and Houlton, now associated with his father. 2. Louise, educated in the town schools and business college; now bookkeeper for the Singer Sewing Machine Company. 3. Resper May, educated at the town schools, Ricker Classical Institute and the Normal School; is a teacher. 4. Ada Marion, a graduate of Ricker Classical Institute. 5. Edith, a student at Ricker Classical Institute. 6. William Bernard, a student at the town schools. The family attend the Baptist church.

JOSEPH J. MICHAUD—A prosperous and widely known citizen and business man of Island Falls, Maine, is Joseph J. Michaud, proprietor of a clothing and furnishing store at Island Falls and owner of a fine farm of two hundred and eighty acres. A man of many interests, he also engages in other lines of business and in various civic and religious pursuits.

Joseph J. Michaud was born at Clair, New Brunswick, March 4, 1874, son of Frank and Chantie (Bouchard) Michaud. The father was a farmer. The son attended public school until he was eleven, when he became a chore boy working as a hired man on a farm for the decade which passed before he attained his majority. He had

learned much in these years and proved his worth so effectively that he was, at the age of twenty-one, made foreman for the Frank W. Hunt Company, an office he filled for eight years. During the next two, he was foreman for Charles Fly. Mr. Michaud then took for Delmont Emerson contracts in logging and wood pulp for fifteen years. It was in March, 1924, that Mr. Michaud established his store in Island Falls, the management of which is in the hands of his son, Eleric. Clothing and furnishings, boots and shoes are sold in his establishment, excellent in quality, diversified in styles, and reasonable in prices. The enterprise is prosperous and is a credit to the town. Besides managing his farm, Mr. Michaud also does a pulp wood business with his brother, Dennis Michaud. He is an independent in politics, voting for the man or the measure rather than the party. For two years he was deputy sheriff of his county. He is a communicant of the Roman Catholic church.

Joseph J. Michaud married Anna S. Sancier, who now spells the name Socia, daughter of Fred and Virginia (Leveresque) Socia. Children: 1. Lena, wife of George Peavey, who lives in Patten, Maine, where the husband is in the ice business; children: Ruth, George, Mary, and an infant. 2. John E., a forester, married to Elizabeth Goodblood, and has a son, Robert Michaud. 3. Eleric, married Laura Berger and has children, Reda and Francis. 4. Leonard, married Erene Cyr, and has a child, Claude. 5. Edmund. 6. Frank. 7. Hilda. 8. Raymond.

SAMUEL P. ADAMS—In the history of the development of this section of the State, the name of Samuel P. Adams is conspicuous among those who had faith and the courage to persevere despite reverses and handicaps until he owned and maintained one of the most interesting farms in this vicinity.

Samuel P. Adams was born in Richmond, New Brunswick, on January 17, 1844. His father was David Adams and his mother Rachel (Long) Adams. After a common school education, at the age of eighteen years, he came to the State of Maine. Determining to be a farmer, he purchased two hundred acres of uncleared land and set about to clear it and put it in condition for crops. The work was hard, but he persevered until at last he owned and managed one of the finest farms near Littleton. While he always called this section his home, he was interested in lumbering and saw mills and spent some time in Bangor, Maine, and some time out in Michigan, then back to his farm here. He was a Republican in politics, and an active member of the Grange. He and his family were members of the Episcopal church.

Samuel P. Adams married Annie Love, a native of Richmond, New Brunswick, daughter of Thomas and Lizzie (Watson) Love, who owned a farm next door to that of Mr. Adams' parents. He and his wife were children and playmates together. They had three children: 1. Lizzie A. (L. Arissia), who was brought up on the farm and owns two hundred acres of the original home place which she operates as a farm for herself. 2. Harvey Johnston, who is a carpenter and lives at home with his sister. 3. Hobart Ellwood Basil, who is a weaver living at Corinna, Maine; he married Dorothy Taylor. Samuel P. Adams died April 10, 1927. He is survived by his widow and three children.

JAMES B. HAGAN—Owner and proprietor of a most fertile and profitable farm composed of one hundred and eighty acres, on the State road to Bangor, near Houlton, James B. Hagan is one of the principal growers of potatoes in the vicinity. These he sells to the market at Houlton, where he likewise disposes of other produce from the farm. He rotates his crops from year to year according to the best scientific farm management, and the very considerable financial success that he has attained is a result. But the activities of Mr. Hagan do not consist of agriculture alone; his assistance in community affairs and in community direction of Houlton is given constantly. For three terms he served as member of the Board of Selectmen. He is well and widely known as a public-spirited citizen, devoted to the welfare of Houlton and the agricultural area surrounding it.

James B. Hagan was born at Houlton, on October 17, 1890, son of James A. and Anna Bell (Thompson) Hagan. James A. Hagan, too, was

born at Houlton; and indeed the name of Hagan ranks with the oldest in the town. Anna Bell (Thompson) Hagan was born at Ludlow, Maine. James A. and Anna Bell (Thompson) Hagan were engaged in farming, in the Porter settlement, and there spent the greater number of their years, James A. Hagan dying there at the age of seventy-eight years. His widow is now (1927) living, at Houlton.

James B. Hagan received his education in the public schools of Houlton, and during the years of attendance in class he assisted his father with the work on the farm. Upon his graduation he associated with his father constantly in this work, until, in 1919, during the month of October, he purchased the farm of one hundred and eighty acres on the State road, from Frank H. Willett, in the town of New Limerick. Here, as well as in Houlton and throughout the countryside, he is well liked and respected. As an agriculturalist and a man of business his opinions on those subjects are in demand. He takes an interested part in political matters, and possesses a considerable influence in them. Fraternally he is prominent in the Independent Order of Odd Fellows, and Houlton Lodge, No. 16, of the Grange. He is a member of the Methodist Episcopal Church, and as a communicant is most devout, generous in his contributions to charitable and other meritorious causes.

James B. Hagan married Rowena McGown, who was born at Oakfield, Maine, daughter of Alfred and Louise (Saunders) McGown, father deceased, mother living at Houlton. Mr. McGown was an outstanding citizen in the Oakfield vicinity, where he was a farmer and miller. Mr. and Mrs. Hagan are the parents of two children: Louise Marie and Ruth Anna.

SAMUEL R. CRABTREE—To the improvement and progress of Island Falls, Samuel R. Crabtree has contributed in a score of ways that partake of vital meaning for the high rating of this township whether in educational or mercantile matters, in particular, though he has always been devoted to whatsoever movement pertains to the excellence of the community and its institutions. He has represented his district in the State Legislature, and kept at the head of the affairs of the school department, as well as made his pharmacy one of the foremost in this part of the State for accuracy of system and attractiveness of display.

Samuel R. Crabtree was born January 5, 1870, at Topsfield, in Washington County, a son of Lorenzo Crabtree, a blacksmith and farmer, born at St. Stephen's, New Brunswick, and Mary (Farrar) Crabtree, a native of Durham. After attending the common schools, Mr. Crabtree was graduated at Lee Academy, and he then taught schools for several years, and assisted Dr. M. L. Porter at Danforth. He then prepared himself for his vocation in taking the course at the Philadelphia College of Pharmacy; and in 1893 he established his drug store at Island Falls, in the same year when the Bangor and Aroostook Railroad tracks were laid in his section, his establishment, the Rexall Drug Store, having a wide repute in this part of Maine. He also conducts an insurance business; and is president of the L. A. Barker Company, groceries and drugs, at Oakfield; and a member of the board of directors of the Katahdin Trust Company. As superintendent of the Island Falls Public Schools, Mr. Crabtree was instrumental in establishing the grade and high schools here.

Prominent in the activities of the Republican party, Mr. Crabtree is secretary of the Republican county committee, and he served in the Legislature two terms. Fraternally, he is affiliated with the Free and Accepted Masons, and has been treasurer of the local lodge since it was instituted; and is a member of the local chapter of the Royal Arch Masons, and of the Knights Templar Commandery at Houlton. With his family, he attends the Congregational church, of which he is a trustee and deacon, and he has held the position of superintendent of the Sunday School for twenty-eight years.

Samuel R. Crabtree married Margaret Kelley, daughter of Albert and Ella M. (Brannen) Kelley. Their children: 1. Leah, who married Ralph W. Emerson. 2. Paul L., who is general manager and treasurer of the P. P. Caproni Company, Boston, Massachusetts; married Julia Hews, and has a son, Samuel R. 3. Mary E., who became Mrs. Morris Reed Robinson on June 23, 1928.

WILLIAM S. ADAMS—One of the prominent men of the town of Littleton, Maine, is William S. Adams. He is the owner of a farm two hundred acres in extent situated along Framingham Road, near Houlton, on which he has built a large potato house. Mr. Adams specializes in the raising of potatoes and other farm produce, selling to local dealers, and in this field he has been very successful. He occupies a high place in the esteem of his community.

Mr. Adams is the son of William H. Adams, born in the province of New Brunswick, Canada, and Mary (Adams) Adams, born in Ireland, who were cousins. Both of his parents came to the United States as children. His father was a blacksmith and a carpenter, but in his later years he owned the farm where Mr. Adams now lives, having cleared it himself and finally sold it to Henry Little, having purchased it from Burleigh and White.

William S. Adams was born on November 27, 1870, at Houlton, Maine. He attended the local public schools, and when he completed his education, began work on a farm. Eventually he was able to purchase the land which his father had once owned, and since that time he has lived there raising potatoes and other products which he sells to the local buyers. Mr. Adams has greatly improved his farm, putting up all the buildings himself, among them a large potato house. Politically he supports the principles and candidates of the Republican party. He is an Orangeman, and a member of the Grange. He and his family attend the Presbyterian church.

William S. Adams married Alice Ross, and they became the parents of one child, Clayton, who is now associated with his father on the farm.

————————

JOSEPH ALLISON SHAW—For many years Joseph Allison Shaw has been prominent in the life of the town of Littleton, Maine. He is the owner of two farms, each one hundred acres in extent, one on Framingham Road and the other on Shaw Road, on both of which he raises potatoes and general farm produce for sale to local brokers. Mr. Shaw is thoroughly familiar with the best farming methods and has been very successful in his chosen occupation. He is a member of the school board of the town of Littleton, and has also served as town selectman and tax collector. A valuable citizen in any community, he is highly esteemed by all with whom he comes in contact.

He was born on February 12, 1876, in Carlton County, Province of New Brunswick, Canada, the son of Tamberlane J. and Julia (Shaw) Shaw, both natives of New Brunswick. When he was only nine months old his parents came to the United States, settling on the farm where Mr. Shaw now lives. His father cleared the land himself and raised his crops there until his death.

Joseph Allison Shaw entered the public schools of Littleton, and later attended the Ricker Classical Institute. When he completed his education he returned to the farm and to this work he has devoted his life. He has effected many improvements on his land, and specializes in the raising of potatoes. Politically, Mr. Shaw is a member of the Republican party. He is a member of the school board of the town of Littleton, and he also served for four years as a member of the Board of Selectmen, and for three years as tax collector. He is a member of the Grange, of which he served as Master for one term.

Mr. Shaw married Lillie I. Miller, who was born at Littleton, the daughter of Z. M. and Ada (Grant) Miller. Mr. and Mrs. Shaw are the parents of four children: 1. Vaughan, educated at the Littleton schools and Ricker Classical Institute, from which he was graduated in June, 1927, and now associated with his father on the farm. He plans to enter Colby College to take up the study of medicine. 2. Phyllis, a student at the Littleton schools. 3. Cedric, who also attends the Littleton schools. 4. Laurel. Mr. Shaw and his family attend the local Baptist church.

REV. CHARLES E. PROULX—The spiritual welfare of a large number of Roman Catholics in Island Falls, Maine, is in the capable hands of Rev. Charles E. Proulx, pastor of St. Agnes Catholic Church. He is a man of much learning and inspiring devotion, keenly interested in his flock and helpful in every phase of their lives. The whole community, Catholic and Pro-

testant alike, appreciates his wholesome influence and his public-spirited participation in all that makes for community advancement.

Rev. Charles E. Proulx was born at St. Pie, Quebec, March 19, 1887, son of Roch and Carolina (De Tonnancourt) Proulx, both natives of Quebec. They moved to Marlborough, Massachusetts, in 1910, and the father established himself there as a farmer. Father Proulx, one of eight children, was educated in his home town and at College Nicolet, Quebec. He studied theology at Laval University in Quebec and was ordained July 10, 1912. His first work in the cause of the church on his graduation was as teacher of history in Laval University. He ended four years of this work and then took his first charge as assistant at Chicopee Falls, Massachusetts, in St. George's Church. After four years there, he went to Biddeford, Maine, where for three years he was assistant at St. Andrew's Church. His next charge was as assistant at Auburn, Maine, in St. Louis' Church. After three and a half years in Auburn, Father Proulx was given his present pastorate. St. Agnes' Church has three hundred and fifty souls, and the numbers and influence of the church have grown since Father Proulx took charge in November, 1926. His large vision and his thorough understanding of men, together with his complete devotion to the tenets of his great church, combine to promise a fine future development for his parish.

CLYDE D. McLAUGHLIN—Chairman of the school board of Dyer Brook, Clyde D. McLaughlin, farmer, owns four hundred acres of fertile land on the Maine State Highway which he rotates in crops, varying in the plantings from year to year in accordance with the most scientific and practical methods, specializing in potatoes, which he sells to dealers in Dyer Brook. Mr. McLaughlin is known throughout the county, and is a popular citizen.

Clyde D. McLaughlin was born at Oakfield, Maine, May 15, 1876, son of Daniel Webster and Effie Mary (Clark) McLaughlin, the former living and the latter deceased, having died in 1921. Daniel McLaughlin has been a farmer all his life. He was born in New Brunswick, Canada; Mrs. Effie M. McLaughlin was born at Smyrna, Maine. Clyde D. McLaughlin was educated in the common schools of Oakfield, and for twenty years, was with his father on the farm, then purchased a tract of one hundred and thirty-three acres within the boundaries of the land he now occupies, from Lavanda Drew. Later he purchased additional acres, until the four hundred acres were completed, making one of the largest and finest farms in this section of the State. Mr. McLaughlin has taken an interested part in affairs of Dyer Brook, and has served the community as road commissioner and member of the Board of Selectmen. He is a Republican in political faith. For eighteen years he was superintendent of the cemetery. Mr. McLaughlin is a member of the Free and Accepted Masons, and member of the Blue Lodge, Island Falls.

Clyde D. McLaughlin married Ella M. White, and they are the parents of seven children: 1. Carl E., married Mary Gerrish, and is the father of five children, Lillian, Berl, Aubray, Margaret and Nadine. 2. Ken P., married Blanche Freel, and is the father of three children: Gertrude, Phyllis, and Donald. 3. Cleo, married Hazel McLellan, is father of three children: Shirley, Margie and Janice. 4. Villard, graduate of Bay Pathological Institute at Springfield, Massachusetts, married Josephine Heisey. 5 and 6. (Twins) Ralton and Janie. 7. Augustus.

GEORGE A. PALMER—One of the most prominent men in the commercial and civic life of Island Falls and for two terms member of the State Legislature, George A. Palmer is a dealer in building materials, and was, for a number of years, contractor. He is a director of the Katahdin Trust Company and chairman of the loan committee of the branch at Island Falls; and, jointly with B. C. Walker (q. v.), is owner and proprietor of a farm of one hundred and sixty acres on Hardin Street and of three hundred acres of timber land on Lake Mattawamkeag.

George A. Palmer was born in Amador County, California, on August 10, 1869, son of Atkins C. and Eunice (Hooper) Palmer, both of whom were of Maine, having departed thence for the West

not long before George A. was born. The family lived in California until 1872, when they returned to Maine, Atkins C. Palmer dying in 1908, Eunice (Hooper) Palmer now (1927) living. George A. Palmer received his education in the public schools of Whitneyville, and served an apprenticeship of three years in the craft of carriage making. He followed this occupation for fifteen years, then he went into the business of building and repairing mills, in which he engaged approximately twenty years, after the conclusion of which period he became a general contractor. While concerned in milling enterprises, Mr. Palmer was for a time superintendent for the N. G. Shaw Company and for Milliken and Emerson, millers. He constructed the mill housing the Northern Wooden Ware Company, at Island Falls. Since he began his residence in Island Falls, Mr. Palmer has been active in political matters; a Republican, he was twice elected to the House of Representatives on that ticket, serving in 1923-24, 1925-26. He is a member of the Blue Lodge, and Past Master, of the Free and Accepted Masons, Island Falls; Past High Priest of the Royal Arch Masons; the Council, Royal and Select Masters; the Commandery, Knights Templar, at Houlton.

George A. Palmer married Annie E. Foss, born at Whitneyville, daughter of William H. and Olive (Day) Foss. Mr. and Mrs. Palmer are the parents of three children: 1. Phillip A., manager of the Joseph Goodnow Lumber Company, Boston, Massachusetts. 2. Kenneth, shipping clerk in the Northern Wooden Ware Company. 3. Wilson, garage man, at Island Falls. Both Mr. and Mrs. Palmer are members of the Congregational church, of which Mr. Palmer is trustee.

JOSEPH E. TARBELL—Out of the wilderness which they found in Maine, Joseph E. Tarbell and his father, Ira Tarbell, created the town of Smyrna Mills. They cut the forests and underbrush away to clear the land for farming, and they established a store to supply the needs of the ever-growing number of residents. Smyrna Mills today is largely the outgrowth of their activities, and its prosperity was reflected in the personal success which came to Joseph E. Tarbell. The business formerly known as J. E. Tarbell and Sons, now incorporated, is one of the largest of its kind in New England.

Joseph E. Tarbell was born in Solon, Maine, December 20, 1837, son of Ira Tarbell, a soldier in the Revolutionary War. The father, with others, broke the trail which led to Smyrna and pushed ahead when his companions were discouraged. He took his family with him to the new home when his son was six years old, and there they continued to reside. As he grew up, Joseph E. Tarbell picked up limited formal education, but improved his mind by wide reading and much study. He worked with his father in taming the wilderness and in farming until the outbreak of the Civil War, when he displayed the patriotism which characterized his family by enlisting for service in the Union Army.

On his return from war, Mr. Tarbell established the business now known as J. E. Tarbell and Sons. Its first headquarters were in the bedroom of the old home, and the goods for sale were brought there by team from Houlton. Groceries were the staple product. In 1913, a copartnership was formed, and the old enterprise of J. E. Tarbell took the name of J. E. Tarbell and Sons. Eight years later, in 1921, with its incorporation, the following officers were elected: Perley H. Tarbell, president; H. J. Tarbell, treasurer; directors: P. H., H. J., L. F., and F. W. Tarbell. A store and warehouse today are located at Smyrna Mills, and a branch is found at Masardis. In the main store are employed fourteen people, and in the branch, two. Like their forebears, Mr. Tarbell's sons continue to be interested in farming, specializing in the growing and shipping of potatoes. The father, a Republican, held many offices of trust. He was a member of the Methodist church and zealous in its support. He died March 3, 1924, at the age of eighty-seven.

Joseph E. Tarbell married Almeda Goodnow, of Maine, and they were the parents of the following children: 1. Lester F., who lives in Bangor, salesman and director of the A. H. Berry Company, of Portland. 2, 3 and 4. Frank, Phoebe, and Jessie, deceased. 5. Elizabeth, wife of M. P. Wright, residing in Boston. 6. Dr. F. W. Tarbell. 7. Perley H. Tarbell, living in Bangor, manager of J. E. Tarbell and Sons, Incorporated, and frequently to be found in Smyrna Mills.

Symbolic of the best traditions of America as a pioneer settler who opens up desirable new regions to the occupancy of his fellow citizens, Mr. Tarbell deserves inclusion not only in a history of Maine, but in one of the United States. In every respect he was a loyal and constructive citizen, whose achievements remain a part of the general progress.

SANFORD S. DUDLEY—For many years Sanford S. Dudley has been prominent in the life of the town of Castle Hill, Maine. A farmer by occupation, he and his brother Melvin A. own four hundred acres of land, the old Dudley homestead, situated on Dudley Road, one mile west of the town of Mapleton, and some one hundred and sixty acres of wood land in the same township. Mr. Dudley and his brother operate the farm together, raising excellent potatoes and other general farm produce for sale to local buyers. He has a distinguished record of civic service, being now in his first term as a member of the Maine State Legislature. For eighteen years he has been town treasurer, and for five years he was a member of the Town of Castle Hill Board of Selectmen, during three years of which period he served as chairman of the board. Mr. Dudley has been otherwise active in civic affairs and is a member of many fraternal organizations.

He was born on the farm where he now lives, on August 25, 1864, the son of Allen M. Dudley, who was born in Kennebec County, Maine, and of Susan A. (Waddell) Dudley, born in Washington County, Maine, both now deceased. His parents came from old and prominent Maine families, his father having served as a member of the Maine State Legislature, and held numerous town offices.

Sanford S. Dudley attended the public schools of his birthplace, and when he completed his education he began work with his father on the farm. To this occupation he has devoted his life, succeeding, with his brother, to the ownership of the farm upon the death of their parents. Mr. Dudley is thoroughly familiar with the best farming methods and is very successful in his chosen occupation. Politically, he is a member of the Republican party, and is now a member of the State Legislature. He has also held many local offices. He is affiliated fraternally with the Ancient Free and Accepted Masons, being a member of the Blue Lodge at Presque Isle, Maine. He is also a member of the Modern Woodmen of America, of the Grange and of the Orangemen. He and his family attend the Baptist church.

Sanford S. Dudley married Lena Hopkinson, who was born at Fort Fairfield, the daughter of William and Eunice (Decker) Hopkinson. Mr. and Mrs. Dudley are the parents of eight children: Verna, Robert, Warren, Milton, Alton, Doris, Lester and Morris.

MELVIN A. DUDLEY—One of the finest farms in the Mapleton section of Maine is the Dudley homestead, owned by Melvin A. Dudley and his brother, Sanford S. Dudley. Some four hundred acres in extent, it is situated along Dudley Road, about one mile west of the town of Mapleton, and here Mr. Dudley and his brother supervise the raising of a variety of products, specializing in particular, in growing potatoes. Mr. Dudley is also part owner of one hundred acres of timber land in the same township. He has been active in the civic and fraternal life of his community, and for the past seventeen years has been chairman of the Board of Selectmen of the town of Castle Hill. He is also chairman of the Republican Town Committee of that place.

His father, Allen M. Dudley, born in Kennebec County, Maine, was a farmer and engaged in this work until his death, December 17, 1908. His mother, who, before her marriage, was Susan A. Waddell, died September 26, 1919. Both parents came from old and prominent Maine families, his father having served as a member of the Maine State Legislature, and held numerous town offices.

Melvin A. Dudley was born on July 21, 1880, on the Dudley homestead. He attended the local public schools and later entered Ricker Classical Institute at Houlton, Maine, from which he was graduated in 1898. When he completed his education he returned to the home farm, where he has since remained, devoting his life to farming work in which he has been very successful. Politically, Mr. Dudley supports the principles and candidates of the Republican party. He is chairman of the Republican Town Committee for his district, and for twenty-one years he has been a member of the local Board of Selectmen, serving as chairman of this board for the last seventeen years. He is affiliated fraternally with the Ancient Free and Accepted Masons, in which organization he has taken the third degree. He is also a member of the Modern Woodmen of America, and of the Grange. He and his family attend the Baptist church.

Melvin A. Dudley married Ethel M. Bearce, who was born at Ashland, Maine, the daughter of Lewis and Elizabeth (Chase) Bearce. Mr. and Mrs. Dudley are the parents of one child, Allen.

FORREST M. DUDLEY—One of the most successful men in his section of Maine is Forrest M. Dudley. A potato grower and shipper by occupation, he owns about three hundred and forty acres of land situated on Dudley Road, some eleven and a half miles from the village of Mapleton, where he raises many barrels of excellent potatoes and supervises their shipment to the large city markets. He is also a director of the Merchants' Trust and Banking Company of Presque Isle, Maine, and he acts as manager and buyer of the Maine section for the Atlantic and Pacific Tea Company, purchasing and shipping potatoes. Mr. Dudley is highly esteemed in his community as a public-spirited citizen. His father, Micajah H. Dudley, who was born in Maine, was a farmer and engaged in this work until his death. His mother, who before her marriage was Hannah Elois, was also born in Maine.

Forrest M. Dudley was born August 16, 1888, in the town of Castle Hill, Maine. He entered the local public schools and later attended Ricker Classical Institute, at Houlton, Maine, where he remained for three years. At the end of that time the illness of his father forced him to withdraw, and in his eighteenth year he returned to the family farm as manager. After his father's death he purchased the farm and has conducted it ever since, gradually adding to his holdings until now they total three hundred and forty acres of fine farming land, well suited to the raising of potatoes. Mr. Dudley is well acquainted with the best farming methods and has been very successful in his chosen occupation. He acts as director of the district manager for the Atlantic and Pacific Tea

Merchants' Trust and Banking Company, and as Company, in charge of buying and shipping potatoes.

Politically, Mr. Dudley is a member of the Republican party, and he is now a member of the local school committee. He is affiliated fraternally with the Ancient Free and Accepted Masons, and is also a member of the Independent Order of Odd Fellows, Encampment and Canton; and of the Knights of Pythias. He and his family attend the Baptist church.

Mr. Dudley married Avis Tilley, who was born in the town of Castle Hill, Maine. They are the parents of four children: Dana F., Willa, Pauline, and Ruth.

GUSTAVUS A. YOUNG—From 1918, Gustavus A. Young, whose various experiences as a business man and a craftsman, in Maine and elsewhere, have given him more than the average knowledge of human nature, has been settled in Island Falls as postmaster and manager of the Katahdin Telephone Company. He was named to the postoffice, which is third class, by President Wilson, and operates a rural route and employs two clerks in the office itself.

Born August 27, 1877, at Crystal, Maine, son of Anson H. and Ida M. (Bradford) Young, he comes of Maine farming stock, his father having been a farmer there all his life, and his grandfather for the greater part of his life. When Gustavus A. Young was two and one-half years old, his father died, and on the marriage of his mother to William C. Hackett, the boy spent much of his time with his maternal grandmother, Sarah Bradford, who died April 4, 1928, at the age of ninety-three years and eleven days. Educated in the public schools of Crystal, Maine, he spent one term in the Business College in Bangor, and then found employment in Bridgewater, Maine, as clerk and bookkeeper for Hunt & Company, lumbermen, tanners, and proprietors of a general store. Transferred to their store in Island Falls, he remained there for a year, after which he married and turned to farming, at Crystal, Maine. Six years later he returned to Island Falls, found work as a carpenter, then joined the Emerson Lumber Company as clerk and bookkeeper, and next went to the West Indies in the employ of the J. W.

Moore Water Company. On his return to Island Falls he spent six years with the Mattawamkeag Lumber Company, and soon after the reorganization of this concern as the Northern Wooden Ware Company, he became postmaster. He had been town clerk of Crystal, and had served some years on the Island Falls School Board. Politically, he is a Republican. He is a Free and Accepted Mason, and belongs to the Blue Lodge and Chapter. With his family, he is active in the affairs of the United Baptist Church.

Mr. Young married Ila L. Ackerson, daughter of Harden and Angie Ackerson, of Bridgewater. Their daughter is Helen Ida, wife of Benjamin Edwards, who is in the employ of the Bangor and Augusta Railroad Company at Oakfield, Maine.

GEORGE F. POMROY—As a boy, George F. Pomroy, of Presque Isle, Aroostook County, was forced by the straitened financial condition of his family to seek employment as soon as he had concluded his studies in the public schools of his community.

Mr. Pomroy was born in Maysville, now part of the town of Presque Isle, November 30, 1851, the son of Cyrus and Elizabeth (Small) Pomroy, the former a native of Sandy River, Franklin County, and the latter a native of the Miramichi District of New Brunswick. The father and mother of Mr. Pomroy came in boats with some other families in early days to settle in Aroostook, taking up locations in Maysville, then a township of its own. There they resided and brought up their families, tilling the ground and living a hard but healthy life. The father of Mr. Pomroy died at the age of seventy-nine years, respected and mourned by his neighbors. As stated, George F. Pomroy was forced to seek employment at an early age and he went to work in the lumber woods, driving logs on the streams. He saved his money and was soon enabled to purchase the rights of a farm in Washburn, Aroostook County, from his brother, Paul A. Pomroy. He operated this farm for two years and then he traded it for another farm near his native town of Maysville, later purchasing a second farm in the same locality. About 1902 his health gave out and he was forced to retire from agricultural pursuits. He

sold one of his farms, keeping the other until
1924, when he disposed of that one. In politics,
Mr. Pomroy is a staunch Republican. He was
road commissioner for the town of Presque Isle
for many years, until ill-health forced him to
resign the office. He is affiliated with the United
Baptist Church.

George F. Pomroy married Frances E. Clark, a
native of Carleton County, New Brunswick, daughter of John L. and Mary A. (Clark) Clark, who,
although bearing the same surname, were not related by blood ties. They came to the United
States in 1861 and spent the rest of their life in this
country. Mrs. Pomroy died February 13, 1926. Mr.
and Mrs. Pomroy were the parents of one child, a
daughter, Eva L., married to Adelbert Lumbard,
a prosperous farmer living in Presque Isle. They
have one child, Ruth, married to Lawrence Hed-
rich, and they have one child, Maxine.

FOREST F. PAGE—A prominent figure in
the farming industry of the State, Forest F. Page,
of Ashland, operates two of the largest farms in
this vicinity, specializing in the raising of seed potatoes, besides growing and shipping large quantities of this product for food consumption. Mr.
Page came to Ashland twenty-one years ago and
at first got out lumber and built a potato house,
rented various farms, engaging in potato raising
and also in the wholesale trade, buying from the
surrounding producers and shipping to the large
markets. Under his capable direction and energetic methods, his business grew and prospered
rapidly and he then bought the large farm of one
hundred and sixty-five acres from L. C. Bearce,
in addition to which he and his wife own a farm
of considerable size on the Sheridan Road. Mr.
Page was born in Fort Fairfield, June 6, 1880, son
of Erastus Page, of Ashland, and Jane (Lannigan)
Page, of Fort Fairfield. Erastus Page, who is
now retired, was engaged for many years in the
business of agriculture and was one of the leading
persons in community affairs.

Forest F. Page received his education in the
public schools of Fort Fairfield, after which he
was associated with his father in farming until he
was twenty-one years old. He then entered on an

independent career, tilling forty acres of land at
Fort Fairfield successfully until he sold out when
he removed to Ashland. Mr. Page maintains a
large warehouse in this town in connection with
his business and gives employment to a number of
people. One of the town's most esteemed citizens,
he has always taken a constructive interest in civic
welfare and progress and is a leader in all projects
that are directed toward the good of the community. In politics, he is an Independent, preferring to make his own choice at election times,
rather than align himself with any specific political
party. He is active in fraternal circles, being a
member of the Blue Lodge, Free and Accepted
Masons, Ashland, and of the Independent Order of
Odd Fellows, and the local Grange. He and his
family are prominent members of the Episcopal
church, where he acts as trustee.

Forest F. Page married Rebecca M. Bearce, of
Ashland, daughter of Durbin and Lavisa (Coffin)
Bearce, and they have six children: 1. Annie,
graduate of Ashland High School, who spent two
years at business college in Bangor. 2. Melvin,
student at the local high school. 3. Alice. 4. Rowena. 5. Bertha. 6. Muriel.

ORIN L. WINSLOW—Proprietor of the flour
and feed mill of Mapleton Village, Mapleton
Township, Aroostook County, Maine, doing business here under the firm style of Orin L. Winslow,
he is one of the most prominent and public spirited
of citizens of the community; and in connection
with his commercial establishment he owns and
operates a fertile tract of farm land amounting to
some two hundred and seventy acres in Mapleton
Township. Mr. Winslow is a native of this township; he was born on February 11, 1891, son of
Frank and Nellie (Chandler) Winslow, his father
having been born at Westbrook, Maine, a farmer,
and his mother at Mapleton Village. Both Frank
and Nellie (Chandler) Winslow are now (1928)
living, residing in Mapleton Township.

Orin L. Winslow received his education in the
public schools, and for one year attended the
Presque Isle High School. Upon quitting high
school he went at once into agriculture with his
father, and so continued until he purchased the

Mapleton flour and feed mill, in 1924. The mill was established by Frank Chandler and was later passed into the control of the Aroostook Federation of Farmers, from which organization Mr. Winslow purchased it. He is a Republican, loyal to the principles of government upheld by the party, and active in the political matters of his community, where he is possessed of a considerable influence. For two years he served as tax collector, and is now (1928) a member of the school committee. He gives of his time constantly to programs designed for the welfare and progress of Mapleton Village, the township and county, and is known as a representative and substantial citizen, conscientious in the exercise of public office and intelligent and successful in the direction of the mill and farm. On the farm, Mr. Winslow employs the most modern of scientific agricultural methods purveyed by State and National departments of agriculture, and under his husbandry the acres yield large return. He engages in general farming, rotating his crops, and disposing of the produce locally. Mr. Winslow was on the farm during the World War and did his utmost to insure the production of ample provision for his country in time of such stringent need; on the various war work committees and boards he served whenever requested, tirelessly, and was active in local Liberty Loan drives. He is a member of the Blue Lodge of the Free and Accepted Masons; Royal Arch Masons, Royal and Select Masters at Caribou; the Knights of Pythias, at Mapleton, and other organizations.

Orin L. Winslow married Marguerite Turner, of Mapleton, daughter of George W. and Margaret (Waddell) Turner. Both the families of Turner and Waddell are old in the history of Mapleton Township; George W. Turner is owner and proprietor of five hundred acres of rich agricultural land in this township, Republican, active in affairs of the community, and retained by the Fruit Growers' Association as agent with authority to purchase produce throughout Aroostook County. Mr. and Mrs. Winslow are the parents of two children: Marion, born in 1927; and Matthew, born in 1928. Mrs. Winslow takes an interested part in affairs of the Methodist Church and is popular in the social life of Mapleton Village.

PERCY RAYMOND WINSLOW—Youth, energy, ambition and quiet determination to make for himself a secure place among his fellows in the busy marts of commerce have brought to Percy Raymond Winslow, of Ashland, their reward at an age when most activities are but beginning. The dignity of high financial office has been achieved, together with the confidence, respect and sincere friendship of those with whom he has been brought in contact. Appreciating the fact that opportunity often lies at hand for the man who elects to invoke it, and that departure from one's native locality is not necessary to accomplishment, Mr. Winslow already has proved the truth of that condition. The result is that he is safely established and may be justified in feeling that his work among those with whom he has all his life abided is assistful to the community as a whole as well as to himself as an individual.

Percy Raymond Winslow was born in West Falmouth, Maine, December 20, 1897. His father was William Everett, a civil engineer, and his mother, Dorcas Ellen Winslow. He was educated at Westbrook Seminary, Portland, from which he was graduated in 1914. He then attended Bates College, at Lewiston, from 1916 to 1917. Then came the World War and the call of his country. Responding promptly, he joined the first army of the American Expeditionary Forces, was made a corporal in the First Provisional High Burst Ranging Section and sent to France. His services continued until March, 1919, when he was honorably mustered out and at once returned to West Falmouth. In that year he was made assistant treasurer of the Katahdin Trust Company, of Patten, serving for one year, when he accepted the post of treasurer of the Ashland Trust Company. He was elected treasurer of the Town of Ashland in 1926 and still holds that office. He is also finance officer of Donald DeLaite Post, American Legion, of Ashland, and is a member of the Pioneer Lodge, Free and Accepted Masons, of Ashland.

He married, in Sherman, Maine, November 25, 1920, Verna Lora Kneeland, daughter of George and Lillian (Perry) Kneeland. They have one child, Dorothy, born April 24, 1922.

HUGH HAYWARD—Before his appointment as postmaster of Ashland, Maine, in 1924, Hugh Hayward had been a clerk there for thirteen years, while W. B. Hallett was postmaster, but resigned to enter business life.

Born at Portage, Maine, November 7, 1879, he was a son of John Halbert and Martha (Brown) Hayward. The elder Hayward, who was born in New Brunswick, Canada, was a lumberman, and had lived in Maine from his sixteenth year, and his wife was born in Maine. Educated in the public schools of Portage and Ashland, Maine, and at the Houlton Business College, Hugh Hayward found his first employment in the United States Post-office, and when he resigned, went to the Penobscot Development Company as division clerk, remaining there three years. Prior to his appointment as postmaster, he was a warehouse clerk for N. C. Howe.

Mr. Hayward, who has always been a Republican, served his community both as first selectman, and as town treasurer. He is a member of the Free and Accepted Masons, Ashland, and Caribou Chapter. He attends the Congregational Church.

Mr. Hayward married Abigail McNally, daughter of George H. and Julia (Butler) McNally, and their children are George Halbert and Hugh Bradford Hayward.

JOHN G. CHADWICK—In point of seniority dean of the architects and builders of northern Maine, John G. Chadwick has been engaged in constructive work in Houlton since September, 1879, and is still active.

Son of Andrew J. and Bessie T. (Gordon) Chadwick, he was born in Holden, Maine, June 26, 1855. The family originally came from New Hampshire, where the elder Chadwick was a surveyor. One of seven children, all of whom are now dead save himself, John G. Chadwick received his education in the schools of Winterport, Maine, and while still going to school, served his apprenticeship to the carpenter's trade, which in those days required seven years. On becoming a journeyman, he worked in several Maine cities, and finally settled in Houlton, where he established himself first as a master carpenter, and then developed into the profession of architect and builder.

Mr. Chadwick is a member of the board of trustees of the Methodist Episcopal Church, fire and building inspector for the town of Houlton, a member of the Independent Order of Odd Fellows and all its branches, in which he has been through all chairs. He is also a member of the Rotary Club. He is a Republican.

Mr. Chadwick married (first) Carrie Lincoln, their children being Harold, who is now a florist in Houlton, Maine; Helen Gordon, who married Russell Britton, cashier of the Farmers' National Bank. On the death of Mrs. Chadwick he married (second) Myrtle B. Bolstridge.

GEORGE RICHARD RANDOLPH KETCHUM—Although born to but few advantages, the late George Richard R. Ketchum, by his own initiative and ability, overcame all obstacles and attained the position of one of the foremost citizens of Aroostook County. Mr. Ketchum was a man of strict probity and unswerving integrity and was accorded the respect and esteem of all who knew him.

He was a native of Canada, born in Woodstock, Carleton County, New Brunswick, June 25, 1849, the son of Ralph and Judith Caroline (Bull) Ketchum. At the age of fourteen years he started out in life, working in various minor positions until he was enabled to start a little country store in his native county in New Brunswick, to which he added the business of buying and selling produce raised by the neighboring farmers. He succeeded in his ventures and attained a leading position in his community.

It was in 1891 that he decided to remove to the United States and in that year he purchased a farm in Garfield, just outside of the village of Ashland, where he engaged in agriculture and in the timber business, cutting long and short lumber. He was also interested in one of Ashland's starch factories. He spent most of his life in Ashland and was one of the prominent figures in the town's activities. In politics he was a Republican and was an active member of the Episcopal church. He was affiliated with the Free and Accepted Masons, and he was an honorary member of Woodstock Lodge, in the New Brunswick jurisdiction.

George R. R. Ketchum was married to Inez A. Clayton, who died, leaving two sons, Ralph and Charles Clayton, and a daughter, Inez, now Mrs. L. L. Adams, of Ellsworth. His second wife was Abbie (Clayton) Smith, the widow of William Smith and sister of Mr. Ketchum's first wife. By her first marriage, Mrs. Ketchum was the mother of two sons, Randolph and H. Neeley Smith.

On March 5, 1927, Mr. Ketchum passed away, to the deep and sincere regret of the many friends he had made in and around Ashland. His funeral was largely attended and there were many expressions of sorrow at the loss of a man who, by example and precept, had done so much for the betterment and uplift of his community. He is survived by his wife, a daughter, and two sons, and his two stepsons.

———————

EDWARD C. DONOVAN—Owner of two hundred and eighty-five acres in Houlton Township, Aroostook County, on the Ludlow Road, Edward C. Donovan is one of the most prosperous farmers and public spirited members of the community. He engages in general farming, raising hay, grain and potatoes, which he sells in the local market.

Edward C. Donovan was born on the farm he now conducts, in Aroostook County, on October 27, 1883, son of Timothy J. and Alice (Hogan) Donovan. Timothy and Alice Donovan were each descended from families long established in New England and well and favorably known, the former having been born on the Houlton farm and the latter at Limerick. Timothy Donovan was active in matters of the community and wielded considerable power in politics. He was high in the estimation of the people of town and countryside, and devoted his entire life to the farm, varying the crops and specializing in the raising of potatoes. Timothy and Alice Donovan were the parents of five children.

Edward C. Donovan attended the public schools of Houlton and went immediately to work upon the

farm for his father. His career has been an honorable one, and his prosperity deserved. He is a member of the Knights of Columbus and of the Catholic church.

Edward C. Donovan married Myrtle Haggerty, born at Littleton, daughter of Charles and Louise (Lafferty) Haggerty, her father having been a native of Houlton and her mother born at Benton, New Brunswick. Mr. and Mrs. Donovan are the parents of five children: John, Wilfred, Albert, Justina, and Timothy.

———————

CLAUDE L. DeWITT—In the ranks of those who produce the country's foodstuffs, which are the most vital requisites in the Nation's existence, Claude L. DeWitt stands high as an important producer of high grade potatoes for food consumption. Mr. DeWitt operates a large farm of two hundred and ten acres on the State road, from Presque Isle to Fort Fairfield, where he is engaged in general farming, specializing in potato growing. He has always been a prominent figure in local agricultural circles, and through his energy and initiative carries on a substantial and prosperous farm organization. He was born in New Brunswick, May 12, 1883, son of James Alonzo DeWitt, who died in 1926, and Mary (Churchill) DeWitt, who is still living. James Alonzo DeWitt came to Presque Isle about 1893, with his family, and settled on the old Smith farm on Center Line Road, engaging in agriculture which he followed for many years.

Claude L. DeWitt received his education in the public schools of New Brunswick, and coming to Maine when ten years of age, attended the Presque Isle public schools, and after high school, entered a business college at Caribou. Finishing his studies, he became associated with his father in farm operation until he was twenty-one. At that time, his father established him in an independent farm venture where he remained for one year, after which he returned to assist his father. Later, he bought his present farm from F. Guiou and he has ever since continued to operate it successfully, using modern and efficient methods of cultivation and always advancing with the progress of the times. In politics, Mr. DeWitt is a member of the

Republican party and takes a deep interest in the civic welfare of the community, being always active in all projects for improvement and advancement. He is prominent in fraternal circles, being a member of the Free and Accepted Masons, Blue Lodge and Council of Presque Isle, Caribou Chapter, and Houlton Commandery; he is a member of the Ancient Arabic Order Nobles of the Mystic Shrine at Anah Temple, Bangor, and of the local Grange and Moosleuk Club. In his religious affiliations, he attends the Congregational church.

Claude E. DeWitt married Evelyn Irving, a graduate of Caribou High School, daughter of H. D. and Pauline (Davis) Irving, and they have four children: Dorothy, Catherine, Gwendolyn and Irving.

WILLIAM J. GRIFFIN—A prosperous potato grower at New Limerick, with postoffice address at Houlton, William J. Griffin owes his success in his business to the fact that he has made a lifelong study of his specialty, and has left nothing undone in order to make his farming property one of the best cultivated in this section of the State. He has succeeded by perseverance and thrift, and he has the well-deserved regard and esteem of his fellow-citizens and all with whom he deals, whether in business or social life.

William J. Griffin was born January 4, 1879, at Benton, New Brunswick, son of William Griffin, a farmer, who is now deceased, and Mary (Howie) Griffin, both natives of New Brunswick, Mrs. Griffin surviving her husband. After attending the New Brunswick public schools, he came to Houlton, where he took a business course, and then, working as a farm hand until 1925, bought his present farming property of two hundred and eighty-two acres, from his wife's father's estate, known as the Willett farm, and situated in the town of New Limerick, on the Bangor State Road. Here he does general farming and sells potatoes to local buyers. Fraternally, Mr. Griffin is affiliated with the Modern Woodmen of America and with the Knights of Columbus. He is a communicant of the Roman Catholic church.

William J. Griffin married, in January, 1904, Eva Theresa Willett, who was born on the Willett farm, daughter of Thaddeus and Catherine Willett, an old established family here; Thaddeus Willett a native of Madawaska, his wife born in New Limerick, and both now deceased. Mr. and Mrs. Willett had three children: 1. Walter F., lives at New Limerick; farmer. 2. Eva Theresa, wife of William J. Griffin. 3. Fred, an automobile salesman. Mr. and Mrs. Griffin have a daughter Phyllis, who was born June, 27, 1905, and received her education at Houlton High School, St. Mary's Academy, at Houlton, and in the University of Maine.

CYRILLE CYR—A man who is known for his interest and activity in good roads is Cyrille Cyr, of Presque Isle, Maine. Mr. Cyr is the son of Richard and Sophia (Jalbert) Cyr. His father was a native of Canada and his mother of the country of Acadia. They made their home in New Brunswick and never came into the States.

Cyrille Cyr was born in New Brunswick on April 12, 1872. When he was twenty-one years of age, he left his native land and came into the State of Maine, settling at what was then Maysville, which has since become the town of Presque Isle. He at first worked as a farm hand and after learning how to handle a farm and by practicing thrift, he was able to own and operate a farm of his choice. This farm, which comprises one hundred acres located on the State road that runs from Caribou to Presque Isle, about five miles from the latter place, he purchased from Ray Danforth and has continued to cultivate and improve it. About ten years ago, Mr. Cyr was made road commissioner and put in charge of the State road that runs from Caribou to Presque Isle and also in charge of the Washburn Road, which is a State aid road. After taking up the duties of the road commissioner, Mr. Cyr began to gradually turn over the running of his farm to his son, who now practically has the management of it. Mr. Cyr is a Republican in his political affiliations and he and his family are members of the Roman Catholic church.

Cyrille Cyr married Clara Belanger. They have seven children: Lena, Ida, Oneal, Florence, Benjamin, Ernest and Clara.

WILLIAM H. COOK—Native of Aroostook County, Maine, and, since 1902 owner of a farm of three hundred and sixty acres near Mapleton Village, township of Mapleton, having purchased it previous to that year, William H. Cook has become one of the substantial and representative agriculturists of his community, here engaging in general farming upon his fertile tract and specializing in the growth of seed and table potatoes, of which he disposes in the local market. William H. Cook was born on a farm in the township of Castle Hill on March 19, 1874, son of Edward C. and Harriett (Gammon) Cook, his father having been born at Windham, Maine, and his mother at Casco, Maine.

Edward C. Cook came from Windham to Aroostook County before the outbreak of the Civil War, and served with valor in that war. When mustered out at the end of hostilities he returned to Maine, but located in Cumberland County, later returning to Aroostook, and here, on a farm, spent the remainder of his days, highly respected by everyone who knew him.

William H. Cook received his education in the public schools of Aroostook and, on completion of studies, at the age of seventeen years, went to Massachusetts, there securing employment without loss of time on the electric street railway and in the railway machine shops at Lynn. He remained in this connection for eight years, during the last three of which he was foreman of the repair shop of the Lynn plant; and in 1902 he came to Aroostook County to manage his farm property. Here Mr. Cook is accounted not only a successful farmer but a business man of foresight and sound judgment. He employs the most modern methods of agriculture recommended by State and National departments of agriculture, and adapts them to crops best suited to his soil; yields are large under his direction. A Republican, Mr. Cook is loyal to the principles of government upheld by that party and is prominent in local political matters. Never, however, has he accepted the suggestion that he become candidate for public office. He is a member of the Baptist church and generous in contributions to charitable and other causes of merit.

William H. Cook married (first) Laila A. Hudson, deceased, and by her was father of seven children, three sons, four daughters. Laila A. (Hudson) Cook was a daughter of Israel Hudson. Mr. Cook married (second) Temmie A. Baird, widow of William Baird and mother of his two sons. Mrs. Temmie A. (Baird) Cook attends the Bible Students' Association.

———

JOHN R. CONLOGUE—A life-long farmer, and a good one, John R. Conlogue cultivates a fine place at New Limerick, on the Bangor State Road, near Houlton, Maine, where he practices general farming, with potatoes as his chief money crop. Son of James and Anna (Donovan) Conlogue, both natives of Ireland who had been brought to America as children by their parents, he was born in New Limerick, April 23, 1877, on a farm his father had himself cleared.

After completing the course in the local public schools, John R. Conlogue went to Houlton, where he took a business course, working for Dr. Dickerson while in school, but the call of the land was too strong for the commercial career he had planned and so he returned to his father's place, saving his earnings, and when twenty-eight years of age, started farming on his own account, buying his first acreage from W. H. Monahan. Mr. Conlogue is a Democrat. He has served for three years as town superintendent, and one term as selectman. He is a communicant of the Roman Catholic church and a member of the Grange.

He married Nellie Shanley, of Bangor, daughter of Thomas and Mary (Cullinan) Shanley, of that city.

———

ORIN E. BECKWITH—Farmer and potato grower, Orin E. Beckwith owns and conducts a fertile tract of seventy acres of land on the main highway between Presque Isle and Mapleton, on the outskirts of Mapleton Village, in the township of Mapleton. Moreover, he owns a farm of sixty-five acres in Castle Hill Township. Both of these he operates in general agriculture, rotating crops according to the most scientific of methods approved by the Department of Agriculture at Washington and by the Department of Agriculture of the State of Maine, and makes a specialty of potatoes, which he markets locally along with other produce. He is known as one of the most progressive and public-spirited of the younger men of the Mapleton countryside.

Orin E. Beckwith was born on October 1, 1898, son of Ernest G. and Jennie (English) Beckwith, his father being a native of Maine, his mother a native of the province of New Brunswick, Canada, both now (1928) living. Ernest Beckwith has devoted his career to farming, and now resides with his wife on a farm abutting on the State road to the village of Castle Hill. Orin Beckwith received his education in the public schools of the neighboring village of Presque Isle, and there graduated from high school in 1915. For the next ten years, until 1925, he worked on the farm with his father. In 1925 he leased a piece of land and went into farming for himself; he readily demonstrated what he could do as proprietor of a farm, and on this favorable showing purchased the two farms, making him owner and operator of a total of one hundred and thirty-five acres. The farm on which he lives (the seventy acres on the highway between Presque Isle and the village of Mapleton) he purchased from Nelson Pearson; the other he purchased from C. C. Smith. A Republican, and loyal to the principles of government upheld by that party, Mr. Beckwith takes some part in political matters of the community. He is a member of the Independent Order of Odd Fellows, the Presque Isle Encampment of Rebekahs, and the Link Club. He attends the Baptist church and is generous in his contributions to charitable and other worthy causes, whether or not they are sponsored by the church of his own choice.

Orin E. Beckwith married Etta Greenlaw, born at Washburn, daughter of Harry and Rose (Griffin) Greenlaw; and they are the parents of one child, a daughter, Joan.

JAMES NOWLAND—An interesting and varied career characterized the life of the late James Nowland, of Ashland, who, coming to this country when a young man to engage in business, soon found himself in the exciting adventures of an Indian war in the Seminole country of Florida.

Mr. Nowland was born in Liverpool, England,

son of James Martin and Catherine (Boyle) Nowland. He received his education in the schools of his native city, after which he became an apprentice in a large business institution and soon became an expert accountant. When he was twenty-two years old, he came to the United States, landing at New York with letters of introduction to a number of prominent American business men. These he was unable to use, owing to the cholera epidemic which was raging at that time. Meeting some officers from the Black Hawk War who were seeking recruits, he enlisted, entirely unacquainted with the country or conditions, but always daring and courageous. He was ordered South with the troops who were going to Florida, and saw active service against the Seminole Indians. After the war, Mr. Nowland was sent North and stationed in the garrison at Houlton, where he remained in the service of the regular army until the expiration of his term of enlistment. After his discharge, his participation in the war having automatically made him a United States citizen, he engaged in farming at Houlton, but after a period of years, gave up this venture and removed to St. John's, New Brunswick, where he accepted a position as bookkeeper with a large mercantile establishment. Here, he soon acquired a reputation for great ability and knowledge and was ever known as a man of sterling character and keen business sense. For eight years, he continued successfully, when the Civil War began in the United States, and as a loyal citizen, he felt it was his duty to return to offer his services. A dramatic incident occurred in connection with his return to this country: On the eve of his leaving New Brunswick to enlist, his sister, his only living relative, arrived at his home from abroad, yet Mr. Nowland, putting his duty to his country above personal feelings, went off to the service, where he was of great value in training the new recruits on account of his previous experience. He received the rank of adjutant and saw active service, distinguishing himself for his bravery and courage, and winning the acclaim of both men and officers. When the terrible strife was ended, Mr. Nowland came to Ashland and engaged in business, acting as bookkeeper for the Jewett and Pitcher Lumber Company for many years. With his great energy and vitality, he was soon known as a leader in the civic affairs of the town, and was always an

eager supporter of all movements for community
welfare and progress. At the time of his death,
the entire town of Ashland mourned him greatly,
realizing what a noble and inspiring influence he
had always exercised in town affairs.

James Nowland married at Houlton (first)
Susan Griffin, who died, leaving three daughters, Katherine, who died when a child; Susan
and Emily, who are deceased. Mr. Nowland married (second) Helen Augusta Parker, daughter of
Alexander Parker, a prominent farmer of Hodgdon, and Lucetta (Soule) Parker, and to this union
were born eight children: Mary P., Carrie, Alice,
Lucy, died when young; James Martin, Nellie,
also died when young; Charles A. and George
D., M. D.

All of the family attended the Episcopal church,
and all, excepting James Martin, who teaches in
Medford, and resides in Franklin, Massachusetts,
are living in Ashland.

EDMUND WELLINGTON MacBURNIE—
Resident in Aroostook County since 1882, when
he was thirteen years of age, Edmund Wellington
MacBurnie, formerly owner of a farm of one
hundred and forty acres in Houlton Township not
far distant from Houlton, and which he has recently sold, now maintains a home in Houlton
Village. Mr. MacBurnie is actively identified
with the civic affairs of the town, and is one of
the prominent men in the community; he is sincerely respected, and has a number of friends.

Edmund Wellington MacBurnie was born at
Rockland, Carleton County, New Brunswick, Dominion of Canada, on April 16, 1869, son of William H. and Annie (Friend) MacBurnie, and was
one of seven children, four of whom are now living.
The family resided at Carleton until Edmund Mac-
Burnie had nearly completed grammar school, then
came to Bridgewater, Aroostook County, Maine.
Here Edmund MacBurnie completed his education, graduating from high school, and entered the
business established by his father, dealing in lumber, and also occupied himself with work upon
the farm, near Bridgewater. When he was twenty-five years of age, in 1894, he purchased the farm
and conducted it with success for twenty years,
then disposed of it. In 1914 he went to Utah with

the intention of settling there in agriculture; he
remained in the West three years, and returned
to Aroostook County to purchase the farm in
Houlton Township. Mr. MacBurnie has enjoyed
prosperity on these acres, for his methods of agriculture are of the most scientific and time tried.
Proprietor of one of the largest farms in the State,
located in one of the richest counties, he devoted
the greater portion of the area under cultivation
to potatoes, for which the valley is known as an
important source supplying the centers of population up and down the Atlantic seaboard. The
farm was well maintained in all respects; the
buildings conveniently plotted and the livestock of
the best. Mr. MacBurnie is a Republican, and
has authority in the political matters of Houlton.
He is a member of the Independent Order of
Odd Fellows, at Bridgewater, and of the Court
Street Baptist Church, of Houlton.

Edmund Wellington MacBurnie married Myra
E. Fulton, born at Bridgewater, daughter of
Charles and Mary C. (Allen) Fulton, and one of
three children, of whom Mrs. MacBurnie is eldest.
The others are married also: Salome W. Fulton
to Adrian Scott, and Elizabeth Fulton to William
Patten. Mrs. MacBurnie received her early edu-
cation at Bridgewater, then, for one year attended
Ricker Classical Institute, and, for a year, the
Farmington Normal School. For several years she
engaged in the profession of teaching, in the Free
High School of Boston, then studied nursing in
the Boston City Hospital. She graduated as a
trained nurse and took up private nursing in New
York City. Her health failed while thus engaged
and she returned to Maine, much to the benefit of
her condition. She resumed nursing, under Dr.
Sawyer, at Houlton, and continued in that capacity
until her marriage. Mr. and Mrs. MacBurnie are
the parents of three children: Charles William,
Gladys Louise, and Ralph Paul.

ERNEST BONVILLE—Contractor for paper hanging and painting, Ernest Bonville, of
Presque Isle, Aroostook County, employs five
helpers the year round, and is accounted among
the more progressive citizens of the community.
He is a native of the State of Maine. Mr. Bonville was born at Jackman in the month of Sep-

tember, 1889, son of Eli Joseph and Louise (Thibault) Bonville, natives of the Province of New Brunswick, Dominion of Canada.

Ernest Bonville attended the public schools of Ashland, and at the age of sixteen years went to work in wood pulp and saw mills. There he continued to be employed for several years, until he reached the decision to go into business for himself. In 1911 he opened a shop for papering and painting in his home at Presque Isle, North Main Street, with a store room for display of paper stuffs and paint swatches. Here he has attained to some prosperity as a contractor; his talents in commerce and ability as contracting paperer and painter are widely recognized. A Republican, Mr. Bonville is loyal to the principles of government upheld by that party and has a considerable following in local political questions. His contributions to charitable causes are readily forthcoming and generous in proportion.

Ernest Bonville married Emma Dionne, and they are the parents of two children: Jeanette Louise and William Thomas.

GEORGE W. MacNAIR—Although he has been a life-long Republican and active locally in the affairs of the party in Houlton, Maine, for many years, the only public office George W. MacNair ever would accept was that of town constable, which he has now held for the last ten years. He is a prosperous contractor and builder, has been in business for himself in Houlton for thirty-nine years, during which time he has accumulated real estate and built several fine residences on various tracts which he still owns, so it is not the salary that attracts Mr. MacNair. The fact is he has always been a "booster" for the town of his choice, invests his money there, knows everybody, and is liked by everyone, even those with whom his badge is by no means popular.

Born in New Brunswick, Canada, January 1, 1855, he was the son of Thomas and Ann (Hill) MacNair. Educated in the public schools of his home town where his father was a carpenter and contractor, he learned the business in his father's shop, and continued with him until he had reached the age of thirty, when he came to the United

States and settled in Houlton. He worked there as a journeyman carpenter for four years before setting up in business on his own account, where his industry and practical ideas insured success from the outset. He is a member of Houlton Lodge of the Benevolent and Protective Order of Elks, and attends the Congregational Church with his family.

Mr. McNair married Mary J. Patten, daughter of John C. and Emily (Crips) Patten, of Sussex, New Brunswick, Canada. Their children are: Margaret, who married Fred Cates; John, Charles, Frank, and Leonard MacNair.

ARTHUR G. ANDREWS—Doing a general household furnishings and undertaking business, Arthur G. Andrews is one of the leading business men of Ashland, Maine, where he is a member of the firm of A. G. Andrews and Company. Mr. Andrews, who is a licensed embalmer, has adopted all the latest methods of embalming, and in connection with his funeral parlors he maintains a fine show room with all up-to-the-minute equipment. He is a native of Maine, and consequently is thoroughly familiar with local conditions and with the people of this part of the country. His knowledge and understanding of his community enable him to take a leading part in its civic and social affairs, in which he is deeply interested, and to participate freely in its fraternal life, as well as to adapt his business with outstanding success to the special needs of this district.

Mr. Andrews was born in Plymouth, Maine, on November 24, 1879, a son of Daniel and Nancy (Allen) Andrews, the former of whom, a granite worker by occupation, was a native of Massachusetts, and the latter a native of Maine. As a boy, Arthur G. Andrews attended the schools of Plymouth, his native town; later became a student at the Maine Central Institute and at Shaw's Business College, in Bangor; and finally at the Massachusetts School of Embalming, in Boston, from which he was graduated. His business career has been extensive and varied. He was assistant bookkeeper for the C. M. Conant Company for two years; then he established a furniture business in Milo, Maine, this enterprise being a partnership

with W. G. Orcutt, with whom he later removed
to Ashland, where they continued the business for
three years, at the end of which time he and his
brother Walter bought the Orcutt interests and
together they continued. the business, and at the
end of two years he bought out Walter's interest
and continued business for himself, remaining
alone from 1910 until 1918. In 1918 he took Carl
L. Hews as his partner, and they established the
undertaking and furniture business which is known
as A. G. Andrews and Company, but in 1928 the
undertaking business was discontinued, Mr. Andrews buying out his partner and is now sole owner
of the business. Mr. Andrews is a Republican in
his party convictions. He is affiliated with the
Free and Accepted Masons, in which order he
belongs to the Blue Lodge, in Ashland; the Royal
Arch Chapter, in Caribou; the Commandery in
Houlton; and Anah Temple, Ancient Arabic Order
Nobles of the Mystic Shrine, in Bangor. He and
his family attend the Protestant Episcopal church.

Arthur G. Andrews married Margaret Hews, a
daughter of Roscoe and Caroline (Bartlett) Hews.

HORACE HASTINGS McGOWN—One of
the outstanding men in public, fraternal, commercial and agricultural affairs of the town of Houlton and its vicinity is Horace Hastings McGown,
who owns one hundred and thirty-five acres of rich
land near the town of Ludlow, not far distant
from Houlton. Here he engages in general farming, employing the best and most modern of scientific methods of management, to considerable profit.
The Ludlow farm has been in the family of Mc-
Gown for more than half a century, and in the
neighborhood the name McGown is well and honorably known. Mr. McGown was born on this
farm on June 14, 1897, son of Llewelyn LeRoy
and Annie B. (Hand) McGown, the father having been born at Ellsworth, Maine, and the mother
at Richmond, New Brunswick, Dominion of Canada. Llewelyn McGown married three times, and
the marriage with Annie B. Hand was his third.
He was extremely popular in Houlton and devoted
his efforts toward the welfare of the community
as a whole and to the comfort and peace of the

citizens individually. He was a kindly and industrious man, and his loss was felt keenly by
his many friends, and especially so by his
widow, Annie B., and his son, Horace H., of whom
further.

Horace Hastings McGown received his education in the public schools of Houlton, then matriculated in the Ricker Classical Institute, whence he
graduated with the class of 1914. Immediately
upon graduation he settled down on the farm with
the intention of giving to its direction in practice
the theories he had mastered in school, and had
made very satisfactory progress in this direction
when the United States entered the World War.
At once he enlisted in the service of his country,
at Houlton with the Infantry. He was sent to
Slocum for training and at its completion to the
Canal Zone, where he served with the machine
gun outfit of the 33d Division of the Infantry Detachment, and there he remained one year. He was
discharged at Camp Devens, and returned to the
farm, where he has been engaged busily since. Although the management of the farm takes the
greater part of his time and application, Mr. Mc-
Gown is well known in the business and political
circles of Ludlow and Houlton, where his reputation for ability in either connection is admirable.
He disposes of the produce of the farm in the
Houlton market, and concentrates on the growing
of. potatoes, though he likewise conducts agriculture of a general character, rotating crops from
time to time. He is a member of the Republican
party and active in the cause of the party locally.
For two years he served on the town board of
selectmen, of Houlton, with distinction. He is
affiliated fraternally with the Independent Order of
Odd Fellows.

Horace Hastings McGown is now (1928) in his
thirty-first year of age, and has not married. He
lives with his mother at the country home, and
with her is a devoted member of the First Day
Adventist church. They are liberal in their contributions to charity and to kindred appeals sponsored by the church or sponsored by the greater
organization; that is, by the kindness of heart and
sympathy for the lowly and needy that is so uni-
versal throughout humanity. Mrs. McGown is
affectionately known by numerous friends.

LLEWELYN L. WILCOX, of Mapleton, Maine, is a buyer and shipper of potatoes, and has done as much as a million and a half dollars worth of business in a single year. He has traveled a great deal in the southern States, buying and inspecting for distribution. He has been associated with a number of important firms engaged in the buying and selling and distribution of farm produce. He ran the first potato house in the town in which he lives. He has now his own business, though he is associated with the distributors of his State as buyer and inspector.

Llewelyn L. Wilcox was born at Hodgdon, Maine, October 23, 1877, son of John A. and Olive M. (Hughes) Wilcox, both now deceased, and both descended from farmer stock. Mr. Wilcox was educated in the log school house at Mapleton, Maine. As a boy he worked on a farm for himself, and when he was twenty-one years old he lost his right hand in a threshing machine, but he continued to engage in farming until the year 1909, since which time he has devoted his time to the potato business, handling, buying, selling, and distributing potatoes. He ran the first potato house in Mapleton for Smith & Hoyt, with whom he was at Boston for a period of two years, handling their business, adjusting claims and selling. He was for twelve years representative of the John Grove Company of Boston, and while with them he traveled through the southern States for ten summers, buying and doing inspection work for that firm. He served for several years in the same capacity with his brothers, Charles and W. G. Wilcox, and he was for several years associated also with Phillips & Company, of Norfolk, Virginia, and he traveled the southern States for them. He has done a volume of business of $1,500,000 a year. He has now his own business and is associated also with the Maine Potato Distributors as buyer and inspector. Mr. Wilcox is a Republican in politics. He belongs to the Independent Order of Odd Fellows, and Encampment; Knights of Pythias; and Modern Woodmen of America.

He married Myrtle E. Rogers, born at Wade, Maine, daughter of Charles and Cora (Ireland) Rogers. There are four children: Leona, Cyril, Crystal, and Harry Keith. The family attends the Methodist church, of which Mr. Wilcox is trustee and steward.

Maine—2—3

STANLEY W. ANNETT—This potato-growing section of the State has in Stanley W. Annett a factor of well known abilities and resourcefulness, who has engaged in farming and potato-raising during the most active part of his career. He has owned fine properties both at Presque Isle and at Houlton, where he now resides, and the science of first class potato culture absorbs most of his time and attention with the result that buyers have recorded his product as one without successful rivalry.

Stanley W. Annett was born in January, 1881, at Carleton County, New Brunswick, a son of William Annett, deceased, and Eveline (Walker) Annett. Upon the death of his father, while Stanley was a small boy, it became necessary for him to leave school when he was only eleven years old, and after spending a few years on the farm, he was employed by a railroad company for a few years. He was then a farm hand for a few years, and after renting a farm for three years, he bought his first farm of three hundred acres at Presque Isle, which he conducted for four years. He afterwards sold out, and bought his present farm of one hundred and fifty-three acres on the State road from Houlton to Bangor. Here he carries on general farming and potato raising, disposing of his product to local buyers. He is a prosperous farmer, a self-made man, highly respected, and a good friend and neighbor. He is a Republican in his political convictions; and his religious faith is that of the Methodist Episcopal church.

Stanley W. Annett married Anna McKinnon, daughter of William and May (Kerr) McKinnon; she was born in New Brunswick while her parents who had resided in the States were visiting in that province, but they lived the rest of their life at Bridgton, Maine. Mr. and Mrs. Annett have three children: Carl, Harold, and Eva.

———

HORACE H. HIGGINS—One of the leading agriculturists of Aroostook County, who has done much to develop the cultivation of high quality seed potatoes, owner of two extensive farms and part owner, with his brother, of three others, is Horace H. Higgins, of Mapleton. Mr. Higgins has certainly done a great deal to establish the potato industry in Aroostook County on a solid and safe basis, and the thanks of the community are due him for the time and thought he has spent on the matter. With his brother, Ray Higgins, and with Mr. Brown, of the United States Department of Agriculture, Mr. Higgins has done much experimenting on seed potatoes and the results have been published in the government publications, with much resulting benefit to potato farmers in general, and particularly to those of Aroostook County.

Mr. Higgins was born in Mapleton, December 12, 1878, the son of Sheppard and Bertha (Smith) Higgins, the former a native of this State and the latter of New Brunswick. After completing his education in the town schools, Mr. Higgins worked with his father on the latter's farm. When his father died in 1897, Mr. Higgins and his brother carried on the farm until 1918, when he sold out his interest to his brother and purchased the property he now occupies. He was always experimenting with seed potatoes and today is known from coast to coast as one of the leading experts in that line. His stock is noted for its fine qualities and it is in demand all over the country.

In politics Mr. Higgins is a Republican. He has held a number of public offices in his community, having officiated as secretary of the Mapleton Board of Trade for a number of years; as selectman for two years; as deputy sheriff of the county for two years, and on the School Board. He is an active member of the local lodge of the Knights of Pythias and is affiliated with the Grange. With his wife and family, Mr. Higgins is an attendant at the local Free Baptist Church.

Horace H. Higgins married Susie Waddell, daughter of John Waddell. Mr. and Mrs. Higgins are the parents of four children, as follows: 1. Lois R., educated at Mapleton High School and Farmington Normal School; is a teacher of home economics in Mapleton High School. 2. Clifton L., a graduate of Presque Isle High School; after spending one year at the Y. M. C. A. College at Springfield, Massachusetts, and a commercial course at the Presque Isle Business College, returned home and now (1928) assists his father in the extensive farming interests. 3. Lawrence, a 1928 senior at high school. 4. Philip, at home.

WALLACE B. WADDELL—Specializing in the cultivation of potatoes, Wallace B. Waddell is one of the leading farmers of Mapleton, Maine, owning three farms totaling five hundred and twenty-five acres in area. Having lived in Maine practically all of his life, Mr. Waddell is thoroughly familiar with local conditions, and is well acquainted with the local people, who respect him highly both for his unusual ability as a farmer and for his square dealing in all business matters. He is keenly interested in the public affairs of his town and his community, especially in matters affecting the farming conditions, and has held important town offices at different times. He sells his goods to local buyers.

Mr. Waddell was born on February 6, 1880, in Castle Hill, a son of John Waddell, who is deceased, and of Hannah (McGlauflin) Waddell, who is now (1928) living. The father, who was a prominent man in this section of Maine, was engaged here in farming for the greater part of his life. As a boy, Wallace B. Waddell attended the public schools of Castle Hill. Then, when he completed his education, he became engaged in farming. The Waddell farm is now one of the most beautiful spots in the vicinity, and from it there is obtainable a fine view over the lovely fertile fields of this section. Mr. Waddell, always a public-spirited man, has evidenced his splendid citizenship by service on the school board and the Board of Selectmen of Mapleton. He is an active member of the Grange; of the Free and Accepted Masons, in which he is affiliated with the Blue Lodge; and the Knights of Pythias. He and his family are affiliated with the Baptist church, being staunch members of the local congregation. Mr. Waddell has sung in the choir of this church since he was fifteen years old, and is credited with being one of the best singers in this section.

He married Phoebe V. Craig, a daughter of Willard and Ellen (Lunn) Craig, both natives of New Brunswick, Canada. Wallace B. and Phoebe V. (Craig) Waddell became the parents of seven children: 1. Dorothy, who is the wife of Carroll Coffin. 2. Chrystal, who is the wife of Homer Ward. 3. Alton, a graduate of the local high school. 4. Willard, a graduate of the local high school, who married Helen Giberson. 5. Kenneth. 6. Woodrow Wilson. 7. Bernard.

WILLIAM J. WEBB—With the exception of three years spent in a mining camp in Colorado, when he was a young man, William J. Webb, of Ludlow, Maine, has been a farmer all his life, and he is the owner of two hundred and two acres, mostly under high cultivation.

Born in Ludlow, August 16, 1859, he was the son of Dr. William and Mary (Abernathy) Webb. His father was the first physician to practice in Houlton, Maine. His mother was born in Kennebec County. The eldest of eleven children, William J. Webb received his education in the school at Houlton, and until he was twenty-seven years old, was his father's assistant on the farm. Then came the western adventure, at the end of which he returned to his original occupation in Maine, and has now owned the property on which he resides for thirty-two years.

Mr. Webb is a Republican and has served three years as selectman. He is a member of the Free and Accepted Masons, and of the Houlton Chapter, Royal Arch Masons. With his family he attends the Baptist church.

William J. Webb married Sarah T. Hussey, daughter of Albert R. and Jane (Tibbetts) Hussey, of Ludlow. Their children were: 1. Bessie, who married Frank H. Jordan (q. v.), a farmer whose place is on the Callahan Road, Houlton. 2. William, who married Dorothy Perkins and is now employed in a store in Houlton. 3. Verna, who is a stenographer in the office of Frank Peabody. 4. Hershell, a high school student.

OWEN H. SMITH—The owner of two hundred and thirty acres of land located near the town of Mapleton, Maine, Owen H. Smith is a very successful farmer of that neighborhood. Although he raises many general farm products, he specializes in handling potatoes, growing many barrels of excellent varieties, some of which are sold to local buyers, and others shipped to the larger city markets. Mr. Smith has served as road commissioner and is generally active in local civic affairs. He is also a member of many fraternal organizations. His father, Edwin Smith, now deceased, was a farm owner and a merchant. His mother, who before her marriage was Zanie M. Chandler, is still living (1928).

Owen H. Smith was born on May 26, 1874, at Mapleton, Maine. He attended the local public schools and when he completed his education he became associated with his father for a few years in business. At the end of that time he became manager of his father's farm, and still later he purchased a tract of land adjoining that which his father owned and started farming for himself. Here he remained for twenty-six years, finally selling and buying what was known as the Lee Stewart farm, which became the nucleus of Mr. Smith's present holdings. Some time later he bought the old Dudley and Smith farm, so that he owns in all about two hundred and thirty acres of fine farming land, on which he chiefly raises potatoes, both the seed and table product being grown only from certified seed.

Politically, he is a member of the Republican party, and has served for a time as local road commissioner. He is affiliated fraternally with the Independent Order of Odd Fellows, in which organization he is a member of the Encampment and Canton. He is also a member of the Knights of Pythias, at Mapleton, of the Three Link Club at Presque Isle, and of the Grange. He and his family attend the Methodist Episcopal church.

Mr. Smith married Flora L. Dudley, the daughter of Micajah H. and Hannah (Elois) Dudley, both of Maine. Mr. and Mrs. Smith are the parents of three children: 1. Harold, who married Hannah Turner. 2. Lionel E., who married Delda Griffin. 3. Dorothea, who attended Mapleton High School and Simmons College at Boston; spent two years in the Boston Conservatory of Music, and is now a teacher of music in New York City.

OSCAR A. STEVENS—Practically all of his life associated with business matters at Ludlow, and now holding the office of postmaster of that town, Oscar R. Stevens is also one of the leading merchants in this progressive community, deeply interested in all matters that pertain to the growth and advancement of this section of the State.

Oscar A. Stevens was born June 6, 1878, at Plymouth, a son of Lewis Stevens, a farmer and carpenter now retired at Ludlow, and Susan A. (Carter) Stevens, who is now deceased. After attending the Ludlow public schools, Mr. Stevens was graduated at Maine Central Institute, Pittsfield, in 1895, and at Bates College with his degree Bachelor of Arts in 1899, when he taught school in Maine and Vermont for two years. Engaging in the insurance business in Boston for awhile, he then returned to Ludlow, where he established his present widely known general store interests, for the sale of farm machinery, the present building being newly constructed as the result of a fire that took place in 1924. Here, also, Mr. Stevens maintains a gas filling station, roadside lunch and overnight camps.

For twenty-four years, Mr. Stevens has held the responsible office of postmaster at Ludlow, and he has the highest regard of the community. He is a member of the school committee; and his fraternal affiliations are with the Free and Accepted Masons, in the Blue Lodge, and with the Royal Arch Chapter of Free Masonry. He attends the Baptist church.

Oscar A. Stevens married Goldie L. Hovey, who is Ludlow town treasurer, and was born in Smyrna, daughter of Ivory A. and Sadie J. (Shirley) Hovey. Mr. and Mrs. Stevens have four children: Gertrude, Oscar, Jr., Sadie, and Patricia.

WILLIAM L. McPHERSON—Since 1924 William L. McPherson has served as road commissioner of the town of Mapleton, Maine. His earlier experience as a builder and contractor has been valuable to him in this position, and he has discharged the duties of his office with his customary energy and ability. Mr. McPherson is a member of several fraternal organizations, and is otherwise active in the civic and social life of his community. He is highly esteemed there as a public-spirited citizen. He was born on May 13, 1881, at Presque Isle, Maine, the son of Isaac A. and Maggie (Wade) McPherson. His mother is now deceased. His father was born at Saint Francis, Maine, and died March 15, 1928.

William L. McPherson attended the public schools of his birthplace, and when he completed his education he began work as a farm hand. Some

time afterward he bought a farm, eighty acres in extent, in the town of Castle Hill, which he operated with considerable success until 1915, when he sold it and went into the construction business. Mr. McPherson contracted for and built many bridges and buildings in the vicinity, and he conducted this enterprise until he took over the duties of road commissioner. In 1924 he was appointed to this office but for a year previously he had performed all the functions of the position, and he has continued to do so until the present time (1928). In his present capacity Mr. McPherson is employed jointly by town and State. Politically he supports the principles and candidates of the Republican party. He is affiliated fraternally with the Independent Order of Odd Fellows at Presque Isle, and is also a member of the Knights of Pythias, at Mapleton. He and his family attend the Methodist Episcopal church.

Mr. McPherson was twice married, first to Hattie Smith, the daughter of E. A. and Zanie (Chandler) Smith, by whom he has three children: Edwin A., LeRoy, and Perley. Mrs. McPherson died and Mr. McPherson married (second) Elizabeth McPherson, the families not being related. By the second marriage there are four children: Glenna, Vinal, Wilda, and Iona.

DONALD M. KILPATRICK—Presque Isle, Maine, has many farmers who are not limiting their activities merely to the growing of crops, but are also engaged in the shipping of their own products, especially potatoes, and among this number of those who find it to their advantage to market their own products, is Donald M. Kilpatrick, who owns and operates a farm of one hundred and twenty-six acres on the State road between Presque Isle and Caribou. Mr. Kilpatrick is the son of Andrew R. and Mary (Easterbrook) Kilpatrick, both of whom are natives of New Brunswick and moved to Presque Isle in 1895, where they continued to reside until the death of Mr. Kilpatrick, since which time his widow has lived in Vancouver. They had five children and two are still living in the State of Maine.

Donald M. Kilpatrick was born at Florenceville, New Brunswick, on April 3, 1893. At the age of two years, he was brought by his parents into the State of Maine and, as they settled at Presque Isle, he was brought up here and got his education in the public schools of this place and graduated from the Presque Isle High School. Just as soon as his school days were over, he gave all of his time to learning to be a good farmer. He had always enjoyed farming and in early life chose it as his vocation and has followed it all along with good success. He worked with his father on the home farm for a number of years and after a while, he purchased the place from his father and has continued to cultivate and to improve it. He has erected a potato house and stores his potatoes until ready for shipment, although he does sell some to the local buyers. He is interested in civic activities but has never held a public office, giving all of his time to the business of farming. He is a member of the Grange, the Moosleuk Club, and the Order of Free and Accepted Masons, where he is in the Blue Lodge, the Chapter and the Council.

Donald M. Kilpatrick married Lucy Beckworth, a native of Presque Isle, daughter of Ernest and Jennie (English) Beckworth. They have had three children: Philip, deceased, Barbara, and Donald. Mr. Kilpatrick and his family attend the Congregational church.

ORIN J. HIGGINS—Potato grower and shipper in Mapleton Village, Mapleton Township, Aroostook County, Orin J. Higgins is numbered outstandingly among the more public-spirited and substantial citizens of the community, and is also associated with I. R. Lenfest in starch manufacturing plants at Washburn, Ashland and Mapleton, Maine; he is a trustee of the Merchants Trust & Banking Company of Presque Isle, Aroostook County. He and Mr. Lenfest also own thirteen potato houses in Mapleton and Washburn. With these diverse connections Orin J. Higgins is well and favorably known in business circles of Mapleton, Washburn, Presque Isle and Ashland, and is respected as a man of sound commercial judgment and high character. Mr. Higgins is a native of Mapleton; he was born here on May 25, 1883, son of Orin J. and Laura T. (Tyler) Higgins, both deceased, his father having been for

many years engaged in farming in Mapleton Township.

Orin J. Higgins received his education in the public schools of Mapleton then graduated from Ricker Institute at Houlton, then one year at Colby, after which he took a business course at Bryant and Stratton Business College, Boston. Leaving the farm, he became interested in varied enterprises with great success and prosperity. He now (1928) conducts the farm in conjunction with his other interests, and under his direction yields are large; he employs the latest of scientific methods of agriculture, applying them as best suited to the character of his acres, rotating crops judiciously, and specializing in the growing of seed and table potatoes. These he ships, and also ships for neighboring farmers, who have confidence in his business ability. Mr. Higgins is a member of the Republican party and is loyal to its principles of government, possessed of a considerable influence in political matters of Aroostook County, and has served with distinction as town clerk of Mapleton and on the school committee. He is fraternally active, with membership in the Blue Lodge of the Free and Accepted Masons, Canton Encampment of the Independent Order of Odd Fellows, and the Knights of Pythias. He is a communicant of the Baptist church, devout in its service, and generous in his contributions to charitable and other worthy causes, whether or not they are sponsored by the church of his denomination.

Orin J. Higgins married, February 29, 1908, at Rudyard, Michigan, Mona Greenleaf, born at Washburn, Maine, daughter of Melvin A. and Nettie C. (Story) Greenleaf. Mrs. Higgins was a teacher for four years in the public schools of Washburn, afterward attending Miss Beal's School of Shorthand and Typewriting in Bangor. To this union have been born five children: 1. Cleo, student at Bates College, class of 1928. 2. Hayward W., graduate of high school and now (1928) a student at Bates College. 3. Melvin, attending high school. 4. Orin, 3d. 5. Dyer.

WILLIE F. PARADIS, one of the most prominent citizens of Van Buren, Maine, was born on October 23, 1864, at Hamlin Plantation. Mr.

Paradis is a son of Damase and Sophie (Parent) Paradis, the former born in the province of Quebec, and the mother was born at Hamlin Plantation, Maine. Damase Paradis, the father, was a well-known farmer of that community.

His son, Willie F. Paradis, received his education in the public schools of his native township. He gave up his studies at an early age, however, to work with his father on the farm. He continued with this occupation until he was thirty-eight years of age. At that time he moved to Van Buren, Maine, where he established a general store, and erected the building which it now occupies. Mr. Paradis is also the owner of several farms, comprising in all some seven hundred and fifty acres. The extent of his business in this line may be judged by the fact that he plants 900 barrels of seed potatoes, a commodity which he deals in extensively. Mr. Paradis has been eminently successful in his business affairs. Despite the curtailment of his schooling, he has educated himself and he is now one of the most learned and respected citizens of Van Buren, Maine, a friend to all, and beloved by those with whom he comes in contact.

Despite the many duties which his work entails, Mr. Paradis has, nevertheless, found time to take a keen interest in the affairs of his community. A supporter of the Republican party, he served for three years as the first selectman of Van Buren, Maine. He also served as chairman of the Light District for two years, and as chairman of the Water District for six years. He is fraternally affiliated with the Knights of Columbus.

Willie F. Pardis married Sophie Cyr, who was born at Hamlin Plantation, a daughter of Hypolite and Marie (Ouellette) Cyr. Mr. and Mrs. Paradis are the parents of two children, both of whom are daughters: Emma and Cecelia. Mr. Paradis and his family attend the Catholic church.

JOSEPH F. HUSSEY—Prominent among the progressive farmers of this district is Joseph F. Hussey, of Ludlow. He is the son of Albert R. and Jane (Tibbetts) Hussey. His father was born at Vassalboro and his mother at Liberty, in the State of Maine, and they have spent all their lives in this State. Albert R. Hussey was by trade a carpenter, but in later life he took up farming and carried on that line of business almost entirely, however, he was constantly doing little jobs in his old trade of carpentry. They had four children: 1. Benjamin T., deceased. 2. Joseph F., of whom further. 3. Sarah T., and one other.

Joseph F. Hussey was born at Ludlow, Maine, on November 4, 1867. He was educated in the common schools of Ludlow and then attended Houlton Academy. After finishing his school work, he returned to the farm and worked with his father. He has never lived at any other place except for two years he was in British Columbia. In 1912, he purchased his present farm from John C. Dorrance and also has other real estate. His largest farm, known as Pine Tree Farm, comprises two hundred acres; he also has one hundred and twenty acres in the town of Houlton and eighty acres in Ludlow. He does general farming and sells potatoes to local dealers, and in addition to his farming interests, he owns a half interest in an eighty acre wood lot in partnership with his nephew. He is a Republican, a member of the Order of Free and Accepted Masons and a member of the Baptist church.

ARTHUR G. COOK—President of the Mapleton Supply Company, of Mapleton Village, Aroostook County, Maine, owner and proprietor of a general store and sawmill, Arthur G. Cook is numbered prominently among the more public spirited citizens interested in the welfare and development of the Mapleton community, and has here been engaged in business since the year 1912. Native of Maine, Arthur G. Cook was born at Castle Hill, June 9, 1882, son of George A. and Lorancy (Morris) Cook, his father a native of Dixmont, Maine, and his mother of the province of New Brunswick, Dominion of Canada.

Arthur G. Cook attended the public schools of Presque Isle, Aroostook County, and graduated from Presque Isle High School. Upon completion of studies then, he entered at once into the commercial world with his first connection as clerk in a hardware store at Portland, Maine. After this experience, through which he became thoroughly conversant with methods employed in retail business, Mr. Cook joined in association with T. F. Phair, and with him was joint owner and proprietor of the general merchandising establishment at Mapleton. In all, Messrs. Cook and Phair were in partnership for nine years; in 1921 they purchased the sawmill, and later Mr. Cook purchased the shares of Mr. Phair, and has since conducted both store and mill independently. In the commercial circles of Mapleton and in other centers where he has contact, such as in Presque Isle, Mr. Cook is highly regarded as a man of character and intelligently directed industry. He is a Republican, loyal to the principles of government upheld by that party, and possessed of a considerable influence in village and county elections; he has never, however, accepted the suggestion that he run for office, preferring to exercise his civic activities as a private citizen. During the World War he served on various boards and committees having as their purpose the prosecution of the war from this country; he served tirelessly and well, and was actively connected with the different Liberty Loan campaigns. He is a member of the Blue Lodge of the Free and Accepted Masons, Royal Arch Masons, Royal and Select Masters; Lodge No. 93, at Washburn, Chapter and Council at Presque Isle. He attends the Baptist church at Mapleton, and is known for the generosity with which he meets requests from charities and other worthy causes, regardless of their sponsorship, emanating from the church or coming to his attention from another source.

Arthur G. Cook married Alice Stevens, native of Wisconsin, who, when she was a child, came to Presque Isle with her parents. Her father was John S. Stevens, a lumberman, who died in 1923, and her mother, Margaret (McGilton) Stevens, is now living.

LOUIS ABEL MARTIN—Ownership of one of the oldest mercantile establishments in his section has brought into prominence Louis Abel Martin, proprietor of Martin Brothers, a general store established more than a half century ago by his father, a merchant of Van Buren, Maine. The present owner is alert and forward-looking, con-

ducting his business with great efficiency and prosperity. The father of the subject of this record is Joe Martin, born in the province of Quebec in 1831 and died May 15, 1927. He had little education and mastered the trade of blacksmith, which he followed until he was thirty-three years old. He then, in 1876, established the store now operated by his son, which began under the title of Joe Martin and Sons. This enterprising man was one of the organizers of the First National Bank of Van Buren and served as its first president, holding office for several years, and he served his town as selectman when a young man. Joe Martin married Marie Cyr, born at St. Anne, New Brunswick, and they had children: J. E., who died in 1924; Louise; George; Celina; David; Melvina; Paul; Anne; Louis Abel, of further mention; and Cecile.

Louis Abel Martin, son of Joe and Marie (Cyr) Martin, was educated at St. Mary College, the Ricker Classical Institute, and St. Joseph's, at Munbrencooke, New Brunswick. His preparation for his life work was rounded out by a course at Shaw's Business College, at Bangor, Maine. He and his brothers, Paul J. and J. E., took over their father's business, Joe Martin and Sons, and changed the name to Martin Brothers, which it now bears. In 1923, J. E. Martin withdrew, leaving Louis Abel and Paul J. Martin in ownership, and started a business of his own in Van Buren, which came to an end with his death in November, 1924. Mr. Martin is a member of the Benevolent and Protective Order of Elks, of Houlton, and a communicant of the Roman Catholic church, as are all the members of the family.

Louis Abel Martin married Delphine Farrell, born in Van Buren, daughter of Leonard and Louise (Martin) Martin, and they have children: Gabriel Romeo Martin, Jacques Clement Martin, and Florence Martin.

WILLIAM EDWARD BELYEA is the proprietor of a general store in the village of Mapleton, Maine. He is also town clerk, so that he manages to combine politics and an interest in public affairs with the successful conduct of a business. He did not establish the store himself; he received it as an inheritance from his father, who founded it and financed it, though he did not take a very active part in its management. William Edward Belyea has operated successfully and his establishment has become something of an institution in the town.

William Edward Belyea was born at Castle Hill, Maine, March 19, 1893, son of John W. and Alice (Tarr) Belyea, the father being a native of New Brunswick, who came to the United States when he was fifteen years old with his parents. They purchased a farm on arrival in the town of Castle Hill and there they made their home and worked the farm. John W. Belyea was in the main a farmer till his death on January 4, 1927. Agriculture was his main interest, and he was never much engaged in the conduct of the general store, which was founded by him in 1915, and which for the first three years was under the management— in the case of the father the nominal management —of John W. Belyea and his son-in-law, J. F. McEachron. At the end of that time this association was discontinued and the store passed under the control of John W. Belyea and his son, William Edward Belyea, the present proprietor and manager. John W. Belyea is described as a good citizen and a good neighbor, who took an active part in any movement and in any work for the town's good. The wife of John W. Belyea, mother of William Edward Belyea, is a native of Castle Hill, and there she still resides on the home farm.

William Edward Belyea was educated in the public schools and attended the high school for two years. He has been in general business all his life, and gradually took over the sole management of his father's store. He is, as aforestated, town clerk of Mapleton. In politics he is a Republican, and attends the Baptist church. He belongs to the Blue Lodge, of Masons; the Independent Order of Odd Fellows, Encampment Canton, and the Knights of Pythias, of Mapleton.

William E. Belyea was united in marriage to Kate Turner, daughter of G. W. Turner.

MAXIME M. PELLETIER—Among the most useful of Maine's foreign born citizens, and they are comparatively few, are those of French Canadian extraction. Apt to be intensely conservative, they are industrious and thrifty, good neighbors and good friends. Of such origin is Maxime M. Pelletier, proprietor of a prosperous men's furnishings store in Van Buren, Maine, known as a careful merchant and a progressive citizen.

Born at Cyr Plantation, Maine, April 20, 1880, his parents, both of whom are now dead, were Maxime and Celine Pelletier, natives of Canada who had settled in Aroostook County, Maine, some years previously. After the usual course in the public schools of Van Buren, Maxime M. Pelletier spent a year and a half at St. Mary's College, and then went to Massachusetts to seek employment. For two years he worked for an electric railway, and then returned to Maine, and obtained a clerkship with the Van Buren Mercantile Company. He remained with this concern two years, and then took a similar post with Jacob Klein Company where, after various promotions, he was taken into the firm, after eight years of service.

In 1923, he sold out his interest in the Jacob Klein Company, and started in business for himself by purchasing the stock of Joseph L. Violette, adding new goods, and removing the establishment to larger and better quarters. The turnover has been increasingly good for several years, and he is now rated as one of the substantial business men of the community. Mr. Pelletier is a Republican and has served on the school board. The family are communicants of the Roman Catholic church, and he is a member of the Knights of Columbus.

He married Artheline Cyr, who was born at Cyr Plantation, daughter of Edward D. and Delina (Ayotte) Cyr. Their children are Fabiola, Hector, Eunice, Dominic, Charlotte, Loraine, Anne Marie, Marcello, Robert, and Jacqueline Pelletier.

ALBERT E. MOOERS—That farming and dairying are profitable has been amply demonstrated in the business record of Albert E. Mooers, of Houlton, well known potato merchant and banker. Mr. Mooers every year plants about five hundred acres of potatoes, and also keeps a herd of thoroughbred Jersey cattle which yield a nice profit in butter, cream and milk. Mr. Mooers has done much to advance the scientific side of farming, and his efforts have yielded such a return that he is enabled to become a director in the Farmers' National Bank of Houlton, in which city he enjoys an enviable standing as a citizen of the first importance.

Mr. Mooers was born at Houlton, May 14, 1868, son of David and Eliza (Abernathy) Mooers, both natives of Canada, who came to this section when young and engaged in the farming business. He received his education at the public schools of Houlton, then entered the employ of the wholesale store of E. Merritt & Sons. He remained with this concern fourteen years, mastering all the details of the business, and by this time had saved up enough to engage in farming on his own account at twenty-nine years of age. He did well from the start and is today one of the largest producers in the city. He is intensely proud of the growth of Houlton, and always stands in the forefront of all constructive movements for its advancement, commercially, socially and spiritually.

Mr. Mooers is a member of the Republican party, and is strongly committed to that organization's policies, which have done so much to build up New England. In fraternal order circles he is a member of the International Order of Odd Fellows and a Master Mason of the Free and Accepted Masons.

Mr. Mooers married (first) Ruth McIntosh; she died, leaving two sons and a daughter: 1. Finley, a farmer in Houlton. 2. Albert E. Mooers, Jr., a sketch of whom follows. 3. Beatrice, wife of Paul W. Jackins. He married (second) Ada E. Atchison, and they have resided in the village of Houlton for four and one half years, and attend the Congregational church.

ALBERT E. MOOERS, JR.—The business of dairying has been one of life-long interest to Albert E. Mooers, Jr., who, in the successful operation of his farm at Houlton, finds his vocation satisfactory and profitable, and has won patrons and made friends in his specialty for the excellence of his product. Besides, he has a large number of cattle, and in all matters is known as a painstaking and enterprising farmer.

Albert E. Mooers, Jr., was born June 25, 1897,

at Houlton, son of Albert E. Mooers and Ruth (McIntosh) Mooers; Albert E. Mooers, his father, is a prominent potato grower and banker at Houlton, keeps a fine herd of cattle, and has an excellent dairy. A review of his life appears in preceding biography. Albert E. Mooers, Jr., after attending the Houlton public schools, began to engage in farming, and he now owns and operates a large dairy and potato-growing farm of two hundred acres. He keeps forty-five head of cattle, besides eight horses, six for working and two for driving.

A Republican in his political views, Mr. Mooers adheres to the principles of that party, though he has not sought the responsibilities of public office. He is affiliated with the Royal Arcanum. His religious faith is that of the Methodist Episcopal church.

Albert E. Mooers married Bessie Burtt, who was born at Burtt's Corners, Frederickton, New Brunswick, a daughter of Edward and Levinia Burtt. He has four children: Ruth, John, Frederick and Albert Emery.

ANDREW P. YOUNG, who was one of the most prominent men of Houlton, Maine, and a member of an old and well-known Maine family, was born January 3, 1846, in Phillips, Maine. Mr. Young was a son of John and Lydia (Harris) Young, both of whom are now deceased. John Young, the father, was a well-known farmer of Phillips, Maine. His son, Andrew P. Young, received his education in the district school of the community in which he was born. As was often the case in those days, his studies were curtailed in order that he might begin his business career at as early an age as possible. As a boy he worked in the local grocery store, later going into business for himself, conducting a combined grocery and general store. This enterprise he carried on for fourteen years in the town of Phillips. At the end of that time he removed to Houlton where he became a trader, travelling through Aroostook County and dealing mostly in horses. This work of buying and selling he followed for some ten years, during which time he had acquired several farms. He then took up his residence at his farm near Houlton, which he worked until the time of his retirement, and his death occurred March 22, 1928. In his political preference Mr. Young was a strong supporter of the Republican party. He was fraternally affiliated with the Independent Order of Odd Fellows.

Andrew P. Young married, in 1871, Mary L. Beedy, who was born in Phillips, a daughter of Nathan and Elizabeth (Winship) Beedy, both of whom were members of old families of Maine. Mr. and Mrs. Young became the parents of two children, a son and a daughter: 1. Fred Arthur, who died in infancy. 2. Edith M., who married John F. Peacock, of St. Andrews, Maine, and who is now deceased. Mr. and Mrs. Young had long been connected with the Unitarian church.

SETH T. CAMPBELL—For more than three decades Seth T. Campbell, attorney, has figured prominently in business and legal affairs in Island Falls, Maine. He has also taken an active part in public affairs and served as Legislator in 1915. Mr. Campbell was born at Eden, now known as Bar Harbor, Maine, November 20, 1867, son of James and Alberta (Remick) Campbell, both natives of Eden. The father was in youth a sea captain and retired to farming during his later years.

Well educated in the excellent grade and high school of Eden, the son studied law in the office of Deasy and Higgins. He was admitted to the bar in 1891 with a wide theoretical insight into legal problems and a practical knowledge of their working in everyday life which has stood him in good stead as he has successfully pursued his career. For a year he practiced law in Colorado, and for six months at Ellsworth, Maine. It was in 1895 that Mr. Campbell settled in Island Falls, Maine, where he has since continued, and where he has become a leader in his profession and in other aspects of community life. He is first selectman of Island Falls. His fraternal affiliation is with the Free and Accepted Masons, the Island Falls Lodge, and the Houlton Commandery, of the Knights Templar. He attends the Congregational church.

Seth T. Campbell married Mary A. Hopkins, of Ellsworth, Maine, daughter of Edward K. Hopkins. Children: 1. Mary Campbell, a musician of

note, a concert performer and teacher in Boston. 2. Madeline, who teaches school at Falmouth, Maine. 3. Clara H., a student. 4. Donald Campbell died in the service of his country during the World War.

NORRIS F. STEVENS—By training and equipment a thorough and capable general legal practitioner, Norris F. Stevens has secured a considerable and well-merited share in the activities of his profession at Van Buren and this section of the State, his attainments being those of an attorney who has rendered a devoted and a broad service to all branches of the law. Van Buren's best community interests are his, and he has represented its progress in his Chamber of Commerce activities.

Norris F. Stevens was born November 18, 1888, at Coaticook, province of Quebec, a son of Frederick Stevens, a woolen manufacturer, and Catherine (Brown) Stevens, the family always having been residents of Coaticook. There Mr. Stevens attended the local schools, finishing his public school course at Berlin, New Hampshire. He was matriculated at Colby College, but he completed his college work and was graduated at the University of Maine, where he received his Bachelor of Laws degree in 1917. Upon his return from his war service, he established himself as an attorney-at-law in Van Buren, where he continued in a successful practice. He has now moved his office to Fort Kent, Maine, and here he plans to build up a practice equally as successful.

Mr. Stevens was ready for service to his country at the call of the World War, and, enlisting at Bangor, he was assigned to the Depot Brigade in the United States Infantry, receiving his discharge December 5, 1918.

Norris F. Stevens married Queenie Archambault, daughter of Dr. John and Emma (Marquis) Archambault.

JEREMIAH SMITH, who is one of the leading citizens of Caribou, is respected not only for his excellent business ability but also for his fine friendliness and his interest in the welfare of his community. He has many business interests, all of which he has developed to a substantial success and has always shown himself willing to help promote any movement which would be for the best interests of the community in which he lives. Born in Fairfield, Maine, in August, 1874, he is the son of Isaac and Mary (Gievie) Smith, both parents deceased. His father, a native of Canada, was a successful farmer and his mother was a native of Maine.

Mr. Smith, due to the fact that both of his parents were invalids, left school at the age of ten years and began work on the farm, took care of his mother and father and laid the foundation of his future success. He now owns two farms, one of two hundred acres and another of one hundred acres, worked by his son. Besides farming he is a dealer in fertilizer and a broker of potatoes with a warehouse on the Bangor and Aroostook Railroad. He ships four hundred to five hundred cars yearly, deals in both table and seed potatoes, and has, in general, a most prosperous business. He is a director of the Aroostook Truck Company. In politics a Republican, he is in his fraternal affiliations a member of the Free and Accepted Masons in the Lodge, Chapter, Council, Commandery of Knights Templar, and Ancient Arabic Order Nobles of the Mystic Shrine. He is also a member of the Modern Woodmen of America.

He married Annie Mabel Spooner, daughter of Ezra and Annie (Brewer) Spooner of Woodland, Maine. They had eight children, seven of whom are living: 1. Eleanor, a graduate of the Caribou High School, married to Luther Hewitt. 2. Fern, also a graduate of that high school and of LaSalle Seminary; married Francis Hodgdon. 3. Cordelia, a graduate of Caribou High School and of the business school at Lewiston, Maine. 4. Ezra, married Lela Whiteneck, lives on his father's farm. 5. Alta. 6. Albert. 7. Barbara. 8. Ernest, died at ten years of age. The family are all members of the Methodist church.

FREDERICK W. BISHOP—A prominent citizen of Houlton, deeply interested in all civic and social affairs of the town, Frederick W. Bishop shares in the prosperity of the farmers and potato growers of this section, having a farm of three hundred acres and specializing in potatoes, in which he deals on an extensive scale.

The son of Amos and Martha J. (Hann) Bishop, both now deceased, Frederick W. Bishop was born in Fort Fairfield, Maine, on November 14, 1864. His father, who was a farmer and a lumberman by occupation, was a native of New Brunswick; while his mother, who was married first to a Mr. Putnam and then to Amos Bishop, was born in Hodgdon. Frederick W. Bishop was educated in the public schools, and when he was sixteen years old he started to work in the woods. All his life he has been in the lumber and farming business. Interested at all times in political and civic matters, Mr. Bishop is a member of the Republican party, and served on the road committee of the town of Fort Fairfield. He is a member of the Independent Order of Odd Fellows, in which he is affiliated with the Houlton Lodge; and also is a member of the Grange, in which he always has been active. He has been living in Houlton only since 1916, but in that time he has shown himself to be deeply concerned with the development of the town.

He married Etta M. Tracy, and they became the parents of five children: 1. Earl, who lives in Waterville, Maine. 2. Effie, who is a graduate of the nurses' school at Newton Hospital, in Newton, Massachusetts, and who is a trained nurse. 3. Pearl, who is a graduate of the high school of Houlton. 4. Paul, a graduate of Houlton High School. 5. Laura, who is a member of the class of 1928 in Houlton High School. The Bishop family attends the Congregational church.

GEORGE EDGAR WANN—As civilization advances, teaching holds out an increased attraction to young men of pronounced talent and ideals of service to mankind. Many of the world's greatest figures have been teachers, and indeed, in a sense, no great world figure has failed to be a teacher, indirectly. He who chooses education for a career chooses wisely and with ambition.

George Edgar Wann has attained to a position in matters of education which is comparable with that of any of his colleagues of like generation.

He was born at Akron, Minnesota, in 1905, son of John and Mary (Willett) Wann. His father, for many years identified with railroading, is at the present time engaged as foreman in Waterville, where the family residence, meanwhile, has been established. When George Edgar Wann was a child his parents moved from Minnesota to Presque Isle, and here he has used the years in founding his career. He graduated from the local high school in 1923, holding scholastic honors, and in the fall of that year matriculated in Aroostook State Normal, whence he graduated in 1925. He is at present connected in helping teacher work obtained at Castine Normal, and in this connection has worked through the terms succeeding to the present (this is written in 1928), now being well launched as an instructor, and with his feet firmly planted upon the ladder of his profession. It is said of him by confreres that his position at teaching will of necessity be large in the future, as he has brought to his career the earnest application without which progress in education is impossible. A natural student, constantly devoted to his books, to observation and reflection, he is at the same time owner of a genial, pleasant spirit, and has a wide friendship.

Mr. Wann is a member of the National Educational Association, the Maine State Teachers' Association, and the Grange, in the workings of which he is active. He is a communicant of the Baptist church, being active in its works as well.

Presque Isle is dear to Mr. Wann. Though he was not born here, he studied here and has made the acquaintance of practically all persons within the community. He supports all movements having to do with the community's welfare, when such support is requested or when an opening offers. And Presque Isle's people have the highest regard for Mr. Wann.

HOWARD WEBB—For many years Howard Webb has been prominent in the life of Houlton, Maine. A farmer and potato dealer by occupation, he owns a two hundred acre farm on Foxcroft Road, which he runs very successfully, and a large potato warehouse on the Canadian Pacific Railroad. He has served for ten years as selectman for the town of Houlton, and is otherwise active in the civic life of the community. His father, William Webb, born in Ludlow, Maine, was a farmer and lumberman and engaged in this work until his death. His mother, who was Mary Abernathy, was born in Merrimack, New Hampshire.

Howard Webb was born on April 16, 1864, at Houlton, Maine. He attended the local public schools, and when still a young man spent three years in the West, during which he tried his hand at mining. He returned to his father's farm where he remained for a year, and at the end of that time he took charge of the estate of Governor Llewelyn Powers. After a number of years in this position he started farming for himself, in which work he has continued since that time. He employs about eight men on his farm and at the warehouse. By political inclination Mr. Webb is a member of the Republican party. He is the second selectman for the town of Houlton, in which position he has served for ten years. He is affiliated fraternally with the Ancient Free and Accepted Masons. He and his family attend the local Methodist Episcopal church.

He married Bertha E. Davis, who was born in St. John's, New Brunswick. Mr. and Mrs. Webb are the parents of seven children: 1. Frederick, a graduate of the University of Maine, now working at home with his father. 2. Howard, Jr., a graduate of Houlton High School, also living at home. 3. Mary, who was married to Reginald Doherty, both of whom are now teaching school at Bridgewater, Maine. 4. Oscar, a student at the University of Maine. 5. William, graduated 1927 from Houlton High School. 6. Freeman, a member of the class of 1928, Houlton High School. 7. Dorothy, who attends the local grade school.

DANIEL WEBSTER McLAUGHLIN—By inclination and preference a farmer, and associated with agricultural interests throughout his career, Daniel Webster McLaughlin has made a thorough success of his farming properties located both at Murrill and Dyer Brook, his farms being maintained in the most satisfactory state of cultivation, and their product being the result of the experience and skill of the owner. Mr. McLaughlin is a public-spirited citizen, and one who has also demonstrated his capabilities in carrying on the duties of those local offices to which he has from time to time been elected.

Daniel Webster McLaughlin was born May 30, 1855, in New Brunswick, son of Daniel McLaughlin, who was born and brought up in that province, and Helen (McGeorge) McLaughlin, a native of Scotland, but who came to New Brunswick when she was six years old. Mr. and Mrs. Daniel McLaughlin came to Aroostook County in 1868, and settling at Oakfield, died there, having had eight sons and one daughter, Daniel Webster McLaughlin being the youngest of their children. After attending the common and high schools, Mr. McLaughlin began life as a hired man on a farm, and when he bought his first farm at Dyer Brook, he worked its gardening activities in the summer, and during the winter season cut and drew the wood, meantime working as a driver on the river, in order to get the property paid for. He now owns this farm of two hundred and forty acres on State road, Dyer Brook, that is worked on shares by his grandson, Kent McLaughlin, and he is also owner of a two hundred acre farm on Moro Road, in Merrill, where he now resides; and since he was thirteen years old, he has passed his life here and at Oakfield and Dyer Brook, with the exception of a short period when he visited in California. In politics a Republican, Mr. McLaughlin has held at Merrill the offices of first selectman, of tax collector, of which he was the incumbent for thirteen years, and of treasurer two years. Fraternally, he is affiliated with the lodge of Free and Accepted Masons at Island Falls, and with the Independent Order of Odd Fellows at Smyrna Mills.

Daniel Webster McLaughlin married Effie Clark, who was born at Smyrna, daughter of John D. B. and Mary Matilda (Young) Clark; and they have two children: Clyde D. and Cornelia A. The family attend the Universalist church.

WILLIAM H. WATTS—The Watts family came to this country in the year 1873, having left Nottingham, England, to settle in St. George, Maine. The father had charge of the contracts of cutting granite for the government.

William H. Watts was born in the year 1806, son of George and Mary A. (Welthall) Watts, both natives of Nottingham. He attended public school in St. George, Maine, and put in one term at business college, after which he started his career in the granite trade, for which he was well suited from having studied under his father. The Billings & Watts Company, made up of L. F. Billings and himself, was established in 1895. After a time Mr. Billings retired and the business as The Houlton Granite and Marble Works has since been conducted by Mr. Watts.

Mr. Watts has spent many years as a pioneer in the granite business, and has never abandoned the hope of finding, in Maine, a stone equal or superior to any, and is now operating a quarry that promises to fulfill his fondest hopes. This quarry is situated in the town of New Limerick, Maine.

Mr. Watts is a Republican, is an assessor of Houlton, and is a member of the Independent Order of Odd Fellows, and together with Mrs. Watts is a member of the Baptist church. Mrs. Watts was Lorena Leeman, daughter of Captain Albert and Elizabeth Leeman, of Bristol.

P. L. B. EBBETT, M. D.—For a quarter of a century, Dr. P. L. B. Ebbett has been engaged in the general practice of medicine in Houlton, Maine, or Hodgdon, Maine, and has been a leading member of the fraternal organizations, and active in the community work of both places.

Born in Gagetown, New Brunswick, Canada, July 28, 1881, the son of Charles H. and Elizabeth Mary (Penry) Ebbett, his boyhood was spent on the ancestral farm. Both parents are now deceased. After the course in the Gagetown Grammar School, he qualified for entrance to the Medical School of McGill University, and was graduated there in 1903. In that same year he passed the New Brunswick and Maine State medical examination, and opened an office in Houlton. On December 1, 1904, he removed to Hodgdon, Maine, where he remained in practice until October, 1918, when he returned to Houlton and took offices in the Masonic Temple Building, which he still occupies. A Republican in politics, he was health officer for the town of Hodgdon during his residence there, and is still medical adviser to the Board of

Health. In Houlton, he is school physician. He is a past president of the Aroostook County Medical Society, and a member of the American Medical Association. He is a member of the Free and Accepted Masons, including the Blue Lodge, Royal Arch, Knights Templar, and is a Shriner. In the Benevolent and Protective Order of Elks he is Past Exalted Ruler of Houlton Lodge and Past District Deputy Grand Exalted Ruler of Eastern Maine. He was president of the Houlton Fair Association, 1926 and 1927, and a member of the Houlton Business Men's Association, and of the Medufnekeg Club. His family attend the Methodist church.

In 1906, Dr. Ebbett married Luella Green, daughter of Charles and Charlotte (Scott) Green, of Hodgdon. They have two children, Charlotte Elizabeth, born in 1907; George Hudson, born in 1909.

OLOF L. STADIG—Since 1898 Olof L. Stadig has been the owner and operator of a first class machine shop in St. Francis, Maine. Mr. Stadig has had a varied experience as a machinist and for twelve years operated a lumber mill, he also operated a farm, along with his other activities, for some years; but since 1920 he has devoted his entire time and attention to his machine shop and to his duties as trial justice of Northern Aroostook.

Olof L. Stadig was born in Sweden, May 28, 1865, son of Lars and Christine (Olafson) Stadig, and came to this country with his parents in 1871, when he was six years of age. His father is still living at the age of ninety-two years, but the mother is deceased. Mr. Stadig received his education in the public schools of New Sweden, where his parents settled one year after the first families located there, and then learned the trade of the machinist and millwright, which line of activity he has followed throughout his life to the present time (1928). He has built mills and starch factories all over the county and for a period of four years was a partner of C. E. Jones in the building and contracting business. In 1898 he removed to St. Francis, Maine, and here he has since resided. For several years after coming to St. Francis he owned and operated a farm, while attending to his

other work, and he also owned and operated a lumber mill for about twelve years. In 1920 he sold his farm, and since that time he has devoted his attention in a business way entirely to his machine shop. His business activities, however, do not include all of his interests and his activities. He is trial justice of the Northern District of Aroostook County, and to that office he is giving the careful and painstaking attention which has won him success in his private business undertakings. His sense of justice and his clear grasp of the essential facts of cases brought before him are characteristic features of his work in this connection, and make his decisions an instrument of righteousness and a cause of fear to wrong doers. Politically, he gives his support to the principles and the candidates of the Republican party, and he is active in local public affairs, bearing his full share of the burdens of local public office. He has served as a member of the board of assessors, is a member of the school board, and, as has already been stated, is also a justice of the peace. His fraternal membership is with the Masonic Order.

Olof L. Stadig was married to Ella Beckline, who was born in Sweden, daughter of Andrew Beckline, and came to this country when she was nineteen years of age. Mr. and Mrs. Stadig have had five children: 1. Francis F., who died at the age of thirty-eight years. 2. Walter L. 3. Randolph E. 4. Alphonse. 5. Adelia. The family are attendants of the Presbyterian church.

CHARLES W. STARKEY—For many years Charles W. Starkey has been prominent in the business life of Houlton, Maine. He is the proprietor of the Houlton Dressed Meat Company, whose business he conducts very successfully, and he is also the owner of several farms in the vicinity, which he rents on shares. Mr. Starkey has been active in the civic and fraternal life of Houlton. His father, James Starkey, was born in the province of New Brunswick, Canada, but later came to Houlton with his family. He was a farmer and engaged in this work until his death. He married Hannah Patterson, born in New Brunswick, and also now deceased, and Charles W. Starkey was their son.

He was born in October, 1866, in Queens County, New Brunswick, and educated in the public schools there. As a young man he was employed in various positions and finally came to Littleton, Maine, when he was twenty-seven years old. Three years later he moved to Houlton and established the meat business which he has continued since that time over a period of almost thirty-five years. He employs several men in his shop in the town and two others in the slaughter house on the outskirts of Houlton. Mr. Starkey has secured possession of several farms in the neighborhood, which he rents to reputable tenants for a share of the produce.

By political inclination Mr. Starkey is an independent voter. He is affiliated fraternally with the Benevolent and Protective Order of Elks, the New England Order of Protection, the Orangemen and the Black Knights. He is also a member of the Houlton Business Men's Association. He and his family attend the local Congregational church.

He married Bertha Dalton, the daughter of James and Susan Mary (McGoldrick) Dalton. Mr. and Mrs. Starkey are the parents of two children: 1. Earl James, a law student at Columbia University, a member of the class of 1928. 2. Alice, now studying at Boston University.

JOSEPH A. OUELLETTE, proprietor of the Van Buren Hardware Company of Van Buren, Maine, was born in 1882 in Caribou, Maine. Mr. Ouellette is a son of Andrew and Lena (Bellanger) Ouellette, both of whom were born in Canada. Mr. Ouellette's father, Andrew Ouellette, is now deceased. Lena (Bellanger) Ouellette, the mother, is living and resides in Caribou, Maine.

Their son, Joseph A. Ouellette, received his education in the public schools of the community in which he was born. Upon the completion of these studies, he took a course at Shaw's Business College during the summer months. During the winter he worked in the woods to defray the expenses of his studies. His training finished, Mr. Ouellette became employed as a clerk for the Briggs Hardware Company of Caribou, Maine. He remained in this position for seven years, after which he travelled as a salesman for the International Harvester Company. Some time later Mr. Ouellette resigned from this position and, joining with John B. Roberts, a lawyer and banker of Caribou, Maine, he started the Van Buren Hardware Company, of which he has been proprietor for seven years. Mr. Ouellette has been eminently successful in this business, to which he has added an agency of the Buick and also Pontiac cars. Despite the manifold duties which his business entails, Mr. Ouellette has nevertheless taken a keen interest in the affairs of his community. In his political preferences he is a strong supporter of the Republican party. He is fraternally affiliated with the Benevolent and Protective Order of Elks and the Knights of Columbus.

Joseph A. Ouellette married Alma Cyr, who was born in Van Buren, Maine, a daughter of Abel and Stella (Morrin) Cyr. Mr. Ouellette and his family attend the Catholic church.

HARRY BURNS SHARP, the proprietor of the lumber mill at Houlton, Maine, was born on November 18, 1866, in the province of New Brunswick, Canada. Mr. Sharp is a son of Henry C. and Eliza (Faulkner) Sharp, both of whom were natives of New Brunswick. Mr. and Mrs. Henry C. Sharp came to the United States while their son Harry was still a young boy, and they lived the remainder of their lives here.

Their son, Harry Burns Sharp, received his education in the public school of Monticello, Maine. Upon the completion of these studies, he went to work in the woods and in the lumber mills. The knowledge he there acquired proved invaluable and he soon rose to high positions in the lumber business until he became the owner of the lumber mill which he now operates. Mr. Sharp handles both rough and finished lumber and his business has increased so that he now employs some thirty men. In his political preference he is a strong supporter of the Republican party. He is fraternally affiliated with all bodies of the Masonic Order up to and including the Shrine, and the Benevolent and Protective Order of Elks.

Harry Burns Sharp married Susan Luce, who was born at Monticello, Maine, a daughter of Charles and Rebecca (Lowell) Luce. Mrs. Sharp is a member of the Daughters of the American Revolution. Mr. and Mrs. Sharp are the parents of two children, a son and a daughter: 1. Henry C., who received his education at Houlton and at the Kents Hill Seminary, and is now in business with his father. 2. Lona, who married Dr. Joseph Toot, and by him became the mother of Martha and Barbara, and who now resides in Canton, Ohio. Mr. Sharp and his family attend the Methodist church.

FRANK H. VAIL—As proprietor of a general store in Hodgdon village, the town of Hodgdon, and as a man actively interested in the affairs of his community, Frank H. Vail has won the confidence and the esteem of his townspeople. He has held many important public offices, having been postmaster of Hodgdon for twenty-five years, resigning from this office in favor of his son, and having been a member of the Lower House in the State Legislature.

Born in Linneus, Maine, on March 4, 1859, he is the son of Israel S. and Nancy P. (Hunter) Vail, both now deceased. His father, a Canadian by birth, was engaged actively in the Civil War in the United States, and was a farmer by occupation; while his mother was a native of Maine. Frank H. Vail attended the public schools; worked for several years on his father's farm; went to Pennsylvania, where he was employed in the pine woods; then returned to Hodgdon and bought from his brother the store which he now operates. It is known as the old Washburn stand. A confirmed Republican in his convictions, Mr. Vail has held several important offices. For twenty-five years he was postmaster, but resigned the postmastership of Hodgdon in 1925 in favor of his son, Lexus I.; he was a member of the Lower House of the State Legislature from 1925 to 1927; has been town clerk and treasurer of Hodgdon since 1895; and has served at different times as selectman and member of the school board. He is active in the fraternal life of his community, being a member of the Free and Accepted Masons, in which order he is affiliated with the Blue Lodge.

Frank H. Vail married Melvina Jackins, who was born in Hodgdon and who was killed in an automobile accident on July 17, 1917. She was the daughter of James and Matilda (Gerow) Jackins. Frank H. and Melvina (Jackins) Vail became the parents of the following children: 1. Lettie M., who is now the wife of Russell Carter, bookkeeper for the Houlton Water Company, by which marriage there are two children, Eleanor and Marion. 2. Lexus I., who received his education in the public schools of Hodgdon and the Ricker Classical Institute, and who is associated with his father in business. The Vail family, in its religious affiliation, holds to the Protestant faith.

DUNCAN LEWIS WOODWORTH—A farmer of large potato-shipping interests on the North Road and at the Littleton Depot, Duncan Lewis Woodworth, a resident of this section, with postoffice address at Houlton, is a man of practical business training, well known among the farmers and their constituency in this part of the State. He is successful in his specialty, and has the esteem of his associates in the business and social world of his township.

Duncan Lewis Woodworth was born November 20, 1885, at Littleton, a son of Lewis H. Woodworth, a farmer, now deceased, born in Richmond, New Brunswick, and Jane (Manson) Woodworth, a native of Littleton, who survives her husband. Mr. Woodworth, one of the three children of his parents, attended the public schools at Littleton, and took the course at the Houlton Business College. He then became associated with his father in farming, from whom he purchased his present farm of one hundred and fifty acres on the North Road in Littleton; and since his father's death he has continued in the business of potato-raising and shipping, also as owner of a third interest in the warehouse at Littleton depot. In political matters, Mr. Woodworth supports the principles of the Republican party. Fraternally, he is affiliated with Monument Lodge, Free and Accepted Masons; and with the local Grange, Patrons of Husbandry. With his family, he attends the Baptist church.

Duncan Lewis Woodworth married Alice L. Livermoore, who was born at Milo, daughter of William Livermoore, a market gardener, and Alice (Stone) Livermoore. They have four children: 1. Preston Hubert, a two-year student at Ricker

Classical Institute, and associated with his father in business. 2. Mary. 3. Julian Edwin. 4. Gene Porter.

T. C. S. BERRY—After a well-rounded business experience in which he showed a remarkable capacity to work his way from the ground up in more than one line, T. C. S. Berry, of Houlton, Maine, operates the Houlton Mills and Light Company, which he owns, together with his son, T. Carroll Berry, and his son-in-law, John B. Maxell. They are general dealers also in flour, feed, grain, hay and straw.

Mr. Berry's people were old time settlers in Maine, who later went to Minnesota, where he was born. But when he was still a child they returned to their native State and settled at Houlton, where T. C. S. Berry attended the public schools, going then to the Ricker Classical Institute. After leaving school he went into the brick making business, but after several years in that trade, he entered the mill of which he subsequently became the owner, and acquired a practical knowledge of the milling business from the purchase of raw material to the sales of the finished product. Then, in partnership with his father, he started in the grocery business as A. H. Berry & Son, and operated successfully for seventeen years. At the end of that period he returned to work in the mill and bought it from E. Merrill & Sons some six years later. Mr. Berry is a Republican and a strong supporter of prohibition. His family attend the Baptist church and he is both treasurer and a deacon.

Mr. Berry married Elizabeth Carroll, who was born in the Province of New Brunswick, Canada. Their children are: 1. Anna, who married John B. Maxell, their one child being a daughter, Gertrude. 2. Dora. 3. T. Carroll, who married Nellie Scott, their two children being Clayton and Marie.

FRANK LOWREY—In the death of Frank Lowrey, July 25, 1923, at his home near Houlton, Maine, Aroostook County lost not only one of its most highly respected citizens, but a farmer who, by industry, thrift and intelligence, amassed a com-

petence, setting a fine example to the younger generation.

Son of Frank and Jane (Bates) Lowrey, he was a descendant of one of the oldest families in Aroostook County, and of his numerous brothers and sisters the only one now surviving is John Lowrey. He was educated in the rural schools of his neighborhood, but passed his youth and early manhood in incessant toil in the effort to obtain land of his own to cultivate, a purpose in which he succeeded so well that he eventually became the owner of three fine farms in the town of Houlton.

Early in life he married Amanda Cuvier, who proved a devoted helpmate, and aided him greatly in his first struggles toward independence. Their children were Frank, Fred and Willis Lowrey and Maude, who became the wife of Otis Oakes. Mr. and Mrs. Oakes make their home with Mrs. Lowrey on the farm on the North Road two miles north of Houlton. There are four grandchildren.

Mr. Lowrey was a member of the Presbyterian Church, of the Grange, and of the New England Order of Protection. He was widely known throughout the countryside, was highly respected and had many friends. The Rev. Albert M. Thompson paid a fine tribute to his character at the funeral, and he was laid to rest in Evergreen Cemetery.

GEORGE H. BENN—As a farmer and a dealer in both lumber and automobiles, George H. Benn is successful in all his different enterprises and is one of the leading figures in the life of Hodgdon. His lumber mill is in Hodgdon Village, and in it he employs from fifteen to twenty hands. He owns several farms, but the home farm of the group, which is in Hodgdon, is three hundred acres in area. In his farm work, he specializes in the cultivation of potatoes, while as an automobile dealer he sells Oldsmobile cars. His automobile and potato business he conducts under the firm name of the George H. Benn Company.

He is the son of Moses and Annie E. (Ingraham) Benn, both now deceased. His father was born in Hodgdon, where he was a farmer; and his mother, although she was born in Prince William, New Brunswick, came as a child to

Hodgdon. George H. Benn was one of their six children, who were: 1. Leander. 2. Frank. 3. Abbie, now the wife of Fred S. Daggett. 4. Jessie E., the wife of Delbert Bither. 5. George H. 6. Sophia, the wife of Amos Farrar, who is now deceased. Born in the town of Hodgdon on January 13, 1877, George H. Benn attended the public schools in that town, following which he spent one year in high school. Then he became engaged first in his agricultural activities, and ever since that time has been interested in the lumber and farming business. His political affiliations are with the Republican party. He is a member of the Free and Accepted Masons, in which order he is affiliated with the Monument Lodge.

Mr. Benn married Ruby E. Hunter, born in Hodgdon, the daughter of George A. and Flora (Young) Hunter, both farmers. George H. and Ruby E. (Hunter) Benn are the parents of one child, Mildred, who is a graduate of Houlton High School and a graduate of the Wheelock Kindergarten School in Boston.

Mr. Benn, who is well and favorably known in his community for his public-spirited attitude and his extensive business activities, has been since 1897 a trustee and a director of the local Methodist Episcopal church, of which he and his family are members.

OSCAR ABRAHAM BENN—Owning a farm one hundred and seventy-five acres in area on Benn's Hill, just off the Walker Road, Oscar Abraham Benn is one of the successful citizens of the town of Hodgdon, and the ability which he has displayed in his agricultural pursuits has caused him to be known as a distinct credit to his community.

He is the son of Abraham and Catherine (Woodward) Benn, both the Benns and the Woodwards having come originally from Ireland. His father, Abraham Benn, came with his brothers Solomon and Ephraim and their mother from Ireland, and settled in this section of Maine. The father of these three men died when they were mere children. Each of the three brothers who came to the United States became prosperous, however, as well as prominent men in their communities, and land owners. Abraham Benn married Catherine

Woodward, who was a daughter of Walter Woodward, also a native of Ireland. His son, Oscar Abraham Benn, who is now a farmer in Hodgdon, was one of eight children: 1. Julia, now deceased. 2. Ezekiel, a veteran of the Civil War who now lives in Oakfield. 3. Mary, living with her brother Oscar Abraham. 4. Augustus, who died in 1925. 5. Emily, who is the wife of Elvin E. Williams and who lives in Hodgdon. 6. Cyrus, who lives in Hodgdon. 7. Clarissa, deceased. 8. Oscar A., of whom further.

Oscar Abraham Benn, who was educated in the public schools of Hodgdon and in the Houlton Academy, is a prominent figure in this section. Politically he is affiliated with the Republican party. He has held the office of superintendent of schools in Hodgdon and participates considerably in the affairs of the Grange.

In 1893 he married Martha May, who was born in Island Falls, Maine, the daughter of Levi H. and Catherine (Thompson) May, the former of whom was a native of Henniker, New Hampshire, and the later a native of Lowell, Massachusetts. They were farmers and pioneers in Maine. Martha (May) Benn was for many years a teacher in the public schools of Aroostook County. Mr. and Mrs. Benn became the parents of the following children: 1. Ray Oscar, now deceased. 2. Catherine, a graduate of the Ricker Classical Institute and of Shaw's Business College, and a trained nurse at Roosevelt Hospital. 3. Oscar Packard, who attended the public schools of Hodgdon, graduated from the Ricker Classical Institute in the class of 1921, and from Colby College in the class of 1925 was employed for one year as clerk in a bank in New York City, then taught for a year, and is now taking a course in history at Columbia University. The members of the Benn family are affiliated with the Methodist Episcopal church, of which Oscar A. Benn is a trustee.

ARTHUR RAYMOND CUMMING has, since 1922, been a member of the firm of Cumming and Barker, electrical contractors of Houlton, Maine. He has had considerable experience in the electrical business, and his energy and ability have contributed greatly to the success of his firm. Mr. Cumming, who has been connected with the Houlton Fire Department for thirteen years, is now chief of that department, and he is also active in the social and fraternal life of his community. His father, Alexander Cumming, born in Scotland, is foreman of the electrical department of the Houlton Water Company. His mother, who was Maude Jordan before her marriage, was born in Sherbrook, Canada.

Arthur Raymond Cumming was born on February 21, 1897, at Houlton, Maine. He attended the local public schools, and when he completed his education, began working with his father to learn the electrical business. In December, 1922, in association with Jasper Barker, he established the firm of Cumming and Barker, electrical contractors, with their store and offices on the Houlton public square. This firm, which employs two other men, all practical electricians, carries a complete line of electrical supplies and equipment, including mechanical refrigerators and farm lighting plants.

By political inclination, Mr. Cumming is a member of the Republican party, and he served for several years as a constable. He has been a member of the Houlton Fire Department for the past thirteen years, acting as foreman of the department for seven years, and as chief of the department since April 1, 1927. He is affiliated fraternally with the Ancient Free and Accepted Masons, having taken the degrees of the Blue Lodge and Chapter in this organization. He is also a member of the Independent Order of Odd Fellows, and the Benevolent and Protective Order of Elks. He is a member of the Business Men's Association of Houlton. He and his family attend the local Baptist church.

Mr. Cumming married Phyllis Josephine Dow, who was born in Benton, New Brunswick, the daughter of Nevers and Jennie (Hazlett) Dow. Mr. and Mrs. Cumming are the parents of two children: Harvard Alexander and Virginia Jennie.

THOMAS H. HENDERSON—Among those foremost citizens of Littleton who have always been identified with the leading business interests of the community, and with the advancement of its institutions, Thomas H. Henderson has long established his repute in matters of good govern-ment as an office holder, and in business as a potato grower he has no successful competitor for the excellence as well as the quantity of the product of his farms.

Thomas H. Henderson was born January 12, 1876, at Littleton, a son of Thomas J. Henderson, a farmer, who was born in Ireland, but spent practically all his life here, and Margaret (Little) Henderson, of whose family of nine but two are living, Jennie Henderson, who married Walter Hanning, and Thomas H. Henderson, of whom further.

Mr. Henderson attended the Littleton schools, and entered upon general farming and the potato-growing specialty early in his career. He is the owner of two farms in Littleton, one of one hundred and seventy-five acres, where he resides, on the Carson Road, and the other, of one hundred and fifty acres on the North Road, on both of which he raises abundant crops of potatoes; and as a well-known shipper, he maintains his own warehouse in Wiley siding. One of the leading and substantial men of this township, he is active in all the community's interests. He is a Republican in his political views, is a first selectman, and has served as a member of the school board. His fraternal affiliations are with the local Grange of the Patrons of Husbandry. With his family he attends the Baptist church, of which he is a liberal supporter.

Thomas H. Henderson married Mabel McArthur, who was born in New Brunswick, daughter of James and Margaret McArthur, both farming people, natives of New Brunswick, but later resided here. Their children: 1. Ernest, born in 1904, received his education in Littleton schools, and is associated in business with his father. 2. Frank, attended the Littleton schools. 3. Gladys, married Elbert Daw, a farmer, and they reside in Littleton. 4. Earl. 5. Irvin. 6. Hartley. 7. Almon.

ALLAN J. CAMPBELL—From his youth interested in farming and particularly in potato raising, Allan J. Campbell has secured a place of leadership in the agricultural region of which Littleton and Houlton are thriving centres, his business being accounted as one of the largest and most prosperous in the section. Mr. Campbell is an expert in his specialty, his farms are extensive, and thoroughly cultivated, and he is well known among the potato brokers in the State.

Allan J. Campbell was born March 22, 1863, in Carlton County, New Brunswick, a son of George Campbell, a farmer, who was born in this State, and Mary (McLellan) Campbell, who was born and died in New Brunswick. When he was twenty-one years old, Mr. Campbell came to the United States, but after two years here he returned to New Brunswick, where he remained to his twenty-seventh year. His first stay in this country was in mining in Montana, but since his return here he has made himself one of the largest landowners in Littleton, his four farms yielding potatoes and general farm produce; and he also has a warehouse at Littleton, where he sells to local brokers.

In the political field, Mr. Campbell is a Republican, his vote and influence being exerted for his party's benefit. Fraternally, he is affiliated with the Independent Order of Odd Fellows, and with the Houlton Grange, Patrons of Husbandry. He has served as a member of the board of trustees of the Methodist Episcopal church.

Allan J. Campbell married Georgia Ann Watson, who was born in Littleton, who died May 11, 1922, daughter of George and Ann (Lowrey) Watson. They were the parents of a son, Don A. Campbell, who is associated with his father in business.

LYNWOOD B. RHODA—Not only does Lynwood B. Rhoda do an extensive business in shipping potatoes and general farm products and in selling fertilizer, making his headquarters on his one hundred acre farm in Hodgdon, but he also has a warehouse on the Bangor and Aroostook Railroad in Houlton.

The son of Samuel B. and Elizabeth (Hone) Rhoda, both farmers and natives of Maine, the former of whom was counted as a prominent and reliable citizen in his community, Lynwood B. Rhoda was born in Hodgdon on July 19, 1879. He was educated in the public schools and took a commercial course to supplement his early training. After he completed his education, he became engaged in farming, which ever since has been his

life work. Ten years after he became a farmer, he established his fertilizer business; and about 1917 he started his potato business. Having his own warehouse in Houlton, he acts as his own broker and sells his goods direct. In his political beliefs he is a Republican. He is a prominent man in the public affairs of Hodgdon, having been for four years chairman of the town's board ot selectmen.

Mr. Rhoda married Grace Howard, who was born in Hodgdon, the daughter of Napoleon and Ada (Gerow) Howard, both of whom were farmers. Lynwood B. and Grace (Howard) Rhoda are the parents of one child, Virginia L. Mr. Rhoda and his family are associated with the Church of England, although Mrs. Rhoda is a member of the Baptist church.

JOHN M. WARD—Prominent agriculturist owning two hundred and forty acres of fertile land in Limestone Township on the Ward Road near the village of Limestone, Aroostook County, John M. Ward is one of the principal men of his community, making his home in the village and conducting his acres in the production of general crops, and notably seed and table potatoes of good grade, which he sells in the local market. For a number of years he owned and operated a starch factory in Limestone successfully, and since 1907 has represented the American Agricultural Chemical Company as local agent. In all matters of civic progress Mr. Ward is interested, and in the majority of such enterprises is personally concerned. In public life he has for many years played an important part.

John M. Ward was born upon the farm which he now (1928) owns, February 17, 1865, son of Josiah and Mary Ann (Towle) Ward, his father having been a native of China, Maine, and his mother of Gardiner. Josiah and his wife, Mary Ann Ward, came to this township in early age, and here lived the balance of their lives and died, greatly respected by all who knew them and mourned sincerely at their passing. Josiah Ward engaged wholeheartedly in matters pertaining to the village and this section of the county and was instrumental in the fulfillment of several most beneficial undertakings for public welfare.

John M. Ward attended the public schools of Limestone and worked upon the farm with his father until the latter's death in 1883, when John M. was eighteen years of age. Then, in association with his brother, I. C. Ward, John M. Ward took charge of the home farm and ran it for four years with sound fortune, after which time he purchased a farm of his own on the State road to Fort Fairfield. This he conducted with great prosperity for thirty years, and disposed of it finally to his son, Herman A. Ward, see accompanying sketch, next purchasing the farm on which he was born, on Ward Road. A Republican, Mr. Ward is loyal to the principles of government upheld by that party and is possessor of a considerable influence in local political matters; and never in his many years of political activity has he misapplied that influence, but always has directed it in channels for the public good. Since 1915 he has been a member of the Limestone Board of Selectmen. As a business man he is known to be able, and is well acquainted in commercial circles of Limestone and nearby points, partly due to his former activity in the starch factory and more widely because of his application of tried business methods in the growth and disposition of his crops. Fraternally Mr. Ward enjoys strong and extensive connections, including membership in the Limestone Lodge of Free and Accepted Masons, Caribou Chapter of Royal Arch Masons, the Fort Fairfield lodge of the Independent Order of Odd Fellows, and Limestone Grange. The family attends the Episcopal church and Mr. Ward gives generously to charitable and kindred worthy appeals, in a spirit truly humanitarian.

John M. Ward married (first) Alice Willey, deceased, daughter of Isaac and Sarah (Forrest) Willey. Mrs. Ward died in 1918, leaving three children: Benjamin Harrison (see following biography); Eva, wife of Glenn Cheney; and Herman A. Five other children were born to this union, and are deceased: Elmer, Mabel, James, Sadie, and Beecher. Mr. Ward married (second) Eva Baird, daughter of Haniford and Sarah (Richie) Baird; and to this union was born one child, Darrell W.

BENJAMIN HARRISON WARD—Owner of a farm tract of two hundred acres abutting on the South Caribou Road in Aroostook County, representing the amalgamation of two farms, the first of one hundred and ten acres which he purchased from Isaac Willey, and the second, adjoining, of ninety acres, which he purchased from John Frazier, Benjamin Harrison Ward engages in agriculture both extensive and general, and specializes in the growing of potatoes, which he markets in Limestone and Fort Fairfield. He is one of the directors of the Limestone Trust Company and is known favorably in business circles of this village and in Fort Fairfield as a man of reliable commercial judgment. He participates actively in affairs of village and countryside, and is accounted one of the substantial and representative citizens having close to the heart a desire for the welfare and advancement of his community.

Benjamin Harrison Ward was born in Limestone Township, May 16, 1888, upon the Ardell Ward farm on Caribou Road, son of John M. and Alice (Willey) Ward (see a preceding biography). He received his elementary education in the grade schools of Limestone, and for three years attended high school. He learned all phases of successful farm management under the direction of his father, and after spending a year in association with him in agriculture, purchased a holding under his own name, the one hundred and ten acres, to which he later added by purchase the complementary ninety acres, making of his total acreage one of the important farming tracts in this portion of Aroostook County. Always a participant in constructive enterprises calculated to improve his community, Benjamin H. Ward is a Republican, loyal to the party's principles of government, and a leader in politics locally. He is also active fraternally, being a Master Mason and a member of the Grange. A husbandman, he combines the latest methods of scientific agriculture with the peculiarities of the soil under his cultivation, adapting the crops best suited to it; and under his care yields are large. With his family he attends the Methodist church, and in this church he is recognized as a principal supporter. Toward appeals of charity Mr. Ward is kindly and sympathetic, giving largely and in a spirit truly humanitarian, without regard for race or creed represented.

Benjamin Harrison Ward married Gladys Cox, native of New York State, daughter of Joseph and Emma (Cox—no blood relationship) Cox, her father's forefathers having been natives of New

York State and her mother's of the province of New Brunswick, Dominion of Canada. To this union have been born three children: Althea, Barry and Valeska.

HERMAN ANDREW WARD—Numbered outstandingly among the younger but none the less progressive and representative landowners and farmers of the Fort Fairfield neighborhood is Herman Andrew Ward, who owns a rich farming tract of some one hundred and sixty-five acres situated on the Fort Fairfield State Road, in Aroostook County. Here he engages in general agricultural pursuits and specializes in the growing of high grade seed and table potatoes, which he disposes of in the Fort Fairfield market.

Herman Andrew Ward, son of John M. and Alice (Willey) Ward (see accompanying sketch), received his academic education in the public schools of Fort Fairfield, having been born on the farm near here one time owned by his father and later owned and conducted by himself, on January 1, 1900. It was here, with his older brother, Benjamin Harrison (q. v.), his senior by twelve years, that the father instructed his sons in all phases of farming, and inculcated in them the principles on which his own success in agriculture had been founded. Herman A. Ward learned rapidly, and upon completion of his studies in the village gave his whole time to the soil and the livestock. In time, after his marriage, the father saw fit to sell out to him, and he has since conducted his affairs on businesslike methods, insuring good return in political matters of Fort Fairfield, and belongs to the Limestone Lodge of the Free and Accepted Masons, and to the Caribou Chapter of Royal Arch Masons. He attends the Baptist church and is most temperate in all ways.

Herman Andrew Ward married Susan Bassett, native of Caswell, Maine; and to this union have been born two children: Thurly Marilyn and Norma Elaine.

ISAAC B. UMPHREY—One of the town's leading citizens and prominent business men, Isaac B. Umphrey has been a successful agriculturist for many years in addition to which he is a leading factor in the financial life of the town, having been a director of the Washburn Trust Company since its inception. Mr. Umphrey owns and operates two large farms, besides which he acts as a buyer for F. Putnam Company, important potato brokers of Boston, having successfully filled this position for eighteen years.

Mr. Umphrey was born in Washburn, December 27, 1871, son of William Umphrey, of Kings County, New Brunswick, and Lorinda (Wilder) Umphrey, of Pembrook, who was brought to Washburn as a child sixteen months old. Her father, Robert Wilder, was one of the founders of this town. Both Mr. and Mrs. Umphrey are now deceased. William Umphrey came to Washburn when twenty-two years of age, first starting in the lumber business, but later entering agriculture, in which he remained all the rest of his life.

Isaac B. Umphrey was educated in the local public schools and while pursuing his studies, worked on his father's farm. After the completion of his formal education, he was engaged for eleven years in the shingle business, where he achieved a reputation for great energy and industry, in which qualities he still excels. After leaving this business, he has always since been engaged in agriculture, and when the railroad was projected through here, he actively entered the potato business on a large scale, as a producer, buyer, and shipper. His venture grew and prospered and today he operates a farm of forty acres in Washburn and another of forty acres in Wade. The potatoes produced are of the highest grade and customers are always sure of their unvarying quality and dependability. A member of the Republican party in his political affiliations, Mr. Umphrey takes an active interest in the progress and welfare of his community at all times, although he has constantly refused to accept public office, preferring to serve the interests of the town as a public-spirited citizen, by his example and influence. A prominent figure in fraternal circles, he is a member of the Free and Accepted Masons, connected with the Blue Lodge of Washburn, Caribou Chapter, Presque Isle Council and Houlton Commandery. He is a member of Anah Temple, Ancient Arabic Order Nobles of the Mystic Shrine,

Bangor, and takes an active part in the Rotary Club of Washburn.

Isaac B. Umphrey married (first) Maud Sweetser, of Presque Isle, who is deceased. Mr. Umphrey married (second) Mabel Wallace, who died, leaving two children: 1. Isaac Malcolm, connected with the Bangor and Aroostook Railroad, married Mildred Duncan. 2. Lucia May, a student in the local high school. Mr. Umphrey married (third) Adella Lacey, widow of William Lacey, who had two children by her first marriage: Harold and Bessie. Both Mr. and Mrs. Umphrey are leading members of the Baptist church.

member of the town committee and fulfills the duties of his office with the best interests of the town in mind. Prominent in fraternal circles, he is a member of the Free and Accepted Masons, being connected with the Blue Lodge of Washburn, Caribou Chapter, and Houlton Commandery. He is also a member of Anah Temple, Ancient Arabic Order Nobles of the Mystic Shrine, Bangor.

Harry E. Umphrey married Hepsie Crouse, of Washburn, daughter of W. J. and Esther (Lovely) Crouse, and their children are. Donald, Phyllis and Ardis. The entire family are members of the Baptist church.

HARRY E. UMPHREY—One of the outstanding young men in the commercial life of the town, Harry E. Umphrey of Washburn has risen to his present position by reason of his thorough business ability and a desire to progress, coupled with an enthusiastic and energetic disposition. In addition to his important business interests, Mr. Umphrey finds time to devote to the civic affairs of the community and he is always an interested and active participant in all projects for its welfare and advancement. As president of the H. E. Umphrey Company, growers of seed potatoes, he is a leading factor in the agricultural prosperity of the vicinity, and the products sold by this company have acquired a reputation for unchanging stability of quality and absolute dependability.

Mr. Umphrey was born in Washburn, October 3, 1894, son of George R. Umphrey of Washburn, whose biography accompanies this, and Myrtle E. (Packard) Umphrey, who is deceased. George R. Umphrey is prominent in the financial and political affairs of the town, having several large farms in the vicinity.

Harry E. Umphrey received his education in the local public schools, after which he entered the business world and upon the organization of the Maine Division of the American Fruit Growers' Association, Incorporated, he was appointed sales manager and he still continues to carry on the duties of this responsible position. In addition to being head of the business which bears his name, he is a partner in the O. K. Story Company. An active member of the Republican party, he is a

GEORGE R. UMPHREY—An important figure in State, financial and political circles, and one of the town's most eminent citizens, George R. Umphrey of Washburn has held a number of important posts in the civic government of the town and commonwealth in addition to attending to his varied business interests, including the operation of two large farms in the vicinity. At the present time, Mr. Umphrey is commissioner of Aroostook County, serving his second term of six years, being reëlected to this office by reason of his capable and intelligent administration of county affairs.

Mr. Umphrey was born in Washburn September 23, 1869, son of William Umphrey of Kings County, New Brunswick, and Lorinda (Wilder) Umphrey, of Pembrook, who came to Washburn with her parents as a child sixteen months old. They are both deceased. William Umphrey came to Washburn as a young man, twenty-two years old, and at first engaged in the lumber trade, but later went into agriculture, in which occupation he remained all the latter part of his life.

George R. Umphrey was educated in the public schools of Washburn, and after the completion of his formal education, worked on his father's farm and in the woods until he was twenty-one years old. Starting independently, he engaged in agricultural pursuits in the summer and in the arduous work of lumbering in the deep woods in winter. Always energetic and earnest in the carrying out of all details, he advanced steadily and today he owns a farm of seventy acres on Caribou Road, and another of forty-five acres in Washburn Village, which he operates as a gentleman farmer, raising potatoes of the highest grade. Mr. Umphrey lives at the present time next the house where he was born. Taking an active part in affairs of finance, he has been vice-president of the Washburn Trust Company ever since its organization, and is a director of the Presque Isle National Bank, having served in that capacity for eighteen years. A popular figure in political circles, because of his having the best interests of his constituents at heart, he was elected a member of the State Legislature and served during the years 1913 and 1914. For twenty-two years he was a selectman of the town and was chairman of the board for fourteen years. To all projects which have been advanced during his career, Mr. Umphrey has always given the advantage of his keen and unprejudiced judgment, coupled with a sincere desire to help the growth and advancement of his community. His political affiliations have always been with the Republican party. Interested and active in fraternal organizations, he is a member of the Free and Accepted Masons, connected with the Blue Lodge of Washburn, Caribou Chapter, Houlton Commandery, also the Independent Order of Odd Fellows, Washburn Lodge. With his wife, Mr. Umphrey attends the Baptist church, and for many years was a trustee. His maternal grandfather, Robert Wilder, was one of the founders of this town.

George R. Umphrey married (first), in 1892, Myrtle E. Packard, who died in 1922; they had three children, two of whom died in infancy, and Harry E., of Washburn, a biography of whom accompanies that of his father. Myrtle Packard was the daughter of George Washington and Amelia (Morris) Packard. He was one of the founders of the town of Mapleton, and was one of the oldest citizens of Aroostook County. In 1925, Mr. Umphrey married (second) Julia L. McLaughlin, a public school teacher, of Caribou, and eldest daughter of John and Margaret (Gallagher) McLaughlin, who were among the pioneer settlers of Caribou.

GEORGE HARE—Owner of a fertile farm of ninety acres on the Hare Road, near the town of Monticello, George Hare is a well-known and respected member of his community. The family of Hare has long been established in the State of Maine, and has given its male descendants liberally to the soil. George Hare was born at Monticello, on the farm, May 14, 1857, son of Henry Harrison and Mary Ann (Gentle) Hare, his mother also having descended from an old and distinguished family, it having been founded in England, whence the American branch sprang early in the history of Maine. Henry H. Hare was a farmer high in the estimation of the people of town and country; he was active in politics in the neighborhood of Monticello, and a member of several fraternal societies. Henry H. and Mary Ann (Gentle) Hare were the parents of nine children.

George Hare received his education in the public schools, and until he had reached the age of thirty-two years worked on the farm with his father. In 1889 he went into business as a farmer for himself. He was successful and on several occasions changed his location. He engages in general farming, grows potatoes extensively, and disposes of his crops in the local markets. Mr. Hare is a member of the Republican party, the Grange, and with his wife attends the Methodist church.

George Hare married (first) Martha Merithew, and this union resulted in the birth of two children, Nettie Mildred and Elbridge Harrison. Upon the death of Martha (Merithew) Hare, Mr. Hare married (second) May Elizabeth (Swart-Bell), widow of William Bell, and by him mother of three children: Nellie, Effie and Arnold.

BENJAMIN FRANKLIN SMITH—One of the highest tributes that can be paid to a man in any community is that of a good citizen and a good neighbor. This is what has always been said of Benjamin Franklin Smith of Presque Isle, Maine. To be a good citizen and a good neighbor, with all that the terms imply, is to express those characteristics with which Mr. Smith was endowed and which he put into his life, in taking an interest in all that pertained to the general welfare and progress of the town and in those beautiful humanities that are expressed in sharing the joys and sorrows of one's fellowmen with a sympathy of understanding that is not always expressed, even though felt. He was the son of Simeon and Eliza (Given) Smith, old citizens of the State of Maine.

Benjamin Franklin Smith was born in Richmond, Maine, and like other boys of his association, he was educated in the public schools. After finishing his school days, he set out to learn the trade of a carpenter and succeeded in mastering this craft and followed it for many years. After a time he felt a great desire to own and operate a farm and in order to carry out his wish, he purchased a tract of one hundred and sixty-eight acres on the road between Presque Isle and Caribou, Maine, and after clearing most of the land himself, he began to get the ground in shape for a farm. All the time that he was preparing his farm, he was working very hard as a carpenter and even after he began the actual operation of farming, he continued to do carpentry work. By diligence, perseverance and thrift, he made a success of his undertaking and was in a position to enjoy the fruit of his youthful labors in the ripeness of mature age. He was a member of the Grange, in which organization he took a keen interest; and he was a member of the Order of Free and Accepted Masons; and of the Congregational church. Mr. Smith died December 23, 1902, and since that time two of his sons have carried on the farm for their mother.

On January 17, 1890, Benjamin Franklin Smith married Ida McNally, who was born at Ashland, Maine, the daughter of Moses and Sarah (Clark) McNally, both natives of New Brunswick, but who had lived in Ashland for many years. Mr. and Mrs. Smith had five children: 1. Milroy, deceased. 2. Roland, who is in business in Bangor, Maine, and who married Alice Pelkey. 3. Earl. 4. Omer. The two younger sons manage the farm.

———

SIDNEY GRAVES—The late Sidney Graves who founded the Graves Hardware Company of Presque Isle, Maine, was one of those retiring, forceful characters whose impress on a community is a lasting influence. He was born at South Thomaston, Maine, on July 13, 1853, the son of William D. and Mary (Graves) Graves. His parents were no relation although they had the same surname. Mr. and Mrs. Graves moved to Presque Isle from South Thomaston when Sidney Graves was a lad of only eight years. His father was a ship builder and part owner of three ships. By a strange coincidence, at different times, all of these ships were destroyed by fire, which loss greatly crippled the finances of the family, and Sidney Graves was then obliged to leave school at the age of fifteen years and begin work to support himself. Up to that time he had attended the common schools at Presque Isle and had done some work at the old Presque Isle Academy.

He started work in the store of George H. Freeman and worked his way in the business and saved his surplus wisely until he was able to buy out the business, which he carried on prosperously for a number of years when he had a complete loss by fire. At that time, he did not reopen the old line, but started in the coal business, which he ran for two years and then established the Graves Hardware Company, which he conducted most successfully until the time of his death, April 9, 1924. The business still continued as one of the best in Presque Isle until July 1, 1928, when it was liquidated and closed. Mr. Graves was an Independent Democrat and, while zealous in his interest in political affairs, he was modest and retiring in his disposition and sought no public political office. He did, however, give of his services as officer in a number of charitable organizations and enterprises. He was a trustee of the Presque Isle General Hospital from the time it was inaugurated until the time of his death. He also had an interest in the Aroostook Wholesale Grocery Company and was president of that enterprise. He was a devoted Mason and very active in the affairs of that order.

On August 21, 1894, Sidney Graves married Laila Etella Smith, who was born in Houlton, Maine, the daughter of George H. and Abbie (Brown) Smith, both natives of the State of Maine, where Mr. Smith operated a farm, and later was in the hardware business and lastly a salesman. Mr. and Mrs. Sidney Graves had one child, a daughter, Dorothy Eulalia, who was educated at the schools of Presque Isle and then finished her undergraduate work at Smith College in 1921 and has since done graduate work at the University of Washington and at Columbia University, New York City. She is now a teacher in the State Normal School at Cortland, New York. Mr. Graves was a member of the Unitarian Society and Mrs. Graves is a member of the Congregational Society.

LYMAN J. PENDELL—Among the successful newspaper men of Aroostook County is Lyman J. Pendell, owner and editor of the "Aroostook Republican," which is published in Caribou, Maine. Mr. Pendell has been identified with the publishing business from the beginning of his active career, and has been the owner of the "Aroostook Republican" since 1904.

Lyman J. Pendell was born in East Brookfield, Massachusetts, February 7, 1865, son of Rev. John R. Pendell, a Methodist minister who was born in New York State, and of Mary J. (Stevens) Pendell, a native of Massachusetts. He received his early education in the public schools of Edinborough, Pennsylvania, and then entered the Edinborough Normal School. When his course in the normal school was completed, he secured a position with a newspaper publishing house in Pennsylvania, and after making himself thoroughly familiar with many phases of the business, came to Maine, and located at Presque Isle, where for seven years he was on the staff of the "Star Herald." In 1904 he purchased the "Aroostook Republican," which had been established in 1880, by Mr. Stickney, and since that time he has been the successful publisher of this well known weekly news sheet. Both Mr. Pendell and his paper are strongly Republican in their political sympathies, and he has built up a long mailing list among the residents of this strongly Republican county, in which it is said that Democrats are as scarce as hen's eggs in January. Fraternally, Mr. Pendell is identified with the Masonic Order, being a member of Lodge, Chapter, Council, Commandery, and Shrine and he is also a member of the Knights of Pythias, and of the Modern Woodmen of America.

Lyman J. Pendell married (first) Ida May Mead. She died leaving one daughter, who is the wife of Attorney O. L. Keyes, and has two children: Marion and Helen. Mr. Pendell married (second) Ethel E. Greenlaw, daughter of Samuel C. and Mary (Sprague) Greenlaw, the first mentioned of whom was county commissioner for a period of eighteen years. To the second marriage three children were born: 1. Louise Evelyn. 2. Philip. 3. Mary Elizabeth. The family attend the Methodist church.

HAMILTON H. DYER—For about twelve years, Hamilton H. Dyer has been associated with the Houlton Trust Company, of Houlton, and since 1923 he has been treasurer of that organization. Mr. Dyer is well known in banking circles of this section. He has spent all of the years of his active career, to the present time (1928), in the banking business, first in Portland, Maine, and since 1916 in Houlton.

Hamilton H. Dyer was born in New York City January 1, 1891, but his parents removed to Portland, Maine, when he was a child and he received his education in the public schools of that city. When he had finished his high school course he found his first employment as clerk with the Portland Trust Company, which later became the Fidelity Trust Company of Portland. That connection he maintained until 1916, when he resigned in order that he might accept the position offered by the Houlton Trust Company, of which he is now treasurer. He came to this company as assistant treasurer, but in 1923 was made treasurer and since that time has filled that official position. Mr. Dyer is known as a man of keen insight and of sound judgment and his advice is much sought in matters of finance. Politically he gives his support to no one party, but reserves for himself the privilege of casting his vote for those candidates whom he considers best qualified to fill the office, regardless of party affiliations. He is a member of the Rotary Club, and holds a high place in the esteem of his many friends and associates. His religious affiliation and that of his family is with the Congregational church.

Hamilton H. Dyer was married to Evelyn Chase, of Portland, Maine, daughter of Dr. George W. Chase. Mr. and Mrs. Dyer are the parents of two children: Hamilton H., Jr., and Phyllis.

WILLIAM B. GIBSON, M. D.—The medical profession is very thoroughly represented at Houlton by Dr. William B. Gibson, whose specialty as a surgeon has received the best training that the medical schools of this country and abroad afford, and whose experience has been attended with results that have secured him the confidence and regard of a steadily increasing practice.

Dr. William B. Gibson was born August 3, 1879, at Benton, New Brunswick, a son of William Gibson, a merchant and native of Scotland, and of Anna (Bryden) Gibson, who was born in New Brunswick. Dr. Gibson, after attending the public schools at Woodstock, New Brunswick, was graduated at the Philadelphia Medical School, now a part of the University of Pennsylvania, with the degree Doctor of Medicine, and, successively, he took post-graduate work in Chicago and New York, and afterwards in Vienna. For a brief period he had his offices in Atlantic City, New Jersey, but since 1904, Dr. Gibson has been established at Houlton, where he is specializing in surgery. He has been a member of the board of directors of the Aroostook Hospital for four years; and during the World War, Dr. Gibson served efficiently as an examiner for the United States Government.

Besides his affiliation with such leading professional organizations as the County Medical Society, the State Medical Society and the American Medical Association, Dr. Gibson held the office of president of the Country Club for two years; and he is a member of the Meduxnekeag Club, the Houlton Chamber of Commerce, and of the Blue Lodge, Free and Accepted Masons. He is a member of the board of directors of the Unitarian church, and all his family are of the Unitarian faith.

Dr. William B. Gibson married Tessie H. Hall, who was born in Houlton, a daughter of G. A. and Tessie M. (Luce) Hall.

WALTER B. CLARK—For nearly two decades Walter B. Clark has been serving in public office in Aroostook County, first as an assistant to his father, and since 1922 as clerk of the courts of Aroostook County and as town clerk of Houlton. Mr. Clark is a graduate of Bowdoin College and is one of the well-known and highly respected citizens of this section of the county.

Walter B. Clark was born in Houlton, July 7, 1882, son of Michael M. and Henrietta (Braden) Clark, the father a native of Woodstock, New Brunswick, whose parents removed to Houlton, Maine, when he was two years of age, and who spent the remainder of his life here, becoming one of the prominent citizens of the place and a public official holding both town and county offices. Walter B. Clark received his early education in the public schools of his birthplace and then prepared for college in Ricker Classical Institute, at Houlton, from which he was graduated in 1900. Later he matriculated in Bowdoin College, at Brunswick, Maine, and completed his course there with graduation in 1906. For a time after completing his college course he was employed on various jobs and then he went to St. Paul, Minnesota, in the employ of the Pittsburgh Coal Company, with whom he remained until 1909, when he returned east and entered the office of his father, who was serving as clerk of the courts of Aroostook County and also as town clerk of Houlton. He served as his father's assistant in these offices until the death of the father, when he was appointed, March 1, 1922, by Governor Baxter, to succeed his father. Since that time he has been most efficiently discharging the duties of both offices, giving to his public most worthy and competent service and winning for himself the commendation of those whom he serves. In addition to taking care of the responsibilities of the two offices which he now holds, Mr. Clark has also served for one term as tax collector. He gives his earnest support to the principles and the candidates of the Republican party, and is well known in Masonic circles, being a member of the Blue Lodge, Chapter, and Commandery at Houlton, and of Anah Temple, Ancient Arabic Order Nobles of the Mystic Shrine, of Bangor. He is president of the Houlton Country Club, and his religious affiliation and that of his family is with the Unitarian church. Mr. Clark is one of the very well known citizens of this section of the county, and he has a host of friends in Houlton and vicinity.

Walter B. Clark was married to Ethel Whitehead, of Minneapolis, Minnesota, and they are the parents of one son, Alan H., who is a student in Bowdoin College. Walter B. Clark, the father, is a trustee of the Unitarian church of Houlton, and has also served as treasurer.

WILLIAM HERBERT ORMSBY—Since 1914 William Herbert Ormsby has been treasurer and manager of The Cochran Drug Store, Inc.,

of Houlton. Before entering the drug business he
engaged in educational work with considerable
success, and when he became associated with the
Cochran Drug Store, prior to its incorporation in
1914, he devoted himself with his customary
energy to building up the business. The financial
position of his company speaks for his ability in
this line.

William Herbert Ormsby was born on January
22, 1876, at Scarboro, Maine. He attended the
local grammar and high schools and later entered
Hebron Academy. After his graduation he taught
for thirteen terms in various Maine schools, and
for three years he served as superintendent of
schools at Dixfield, Maine. At the end of this
time he entered the University of Maine to study
pharmacy, and was graduated from this institution in 1908. Coming to Houlton he became connected with the Cochran Drug Store, and later
became manager for Mrs. Cochran, who was carrying on the business after her husband's death,
and later as a partner. On August 6, 1914, this
business was incorporated under the name of The
Cochran Drug Store, Inc., with Mrs. M. B. Cot-
ton as president; Mrs. Doris Cochran Sullivan of
Springfield, Massachusetts, as vice-president, and
Mr. Ormsby as treasurer and manager. This arrangement has continued since. Fraternally, he is
affiliated with the Free and Accepted Masons as
a member of Monument Lodge. He is also a
member of the Order of the Eastern Star and attends the local Baptist church.

Mr. Ormsby married Ethelyn May McKenney,
born in Cape Elizabeth, Maine, the daughter of
Horace B. and Elizabeth McKenney.

FRED E. HALL—Well known among the
business men of Houlton, is Fred E. Hall, president and treasurer of the Fred E. Hall Company,
distributors of the Buick cars for southern Aroostook and northern Penobscot counties. The company also deals in hay and farm produce. The concern was established by Mr. Hall about 1907, and
is now (1928) one of the thoroughly well known
and prosperous firms of its kind in this section of
the State. In addition to the operation of this
business, Mr. Hall owns a big farm on the State
road and also operates two farms in the town of

Littleton and another in the town of North Limerick. He is active in public affairs, and one of
the representative citizens of Houlton.

Fred E. Hall was born in the town of Chester,
Maine, in September, 1874, son of Eben and Emily (Weed) Hall, both natives of Maine, and farmers. After attending the local public schools, Mr.
Hall continued his studies in the Maine Central
Institute and then matriculated in the University
of Maine, at Orono, from which he graduated in
1898. After the completion of his college course
he went to Portland, Maine, where he entered the
employ of the Schottleback & Foss Company, a
drug concern, with which he remained for about
two and a half years. At the end of that time he
returned to Houlton, and after a few years, in
1907, he established the Fred E. Hall Company,
of which he is president and treasurer, and of
which Frank B. Cassidy is secretary. For three
years after founding the business he handled only
baled hay and fertilizer, but at the end of that time
he added the agency for Buick cars. Mr. Hall is
a man of integrity and resourcefulness, and is of
the versatile type which can handle several lines
of business activity at the same time. He owns
a four-hundred-acre farm on the State road, and,
as has been stated, operates three other farms,
two in the town of Littleton, and another in the
town of North Limerick. Along with his varied
business activities Mr. Hall has also found time
for local public service, and for the past eight
years has served as school commissioner of Houlton. He gives his support to the principles and
the candidates of the Republican party, and fraternally is identified with the local lodge, Free and
Accepted Masons, and with the Commandery and
Shrine. He is a member of Meduxnekeag Club
and of the Rotary Club, and his religious affiliation and that of his family is with the Congregational church.

Fred E. Hall was married to Georgia Soiett,
who was born in Portland, Maine.

GEORGE H. KNOX, sheriff of Aroostook
County, Maine, was born on October 17, 1887, in
New Brunswick, a son of the late Isaac and Isabel (Boviard) Knox. The father died in 1901
and the mother still lives in New Brunswick.

Isaac Knox, who was a native of New Brunswick, was a blacksmith and a farmer.

George H. Knox received his education in the district schools of New Brunswick. Upon the completion of these studies, he moved to Caribou, Maine, where he learned the blacksmith trade while working with his brother, and he has followed this line of endeavor for over twenty years. On January 1, 1927, he took office as sheriff of Aroostook County. During the World War, Mr. Knox enlisted in the infantry on October 13, 1917. After a time he was transferred to the 103d Ordnance detachment, with which he served for some fifteen months. He was honorably discharged from military duty on January 4, 1919, at which time he returned to Caribou.

Despite the arduous duties of the work in which he has been engaged, Mr. Knox has found time in which to serve the people of his community in other than a private capacity. For some time he served on the local police force of Caribou. In his political preferences he is inclined toward the Republican party and he is fraternally affiliated with the Ku Klux Klan.

George H. Knox married Jennie Dieves, who was born in Washburn, Maine, an adopted daughter of Thorwell and Jessie (Steves) Dieves. Mr. and Mrs. Knox are the parents of two daughters: Helen Marie, and Ruby Elizabeth. Mr. Knox and his family maintain their residence in Houlton, Maine, in which community they attend the United Baptist church.

JOSEPH A. BROWNE—As first vice-president of the Farmers' National Bank of Houlton, Joseph A. Browne has been efficiently serving for over twelve years, being at the present time (1928) the only active member of the original incorporators of the bank. Up to 1922 he was also actively engaged in business as a merchant, founder and owner of the concern which still operates under the name of J. A. Browne & Company.

Joseph Browne, grandfather of Joseph A. Browne, was born June 15, 1779, and died May 20, 1812. He married, March 17, 1799, Elizabeth Pine, who was born in Liverpool, England, September 27, 1782, and died September 15, 1872. They were the parents of the following children:

Mary Ann, James P., Margaret, Henry P., Joseph P. (of further mention), and Priscilla.

Joseph P. Browne, son of Joseph and Elizabeth (Pine) Browne, was born in New Brunswick, Canada, and died in September, 1854. He received his education in Frederickton, New Brunswick, and became a well-known mathematician and penman. His son, Joseph A. Browne, has in his possession an unique little music book, all done by hand with pen and ink, and containing old time hymns, but small enough to fit snugly in a vest pocket. This was all done by the father, Joseph P. Browne, and is highly prized by the son. Joseph P. Browne married Mahitable Ebbett, who was born in New Brunswick, Canada, and a few months after the death of her husband, when Joseph A. Browne was a year old, removed to Houlton, Maine.

Joseph A. Browne, son of Joseph P. and Mahitable (Ebbett) Browne, was born in Hampstead, New Brunswick, Canada, in 1853. His father died when he was seven months of age, and a few months later, when he was about a year old, his mother removed to Houlton, Maine, where all his life, with the exception of four years spent in Boston, has been passed. He received his education in the public schools of Houlton and in Houlton Academy, and during the last three years spent in school he also worked in the store of R. G. Rollins after school and on Saturdays and holidays. In 1870, when he was seventeen years of age, he went to Bangor, Maine, with Mr. Rollins, who had removed his business to that place, but nine months later made a change and went to Boston, where he entered the employ of the C. F. Hovey Company, with whom he remained for a period of four years. At the end of that time he returned to Houlton and again associated himself with Mr. Rollins, proprietor of one of the local stores, who had returned to Houlton. After serving for a year as clerk he was admitted as a partner with Mr. Rollins, in which connection he served also as manager of the business. After continuing as manager for a period of three years he purchased the interest of Mr. Rollins, and under the name of J. A. Browne & Company continued to successfully conduct the business until 1922, when he retired, selling the business to his son-in-law, Percy L. Rideout, who is still (1928) conducting it. Although retired from the active management of his business, Mr. Browne still re-

tains his official position as first vice-president of
the Farmers' National Bank of Houlton, of which
institution he is one of the incorporators. He has
been associated with the bank continuously since
its organization; first as a director, and as clerk of
the board of directors, and for the past thirteen
years as first vice-president. He is at the present
time (1928) the only one of the original incorporators of the bank who is active in its management. In 1893 he became a director of The Houlton Water Company and in 1902 was elected secretary and treasurer of The Houlton Water Company and the Houlton Sewage Company and still
holds those positions.

Mr. Browne gives his support to the Republican party. He is a member of the Benevolent
and Protective Order of Elks, of which he is
Past Exalted Ruler; and also of the Country Club,
of which he is one of the governors. Mr. Browne
is held in high esteem among his associates, and
has a host of personal friends in Houlton and
vicinity.

Joseph A. Browne married, in 1878, Lydia
Burnham, who died in 1883, daughter of John and
Lydia (Perkins) Burnham, and they became the
parents of two children: 1. Beatrice, who married Percy L. Rideout, who now operates the
business of the J. A. Browne Company; and they
have three children: Lydia, Joseph Marion, and
David. 2. Clair L., employed in Boston.

PARKER P. BURLEIGH, Register of the
Probate for Aroostook County, has been a practicing attorney of Houlton for over thirty years.
Born at Oakfield, Maine, he is a son of Albert A.
and Lucinda G. (Collins) Burleigh. The father,
Albert A. Burleigh, was a civil engineer and railroad man, and for many years he held the office of
president of the Bangor & Aroostook Railroad.
Mr. Burleigh's brother, Preston N. Burleigh,
whose biographical history appears elsewhere in
this work, is United States Postmaster at Houlton.

Parker P. Burleigh received his preparatory
education in the public schools of Houlton, later
attending Ricker Classical Institute, from which
he graduated in 1885. He then entered Colby College and graduated from there with the class of
1889. He took up his legal training at Harvard

Law School, and graduated from there with the
class of 1892, when he received his degree as
Bachelor of Laws. The following year, in 1893,
he was admitted to the bar. Immediately thereafter he began the practice of his profession in
Houlton. His efforts met with ever increasing
success and now he is one of the most prominent
attorneys of Houlton.

Despite the many exacting duties which his
profession entails, Mr. Burleigh has found time
for active participation in the affairs of the community. In his political preferences he is a supporter of the Republican party, and is chairman of
the Republican County Committee. He is fraternally affiliated with the Blue Lodge, Free and
Accepted Masons; the Chapter, Royal Arch Masons; the Council, Royal and Select Masters; the
Consistory, Ancient Accepted Scottish Rite; the
Commandery, Knights Templar, and the Temple,
Ancient Arabic Order Nobles of the Mystic
Shrine. He is a member also of the Benevolent
and Protective Order of Elks, the Independent
Order of Odd Fellows, Houlton Country Club,
and the Woodstock Country Club, at Woodstock,
New Brunswick.

Parker P. Burleigh married Bertha Cushing,
who was born in New Brunswick, a daughter of
Allston and Clara L. Cushing. Mr. and Mrs. Burleigh are the parents of three children, twin daughters and a son: 1. Helen, who married Irving E.
Hand, who is engaged in the meat packing business in New York City. 2. Dorothy, who married
Henry Heston, who is engaged in the oil business
in Philadelphia, Pennsylvania. 3. Parker P., Jr.,
who received his education at the University of
Pennsylvania and at Bowdoin College, and who
now assists his father. Mr. Burleigh and his family maintain their residence in Houlton, Maine, in
which community they attend the Episcopal
church.

CHARLES B. MARGESSON has, through
his own efforts, achieved a prominent position in
the business and public life of Caribou, Maine.
Mr. Margesson was born in August, 1861, son of
William H. and Ellen (Patterson) Margesson.
The father was a native of England, the mother of
Scotland, and both came to this country at an early

age. As a boot and shoe manufacturer the father was, for years, prominent in the business life of Bangor, Maine.

Mr. Margesson was educated in the public schools and in the high school of Bangor after which he worked for several years in the Mill Furnishing Store. He then obtained clerical work with a railroad in Bangor and then in Boston, later going with the same road in St. Paul, Minnesota. In 1890 he moved to Caribou and opened books for the Aroostook Trust Company at the time of its establishment in that city. After this company was well established he left them to go with the Caribou National Bank as cashier. Mr. Margesson is affiliated with the Free and Accepted Masons, in Chapter and Council, Commandery of Knights Templar, and Ancient Arabic Order Nobles of the Mystic Shrine. He is a member of the Matooko Club and the Chamber of Commerce of Caribou, and is an Episcopalian.

Charles B. Margesson married (first) Helen R. Boyd, of Bangor, Maine, who died; (second) Leola Chaison, of Whitefield, Maine, who also died leaving a son, John L., twenty-four years old, who is employed by the United Fruit Company and is located at Puerto Castillo. He received his education in the public and high schools of Caribou and at Milton Academy, at Milton, Massachusetts. Later he attended Bowdoin College.

HOWARD OTIS SPENCER, owner of one of the leading jewelry firms of Caribou, has always shown himself ready to promote any plan which was for the best good of his village. He has a wide understanding of the elements of progressive business and of what constitutes substantial success. Son of George and Lydia (Dennis) Spencer, he was born in Carroll, Penobscot County, Maine, December 8, 1863. His father, who early in life was a farmer and lumberman, was for many years in the mercantile business where he showed himself an able business man.

Educated in the common schools, Mr. Spencer began as a boy to work, and at the age of twenty-three years went to Lancaster, and Berlin, New Hampshire, working at various lines of trade but always with the dream of having his own business in mind. He finally decided on the jewelry business and to that end took a job as apprentice at four dollars a week in spite of the adverse advice of some of his friends. He had, however, the support of the older and wiser men for his plans and, after serving his apprenticeship, found himself able to come to Caribou and buy the business of H. E. Jones. This business he enlarged and secured for himself a good following. Today his firm carries a full line of jewelry, china, cut-glass and crockery. There are also a gift shop and lamp department.

Mr. Spencer is, politically, of the Republican party and is a member of the Free and Accepted Masons in the Lodge, Chapter, Council, the Commandery of Knights Templar, and Anah Temple, Ancient Arabic Order Nobles of the Mystic Shrine, at Bangor. He is a member of the Universalist church.

Howard O. Spencer married Minnie A. Marshall, daughter of Anthony P. and Emma A. (Osgood) Marshall, of Lancaster, New Hampshire.

FREDERICK W. MITCHELL, M. D.—A well-known eye, ear, nose and throat specialist, and one of the foremost physicians of Houlton, Dr. Frederick W. Mitchell was born on September 14, 1873, at New Glasgow, Nova Scotia, a son of James and Jane (Grant) Mitchell, both of whom were natives of Nova Scotia. James Mitchell was a merchant of New Glasgow.

Frederick W. Mitchell received his preliminary education in the public schools of the community in which he was born, and came to the United States to enter the University of Maryland, from which he graduated with the class of 1898, with the degree of Doctor of Medicine. He took a postgraduate course at Harvard University and later studied at the New York Eye and Ear Infirmary. Following this he began his practice at Island Falls, Maine, where he remained for eight years. In 1907 he removed to Houlton, where he has been eminently successful as a specialist on eye, ear, nose and throat affections. Dr. Mitchell has not confined his energies to his private practice alone but has been very active in a number of civic activities. He is a Fellow of the American College of Surgeons; he served as chairman of the Medical Advisory Board of the South Aroostook District;

he is past president of the Maine Eye and Ear Association, and is now (1928) president of the Aroostook Hospital Corporation.

Despite the manifold duties of his profession, Dr. Mitchell has found time in which to take an interest in civic affairs. Politically, he is a supporter of the Republican party, having served as chairman of the Republican Town Committee and he is serving as a member of the State Legislature, to which he was elected in 1927. He is affiliated with the Masonic Order, including the Commandery, Knights Templar, and the Temple, Ancient Arabic Order Nobles of the Mystic Shrine. He is a member of the Benevolent and Protective Order of Elks, and of the Independent Order of Odd Fellows.

Dr. Frederick W. Mitchell married Florence Eaton, who was born in Portland, Maine, and they have two daughters: 1. Dorothy, who married the Reverend Clifford Grant. 2. Helen, a graduate of Colby College. Dr. Mitchell and his family attend the Congregational church, of which he is auditor.

Municipal Court Recorder and gained a most valuable experience in close contact with the many characters who came before him. He resigned this place to become a member of the State Legislature in 1913, and in this body, where he sat with the Democratic members, he learned much that has subsequently been of great value to him and has enabled him to contribute substantially to the advancement of the science and the ethics of his profession. He is a member of an old family, well established in this section, and noted for its constructive works in all fields of endeavor. He and his family are members of the Unitarian church, and he belongs to the Meduxnekeag Club and the Houlton Rotary Club. His parents, Albert and Cordelia (Putnam) Putnam, engaged for years in farming, and they are now retired, living at Houlton.

Mr. Putnam married Maria Louise Hacker, of Fort Fairfield, Maine, daughter of Jerry and Elizabeth E. (Trafton) Hacker, and their union has been blessed with four children: Elizabeth, Aaron Hacker, Maria Louise and John Libby.

AARON ALBERT PUTNAM, of Houlton, brings to the law an unusual equipment, having served for a year and a half as recorder of the Municipal Court and for one term as a member of the Legislature of the State of Maine. He is an able lawyer, now (1928) in private practice, and his interest in civic affairs has won him an enviable place in community life.

Mr. Putnam was born at Houlton, July 23, 1886, son of Albert Temple and Cordelia Putnam. He began his education in the grammar and high schools of Houlton, and graduated from Bowdoin College at Brunswick in the class of 1908, with the degree of Bachelor of Arts. While a student at Bowdoin he became a member of the Delta Kappa Epsilon Fraternity, and has since been a prominent member of the alumni association of that organization. Upon arriving at the decision to follow the legal profession, he matriculated at the University of Maine Law School, from which institution he was graduated in the class of 1912, with the degree of Bachelor of Laws. Thereupon he opened an office at Houlton and has practiced here ever since. In 1911 and 1913 he served as

RAY N. L. BROWN—It is very largely through the mercantile enterprise and business influence of men of the type of Ray N. L. Brown that Caribou has its well-recognized position among the progressive communities of the State, Mr. Brown throughout his career having allied himself with its fundamental business activities, and, indeed, with whatsoever movements and interests have related to Caribou's prosperity. He is the present head of the extensive department store that bears his name, and also a store at Fort Fairfield, and has a host of friends and patrons throughout this region.

Ray N. L. Brown was born March 21, 1877, at Hodgdon, a son of Noah Brown, a farmer, and Hessie (Crory) Brown, both parents natives of the State. The grade schools and the Caribou High School were the source of Mr. Brown's public school training, and after graduating he taught school for two terms. With the arrival of the business opportunity, Mr. Brown, in company with A. V. Goud, established the firm of A. V. Goud and Company, in 1904, a general department store concern that gradually developed into its present leadership and high rating. The firm name was thus continued for seven years, when the entire business was purchased by Mr. Brown, who has continued the establishment to the present as Ray N. L. Brown & Company, with the employment of five clerks. Mr. Brown also operates a store at Fort Fairfield along the same up-to-date lines as the Caribou store, under the name of G. E. Bartlett & Company.

Affiliated with the Republican party, Mr. Brown with his vote and influence supports the principles of that party, though he has never been a candidate for public office. Fraternally, he is a member of the Free and Accepted Masons; Royal Arcanum; Modern Woodmen of America; and the Chamber of Commerce, the Rotary and Matoka clubs.

Ray N. L. Brown married, February 28, 1905, Mary Goud, daughter of A. V. Goud, a prominent merchant and at the time a partner of Mr. Brown, and of Mary (Teague) Goud. Their children: Cecil J., Natalie G., and Adelaide and Alletta, twins. The family are attendants of the Universalist church.

ARCHIBALD B. HAVEY—A landmark in this section of the State for whatsoever appertains to a high-class pharmacy, the business in the ownership and under the direction of Archibald B. Havey at Caribou is representative of the best things that the druggists of both the past and the present have combined for the medical profession and the general public. Mr. Havey, sole owner of the establishment, is accounted one of the most popular men in his profession, as well as in the various activities of Caribou, business or social, with which he is concerned.

Archibald B. Havey was born May 8, 1884, in Sullivan, a son of Barney Havey, for many years a granite cutter at Sullivan, and Sarah (Hooper) Havey, both parents natives of this State. Mr. Havey went to school in Sullivan, where he was graduated from high school, and he also graduated at Hebron College. In 1907 he removed to Caribou to engage in the management of his brother, F. A. Havey's, drugstore here; his brother later going to Eastport to establish himself in a pharmacy there under the firm name Havey and Wil-

Maine—2—5

son. Archibald B. Havey, who had meantime made a special study of the business and was admitted as a registered pharmacist in 1916, bought a half interest in the store at Caribou in 1917, and but a short time afterwards purchased the entire establishment. In his political views a Democrat, Mr. Havey with his vote and influence supports the principles of that party. Fraternally, he is affiliated with the Free and Accepted Masons, in all the bodies of the York and Scottish Rite, as well as the Ancient Arabic Order Nobles of the Mystic Shrine; and he is also a member of the Caribou Rotary Club and the Chamber of Commerce.

Archibald B. Havey married, November 26, 1906, Ethel Gary, also a native of Caribou, daughter of Joseph W. and Inez Gary; and they have one son, Joseph Gary, a student in the Caribou High School. The family are communicants of the Protestant Episcopal church.

GEORGE H. HOWE—Caribou owes considerable of its repute as an enterprising and present-day township to the excellence of its local postoffice system and the intelligent manner in which the duties of that office are directed by George H. Howe, the postmaster. Mr. Howe, who has always been engaged in business here and is intimate in a very practical way with the progress of the general business and social life of this community, is an official of proven capabilities. George H. Howe was born August 23, 1858, in Boston, Massachusetts, a son of George H. Howe, who died when his son, the postmaster, was four years old, and Myra (Morton) Howe, who later married Alva Holmes. George H. Howe, Sr., who brought his family here from Medford, Massachusetts, where they continued to reside, is recorded as having been the first man to engage in the potato starch business in Aroostook County.

Mr. Howe received his early education in the grammar and high schools at Medford, Massachusetts, and he was afterwards graduated at Bryant and Stratton's Business College, in Boston. He removed to Caribou when he was about twenty years old, where he obtained a position as a clerk in a general store, and afterwards engaged in the lumber and the starch businesses.

In 1922, Mr. Howe received from President Harding his appointment to the postmastership of Caribou, and he has continued in that office to the present. This office is of the second class, with its parcels post delivery, two city carriers and six rural routes, as well as four office clerks. Postmaster Howe's assistant is Napoleon Levasseur. The Republican party claims Mr. Howe's political allegiance, and with his vote and influence he supports its principles. Fraternally he is affiliated with the Free and Accepted Masons.

George H. Howe married, February 10, 1887, Isabel A. Cary, of Fort Fairfield, daughter of A. C. and Anna (Priestly) Cary. They have one son, George H. Howe, Jr., graduate of the Caribou public schools and the University of Maine, and is now department manager for the firm of Swift & Company, Chicago, Illinois; he married Della Drake, who taught in the Caribou public schools. The family attend the Universalist church.

FREDERICK W. MANN, M. D.—Houlton and this section of the State has no better known and more highly respected physician than Dr. Frederick W. Mann, rightly regarded as one of the veterans in his profession here, a successful guardian of the interests of public health throughout his career, honored associate of many medical fraternities, and welcome friend in the families and neighborhoods of township and county.

Dr. Frederick W. Mann was born May 18, 1868, in Charlotte County, New Brunswick, son of Thomas A. Mann, a carpenter and farmer, and of Sarah A. (Gilmore) Mann, both parents natives of New Brunswick. Dr. Mann attended the public schools of New Brunswick and was graduated from Horton Academy. He studied at the College of Physicians and Surgeons (now University of Maryland), and at the College of Physicians and Surgeons, Baltimore, Maryland, receiving his degree of Doctor of Medicine in 1892. He later entered Bishop's College, Montreal, Canada, where he was graduated Medical Doctor *cum laude*, in 1900. In 1919-20 he spent ten months in post-graduate work at Boston University. He went to Monticello, Maine, where he practiced for eight years, afterwards removing to Houlton, where he is one of the leading physicians. His professional affiliations include the American Medical Association, Maine Medical Association, of which he served as president in 1924-25, and Aroostook County Medical Association. He is also a member of the Free and Accepted Masons, Independent Order of Odd Fellows, and Benevolent and Protective Order of Elks. He is an independent Republican in his political views.

Dr. Frederick W. Mann married Ida H. Baird, who was born in Woodstock, New Brunswick, a daughter of Henry R. and Charlotte (Drake) Baird, and they have one daughter, Dorothy Baird, a student at Boston University, and graduate of Mount Alison University, New Brunswick, with the degree of Bachelor of Arts. The family attend the Congregational church.

MURDOCH B. McKAY—Starting in the general insurance offices of the George S. Gentle Company in Houlton, Maine, in 1910, Murdoch B. McKay succeeded to the ownership of the business on the retirement of Mr. Gentle, over ten years, and has since taken in as a partner Berlin H. Brown. The firm represents the most important American fire insurance companies in Houlton and surrounding territory.

Born in Richmond, New Brunswick, Canada, March 15, 1883, Murdoch B. McKay received his education in the public schools of Houlton, Maine, and while still in school was made a clerk in the Houlton postoffice. Later he was made assistant postmaster and served in that capacity for six years. He then resigned to enter the insurance business with Mr. Gentle. A Republican in politics, Mr. McKay is one of the local leaders of his party and a trustee of the Houlton Savings Bank. He is a member of the Free and Accepted Masons, a Knight Templar, and a Shriner. He is also a member of the Benevolent and Protective Order of Elks, of the Rotary Club, the Chamber of Commerce, the Business Men's Association, and of the Meduxnekeag Club. He and his family attend the Congregational church.

Mr. McKay married Bertha E. Hemphill, of Presque Isle, Maine, and they have a son, Joseph H. McKay.

WALTER P. MANSUR—Among the constructive business men of Maine, Walter P. Mansur, real estate operator of Houlton, is easily in the foremost ranks, for he has always been ready to lend a hand in any forward movement relating to the progress of his home town.

Born at Houlton, in March, 1876, son of Walter and Carrie (McAllister) Mansur, he is of sturdy Maine stock on both sides. His father, a native of Houlton, was one of the organizers of the First National Bank of Houlton, and its president for many years. He was also an organizer of the Houlton Water, Sewage & Light Company. His mother was born in Milltown, Maine.

After the customary training in the public schools of Houlton, Walter P. Mansur attended Eastman College, and on completing his education, became identified with the management of the Houlton Water, Sewage & Light Company, where he continued for many years. In politics Mr. Mansur has always been independent. His family are Unitarians. He is a member of the Free and Accepted Masons, the Chapter, Commandery and Shrine, and of the Benevolent and Protective Order of Elks.

Mr. Mansur married (first) Minnie Yerxa, and after her death (second) Rose Dobbins. Two children were born of the first marriage: 1. Marjorie, student in a school for trained nurses at Pawtucket, Rhode Island. 2. Jean, who lives at home.

GEORGE Q. NICKERSON, D. D. S.—A lifelong record of service in his profession to the one community wherein he has been associated in dental practice, is that of Dr. George Q. Nickerson, who, from the beginning of his career, has resided in Houlton and had his offices there, with a steadily increasing practice, marked with all the elements of success. Dean among the dental practitioners in this section, Dr. George Q. Nickerson was born May 20, 1860, at New Limerick, son of Charles Nickerson, a farmer, and Martha Nickerson.

After attending the public schools at New Limerick, Dr. Nickerson continued his elementary education in Houlton, and preparing for his profession at the Philadelphia (Pennsylvania) Dental College, he was graduated there with the degree

Doctor of Dental Surgery. He came direct to Houlton, where he established his present office, and here has continued, known and highly regarded as a dentist of pronounced capabilities and leadership. He is a Republican in his political views and his fraternal affiliations are with the Benevolent and Protective Order of Elks.

Dr. George Q. Nickerson married Maude Farnum, a native of Springfield, Massachusetts. They attend the Unitarian church.

THOMAS V. HOLDAWAY, proprietor of the Houlton Meat Supply and a prominent business man of Houlton, was born in 1881, at Croydon, England, a son of William Henry and Emily Holdaway, neither of whom ever journeyed to the United States.

Thomas V. Holdaway received his education in England and at the age of twenty-four he voyaged alone to this country. His first position in the year of his arrival, 1905, was with Swift & Company, meat packers. The following year he resigned from this position to become associated with C. W. Starkey in the meat business. At the end of three years Mr. Holdaway established his own meat business on Main Street, Houlton. In this enterprise he met with marked success and later was able to buy the property on Main Street where his principal store is now located. As his business increased, he found it necessary to establish another store on Kendall Avenue known as "The Annex," and the extension of his business requires the services of six clerks.

Despite the restrictions of his business duties, Mr. Holdaway has found time to participate in other activities. Politically, he is a supporter of the Republican party, and fraternally, he is affiliated with the Masonic Order, including the Shrine; being also a member of the Benevolent and Protective Order of Elks; the Houlton Progressive Club, and the Business Men's Association, of which latter he has served as president. Mr. Holdaway is particularly interested in racing and he is the owner of several race horses, one of which is the well known "Albert King."

Thomas V. Holdaway married Blanche Clayton, who was born in Fredericton, New Brunswick. Mr. and Mrs. Holdaway attend the Episcopal church.

BERNARD ARCHIBALD, prominent attorney of Houlton, who has often served the people of his community in other than a private capacity, was born on October 7, 1881, at Conticello, in this State. He is a son of the late James and Ellen A. (Nelson) Archibald, both natives of Maine. James Archibald, the father, who was also an attorney, practiced with his son until his death, December 27, 1927.

Bernard Archibald received his early education in the public schools of Houlton and attended Ricker Classical Institute, graduating in 1900. He then studied at Bowdoin College, graduating with the class of 1904, after which he pursued his legal training at the Law College of the University of Maine, graduating from there with the class of 1907. He was formally admitted to the bar of Maine in that same year, since which time he has carried on an increasingly successful practice at Houlton. He is now serving as general counsel for the Houlton Trust Company and for the Aroostook Valley Railroad.

In his political views, Mr. Archibald is a staunch supporter of the Republican party, and as such filled the office of county attorney for a period of five consecutive years; he was elected a Representative to the Eighty-first Legislature of Maine; he is now counsel for the town of Houlton; and for some years he was chairman of the Houlton School Board. Mr. Archibald is affiliated with Monument Lodge, Free and Accepted Masons; Aroostook Chapter, Royal Arch Masons; the Council, Royal and Select Masters; the Commandery, Knights Templar, and the Temple, Ancient Arabic Order Nobles of the Mystic Shrine. He is a member of the Rotary Club and has just been elected as district governor of the thirty-eighth district of Rotary International, comprising Maine and parts of New Hampshire and Massachusetts. He is also a member of the Meduxnekeag Club.

Bernard Archibald married Emma Ruth Putnam, of Houlton, and they are the parents of a son and two daughters: James Putnam, Ruth, and Mary Cordelia. Mr. Archibald and his family maintain their residence in Houlton and attend the Unitarian church.

SAMUEL A. BENNETT—Highly regarded by his fellow merchants of Houlton, who elected him president of the Business Men's Association for 1927 upon his record of service as vice-president of that organization during the previous year, Samuel A. Bennett is popular with all classes of the people. He is proprietor of Bennett's Woman's Wear Shop, a favorite establishment with the ladies, and he also is a member of the firm of Green & Bennett, farmers, noted for their production of potatoes, and dealers in fertilizers.

Born at Charlestown, Massachusetts, November 6, 1891, son of Robert and Margaret (Nicholson) Bennett, he comes of well known New England families on both sides. The elder Bennett died some years ago, but his mother lives in Boston. Samuel A. Bennett was educated in the public schools of Medford, Massachusetts, where his parents resided for a time, and then took a course in a business college at Winter Hill, Massachusetts, after which he obtained employment as a bookkeeper, and continued to do clerical work of various kinds for several years. G. R. Richards & Company, of Houlton, made him a liberal offer to enter their service, which he accepted, and having been with this concern for thirteen years, he was admitted to partnership. Eight years later he sold his interest in the firm and in March, 1925, went into business for himself, opening the women's wear establishment he still conducts.

Mr. Bennett is a Republican, but is not active politically. His only fraternal affiliation is with the Benevolent and Protective Order of Elks. He is a Unitarian, one of the trustees of the Unitarian church, and president of the Laymen's League.

Mr. Bennett married Lelia Bubar, daughter of Samuel and Alma Bubar, and they have one son, Robert.

CLAUDE C. CLARK, chief of the Houlton Fire Department and also owner and proprietor of a large wagon manufacturing and automobile shop, was born at Lincoln, Maine, in 1877, son of Joseph A. and Susan M. (Stultz) Clark, his parents having been farmers. His father was a native of New Brunswick and his mother of Nova Scotia, Canada.

Claude C. Clark came to Aroostook County when young and received the benefit of only a limited schooling, at the conclusion of which he cheerfully took charge of the farm as assistant to his father and thus worked until he was twenty-five years of age. He now owns and operates this farm. Determined to better his condition, he entered the shop he owns now, starting at the bottom and carefully learning his trade. He started out with S. W. Taber, and when that official died he bought out the heirs of the business, including Clarence H. Pierce.

Mr. Clark is prominent in secret order circles, being a Master Mason, member of the Orange Lodge at Houlton; and connected with the Modern Woodmen of America and the Benevolent and Protective Order of Elks. He has always taken a great deal of interest in civic affairs and in many ways proved himself a good citizen in any movement for the good of the community.

Mr. Clark married Ella M. Niles, native of Houlton and daughter of Judson and Mary (Peters) Niles, and their union has been blessed with two children: 1. Frank C., linotype operator at Salem, Massachusetts. 2. Philip E., a mechanic in the employment of his father's firm. Mr. Clark and his family are members of the Congregational church.

T. S. DICKISON, M. D.—One of the foremost physicians of Houlton, Dr. T. S. Dickison has the distinction of having practiced in that community for more than thirty years. He was born in 1868, in Carden County, New Brunswick, a son of Adam and Jennette (Gibson) Dickison, both of whom are now deceased. Adam Dickison, the father, was a farmer and spent his life in New Brunswick.

Dr. T. S. Dickison received his preliminary education in the grammar and high schools at Woodstock, New Brunswick. He later attended the University of New Brunswick. Upon the completion of these courses of study, he journeyed to New York, where he entered the Bellevue Hospital Medical School, and graduated from there in 1893, receiving his degree of Doctor of Medicine. He located at Houlton, Maine, where he began the practice of his profession. Dr. Dickison has been practicing in Houlton since 1893, has built up a large and aristocratic clientele, and has won the affection and respect of his community.

Despite the many arduous duties of his practice, Dr. Dickison has found time to take an interest in civic affairs. A supporter of the Republican party, he served as health officer of Houlton for twelve years. He is also a member of the Chamber of Commerce. Among the professional societies in which he holds membership are the American Medical Association, the Maine Medical Society and the County Medical Society. He is affiliated with the Benevolent and Protective Order of Elks and the Independent Order of Odd Fellows.

Dr. Dickison married Almatia Nelson, who was born in Bridgewater, Maine, and they have two children: 1. Horace E., who attended the University of Maine, and is now a farmer; married Clara Kennedy and is the father of Jean and Joice. 2. Jean, who married Robert Miller and is the mother of one son, Robert, and one daughter, Marion. Doctor Dickison and his family attend the Congregational church.

JOSEPH A. DONOVAN, M. D.—It is no play on words to say that the physician's services are vital to the smaller cities of the country, for the general practitioner is often the personal friend and adviser of his patients and their families. Typical of his profession is Dr. Joseph A. Donovan, of Houlton, health officer of the town, physician to the schools for ten years, and with a practice which brings him contact with wealthy and indigent alike.

Born in Houlton, November 14, 1882, son of William and Ann (Smith) Donovan, his boyhood was spent on his father's farm, and he was educated in the public schools. His father is still living there (1928), although the mother is dead. After taking the classical course at Bates College, where he was graduated in 1908, he entered the Medical School of Harvard University, and received his degree of Medical Doctor in 1912. He then spent a year in the Boston City Hospital as an interne, and next joined the house staff of the Carney Hospital, in Boston, where he remained sixteen months.

With this experience he returned to Houlton in 1913, and has been in active practice there ever since, being one of the surgeons for the Madigan Memorial Hospital. He is a member of the American Medical Association, of the County Medical Association, and of the Medical Association of the State of Maine. A communicant of the Roman Catholic church, his only fraternal affiliation is with the Benevolent and Protective Order of Elks. In politics he has always been an independent.

Dr. Donovan married Mary Alice O'Hare, of Boston, Massachusetts. Their children are: Alice Ann, Frances Marie, Thomas Joseph, and James Frederick Donovan.

DONALD HARTLEY DUNN, manager of the Square Deal Furniture & Undertaking Store at Houlton, and coroner of Aroostook County, both of which positions he entered as a heritage from his father, is a constructive and popular citizen whose achievements have won him the high regard of his neighbors and contemporaries.

Donald Hartley Dunn was born at Houlton, son of Frank Dunn, who was a native of New Brunswick, Canada. His father received his education in the common schools of Jensag and also attended business college, where he further equipped himself for his subsequent career. He became an expert accountant, was head bookkeeper for the John Watson Company at Houlton for many years, and was known as one of the best financiers in the city. With Dr. P. M. Ward and A. E. Astle, he organized the Dunn Furniture Company, known as the "Square Deal Store," which he successfully managed up to the time of his death. He was a member of the Republican party, in whose circles his counsels were considered of great value. He was popular as a member of the Independent Order of Odd Fellows, of which he was Past Noble Grand; the Free and Accepted Masons; and the Benevolent and Protective Order of Elks, in all of which organizations he held office. He was also a member of the Meduxnekeag Club, the Maine Undertakers' Association, and for one term served as its president. He married Jerusha Sharpe, who was born at Norton, New Brunswick, Canada, and their union was blessed with two sons: 1. Donald Hartley, of whom further. 2. Raben Dunn, a student at the University of Pennsylvania, Philadelphia.

Donald Hartley Dunn received his education at the Houlton High School and followed this with a course in the Renouard Training School at New York City, after which he became associated with his father in the store and is now manager of the business. He is a member of the Free and Accepted Masons, Royal Arch Masons, and the Commandery, Knights Templar; and is Esteemed Loyal Knight of the Benevolent and Protective Order of Elks. He is a leading member of the Houlton Rotary Club, in which his civic activities center, and in a social way belongs to the Houlton Country Club.

Mr. Dunn married Ella Barrett, and he and his wife are devoted members of the Protestant Episcopal church.

LEWIS S. BEAN—For many years Lewis S. Bean has been prominent in the life of Aroostook County, Maine. He is Buick dealer in this county for the territory lying north of Monticello, and he maintains a repair shop and service station at Presque Isle, and another at Caribou, employing altogether about twenty-five people. In association with Harry D. Allen, he also owns and operates a farm on the Houlton Road, specializing in dairying and the raising of seed potatoes. Mr. Bean is a man of great energy and ability, active in social and civic affairs, and highly esteemed as a public-spirited citizen. His father, Osias B. Bean, was a farmer and engaged in this work until his death. His mother, who before her marriage was Marcella S. Duff, is also deceased.

Lewis S. Bean was born on October 24, 1874, at Presque Isle, Maine. He attended the local public schools, and when he completed his education, was employed in various capacities for a number of years. Finally, in 1909, he became Buick agent for the northern part of Aroostook County, establishing service stations and repair shops at both Presque Isle and Caribou. Since that time he has built up his business into one of the most prosperous of its kind in the State. He is part owner of a very successful dairy farm, on which he also raises seed potatoes. Politically, Mr. Bean is a member of the Republican party, and he served for a number of years as tax collector. Under appointment of Governor Brewer, he has served as a member of the Maine Development Commission, and is a member of the local Merchants' Association. He is prominent in club life, being a member of the Rotary, the Mooseleuk at Presque Isle, and the Matoka at Caribou. He and his family attend the Congregational church. Mr. Bean has been twice married. He married (first) Annie Burpee, who died in 1915. By this union one child was born, which died in infancy. He married (second) Edith Topham, who was born at Perth, Province of New Brunswick, Canada. They are the adopted parents of one child, Hope, who attended the Presque Isle High School, Lasell Seminary at Auburndale, is a (1928) graduate of the Wheelock Kindergarten School, at Brookline, Massachusetts, and is to teach at Wainfleet, a private school at Portland, Maine.

SAMUEL LANE, who was born on December 8, 1850, at East Sangerville, Maine, and who died on December 19, 1923, at Houlton, Maine, for over forty years was one of the most prominent business men of Houlton. He was a man of great talent and of wide and varied experience, and at the time of his death was senior partner in the firm of Lane and Pearce, dealers in dry and fancy goods. Mr. Lane was active in all phases of Houlton life, kind and generous, and interested in the welfare of his community and its members. He was a member and a liberal supporter of the Unitarian church. His father, Benjamin Lane, was at various times a farmer and a merchant, and he served for many years as postmaster at East Sangerville. His mother was Hannah Adams before her marriage.

Samuel Lane attended the public schools of East Sangerville and later he was graduated from Foxcroft Academy. He enrolled as a member of the second class of the University of Maine, but ill health forced his withdrawal before the completion of his course. Some time afterwards he became a teacher in the schools of Garland and Houlton, and he acted for a time as principal of the high school at Linneus, Maine. For several years he was employed as a clerk by A. J. Chase & Company at Sebec Station, Maine, and for one year he was in the insurance business at Houlton, associated with J. H. Bradford. At the end of that time he went back to Sebec Station, and after only a year, returned again to Houlton, where he remained until his death. He bought out the boot

and shoe business of E. C. Blake, which he conducted himself for several years, and then took as a partner Mr. Varney Pearce. Some time later they added the dry goods stock, and finally disposed of the shoe store altogether, continuing under the firm name of Lane and Pearce, dealers in dry and fancy goods, which became so well known in Houlton.

By political inclination, Mr. Lane was a member of the Democratic party. He served as selectman for the town of Houlton, and was also a candidate for Senator. He was affiliated fraternally with the Independent Order of Odd Fellows, and was a member of the Meduxnekeag Club. He and his wife attended the local Unitarian Church.

In 1880, Mr. Lane married Mary Alice Bradford, who was born in Houlton, the daughter of John H. and Mary Frances Bradford. Mr. Bradford conducted an insurance business at Houlton, and he was one of the organizers and for many years the treasurer of the Houlton Savings Bank. There were three daughters in his family: 1. Eudora Frances. 2. Mary Alice, who married Samuel Lane. 3. Hattie May.

CLARENCE E. HALL—As manager of the general store in Crouseville, Maine, Clarence E. Hall is one of the outstanding business men of his community. He is thoroughly conversant with the work that is to be performed by this type of store, having been engaged in the same line of business in different towns; while his long residence in Maine has given him a complete knowledge of the local people and of conditions in the industrial make-up of the State. He is keenly interested in the civic and social affairs of the town and of the surrounding community, and is willing at all times to lend his support to whatever measures he believes will bring about some betterment.

Mr. Hall was born in Portland, Maine, on October 2, 1895, a son of Frank and Abbie (Junkins) Hall, both of whom are natives of Maine and who reside in Portland. The father, Frank Hall, is a woodworker by occupation. As a boy, Clarence E. Hall attended the public schools of Portland, his native city, and subsequently took a four-years' course in the International Correspondence School.

His first work was as a clerk in a wholesale dry goods house, and when he completed this work he went on the road as a dry goods salesman for three years. In 1918 he enlisted in Houlton in the Machine Gun Battalion as a private, and spent one year overseas. When he was discharged from the military forces of the United States, he returned to New England. With W. R. Hale, he bought a general store in Jefferson, New Hampshire, where he remained for three years. Next he became engaged in the wholesale grocery business with Milliken-Tomlinson Company, of Presque Isle; and after four years with this company, he assumed the management of the general store which he conducts in Crouseville.

Clarence E. Hall married Minnie Munson, a native of Presque Isle, a daughter of George and Annie (Keirstead) Munson, who operate a grocery store in Presque Isle. Clarence E. and Minnie (Munson) Hall are the parents of one child, a son, Donald Keith.

RALPH W. HARDY—As one born to his profession, and one who has progressed in the promotion of farming, Ralph W. Hardy, of Presque Isle, Maine, is prominent among the successful farmers of this district in continuous cultivation of one of the best established farms around here. The farm which Mr. Hardy operates was owned for years by his late father, Weston Hardy, who purchased it when he was a young man of thirty-five years of age. Mr. Hardy continued to operate this farm until his son relieved him of the responsibility at the time of his retirement.

Ralph W. Hardy was born on the farm he now runs, January 12, 1888, son of Weston and Lulla (Turney) Hardy, the former died in April, 1923, and the latter lives in Presque Isle. He had a good public school education in the schools of Presque Isle, including one year in the high school of this place. After that, he went to Bangor, Maine, where he attended a business college and then went to work on the farm with his father. When he had become proficient in the management of the farm, his father retired from activity in agriculture and left his son to take care of his interests. When Weston Hardy died, the farm was left in his estate and so remains, but Ralph

Hardy continues to manage it and to dispose of the products. The farm comprises about two hundred acres which are planted with diversified crops, but a great part of the cultivation is in growing potatoes, which are sold mostly to local dealers. Mr. Hardy's father and grandfather were well known as staunch members of the Republican party and strict adherents to its principles, but Ralph W. Hardy is in the ranks of the independent Republicans and, while active and interested in political affairs, he has never been persuaded to hold office. He is a member of the Order of Free and Accepted Masons, from the Blue Lodge to the Shrine; the Independent Order of Odd Fellows and the Mooseleuk Club.

Ralph W. Hardy married Sarah Brennan, a native of Presque Isle, daughter of Harvey and Ella (Fraser) Brennan. They have four children: Weston R., Alice, Ralph, Jr., and Dana. Mr. Hardy and family attend the Congregational church.

HOWARD L. GOOD—One of the most prominent and public-spirited men in his community is Howard L. Good of Monticello, Maine, a well-known farmer and potato dealer. He is the son of Archibald and Hannah (Burgoyne) Good, both natives of New Brunswick but who came in early life to Fort Fairfield, Maine, where Archibald Good was a farmer and hotel keeper for years and where he brought up a family of five children. 1. William. 2. Mary, widow of George H. Everett. 3. Howard L., of whom further. 4. Walter T. 5. Eliza, wife of Charles Gallagher.

Howard L. Good was born in the Province of New Brunswick, Canada, November 13, 1860. When quite young, he came with his parents to the State of Maine, where he continued to reside and to carry on the business of farming and dealing in potatoes. He has at this time practically retired from the farming business. He began his farming career when a lad of fifteen years in association with his father, but at the age of twenty-three, he started out for himself and continued to progress in that line and in dealing in potatoes until his business has grown to considerable proportions and today he is one of the most prosperous men in the community. In politics, he is a

Republican and has given much time to filling public offices in the town where he has been selectman and on the school board. He is a member of the Benevolent and Protective Order of Elks. He and his wife are members of the Methodist church.

Howard L. Good married Climena A. Jewell, daughter of Josiah B. and Emeline (Moore) Jewell of Monticello. They have no children.

Fort Fairfield, the daughter of John and Mira (Woodward) Shaw. They are the parents of the following children: 1. Herbert, who went through the local high school and who is now employed with the Bangor and Aroostook Railroad. 2. Earl, who is a graduate of Ricker Classical Institute. 3. Dorothy, who is attending the local public schools. The Curtis family's religious affiliation is with the Baptist church.

JOEL H. CURTIS—Engaged for the greater part of his life in the railroad business, Joel H. Curtis, of Houlton, is now superintendent of the northern division of the Bangor and Aroostook Railroad, with his headquarters at Houlton. A native of Maine, he has been, with the exception of two years of his life, a railroad man, and his interests have almost always been centered in this State.

The son of Chester and Carrie (Crosby) Curtis, the father a native of Maine and the mother of New Brunswick, Joel H. Curtis was born in North Newport, Maine, June 20, 1880, and was educated at the Corinna High School and at the Corinna Academy, from the latter of which he was graduated in 1897. Then, after two years in the corn shop of the Northern Maine Packing Company, the only years of his life in which he was not a railroad man, he started his railroad career as station baggage master at Greenville, Maine. While there he learned telegraphy in his spare time and was subsequently made telegraph operator at Sherman. Later he worked in several different places as an operator, and in 1905 was employed in the train dispatcher's office in Bangor. After having remained for six months in this work, he was made train dispatcher, in which capacity he served until 1911, when he became car distributor. In 1912 he was made superintendent of car service in Bangor; in 1917 he went with the United States Government car service in Washington, D. C.; in 1919 he came to Houlton, Maine, as train master; and in 1923 was made division superintendent. Politically he is affiliated with the Republican party. He is a member of the Free and Accepted Masons, in which order he holds the thirty-second degree and is a Shriner.

Mr. Curtis married Iva Shaw, who was born in

DANIEL WINFIELD HOEGG—During an editorial career of less than twenty years, Daniel Winfield Hoegg, of Portland, has held every post in the editorial department and has contributed a full share to the progress that has been made by the press of the city. He has always been actively interested in all affairs that attracted the progressive element of the community and has shown his appreciation of the duties that go with good citizenship by lending his aid to all causes calculated to benefit the entire body politic. He has refused public office, but has acted in advisory capacities in numerous civic enterprises, and was very active in patriotic work for the country during the World War.

He was born in New Mills, New Brunswick, Canada, August 26, 1876, a son of Daniel Warren and Mary Ann Hoegg, his father being a native of Cambridge and his mother of Leominster, Massachusetts. The elder Hoegg was associated with Nathan Winslow in the discovery and application of meat and vegetable canning and operated in that business for many years, having been excused from service in the Civil War by the United States Government in order that he might devote his time to packing food for the army. At that time he operated the world's largest canning factory at Westbrook, Maine, now Portland, and later became the pioneer canned goods packer of Canada. He and his wife spent half the year in New Brunswick, where their son was born. Daniel W. Hoegg was educated in the Portland public schools and was graduated from Westbrook Seminary, Portland, in 1898. In the following January he became associated with the "Evening Express" as suburban reporter and continued with that newspaper until August 1, 1925, when its owner, Colonel Fred N. Dow, sold it to Guy P.

Gannett. During his term with the paper he held every position in the reportorial and editorial departments up to and including the post of assistant managing editor, and became managing editor under Mr. Gannett, holding that position until September 12, 1927, when he resigned to become managing editor of the Portland "Evening News." In politics he is an independent Republican. During the World War he was unable to enlist in either the army or the navy, but devoted the major portion of his time to war work. He was State publicity chairman of several of the great campaigns, as well as local chairman of many. He is a charter member and secretary and former vice-president of the Portland Rotary Club; member of the Economic Club; of the Maine Historical Society; Naples Golf and Country Club; of which he is a director; Cape Shore Community Club, Cape Elizabeth, of which he was one of the organizers. His parents are Methodists and his wife is a member of the First Church of Christ Scientist, of Portland. He assisted in organizing the Portland Boys' Club, of which he is a director. He is also a director of Opportunity Farm, New Gloucester Maine, an institution for under-privileged boys, and in 1927-28 was a member of the Community Service and Boys' Work Committee of Rotary International. He is also a member of the board of directors and executive committee of the State of Maine Publicity Bureau, and is secretary and one of the founders of the Maine Automobile Association, as well as director and member of the executive committee of that organization. He is a member of the Salvation Army Advisory Board for Maine, a member of the Portland Traffic Advisory Board, and director and secretary of the Falmouth Hotel, Portland; president of Naples Realty Company and director of Maine Lake Shores, Incorporated.

Daniel Winfield Hoegg married, in Portland, Maine, July 24, 1909, Florence Isabel Moseley, daughter of Frank Leslie and Emma (Wyer) Moseley.

AUGUSTUS ORLOFF THOMAS, LL. D.— Although now (1928) having filled the difficult position of Commissioner of Education for the State of Maine for twelve years, Dr. Augustus Orloff Thomas already has demonstrated that school authorities made no mistake in choosing him for this important post. He has taken hold of his work with vigor and confidence, and through his example and personality, he has gained the confidence of superintendents and other subordinates, and, what is more important, is receiving full co-operation from them. Dr. Thomas came to Maine with excellent training and broad experience; he is a splendid public speaker, and makes friends easily; and he is a thoughtful, enthusiastic worker. What is more important, however, Dr. Thomas is well versed in the rural school problem, one that long has been of prime interest to Maine, while at the same time he is fully qualified for the supervision of city schools. He is especially concerned with industrial education and trade schools, the development of which was made possible in the large towns and cities of the State by the Smith-Hughes Act.

Dr. Thomas was born in 1863, in Mercer County, Illinois, son of William Lee and Mary Elizabeth (Cox) Thomas, the father was a farmer. Augustus O. Thomas attended the public schools in boyhood, after which he entered upon the training that was to fit him for the honored profession of teaching, upon which he early had decided for his life work. From the country schools he went to Shenandoah, Iowa, where he entered Western Normal College, where he took a business course and later the scientific course in that institution, and was graduated therefrom in 1891, with the degree of Bachelor of Science. Later Dr. Thomas won the degree of Bachelor of Philosophy and still later the degree of Doctor of Philosophy from Amity College. He was granted the degree of Bachelor of Education from the Nebraska State Teachers' College of Peru. In 1925 Bates College conferred upon him the degree of Doctor of Laws, while in the Educational Institute of Scotland he was made a fellow. Added to this splendid theoretical training were several years of practical experience as a teacher, and then Dr. Thomas began his climb in educational circles that culminated in his being brought to Maine. However, he never has ceased to be a student, and is indefatigable in his search of knowledge. His first official position of major importance came to him about 1905, when he was made president of the State Normal School, at Kearney, Nebraska. Dr. Thomas made a splendid record there during his nine years' régime, and following this was elected to the post of State Superintendent of Public Instruction in Nebraska. Two years in that capacity brought renown to Mr. Thomas that spread to Maine, and in July, 1917, he came to Augusta and took up his work as Commissioner of Education of Maine, having supervision over the entire public school system of this State. Dr. Thomas is a Republican in politics but his public offices have been confined almost entirely to those dealing with his profession, and he ever has been connected with some form of educational work. He has been identified with fraternal organizations for many years, being a member of the Lodge, Free and Accepted Masons (Junior Warden) ; is a Past Chancellor Commander of the Knights of Pythias, and a member of Phi Delta Kappa college fraternity. The Kiwanis Club finds him a helpful member, and he is a communicant of the Christian church.

Augustus O. Thomas married, at Arapahoe, Nebraska, in 1893, Ellamay Colvin, daughter of George and Euceba (Davis) Colvin, and they reside at No. 44 Green Street, Dr. Thomas' offices being located in the State House here.

HAROLD SHERBURNE BOARDMAN, LL. D.—The State of Maine has within its boundaries many institutions devoted to higher education which are renowned throughout the entire North American Continent, and undoubtedly one of the largest contributors to the upbuilding of these colleges and universities has been Harold Sherburne Boardman, who, after one year as acting president, was elevated to the presidency of the University of Maine, the honored position he now (1928) fills. It is extremely doubtful if any educator ever came to his post so well equipped, through training and actual experience, as did Dr. Boardman. A native of this State and here educated, his career has encompassed periods devoted to instruction and tutoring, specializing in civil engineering, and also many offices and committee memberships, wherein he obtained actual contact with engineering problems. On many occasions he has served his State and Nation in field operations, covering geological and hydrographic work, and at other times he has contrib-

uted materially as consulting engineer in the erection of bridges and other highly technical tasks. A full listing and description of his innumerable connections in engineering and allied organizations would require far more space than is available in a volume of this kind.

Dr. Boardman was born March 31, 1874, at Bangor, Maine. His elementary and preparatory courses disclosed his special aptitude for engineering and this led to his concentration of his faculties on this subject during his later scholastic career. In 1895, at the age of twenty-one years, Mr. Boardman had completed the courses at Maine State College and in that year was graduated with the degree of Bachelor of Civil Engineering. Then followed one year as a graduate student of Massachusetts Institute of Technology, this occupying him during the academic year 1895-1896. Later, in 1898, the University of Maine conferred upon him the degree of Civil Engineer, and in 1922 he was honored with the degree of Doctor of Engineering. The honorary degree of Doctor of Laws was bestowed upon him in 1927 by Colby University, and the following year Rhode Island State College gave him the degree of Doctor of Engineering. In the meantime, shortly after his graduation from Maine State College in 1895, Dr. Boardman had launched into the teaching profession. In 1896-1899 he was tutor in drawing in the University of Maine ; in 1899-1900 he was employed as a draftsman by the Union Bridge Company, at Athens, Pennsylvania, and from 1899-1900 served in a similar capacity with the American Bridge Company, at Philadelphia, Pennsylvania. This practical experience served to round out Mr. Boardman's theoretical training, and he returned to teaching in 1901. From that year until 1903 he served as instructor in Civil Enginering at the University of Maine, and his professional positions thereafter included: Associate professor and head of the department of civil engineering, 1903-04; professor of civil engineering, 1904-26; dean, College of Technology, 1910-26; acting president of the University of Maine, 1925-26, and as a fitting climax, in June, 1926, he was made president of the University of Maine, at Orono. Although Dr. Boardman has included many outside achievements during his professional career, and is still carrying on in non-professional circles, he is giving to the University of Maine his very best efforts,

76   MAINE—A HISTORY

and that institution's steadily increasing efficiency and prestige testify to this fact.

From 1903 until 1905, Dr. Boardman had charge of important water storage investigations in Maine; was in charge of hyrographic field operations with the United States Geological Survey, in connection with the Maine Survey Commission and the Maine Water Storage Commission, from 1905 until 1911; served as consulting engineer on bridges for the Maine State Highway Commission, from 1913 until 1917, and was in charge of materials, testing laboratories of the State Highway Commission during the years 1913-26. Dr. Boardman was a member and vice-chairman of a special committee on Hydraulic Power Data of the Boston Society of Civil Engineers, from 1917 until 1920; was chairman of the Engineering Section, Land Grant College Association, 1923-24; vice-president of the Society for Promotion of Engineering Education, 1923-24; chairman of the Division of Deans and Administrative Officers, Society for the Promotion of Engineering Education, 1924-26; secretary of the New England Section, Society for the Promotion of Engineering Education, 1921-26; and past president of the Maine Association of Engineers. He is a member of the American Society of Civil Engineers, Boston Society of Civil Engineers, Society for the Promotion of Engineering Education, Maine Association of Engineers, Beta Theta Phi, Phi Beta Kappa, Tau Beta Pi, Phi Kappa Phi, and Scabbard and Blade.

———

CLIFTON DAGGETT GRAY, LL. D.— Called to the presidency of Bates College, at Lewiston in 1920, Dr. Clifton Daggett Gray came eminently qualified for this highly responsible office and has since the beginning of his work here established a very high reputation as an educator and administrator. Proud of her higher educational institutions, Maine has found in Dr. Gray a vital force in the system. He is a man of finished culture and university education, has been honored with high degrees from noted seats of learning and has established a reputation in the field of Assyriology through research work in the British Museum. He has traveled extensively both in Europe and Latin America. He is a member of several fraternal and social organizations and thoroughly enjoys intimate

intercourse with his fellow men, taking an abiding interest in civic affairs that engage the attention of the progressive element of the community and ever alert to aid in such enterprises as are promoted for the general welfare.

His birthplace was Somerville, Massachusetts, July 27, 1874, and he is a son of Jefferson Jenness and Alida Mazella (Daggett) Gray, his father having been a manufacturer. His education was attained at Harvard University, where he received his degrees of Bachelor of Arts and Master of Arts; Newton Theological Institution, which granted him the degree of Bachelor of Divinity; University of Chicago, which graduated him with the degrees of Bachelor of Sacred Theology and Doctor of Philosophy, and the University of Maine, where he received the degree of Doctor of Laws. He is a member of the college fraternity of Phi Beta Kappa and belongs to the order of Free and Accepted Masons, the Rotary Club and to the University Club of Boston, Massachusetts, and the Harvard Club of New York. He is a Republican in politics and a Baptist in religion. His prior work was as pastor of the First Church of Port Huron, Michigan, 1901 to 1905; pastor of the Stoughton Street Baptist Church of Boston, Massachusetts, 1905 to 1912, and editor of "The Standard," of Chicago, Illinois, 1912 to 1919. He was then called to Bates, where he still administers his office of president.

Clifton Daggett Gray married, at Hampton Falls, New Hampshire, June 28, 1900, Neva B. Ham, daughter of Albert H. and Maria (Davis) Ham. Their children are: 1. Malcolm Jefferson, born March 1, 1903. 2. Paul Judson, born March 25, 1906. 3. Clifton Daggett, Jr., born August 21, 1916.

———

CATHERINE OUELLETTE—One of Maine's most prominent women in educational circles, Catherine Ouellette, of Fort Kent, spent a number of years in the noble profession of teaching and is at the present time (1928) superintendent of the schools of Fort Kent, which have made such consistent progress under her efficient and capable administration. The welfare and prosperity of the country depend so greatly upon the education and training which its children receive in the formative years of their lives, which enables them to grow into useful and responsible citizens, and the people of this town and vicinity are fortunate in having such an able executive and brilliant educator as Miss Ouellette at the head of the school organization. She has ever demonstrated her deep interest in the children under her supervision, careful to see that nothing is left undone to provide them with the benefits of the best schooling possible and to train their minds and assist in shaping their characters so that the State and country, as well as the pupils themselves, will be benefited in the future.

Miss Ouelette was born in Fort Kent, September 18, 1892, daughter of Onezime and Sophia (Daigle) Ouellette. Onezime Ouellette has been engaged in the agricultural industry all his life, and is one of the prominent and respected citizens of this community.

Catherine Ouellette was educated in the rural schools at Fort Kent, after which she entered Madawaska Training School, spending four years of diligent study, and graduating valedictorian of the class of 1910. After teaching in the rural schools she later matriculated at Aroostook State Normal School, where she graduated with the class of 1916. After graduation from Normal School she taught in the schools of Maine for some time, winning the praise and acclaim of her superiors from the very first, and steadily advancing until she was accorded the deserved recognition of her talents and ability by being appointed to her present honored position of superintendent. Prior to her appointment as superintendent, Miss Ouellette was selected as one of the first one hundred rural helping teachers at Castine and gained much experience by acting as a helping teacher for one year. In 1925 she studied at Columbia University, New York, taking a special six weeks' summer course.

Although Miss Ouellette is primarily interested in scholastic work and its ramifications, she finds time to devote to local affairs, taking an active interest in everything which tends to promote the welfare and advancement of the community. Her religious adherence is given to the Roman Catholic church, in the affairs of which she is prominently identified.

HORATIO SETH READ—All the schools of the Presque Isle District, which consists of Presque Isle and Westfield, Aroostook County, are under the superjntendency of Horatio Seth Read, who has a splendid record in the educational field and who, in the few years he has held his official position here, has gained the respect and esteem of all by his scholarly attainments and genial presence. He has a total of forty schools under his superintendency, thirty-five in Presque Isle and five in Westfield.

Mr. Read was born in Williston, Vermont, February 27, 1885, the son of Alfred and Sarah J. (Johnson) Read, the former a prominent provision and meat merchant of that town. Both parents of Mr. Read are deceased. Following his preliminary education in the public and high schools of his native town, Mr. Read entered the university of Vermont, from which institution he graduated in 1907. Following his graduation he was employed on engineering work for the United States Government for about two years, after which he worked for four years with a large firm of contracting engineers. It was at the close of this latter engagement that the profession of teaching attracted Mr. Read and he obtained the post of principal of the high school at Hinesburg, Vermont. He held this post for three years and was then appointed superintendent of the schools of Richmond, Vermont. At the end of eight years in this office he was offered the post of principal of Presque Isle High School, which he accepted and, after two years of service, was appointed superintendent of all the schools of Presque Isle and Westfield, which office he now holds.

In politics Mr. Read is a Republican and he is an active member of the local Congregational church, being one of the leading choristers. He is a prominent member of the Free and Accepted Masons and is affiliated with the thirty-second degree, Ancient Accepted Scottish Rite, and a member of the Mooseleuk and Rotary clubs.

Horatio Seth Read married Mary Elizabeth Wright, a native of Vermont, daughter of Charles R. and Arabell (Patrick) Wright. Mr. and Mrs. Read are the parents of four children, as follows: 1. Seth, a student at Presque Isle High School. 2. Richard, also at high school. 3. Paul. 4. Mary.

ARTHUR J. LIBBY—A man of wide experience in raising and handling potatoes is Arthur J. Libby. He has been connected with several different firms of potato shippers, acting as manager of the Maine territory for many years, and in 1919 he started into the business for himself at Presque Isle. He is part owner of a number of farms, whose operation he supervises, and is also a director of the local Merchants' Trust and Banking Company. Mr. Libby has been active in civic and fraternal life, and is a public-spirited citizen of great value to his community. His father, David Libby, born at Eddington, Maine, was a carpenter and farmer, and engaged in this work until his death. His mother, who before her marriage was Martha Shaw, was born at Sebago, Maine, and is also now deceased.

Arthur J. Libby was born on March 30, 1867, at Greenbush, Maine. He attended the local public schools, finally leaving to begin work for the Maine Central Railroad. For thirteen years he was station agent at Olamon, Maine, coming to Presque Isle at the end of that time as freight agent for the Bangor and Aroostook Railroad. From 1905 until 1912 he was manager of the Maine territory for the R. T. Prentice Company, dealers in potatoes and fertilizer. In 1913 and 1914 he was manager for Oscar Frommell and Brother, large potato handlers in New York City, and in 1915 he was manager for the E. S. Woodward Company, potato dealers. In 1916 he returned as manager to the firm of Oscar Frommell and Brother, remaining, after Mr. Frommell's death in 1918, with his successors, Sullivan, Young and Russell. Finally, in the fall of 1919, he started into business for himself. In this field he has been very successful, his keen judgment and thorough knowledge of every detail of the work proving of great value.

Politically, he is a member of the Democratic party. He is affiliated fraternally with the Ancient Free and Accepted Masons, in which organization he has taken all degrees of the Scottish Rite, and is also a Knight Templar and a member of the Mystic Shrine. He is a member of the Independent Order of Odd Fellows, the Rotary Club and local Merchants' Association, the Three Links Club, and the Mooseleuk Club. He and his family attend the Congregational church.

He married Zyphia H. Coffin, who was born at Ashland, Maine, the daughter of Nathaniel and Manira (Greenlaw) Coffin. Mr. and Mrs. Libby are the parents of two children: Mary Elizabeth and Anna Christine.

EARLE H. ROBERTS—Uncle Sam's postal business in Fort Kent, Maine, is taken care of by Earle H. Roberts, who was appointed postmaster here first by President Harding in 1921, and then by President Coolidge. The Fort Kent postoffice is a second-class office, and has two regular clerks, two village carriers, and four rural mail routes.

Earle H. Roberts was born in Caribou, Maine, December 12, 1894, son of Fred P. and Lucy (Bloodsworth) Roberts, both now deceased. The parents removed from Caribou to Fort Kent when Mr. Roberts was twelve years of age, and his life since that time has been spent mostly here in Fort Kent. He attended the public schools of Caribou and of Fort Kent, and when his high school course was completed secured a position as clerk in a grocery store, of which he later was made manager. That position he continued to fill until the entrance of the United States into the World War, when he enlisted for service and was assigned to the 103d Infantry, at Augusta, Maine, as a private. From Camp Keyes, Augusta, Maine, he was sent overseas, where he served for fifteen months and was promoted to the rank of first lieutenant. He returned at the end of fifteen months, having been in service for a total period of twenty-two months. Upon his return he secured a position as manager of a store at Bradbury, Maine, where he continued until 1921, when he was appointed to his present position as postmaster of Fort Kent by President Harding. When his first term had expired he was reappointed by President Coolidge, and he is now serving the second year of his second term. Politically, Mr. Roberts supports the principles of the Republican party, as do most of the residents of this section of the State of Maine. He is a member of Fort Kent Lodge, Free and Accepted Masons; also of Caribou Chapter, Royal Arch Masons; and he is an interested member of the Fort Kent Chamber of Commerce. He and his family are members of the Congregational church, which he serves as a member of the Board of Trustees.

Earle H. Roberts was married to Augusta Pinkham, who was born in Fort Kent, Maine, daughter of Asa M. and Ella A. (Sears) Pinkham. Mr. and Mrs. Roberts have two sons, Kenneth Pinkham and David Clark, and a daughter, Ruth May.

ARTHUR J. NADEAU—One of the leading young attorneys of Fort Kent, Maine, is Arthur J. Nadeau, the son of the late John A. and Sarah (McSweeney) Nadeau. His mother who is still living, was born in New Brunswick, his father was born in the State of Maine, where he was engaged in the insurance business and for years was Collector of Customs and one of the promotors and the first president of the Fort Kent Trust Company.

Arthur J. Nadeau was born at Frenchville, Maine, on September 9, 1880, and was educated here and at Saint Mary's Academy at Vanburen, Maine. He graduated from Saint Mary's Academy in 1900, and then entered Georgetown University, from where he graduated in 1904. Mr. Nadeau was admitted to the bar in 1905 and immediately began the practice of law here at Fort Kent. He was judge of the Northern Aroostook Court for four years. He is a director in the Rotary Club; a member of the Knights of Columbus, and was Grand Knight of the Council here for the first two years after its formation.

Arthur J. Nadeau married Maud S. Smart, who was born in Millinocket, the daughter of Alexander and Frances (Pelletier) Smart, her father living and her mother deceased. They have three children: Virginia, Arthur J., Jr., and Bernadette. Mr. Nadeau and his family are members of the Roman Catholic church.

PAUL D. THIBODEAU—One of the important citizens in the business and industrial life of Fort Kent and Vanburen, Maine, is Paul D. Thibodeau, who holds a prominent position in banking and insurance work, and has held for many years influential public offices. He is president of the First National Bank, of Fort Kent, as well as the organizer of it, in which capacity he has served since the organization of that institution; and is the proprietor of the Paul D. Thibodeau Insurance Agency, which handles general insurance. Since 1908, he has been town treasurer of Fort Kent; since 1917, treasurer of the Village Corporation; and has been a member of the town's Board of Selectmen and is a member of its school committee. He is a director of the National Bank of Vanburen; a member of the firm known as Saint Froid's Land Company; and a member of Thibo-

deau and Cyr, an insurance agency dealing in general insurance in Vanburen, and a member of the insurance agency of Pelletier & Thibodeau at Madawaska.

Mr. Thibodeau was born in Grand Isle, Maine, on June 5, 1880, a son of Vital F. and Methaide (Dublissie) Thibodeau, both of whom are natives of Maine, farmers, and the mother still living, the father having died in 1913. As a boy, Paul D. Thibodeau attended the public schools of Caribou, and subsequently became a student at Saint Mary's College, in Vanburen. When he completed his academic education, he became interested in the insurance business. First he acted as an agent; and later, in 1908, he established his own agency in Fort Kent, which has grown continuously and steadily over the passing years and is now one of the leaders of its kind in this section of Maine. In this business he employs three stenographers, his son, Romeo J., also now working in this business, and his offices present constantly a scene of industry and thrift. In his political convictions, Mr. Thibodeau is aligned with the Democratic party, of whose principles and candidates he is a staunch supporter. He was a member of the Legislature of 1915 from this, a Republican stronghold. A prominent Rotarian, he is a member and vice-president of the local Rotary Club; and he holds a membership in the Knights of Columbus, in which society he holds the fourth degree. Mr. Thibodeau is the first president of the Fort Kent Historical Society, organized in 1927. He and his family are members of the Roman Catholic Church.

Paul D. Thibodeau married Mary A. Nadeau, who was born in Fort Kent, a daughter of Henry W. and Zeline (Audibert) Nadeau. Paul D. and Mary A. (Nadeau) Thibodeau are the parents of the following children: Juliette C., Romeo J., Bernice A., Ludger P., Henry C., Omar A., Phillip J., Gertrude, and Winifred.

ALBERT M. HUSTON—For many years Albert M. Huston has been prominent in the life of Perham, Maine. He is the owner of a large farm, four hundred and eighty acres in extent, situated in the town of Perham, which was originally cleared by his father, Elbridge Huston, and which Mr. Huston himself has added to from time to time. This farm comprises some of the most fertile land in the vicinity, well suited to the raising of potatoes, in which Mr. Huston specializes, and in which occupation his wide experience and careful study of all the factors involved have made him very successful. He is also a director and stockholder of the Washburn Trust Company, and has been since its organization. In his community he is highly esteemed as a public-spirited citizen.

Albert M. Huston was born June 8, 1867, in the town of Weld, Franklin County, Maine, the son of Elbridge and Cynthia J. (Stearns) Huston, both born in Maine and both now deceased. His father, in his early life, was a lumber man and the owner of a sawmill, but later he became a farmer and spent his last years in Aroostook County, where he died. Mr. Huston attended the public schools of his birthplace, and when he completed his education, he began work with his father on the farm, where he remained until he was twenty-one years old. At that time he went to California, spending one and a half years there, and finally returning to Maine to his father's farm. He continued to work there until his father's death, when he inherited the farm and has operated it since. Mr. Huston raises annually many barrels of excellent potatoes which he sells to local buyers.

At the time of the organization of the Washburn Trust Company, Mr. Huston became a stockholder, and some time later he was elected a director, a position which he still holds. Politically, he is a member of the Republican party, and is also a member of the Grange. He and his family attend the Baptist church.

Mr. Huston married Lillian King, who died in 1916, the daughter of Cyrus and Mary (Crocket) King. Mr. and Mrs. Huston became the parents of eleven children: 1. Helen, who was married to Newton Spear. 2. Hester, the wife of Perley Johnson. 3. Lena, who was married to Woodbury Harris. 4. George. 5. Phillip. 6. Walter. 7. and 8. Gerald and Margaret, twins. 9. Lee. 10. Carl. 11. Madeline.

WILLIAM E. WATSON—Popularity and progress have gone hand in hand in the course of the life work of William E. Watson, long established as a general store merchant and farmer at Van Buren, where he has a host of friends and well-wishers who address him on the familiar footing as "Willie," and are well aware of his value as a citizen and the lifelong interest that he has taken in whatsoever has had to do with the standing and the prosperity of his native town.

William E. Watson was born May 22, 1875, at Vanburen, a son of George E. Watson, who was born in Calais, and Eulalia (Farrell) Watson, a native of Van Buren. George E. Watson first removed to this county in the capacity of inspector of lumber and shave shingles, where he was also a merchant, and for many years held the office of sheriff. He was the father of nine children.

After attending Calais public schools, William E. Watson entered the sawmill business. Later he established his present general store in Vanburen, where he employs five men throughout the year, and where he carries an up-to-date line of general merchandise. Mr. Watson also owns two farms on the Caribou Road. In the political field he is a member of the Republican party, voting for the ticket of that party, but never having sought public office.

William E. Watson married Iva V. Dunlap, who was born at Melville, New Brunswick, and they are the parents of four children: Winifred, Margaret, Ruth and Thelma. The family attend the Baptist church.

SAMUEL P. ARCHIBALD has, since 1913, been serving continuously as county commissioner of Aroostook County, being at the present time (1928) in his third term of six years each. Mr. Archibald has been engaged in farming for more than forty years, and has served in various public offices, including those of tax collector and superintendent of schools. Isaac L. Archibald, father of Mr. Archibald, was born in Truro, Nova Scotia, and came to the village of Monticello, Maine, in 1855, when his son, Samuel P., was a child. He operated a hotel in Monticello for a period of fifteen years and then engaged in farming, in which line of activity he continued to the time of his death. His wife, Margaret C. Archibald, was also a native of Truro, Nova Scotia.

Samuel P. Archibald, son of Isaac L. and Margaret C. Archibald, was born in Richmond,

New Brunswick, June 12, 1849, but was brought to the village of Monticello, Maine, by his parents when he was a child. He received his education in the district schools and in the old Houlton Academy, and then engaged in farming, which occupation he followed for more than forty years. While successfully conducting his farming operations, however, he was also giving considerable time to local public service. After the death of his wife, in August, 1917, he removed to the village of Monticello, and here he was active as chairman of the Board of Selectmen from 1887 to 1894, as a member of the school board, as tax collector, and as superintendent of schools at Monticello. He is a member of the local Grange, Patrons of Husbandry, and is very well known in this section of the county. In 1920 he removed to Houlton, where his home is located at No. 22 Highland Avenue. Mr. Archibald is a member of the Congregational church.

Samuel P. Archibald was married, March 29, 1871, to Christiana Alexander, who died in August, 1917, daughter of Hugh and Christiana (Carl) Alexander. Mr. and Mrs. Archibald became the parents of nine children, seven of whom are: 1. Edith, who is a teacher in the public schools of Waltham, Massachusetts. 2. Margaret C., who is in charge of the Lowell office of the Massachusetts Mohair Plush Company, of Lowell, Massachusetts. 3. Kenneth, who resides in Bangor, and is employed as a railroad clerk, between Boston and Bangor. 4. Ida Ethel, who is a trained nurse and resides with her father. She is a graduate of Maine General Hospital and also completed a post-graduate course in the New England Hospital in Boston. 5. Arnot, who is a woodsman in the employ of the Great Northern Paper Company. 6. Marion, a rural mail carrier, who lives in Monticello, Maine. 7. Hope, who married Walter Melvin, a farmer of Monticello.

REV. J. L. DUCLOS, S. M.—As pastor of St. Bruno's parish, Vanburen, Maine, Rev. J. L. Duclos has been serving his people faithfully and well since 1923. Father Duclos has had thorough preparation for his work and had had considerable experience before coming to his present charge, and the results of preparation and experience are

plainly discernible in his work here. In Vanburen and vicinity there are about four thousand souls to whom he ministers, and since his coming he has built up and strengthened both the spiritual and the material resources of the church. Father Duclos was ordained in 1901 and was engaged in teaching for some years before taking charge of a parish.

Rev. J. L. Duclos was born in Medford, Massachusetts, January 1, 1877, son of Louis and Emily A. (Hebert) Duclos, and received his early and preparatory training in the public schools of Cambridge, Massachusetts. Later he became a student in St. Mary's College, at Vanburen, and then went to Maryland, where he spent two years and then entered college at Washington, D. C. He was ordained in 1901, and after his ordination accepted a position as a teacher in Atlanta, Georgia, where he remained for a period of three years. At the end of that time he made a change, becoming a teacher in Jefferson College, in Louisiana, and later he taught in St. Mary's Seminary, in Washington, D. C. He was then transferred to Salt Lake City, Utah, where he remained until he returned to New England as assistant in St. Ann's parish at Lawrence, Massachusetts, where he remained for a period of three years. He was then made pastor of Sacred Heart Parish, Lawrence, in which capacity he served faithfully and well for a period of seven years. In 1923 he came to Vanburen, Maine, as pastor of St. Bruno's Parish, and here he has since been serving. Faithful and painstaking, he spares no effort to keep his flock spiritually vigorous and to render to them whatever service a pastor may extend. His parishioners regard him as their friend as well as their spiritual leader and advisor, and entertain for him both affection and reverence. He is chaplain of the Madawaska Council, Knights of Columbus, of Vanburen, and with his first assistant, Rev. Charles Bedard, is giving to the parish of St. Bruno faithful and devoted care.

JUDGE FREDERICK ALTON POWERS —In the early history of the family of Powers there is a record of one "le Poer" being an officer in the army of William the Conqueror, and later, in 1187, a Richard le Poer was high sheriff of

Gloucestershire, England. The name recurs many times in the history of England after that time and finally becomes Anglicized into the modern spelling of Power and later to Powers. The name first appears in early New England history in the "Genealogies and Estate of Charlestown, 1629-1818, and in Boston, 1879." However, following the history of the family at that time it seems that a certain John Power and his wife Sarah, who had one son, Peter, were in this country for a time and then returned to England. John Poer was a hosier.

At a later date there appears a Thomas Power, a blacksmith, at Charlestown, who married Abigail Fosketh, on February 17, 1714, and had a number of children; but the male line of the family does not seem to continue from this family, so again there comes Walter Power, who was born in England and married Trial, a daughter of Deacon Ralph and Thankes Sheppard. After the marriage of these two, they settled on a tract of land in Concord Village, Middlesex County, Massachusetts. From this couple the line comes directly down to the illustrious Judge Frederick Alton Powers, of Houlton, Maine. Daniel was the fourth son of Walter and Trial (Sheppard) Power and married Elizabeth Whitcomb. Peter, known as Captain Peter Powers, was the fourth son of Daniel and Elizabeth (Whitcomb) Powers, and married Anna Keyes. Levi, the fourth son of Captain Peter and Anna (Keyes) Powers, of Coos County, New Hampshire, was born June 3, 1739, married and moved to Sidney, Kennebec County, Maine, where Philip, his second son, was born. Phillip married Lucy Hood. They had seven children. Arba, the third son of Philip and Lucy (Hood) Powers, was born at Sidney, Maine, April 11, 1811. He married, in the spring of 1836, Naomi Matthews, who was born in July, 1813. They made their home in Pittsfield, Maine. They had ten children: Llewellyn, Cyrus M., Gorham, Amos, Seeva, Cassius Caly, Hortense B., Don Arba Horace, Loantha A., and Frederick Alton, of whom further.

Frederick Alton Powers was born at Pittsfield, Maine, on June 19, 1855. He was the youngest of ten children whose parents were ambitious to give them every educational advantage that could be procured and he was sent to the best institutions of learning available in his native State at that time. He went to the Maine Central Institute at

Pittsfield, where he graduated in the class of 1871. Being then prepared for college, he matriculated at Bowdoin College and graduated from that institution in the class of 1875. After becoming one of the most prominent lawyers in Maine, he was given an honorary degree of Doctor of Laws by Bowdoin College. This was in 1906, and in 1908 he was further honored by his *alma mater* in being made one of its board of overseers. He chose law as his profession and was admitted to the Maine bar in September, 1876. He was later admitted to practice before the District Court and the Circuit Court of the United States. He began his practice in Houlton, Maine, with his brothers, the Honorable Llewellyn Powers and the Honorable Don A. H. Powers, both able lawyers, and the firm bore the name of Powers and Powers. He continued in this partnership until 1900. During the time that he was in partnership with his brothers, he became recognized as one of the leading attorneys in the State of Maine, and much of the more important litigation was handled through his office. But, as important as was his work as an attorney, it is through his political achievements that he is best known. He was a most loyal and active member of the Republican party, was elected on that ticket to the Maine Legislature in 1885, and served four years in that body. In 1891, he was elected to the Maine Senate and in 1893 he was chosen as Attorney-General of the State of Maine and held that position until 1896. On January 2, 1900, he began his duties as Justice of the Supreme Court of Maine and held that honorable and responsible position until his resignation, on April 1, 1907. As one of the leaders of the Republican party in Maine, Judge Powers was a member of the Republican State Committee from 1883 to 1887, and again from 1891 to 1895. He was a delegate to the Republican National Convention in 1888 and received the Republican nomination for United States Senator in 1911. Mr. Powers was also interested in several of the important business and financial institutions of Houlton and vicinity. He was for a long time a director and later president of the Farmers' National Bank of Houlton. He was a member of the Unitarian church. Judge Frederick Alton Powers died in Saint Petersburg, Florida, on February 13, 1923. His death brought a loss to Maine of one of her greatest sons and the record of his good deeds and works will ever remain an important part of her history.

Frederick Alton Powers married (first), on January 7, 1879, at Houlton, May Hussey, daughter of Sylvanus H. and Mary J. Hussey, of Houlton. They had three children: 1. Llewellyn H. 2. Paul H. 3. Marion, who died in infancy. Mrs. May (Hussey) Powers died May 28, 1901, and on November 3, 1903, at Danforth, Maine, Frederick Alton Powers married (second) Virginia P. Hewes, daughter of Benjamin W. and Cora (Tupper) Hewes of Danforth.

ALBERT M. SMITH—Prominent in public affairs as well as owner of several farms, Albert M. Smith, of Ludlow and Houlton, Maine, is one of the most active men in this community. He is the son of John and Marjory (McLachlan) Smith. His father was born in Scotland and his mother was born in Kings County, New Brunswick. They came to Mars Hill, Maine, when Albert M. Smith was seventeen years of age and always lived in Aroostook County, spending their last years in the town of Ludlow. They had three children: Emily, Albert M., of whom further, and William.

Albert M. Smith was born in Kings County, New Brunswick, June 18, 1867. At the age of seventeen he moved to Maine with his parents and has made this his home ever since. He had his early schooling in New Brunswick, and after coming to Maine he took a short course at Ricker Classical Institute and after that he followed the trade of a carpenter and did some mill work. Later, in association with his father, he bought this farm of two hundred and forty acres, one hundred and sixty of which are in Ludlow and eighty in Limerick. In 1921, Mr. Smith was elected to the State Legislature where he served through 1923. He was superintendent of schools for two years, town treasurer for two years, and town clerk for ten years. He is now first selectman. He is a Republican in politics and a member of the Presbyterian church.

Albert M. Smith has been married twice. His first marriage was to Esther Ogilvy, who died leaving one child: Orvin F., who married Alice Hunter, now living in Flint, Ontario, Canada, and they have four children: Nella, Boutwell, Albert and Patricia. Albert M. Smith married a second time, to Elinor Henderson, who was born at North Lake, New Brunswick.

HOWARD B. SMITH—Broad experience in lumber manufacturing and an excellent technical education have enabled Howard B. Smith to direct along highly prosperous lines the important concern known as the Northern Woodenware Company, at Island Falls, Maine. Mr. Smith is vice-president and general manager of the company. In the promotion and expansion of this industry, as in his manifold public-spirited methods of supporting town improvements, Mr. Smith has proved himself a progressive and loyal citizen.

Howard B. Smith was born at Ludington, Michigan, in March, 1882, son of Henry B. and Nellie (Shackelton) Smith, both natives of Michigan who have never resided in Maine. After he completed his education in the Michigan State University, the son entered the lumber and woodenware industry, with which he has since been connected. He was for many years treasurer and general manager of the Ludington Wooden Ware Company. Nine years ago, in 1919, he moved to Island Falls and assumed the management of the Northern Woodenware Company, which has greatly benefited by his ambitious and astute direction. He is a good executive and a clever marketer of the wares produced by his plant, and acquainted with every angle of his business. Mr. Smith belongs to the Free and Accepted Masons, both York and Scottish, and to the Knights Templar, the Ancient Arabic Order Nobles of the Mystic Shrine, as well as to other fraternal orders, including the Knights of Pythias, and the Benevolent and Protective Order of Elks. He attends the Congregational church.

Howard B. Smith married Agnes M. Ackersville, of Michigan, daughter of George and Emma (Goodsell) Ackersville. Children: Jeanne Mary, Howard B. Smith, Jr., and John W. Smith.

JOHN EDWARD BRITTON—A farmer of enterprise and experience, conducting a well-cultivated farming property on one of the roads near Monticello, John Edward Britton is a representative agriculturist in this part of the State, all his life having been spent in farm routine and direction of farming activities. John Edward Britton was born February 11, 1885, in Monticello, a son of John Alexander Britton, a farmer, now deceased, who was born in New Brunswick, and Harriet (Rideout) Britton, who was born in Bridgewater, and who survives her husband. After attending the Monticello public schools, Mr. Britton assisted his father on his farm, and at his father's death he came into possession of the two farms, one of seventy-five acres on the Fletcher Road, which he has since sold; the other of one hundred and sixty acres on the Britton Road, and the warehouse at Monticello Depot; he carried on general farming, raising grain for his own feeding, and dealing mostly in potatoes, and he has bought a house in the village.

In the political field, Mr. Britton has not sought public office, but he votes for the principles and the candidates of the Republican party. He is a member of the Loyal Order of Orangemen, and of the local Grange, Patrons of Husbandry. He is a member of the board of trustees of the Methodist Episcopal church.

John Edward Britton married, April 27, 1910, Lena Folsom, who was born in Monticello, daughter of Blackhawk Folsom, a farmer, and Maggie (Bridges) Folsom. Their children: Bernard and Lois.

PERCY M. PORTER—Combining practical farming with road building, Percy M. Porter, of Presque Isle, Maine, finds time for public service when called upon, and for activity in several of the fraternal orders.

Born at Castle Hill, May 23, 1871, he was the son of Simon and Emily F. (Smith) Porter. His father, who was born of farming stock in New Brunswick, Canada, came to the United States when a young man, and married in Weston, Maine, of which town his wife was a native. Educated in the schools of his home town, Percy M. Porter spent the next few years at work on his father's farm, and then went to the Portland State School for Boys, where he spent the next ten years, the latter part of the time as superintendent of Farmington Cottage of that institution. He then re-

turned to farming, and produces a fine crop of potatoes on a one hundred and fifty acre tract in Mapleton. He was road commissioner for Mapleton, and served there as first selectman for eight years, and represented the town in the State Legislature in 1909, 1911 and 1918. He now lives in Presque Isle, where he is also road commissioner, and besides having charge of all the roads in this town, does a great deal of work on the State roads. Mr. Porter is a member of the Free and Accepted Masons, a Knight Templar and a Shriner; he is also a member of the Grange. He attends the Congregational church, and is a Republican.

Percy M. Porter married Elvira Carter, of Mapleton. His three children are: Burton, Esther and Manton, by a previous marriage.

HARRY M. HUGHES, of Mapleton, Maine, is head of the H. M. Hughes Company of the same town, handling farm machinery, automobiles, and accessories. He is also associated with his father, who is president of the Mapleton Electric Company, of which Mr. Hughes, Jr., is treasurer and general manager. The whole business of both companies is centered in Mapleton. However, Mr. Hughes is several other things besides a prominent business man and merchant. He was a member of the last Legislature; he was six years chairman of the Board of Selectmen; and he was a school commissioner for one term. He has been a trial justice for seven years, a justice of the peace and deputy sheriff, and he has been secretary of the Republican town committee for twenty-five years.

Harry M. Hughes was born at Presque Isle, Maine, December 23, 1878, son of Benjamin L. and Etta L. (Fields) Hughes, of whom the father was a farmer, but now retired, though preserving a financial interest in some concerns. Mr. Hughes came with his parents to Mapleton when six months old, and received his education in the common schools of the town. When he was seventeen years old he started in business for himself and gradually became a success as a merchant. He tried his hands in various lines of business and in course of time built up his present concern, which supplies the farmers of the district with tools of every kind. Mr. Hughes, as is apparent from the numerous offices held by him, has always taken a great interest in public affairs, and is an active Republican. He belongs to the Independent Order of Odd Fellows and the Grange.

Mr. Hughes married Gladys H. Nickerson, born in Nova Scotia, daughter of Edwin Nickerson. There have been no children to the marriage, but Mr. Hughes adopted a girl, Crystal S., who is a graduate of the University of Maine, and who is a teacher in the Skowhegan High School, 1927-28. Mr. Hughes also raised another child, a boy named Lee. The family attends the Methodist church, of which Mr. Hughes is a trustee.

DANIEL W. HAINES is a farmer and a potato shipper, according to the season of the year, for he devotes himself to farming in summer, while he ships potatoes in the winter. He raises, in addition, certified seed. He is the owner of some hundreds of acres in the town of Fort Fairfield and an area almost as large again in the town of Chatham, and he has a series of warehouses located in different towns. Mr. Haines' time, however, is not given wholly to farming and business. He takes considerable interest in public affairs, and has held public positions, and he has also numerous fraternal and social connections. He is director also of a National bank.

Daniel W. Haines was born at Fort Fairfield, Maine, June 29, 1871, son of John W. and Margaret (Finland) Haines, of whom the father was a farmer, and both of whom are now deceased. Mr. Haines received his education at the public schools and high school of Fort Fairfield, and then went to work on the farm. He has thus been devoted to farming all of his working life except for the time devoted to public affairs. He was on the Board of Selectmen three years, and he was in the Maine Legislature in 1913 and 1914. However, farming and raising and shipping potatoes have been his leading occupations, and this he does in conjunction with the area of three hundred acres which he owns in Fort Fairfield, and the area of five hundred acres which he owns in the town of Chatham. Of his four warehouses, one is at Houghtonville, one at Chatham, one at Murphy Road, and one at Fort Fairfield. Mr. Haines is a Republican in politics. He belongs to the Blue

Lodge, Free and Accepted Masons, of Fort Fairfield; Caribou Chapter, Royal Arch Masons; Presque Isle Council, Royal and Select Masters; Houlton Commandery, Knights Templar; Anah Temple at Bangor, charter member; the Grange; Independent Order of Odd Fellows; Knights of Pythias, and the Rotary Club.

Daniel F. Haines married Nina Clarke, born at Springfield, Maine, daughter of Henry and Adeline (Lewis) Clarke. There have been no children to the marriage, but Mr. and Mrs. Haines have adopted a daughter, Clarice, who is a graduate of the Fort Fairfield High School and La Salle College. The family attends the Congregational church, of which Mr. Haines is on the finance committee. He is a director of the Fort Fairfield National Bank.

LOUIS L. THERIAULT, M. D.—Although coming to Patten only recently, Dr. Louis L. Theriault has been known by reputation of his good work in other fields and needed no special introduction to this community. He is the son of Joseph E. and Euphemia (Farrell) Theriault. His father was born in the Province of Quebec, Canada, and came to this country when a little lad of only five years and has made his home here ever since; he is a merchant, a potato shipper and a cattle dealer in Vanburen. His mother was born in Vanburen.

Louis L. Theriault was born in Vanburen, Aroostook County, Maine, April 10, 1892. He was educated first in the town schools at Vanburen and then he attended St. Mary's College at Vanburen and, after finishing his work there, he went to Philadelphia, Pennsylvania, where he entered the Jefferson Medical College, from which institution he was graduated with the degree of Doctor of Medicine in the class of 1918. He immediately began the practice of medicine as an interne in the St. Joseph's Hospital in Philadelphia, where he worked for one year, and at the expiration of that time he returned to his native town and opened an office as a doctor of medicine. He soon built up a creditable practice and had calls in many different parts of the county of Aroostook. He continued to have his office at Vanburen from 1918 until 1924, a period of six years, and then found it advisable to make a move. He chose Stockholm as the place for his office and moved there in April, 1924, where he continued the general practice of medicine until March, 1927, when he removed to Presque Isle, later coming to Patten. He is an independent voter without identification with any political party. He is a member of the County Medical Society, the State Medical Society and the American Medical Association. He is a member of the Madwaska Council, Knights of Columbus, and of the Roman Catholic church.

Louis L. Theriault, M. D., married Catherine Riehil, a native of Pennsylvania. They have two children: Robertine and John.

GEORGE B. DUNN—One of the best known citizens of Houlton is George B. Dunn, who has been a farmer and a dealer in timber lands during the greater part of his life, and who is also one of the well-known banking men of this section, being a member of the board of directors of the First National Bank of Houlton, of the Presque Isle National Bank, of Presque Isle, Maine, and of the Ashland Trust Company, of Ashland.

Eldridge G. Dunn, father of George B. Dunn, was born in Mount Vernon, Maine, and in early life learned the carpenter's trade. Later he engaged in farming in Ashland, where he was also engaged in the lumber business. Still later he removed to St. Johns, New Brunswick, where for many years he operated a lumber manufacturing plant. He married Louise Bracket, a native of China, Maine, and they became the parents of children, among whom was George B., of further mention.

George B. Dunn was born in Ashland, June 18, 1849, and received his earliest school training in the local district school. Later he continued study in Houlton Academy, which is now known as Ricker Classical Institute, and after completing his course there he studied for one year in the Massachusetts Institute of Technology, at Boston. When his technical course was finished he returned home and associated himself with his father's lumber business, working in the woods, getting out timber for his father's mill. After a time, in association with his brother, Eldridge G., Jr., he organized the firm of Dunn and Dunn, lumber

dealers, and engaged in business for himself. The enterprise met with success and as the years passed the brothers built up a large and important business. In later years the brothers took over the mill of their father at St. Johns, New Brunswick, which they conducted for many years. Eldridge G. Dunn, Jr., is now (1928) deceased, and Mr. Dunn has been living at Houlton for about forty-one years. In addition to his extensive lumber interests and his farming activities, Mr. Dunn has for many years been interested in banking, in which field he is still actively engaged. He is a member of the board of directors of the First National Bank of Houlton, and he is also a director of the Presque Isle National Bank of Presque Isle, and of the Ashland Trust Company of Ashland. Mr. Dunn is a Republican in his political allegiance, and fraternally is identified with the Benevolent and Protective Order of Elks. He is a member of the Meduxnekeag Club and of the Houlton Country Club, and is an attendant of the Unitarian church. Few of the residents of Houlton are better known or more highly esteemed than is Mr. Dunn, and he has a very large number of friends in this community.

George B. Dunn was married to Lucinda R. Cushing, who died September 18, 1925, daughter of Andrew and Delia (Rich) Cushing, and to their marriage were born three children: 1. Louise D., who married Robert Sawyer. 2. Deborah B., wife of Dr. Henry M. Chapman, who died in September, 1925. 3. George E., engaged in the stock and bond business in Boston.

GEORGE W. WELTON—In 1922 George W. Welton bought the general store of R. D. Adams at Hodgdon Corner, near Houlton, Maine. With his customary energy and ability he has built up a very successful business there, and has since become the owner of a lumber mill at Cary Plantation which he also runs. Mr. Welton has served as tax collector for the town of Hodgdon, and he takes an active part in the civic and fraternal life of his community. He is the son of Erie and Mary Jane (Bunnell) Welton, both of the province of New Brunswick, Canada.

George W. Welton was born April 16, 1883, at Union Corner, province of New Brunswick, Canada, one of a family of nine children. He attended the local public schools for a time but was soon forced to find work. As a boy he was employed in various capacities, finally settling on a farm where he remained until 1922. In October of that year he took over Mr. Adams' general store at Hodgdon Corner, which he has continued to run since that time. In September, 1926, he purchased the starch factory at Cary Plantation and converted it into a lumber mill, which is now in operation under his direction.

Politically, Mr. Welton is an independent voter, and he served for some time as tax collector for the town of Hodgdon. He is affiliated fraternally with the Ancient Free and Accepted Masons, having taken the degrees of the Chapter, Council, and Commandery in the York Rite. In this organization he is also a Knight Templar, a member of the Mystic Shrine, and a patron of the Order of the Eastern Star. He attends the local Baptist church.

Mr. Welton married Sadie M. Kelley, who was born at Dyer Brook, Maine, the daughter of Lyman and Delia (Townsend) Kelley, both of Maine. Mr. and Mrs. Welton are the parents of two children: 1. Earl W., a graduate of Ricker Classical Institute, now associated in business with his father. 2. Marion T., a student in the local high school.

F. CLIFFORD WHEELER—Following in the same line of business as his father, F. Clifford Wheeler began his business career as a farmer and has since branched out into other lines and interests. He is the son of William E. and Mary A. (Kneeland) Wheeler. His father and mother were both born in Maine. His father was a farmer but did not confine his activity altogether to work on the farm, as he also dealt in livestock and was known in the early days as a drover. This progressive spirit is noticed in his son, who is now one of the most prosperous farmers in this section.

F. Clifford Wheeler was born at Easton, Maine, March 17, 1878. He received only a common school education in the schools of Easton and then went to work for the firm of Richardson Company, dealers in livestock. He soon learned to be a good

judge of cattle and sheep and was promoted to the position of buyer of sheep and cattle for the firm. He remained in this position until he was twenty-one years old and then came to Presque Isle and started in the farming business with T. M. Hoyt. He has continued to operate farms ever since. He owns one farm of six hundred acres on the Beach Road and another of one hundred and forty acres on the old Houlton Road. While doing general farming, he also raises a large crop of potatoes and is known as one of the biggest potato growers and shippers here. He also has a fertilizer business, dealing extensively in that commodity. He is interested in financial institutions and is a director of the Presque Isle National Bank. He is an advocate of the doctrine of the Republican party and takes an active interest in the affairs of that organization. He is a member of the United Baptist church.

F. Clifford Wheeler married Madona F. Briggs, a native of Blaine, Maine, daughter of George T. and Agnes (Hardy) Briggs. They have two children: 1. Arno R., who married Lottie Geeky, and has one son, Frank Clifford. 2. Lile C., a student in the Presque Isle High School.

J. HARRY B. CRAWFORD—Living on his farm on the Woodstock Road, one and one-half miles from the village of Houlton, J. Harry B. Crawford cultivates potatoes and does a general farming business, and takes an active part in the affairs of his community. He holds an important place in the State Grange.

He is a Canadian by birth, having been born in Woodstock, New Brunswick, on January 10, 1886, the son of Joshua and Lydia (Brown) Crawford, the former of whom, now deceased, was during his life a harness maker by occupation. His mother is still living. J. Harry B. Crawford was educated in the public schools of Woodstock, New Brunswick; then, for seven years, he worked as moulder in a foundry; and in 1907 took up farming, which he continued ever since. On his farm on the Woodstock Road he raises potatoes as a leading portion of his business, does general farming and dairying, keeping about eight head of cattle. He is Overseer of the State Grange. In addition to his activities in the Grange, he is a

member of the Foresters of America, and is affiliated with the Republican party in his political
views. In 1927 he was chosen as a member of the
State Legislature.

J. Harry B. Crawford married Pearl Drake,
the daughter of James and Ruth (Sherwood)
Drake, both now deceased. Her parents, originally from New Brunswick, spent most of their
lives in Maine as farmers. Pearl (Drake) Crawford, as a matter of fact, was born on the farm
where she and her husband now live, it having
been known as the Drake farm, and having
been the residence of her family for years. Mr.
and Mrs. Crawford are members of the United
Baptist church.

FRANK GILMAN WEBSTER—One of the
town's most prominent citizens and leading business men, Frank Gilman Webster, of Ashland,
has conducted the flourishing hardware store,
plumbing and tinsmith business for a number of
years. Two clerks are employed to take care of
the prosperous Webster business, built up through
years of honest and satisfactory service to the
community. Mr. Webster was born in Orono,
September 1, 1862, son of James and Annie B.
(Baker) Webster, both residents of Maine who
are now deceased. James Webster was engaged in
the lumber business for many years, and was
prominent in commercial circles in his vicinity.

Frank Gilman Webster received his early education in the public schools of Orono, and after
high school, entered the University of Maine,
where he studied for two years, after which he
attended Eastman's Business College at Poughkeepsie, New York. After the completion of his
college career, he engaged in the lumber business
with his father, familiarizing himself with all its
details and steadily advancing during the four
years of his association. For six years, he then
carried on an independent lumber business, during
which time he built up a substantial and prosperous trade. He then came to Ashland to superin-
tend the erection of the mill of the Ashland Manufacturing Company, where he remained for five
years as foreman and bookkeeper, after which he
resigned and bought his present business from
George S. Orcutt. Ambitious and energetic, he

has made his organization a leading factor in the
commercial life of the town, conducting his business on a splendid policy of service and honest
dealing. He also acts as agent for the American
Express Company, handling the details of this
concern in the most efficient manner. Mr. Webster has always taken an active interest in civic
affairs and is a prominent figure in all local projects for town welfare and advancement. For
eight years, he served as auditor of the town books
and in this position gave the town the value of his
mathematical and systematic ability. In fraternal
circles, he takes a deep interest, being a member
of Pioneer Lodge, Free and Accepted Masons,
Ashland; and Caribou Chapter, Royal Arch Masons.

Frank Gilman Webster married Annie J. Mc-
Millan, of Orono, daughter of David McMillan.
They are both members of the Episcopal church.

ORA W. CLARK—In common with many
officials of the same grade, Ora W. Clark, postmaster at Dyer Brook, Maine, which is a fourth
class office, combines his duties to the government
with the management of a general store, of which
he is proprietor.

Born in Dyer Brook, August 20, 1900, he was
the son of Isaiah and Lucy (White) Clark. Educated in the public and high schools of Island
Falls, Ora W. Clark found his first employment
with the Atlantic & Pacific Tea Company, in
whose store at Millinocket he was a clerk for
some time. Then he engaged in farming until the
opportunity was afforded him to buy the general
store in Dyer Brook from Herbert Donald, of
Houlton, who owned it, and soon afterwards E. L.
Cookson, the postmaster, resigned, and Mr. Clark
obtained the appointment as his successor.

JOHN HERBERT CHASE was a farmer at
Presque Isle, Maine, very well known, and taking
a prominent part in town affairs. He died July
28, 1925. He was particularly well known for his
love of horses, always having the finest horses in
that section of the State. He was a progressive
farmer and had a farm of two hundred and twenty-

five acres devoted, in the main, like so many farms in the district, to the raising of potatoes. But he always cultivated enough grain for his own use.

The farm which John Herbert Chase left is now owned by the mother and three of the sons, and the three sons carry it on. They do as their father did, sell potatoes to local buyers. Milford, the eldest of the sons, is manager of the farm. The mother resides in the town.

Mr. Chase married Effie Hatch, who survives him and resides on State Street, Presque Isle. Children: 1. Alena, now the wife of Walter Wray. 2. Milford, who married Beatrice Manzer, born at Presque Isle. 3. Eunice, now the wife of Raymond Knight. 4. Allen, who married Gladys Jones, having one child, Carleton. 5. Pauline, now wife of Ralph Bowker. 6. John. 7. Wallace. 8. Linwood.

CHARLES F. DREW and LESTER H. DREW

CHARLES F. DREW and LESTER H. DREW—Prominent in the affairs of Dyer Brook are Charles F. and Lester H. Drew, brothers, who, with their mother, own a prosperous farm of one hundred and ten acres near this community. Their father, Hannibal Hamlin Drew, was a native of Maine. Born at Lineus, on December 29, 1859, he acquired a common and high school education at the place of his birth, and all his life was a farmer and teacher, in winter engaging in the latter capacity. Most of his life he spent at Oakfield, Maine. He purchased the Dyer Brook acres in 1906, and was active in civic and social life, highly respected in every way by those who knew him. Hannibal Hamlin Drew married Annie Randall, native of Lineus, and by her was the father of four children: 1. Basil, a farmer residing near Unity, Maine, married Anna Tidd. 2. Effie, wife of William Randall. 3. Charles F., of whom later. 4. Lester H., of whom later. After a long and honorable career as teacher and farmer, Hannibal Drew died on May 2, 1921, at the Dyer Brook farm home. The two sons, Charles F. and Lester H. Drew received their educations in the public schools of Dyer Brook, and since boyhood have been engaged in farming, with successful results. The pride which they have in their extensive and fertile land is justified; for the farm yields richly under their diligent care. Buildings

are well arranged for scientific handling of produce, and for living; livestock is of the best. Both Lester H. and Charles F. Drew take part in the social and business life of Dyer Brook, where their mother, Annie Drew, is likewise well known and popular. Mrs. Annie Drew has a commercial position at Houlton, county seat of Aroostook County. The family are members of the Baptist church, and give liberally of time and funds in the service of causes sponsored by it.

Charles F. Drew married Marion Shields, and they are the parents of one child, a son, Hilton H. Lester H. Drew married Madelyn McDonald. Both families make their homes on the Dyer Brook farm, which is located on the State road.

FRANK H. JORDAN—Industry and perseverance, combined with a very practical knowledge of general farming matters, have been the basis of the success that has come to Frank H. Jordan in the course of his all-round agricultural activities at his farming property on the Callahan Road in Houlton. Mr. Jordan knows the business he deals with, because of his lifelong association with agriculture on this, the family homestead, and he has the highest regard of his neighbors and patrons for his skill and integrity.

Frank H. Jordan was born July 16, 1888, in Houlton on the farm he now owns, a son of William Henry Jordan, throughout his life a respected farmer in this section, now deceased, and Harriett (Taggett) Jordan, who survives her husband, and resides on the North Road in this township with her daughter, Mrs. Fred R. Logan. Mr. Jordan is owner of one hundred acres of land on the Callahan Road, where he engages in general farming, marketing his product to local buyers. He attended the common schools in Houlton, and then with his father engaged in farming, afterwards coming into the homestead, which he keeps up to date, and in the best state of cultivation. In political matters, Mr. Jordan votes the Republican ticket. Fraternally, he is affiliated with Monument Lodge, Free and Accepted Masons, at Houlton, and with the local Grange, Patrons of Husbandry. He attends the Baptist church.

Frank H. Jordan married Bessie Webb, daughter of William J. Webb, a review of whose life appears elsewhere in this work, a prominent farmer of Ludlow, and Sadie T. (Hussey) Webb. They have one son, Lawrence, born in 1916.

JOHN WATSON—One of the most loved and highly respected men in the vicinity of Houlton was John Watson, who started the business which now bears the name John Watson Company (although it has been sold to interests outside of the family), and who during his life was one of the prominent citizens of his community.

Mr. Watson, who was born in Andover, New Brunswick, Canada, when he was about twenty years old came to Houlton, where he died. Although he followed an independent course in his political opinions, choosing to be free from the partisan type of politics, and remained likewise independent of fraternal societies, Mr. Watson was a charitable man, loved by all who knew him and respected for his sound business judgment and ability.

He was educated in the public schools of his native town, Andover, New Brunswick, and in those of Grand Falls, New Brunswick. Then, when about twenty years old, he came to Houlton, starting, without friends or money, a career which in later years was destined to become very successful. After several years, during which he worked for other people, he became engaged in business on his own accord. With Mr. Kinney, he started the firm which today carries his name— the John Watson Company, dealing in hardware and farm implements. After some years of successful operation with Mr. Kinney, Mr. Watson purchased the entire business, which he conducted for some time with two clerks, whom he trained and helped to educate—William E. Martin and Heman Whitehead, who are now deceased. After the death of these two men, Mr. Watson carried on the company himself until his death, December 19, 1919, whereupon his widow sold it. During Mr. Watson's administration of this business, he conducted nine starch factories in Aroostook County. As he continued to add to the factories, other men told him that he would fail through not possessing large capital, but undaunted, he persevered, and his hard work and sound business judgment carried him to success. In addition to his own business enterprises, he was a director of the First National Bank and of the Bangor and Aroostook Railroad.

John Watson married Kate L. (Carpenter) Hammond, widow of William C. Hammond, and a daughter of Frank B. and Rebecca S. (Hammond) Carpenter, both of Maine, the father having been a lumberman and a mill owner. The children of Mrs. Watson's first marriage follow: 1. Rebecca Pillsbury, wife of Samuel W. Andrews. 2. Laura K., married Horace Ward. 3. Caroline G., who married Winfield Scott Webb. 4. Elbridge, an electrical engineer in Hamilton, Montana.

Mr. Watson was a liberal supporter and a communicant of the Episcopal church, having built and given to the church "Watson Hall." Mrs. Watson also is liberal in her support of that church, and is an active member, having worked in the Houlton Episcopal parish under four bishops.

AZIAL ROACH—An owner of extensive lands in Merrill Township, Aroostook County, is Azial Roach, whose principal farm area, comprising three hundred acres, is located north of the Rockabenia Road, and whose other farms, small, are several in number, aggregating some five hundred acres. Mr. Roach is interested in potatoes. He devotes nearly all of his land to the crop and ships to Smyrna Mills, where his trade is of such size as to warrant a special warehouse, which he owns and maintains exclusively for the produce of his farms. Azial Roach was born in Merrell Township on April 13, 1870, son of James and Margaret (McKee) Roach, his father having been a native of Waterford, Ireland, and his mother also of Irish origin, born in Ireland. James Roach came to the United States when but a few years of age, the voyage, in an old-time sailing ship, lasting three months. He secured work on a farm near Hersey, Maine, and finally bought a farm of his own in that locality; then he disposed of it and bought another, in Merrill Township, not more than a mile from where his son Azial now (1928) lives. James and Margaret (McKee) Roach were the parents of six children, four sons and two daughters.

Azial Roach received his education in the public schools of Merrill and went to work for his father on the farm. Later, with his brother William, he purchased a homestead, carrying on an agricultural business under the firm name of W. H. and A. Roach. In 1915 William Roach disposed of his interest to Azial, and in 1925 died. Azial Roach has become one of the most important agricultural operators in Aroostook County, and has taken an active part in community affairs, both fraternal and civic. An Independent in National and State as well as in local politics, Mr. Roach has served as a member of the Board of Selectmen on a number of occasions, and is now (1928) second selectman. He is interested in education and has served on the school board; and is a member of the Grange and the Benevolent and Protective Order of Elks, both lodges at Houlton, and of the Catholic church.

Azial Roach married Mary E. Fitzgerald, born in the post-town of Merrill, daughter of Maurice and Bridget (McCluskey) Fitzgerald. Mr. and Mrs. Roach are the parents of four children: 1. George E., a student in the Ricker Classical Institute, student at Colby College, class of 1927. 2. Herbert A., graduate of the Ricker Classical Institute. 3. Asa H., Merrill High School, class of 1932. 4. Harry Quentin.

DON A. H. POWERS—First selectman for the town of Dyer Brook, Don A. H. Powers, farmer, owns one hundred and twenty acres of rich land on the Maine State Highway, on it engaging in general crop raising and the raising of potatoes as a specialty, disposing of them in the convenient market afforded by the proximity of Dyer Brook and the fine road connecting it with his acres. Mr. Powers plays an important part in affairs of the town, where he has been selectman since 1912, continuously, and deputy sheriff since the election of 1926.

Dor A. H. Powers was born in Township Eight, Range Five, on the Aroostook Road between Patten and Ashland, March 27, 1880, son of Elbridge G. and Ida (Wade) Powers, the former born at Masardis and the latter at Benton, in Kennebec County, both deceased. Elbridge and Ida (Wade) Powers were farmers, and moved to Dyer Brook when Don A. H. was ten years of age. He received his education here, in the public schools, and afterward went to work as scaler in the woods, and in the timber on the farm. His father also was employed as scaler, and used to go to work with the son. Don A. H. Powers went to work at this strenuous calling when he was in his 'teens, and continued in various employments at lumbering and farming thence onward. The first farm to come under his ownership comprised fifty acres, and the second, the one he now (1928) owns, was sold to him in 1920 by R. H. Howard. This tract of one hundred and twenty acres is accounted one of the most fertile in the county, and because of his intensive methods of farming, it yields most satisfactory crops, affording the owner much pleasure, for he loves the soil, and considerable profit. Mr. Powers is a Republican, and in political matters exerts wide influence, as his opinions are well founded and sound; and his record as selectman and deputy sheriff has amply demonstrated an ability in community management. He is a member of the Blue Lodge of the Free and Accepted Masons, at Island Falls, and of the Independent Order of Odd Fellows, Smyrna Mills, Encampment at Houlton.

Don A. H. Powers married Eva Robinson, born at Houlton, daughter of Duncan and Mary (Maynard) Robinson. Mr. and Mrs. Powers attend the Baptist church.

JAMES M. WHITE—A long and honorable record as a public servant in various capacities has brought cordial recognition to James M. White, of Dyer Brook, Maine, now Representative in the State Legislature from the district including Dyer Brook, Oakfield, Merrill, Smyrna, New Limerick, Ludlow, Littleton, Moro, and Hamilton Plantation. Mr. White was born in Smyrna, April 29, 1873, son of Charles and Betsy (Lilly) White, both natives of Maine and now deceased. The father was a carpenter and mason.

Educated in the Dyer Brook schools, the son continued his studies at a private school in Bangor in preparation for college, but did not matriculate. Instead, he took a course in the Bangor business college. Mr. White then followed his father's trade of carpenter for two years, after which he

bought from A. C. R. Hall a valuable farm. He
has since devoted himself to general farming and
to growing potatoes, which he sells to local dealers. A Republican in politics and a civic-minded
man, Mr. White served his community as first
selectman, town treasurer, and superintendent of
schools. Last fall he was elected to a two-year
term in the Maine Legislature. He knows his
State and its potentialities and problems well and
honestly represents the best interests of his constituents.

James M. White married Jennie M. Parker,
born in Milltown, New Brunswick, daughter of
William and Phoebe (Travis) Parker, who spent
their latter years in Maine. Mr. White and his
family are communicants of the Baptist church,
and the former is superintendent of the Sunday
school and a teacher in the institution. Children:
1. Enoch J. White, working with his father and
married to Evelyn Virginia Webb. 2. Alfred H.,
soon to become a student at the University of
Maine.

FRITZ C. SOULE—Farming interests of an
extensive scope, in general agriculture, but with a
leading specialty in potato-growing are supervised
with the greatest success by Fritz C. Soule at his
considerable farming properties in Smyrna Mills,
where Mr. Soule is a prominent citizen, owner of
a well-known warehouse in this section, and a
favorite with buyers throughout the section. He
is a citizen of enterprise and of substantial value,
and has represented his constituency in public
office with great credit.

Fritz C. Soule was born July 13, 1888, at Oakfield, a son of Benjamin Franklin Soule, who is
now deceased, and Angie F. (Grant) Soule, who
resides in Oakfield. After attending the public
schools there, Mr. Soule took a course at a business college at Bucksport, and meantime, with his
brother, he rented his father's farm for four years.
Mr. Soule continued in the farming business
throughout his career, and he is now the owner of
a two-hundred acre place on the North, or Rock-
abema Road, and is proprietor of eighteen hundred
acres of timberland in the same township, with his
postoffice address at Smyrna Mills. In joint account with William H. Martin, of Bangor, he has

a commodious warehouse at Smyrna Mills, where
he is a grower and shipper of potatoes; and he is
also a fertilizer and pulp wood merchant.

In political matters a Republican, Mr. Soule has
served as a member of the school board. Fraternally, he is affiliated with the Free and Accepted Masons, and the Royal Arch Chapter of
Masons, at Island Falls; and with the Independent
Order of Odd Fellows at Smyrna Mills. With
his family, he attends the Methodist Episcopal
church, of which he is the treasurer.

Fritz C. Soule married Lou B. Smart, who was
born at Bancroft, daughter of Edwin W. Smart,
a Bancroft farmer, and Celia B. (Moore) Smart.
They have two daughters, Rita E. and Mary Elizabeth.

GEORGE WASHINGTON ESTES—One of
the most widely respected and most useful citizens
of Dyer Brook, Maine, is George Washington
Estes, a farmer and deputy sheriff of the county.
He is an able agriculturist, a good business man,
an active supporter of the church, and a constructive citizen. Mr. Estes was born at Milford,
Maine, February 22, 1866, son of George and
Hannah (Miles) Estes, who died when their child
was in his infancy. The boy lived with his grandmother, Mrs. Abbie Miles, wife of Abraham Miles,
and lost his grandmother at the age of ten, moving
then to the home of his uncle, Fred Miles, where
he stayed until fourteen.

Thrust out into the world at that tender age, Mr.
Estes found what work he could on various farms,
earning mostly just enough to pay for his food
and lodging and clothes. He also eagerly availed
himself of whatever schooling he could get. He
was thus busy as a hired hand until he was twenty-
one, having worked for a time also as hostler in
Houlton, for T. P. Clough. After his marriage
he ran the farm on which he continues to live, a
valuable tract of land belonging to his wife's family. Mr. Estes is a Republican in politics and fills
the office of deputy sheriff with courage and good
judgment. His fraternal affiliations are with the
Blue Lodge, Free and Accepted Masons. He is a
director and trustee of the Methodist church and
always active in his support of the institution and
its program.

At Island Falls, George Washington Estes married Mary A. Gerry, born on the farm on which she now lives, daughter of Benjamin and Nancy (Goodnow) Gerry. Her father acquired the land when it was wilderness, cleared it, and spent the rest of his life there. Mr. and Mrs. Estes have children: 1. Walter I., educated at high school, a farmer and potato buyer, now residing with his parents; he married Gladys Sharp, who died, leaving a daughter, Gladys. 2. Irma N., educated at Houlton High School and at the Normal School at Castine, Maine, where she spent a year; wife of Charles Hinckley, mother of one son, George. 3. Herbert E., educated at Houlton High School and living at home; married Florence Pond, and has two children, Carl H. and Phyllis Estes.

LEON C. TARBELL, D. D. S.—Conducting his profession and making his residence in the house where he was born, on the farm where his father and grandfather before him were born, on a tract first settled by his great-grandfather, paternal side, comprising one hundred and ten acres near the post-town of Merrill on the Moro Road, Aroostook County, Leon C. Tarbell, Doctor of Dental Science, belongs to one of the oldest families in this part of Maine. George Washington Tarbell, born in Solon, first of the family to be born on this farm, grandfather of Leon C. Tarbell, D. D. S., was a man and farmer high in the estimation of the folks for miles around, as was his son, Ira K. Tarbell, farmer on those same acres and prominent in the political life of the township and the town of Merrill. Ira K. Tarbell married Elizabeth Clark, and of this union Leon C. Tarbell was born, on June 17, 1888.

Dr. Leon C. Tarbell received his early education in the schools of Merrill and then matriculated in the Ricker Classical Institute and University of Maine. From the Philadelphia Dental College, at Philadelphia, Pennsylvania, he graduated with the degree of Doctor of Dental Science in 1911. He opened his first dental office at Smyrna Mills, and there retained his practice for some time after he had moved back to the farm near Merrill, where he equipped a second office. In due course he closed the Smyrna Mills office, but the distinguished reputation established through his prac-

tice there brought the patients to his new address; so that, in confining his professional activities to the office in Morrill Township, he has suffered no decline in clientele. Dr. Tarbell has an innate love of the soil and in particular of the soil belonging to the Merrill farm, and in conjunction with his professional duties he combines those of agriculture. An Independent Republican, he has taken an active part in the political guidance of the community, and served as a member of the board of selectmen for seven years; moreover, he has shared prominently in the functions of the Board of Health. He is a member of the Blue Lodge of the Free and Accepted Masons, at Island Falls; member and Past Grand Master of the Independent Order of Odd Fellows, at Smyrna Mills, and member of the National Dental Fraternity, Xi Psi Phi.

Dr. Leon C. Tarbell married Alma M. Leader, born at Philadelphia, Pennsylvania, daughter of Vermont Harrison and Mary Leader. Dr. and Mrs. Tarbell are the parents of one child, Ira King. They attend the Episcopal church.

CHARLES HOULTON FOGG—The editor of so widely read a weekly newspaper as the "Houlton Times," of Houlton, Maine, has great potential influence in directing the development of his community, and to this position Charles Houlton Fogg has brought wide business experience and a sense of civic responsibility handed down by a long line of ancestors prominent in the making of Maine. His hearty support is given to every worthwhile civic movement, and his vigorous personality enters into the social and fraternal phases of progress as well as into its business development.

The surname Fogg, or Fogge, possibly identical with Fagge, is of ancient origin, among the early surnames in use in England. The family was found in County Kent as early as 1400, when the residence was at Ashford, some fifty miles from London. Sir John Fogg was the founder of the college at Ashford, and his descendants continued there, although the principal family seat was at Richbury, where is found the coat of arms. The American progenitor was Samuel Fogg, born in England, February 20, 1600, who came to this country with John Winthrop in 1630 and settled about eight years later in Hampton, New Hampshire. There he died April 16, 1672. Of the considerable landed property owned by this prosperous farmer, one hundred acres, drawn in 1669, have since remained in the ownership of his descendants. Samuel Fogg married (first), October 12, 1652, Anne Shaw, who died December 9, 1663, daughter of Richard Shaw. He married (second), December 28, 1665, Mary Page, daughter of Robert Page of Hampton. Children of both marriages carried the line of descendants which included, several generations removed, Almon H. Fogg, son of Joseph and Esther Fogg. He was born in Bangor, Maine, in 1836, and died in Boston, October 18, 1908. After finishing his education in the Bangor public schools, he entered the hardware business and then, in 1859, established himself as a hardware merchant at Houlton. Prospering, he was a charter member and became a director of the First National Bank, as well as being also a charter member and first president of the Houlton Savings Bank, town treasurer, and a member of the board of directors of the Bangor & Aroostook Railroad, when it was first organized. He was a Republican in politics and affiliated with the First Congregational Church of Houlton.

Almon H. Fogg married Lucy Webster Hasey, a native of Houlton and a descendant of the first settlers of this town, daughter of William Hasey, and they had two children: J. Etta, who was born February 14, 1864, and died in November, 1888; and Charles Houlton, of further mention.

Charles Houlton Fogg, son of Almon H. and Lucy Webster (Hasey) Fogg, was born at Houlton, Maine, July 8, 1866. He was educated in the public schools of Houlton, at Riverview Military Academy, Poughkeepsie, New York, and Bowdoin College, from which he graduated in 1889 with the degree of Bachelor of Arts. After a year in Lowell, Massachusetts, spent in gaining a knowledge of the hardware business, Mr. Fogg became associated with the Almon H. Fogg Company, hardware, in 1890, where he remained until 1906, when he purchased the "Aroostook Times," at Houlton, which name was later changed to Houlton "Times." The paper has prospered and expanded under his ownership and management.

In 1910 the paper was incorporated under the name of the Times Publishing Company, with Mr. Fogg as its president and treasurer and since being taken over by the present company has more than doubled its circulation, and won several prizes for excellence in newspaper production. The following are among the outstanding awards: First prize in Maine Press Association, 1922, for best weekly paper; in National Editorial Association, 1924, first prize silver cup for best community work; 1925, first prize silver cup for best front page, second prize for best editorial page, honorable mention for best community work, and in 1928 was selected as one of eleven outstanding weekly papers in the United States by a professor of journalism in the University of Oklahoma.

Mr. Fogg is a trustee of the Houlton Savings Bank, and a member of the board of trustees of the Houlton Trust Company; a member of the Psi Upsilon Fraternity of Bowdoin, Past Master of Monument Lodge, No. 96, Free and Accepted Masons, a holder of the thirty-second degree in that order, and a member of Anah Temple, Ancient Arabic Order Nobles of the Mystic Shrine. He is also a member of Houlton Lodge, No. 835, Benevolent and Protective Order of Elks; a charter member of the Meduxnekeag Club, as well as the Houlton Country Club. Like his father, he is a Congregationalist in religious faith, and a Republican in politics.

On December 7, 1894, Charles Houlton Fogg married, at Houlton, Rosina Hodgdon Kidder, daughter of James H. and Rose S. Kidder. Her father, who had served during the Civil War as a member of Company C, 14th Regiment, Maine Volunteer Infantry, was later register of deeds of Aroostook County. Mr. and Mrs. Fogg reside on Main Street, Houlton.

HENRY WHEELER COBURN—One of the very well known educators of the State of Maine is Henry Wheeler Coburn, superintendent of schools of Fort Fairfield and of Easton. Mr. Coburn has filled this position since 1924, and is very active in the educational organizations of the county and State, and is a member of the executive board of the Maine State Teachers' Association.

Henry Wheeler Coburn was born in Weld,

Maine, April 3, 1873, son of George N. and Olive (Wheeler) Coburn, the first mentioned of whom was born in Maine and the last mentioned of whom was a native of Vermont, both now deceased. Mr. Coburn attended the public schools of his home town and then prepared for college in Wilton Academy, where he completed his course with graduation in 1892. He then matriculated in Bowdoin College, at Brunswick, Maine, from which he was graduated with the class of 1896. For several years after his graduation he was engaged in teaching, but later he engaged in the electrical business in Boston, in which line he continued for a period of two years. He then returned to the homestead farm in Weld, Maine, where he was successfully engaged in farming and lumbering for a period of fourteen years. His love for educational work, however, had persisted through all these years, and after his fourteen years of agricultural and lumbering activities, he returned to the work he loved, taking a position as superintendent of Union No. 27, which includes the towns of Carthage, Dixfield, Peru, and Weld. That responsible position he held for eight years, at the end of which time he came to his present position as superintendent of the schools of Fort Fairfield and Easton. Mr. Coburn is a member of all the school organizations, local, county, State and National, and as a member of the executive committee of the Maine State Teachers' Association is influential in the affairs of that organization. He is a Republican in his political faith, and in the town of Weld served as a member of the Board of Selectmen. He also served as a member of the school board for four years, being chairman of the board for three of the years, and he was county commissioner of Franklin County for six years, and also served as tax collector. He is vice-president of the School Superintendents' Association of Maine, and is well known as one of the able and skilled educators of the State. Fraternally, he is identified with the Mystic Tie Lodge, No. 154, Free and Accepted Masons, of the town of Weld; and he is a Past Worthy Patron of Mystic Star Chapter, Order of the Eastern Star at Weld, of which his wife is a Past Worthy Matron. He is also a member of the Independent Order of Odd Fellows, and of the Order of Rebekahs, also of the Junior Order United American Mechanics. He is a member of the Weld Grange, Patrons of

Husbandry; and of the Masonic Club, of Fort Fairfield. He is secretary of the Rotary Club, and his religious affiliation and that of his family is with the Congregational church.

Henry Wheeler Coburn is married to Minnie E. Holt, who was born in Weld, Maine, daughter of David and Elmira (Fuller) Holt. Mr. and Mrs. Coburn are the parents of one daughter, Grace Olive, who married Robert E. Ames, of Dixfield, Maine. They have two children: Caroline Joyce and Olive Jean.

ORA GILPATRICK, president of the Houlton Trust Company, and one of the most prominent men in the business world of Houlton, Maine, was born on March 21, 1859, in Danforth, Washington County, Maine. Mr. Gilpatrick is a son of Elisha and Ann M. (Foster) Gilpatrick, both of whom are now deceased. Elisha Gilpatrick, the father, was well known as a dealer in lumber and in timber lands.

Ora Gilpatrick received his preliminary education in the public schools of the community in which he was born. Upon the completion of his studies, he went into the woods with his father, for even at that early age he had commenced to take a keen interest in the lumber and timber land work. This gave him invaluable training and experience for the business career he was to follow, and in which he has met with much success. All of his active life he has been engaged in lumber and timber land dealing. Mr. Gilpatrick was one of the incorporators of the Houlton Trust Company and for the past twelve years has served this institution as president. He is also president of the Summit Lumber Company, George A. Gorham being secretary, while the directors are Mr. Gilpatrick's two sons, Rex E. and Victor A. He is president of the Northern Woodenware Company at Island Falls, Maine; a member of the firm of Gilpatrick & Morehouse Last Block Company; a director of Bangor & Aroostook Railroad, and manager of Keswick Land and Lumber Company.

Despite the many varied and often exacting duties of the work in which he has been engaged, Mr. Gilpatrick has, nevertheless, found time in which to take a keen interest in the affairs of his community, although he has never consented to hold public office. In his political preferences, he is a strong supporter of the Republican party. He has been equally active in his club and social life. In his fraternal affiliations he is a member of Houlton Lodge, Free and Accepted Masons; the Chapter, Royal Arch Masons; St. Aldamer Commandery, Knights Templar; and the Independent Order of Odd Fellows. His clubs are the Houlton Country and the Meduxnekeag.

Ora Gilpatrick married Carrie L. Trask, who is a native of Maine, a daughter of Elias Trask. Mr. and Mrs. Gilpatrick are the parents of two children, both of whom are sons: 1. Victor A., associated in business with his father. 2. Rex E. Mr. Gilpatrick and his family maintain their residence in Houlton, in which community they attend the Unitarian church, of which Mr. Gilpatrick is a trustee.

ALBERT K. STETSON, publisher and owner of the Aroostook "Pioneer," published by the Pioneer Publishing Company, was born on January 26, 1884, at Clyde, New York. His parents removed to Houlton while he was very young, however, and he received his primary education in the public schools of that community. He later attended Colby College, graduating from there with the class of 1907, when he received the degree of Bachelor of Arts.

Since about 1915, Mr. Stetson has been owner and editor of the Aroostook "Pioneer," one of the thoroughly clean and reputable newspapers of this part of the State. The "Pioneer" was the first weekly paper published in Aroostook County, having been founded at Presque Isle, Maine, by W. S. Gilman and the late Hon. Joseph B. Hall. Shortly after the paper was started Mr. Hall withdrew from the partnership but the publication was carried forward by Mr. Gilman who, in 1868, removed it to Houlton. In 1915 it was sold to the Pioneer Publishing Company, of which Mr. Stetson is the head.

Despite the many exacting duties of the work in which he is engaged, Mr. Stetson has found time in which to take a keen and active interest in the civic and general affairs of his community. In his political views he is a Republican, and as such he is a member of the State Republican Committee. He has served for over sixteen years as court recorder, and from 1916 to 1921 he was a member of the Houlton School Board. He is also a member of the board of trustees and treasurer of the Cary Library, and is secretary of the Houlton Business Men's Association. He is president of the Merchants' Press, Incorporated, at Millinocket, Maine. Mr. Stetson served as a delegate to the National convention held at Cleveland, Ohio, and he was appointed county treasurer by Governor Brewster, but resigned before being qualified. He is now chairman of the executive committee of the Maine Press Association and a member of the National Editorial Association.

Albert K. Stetson married Hazel Hewes, and they are the parents of a daughter, Sally Stetson. Mr. Stetson and his family reside in Houlton and attend the Baptist church.

ALBERT TEMPLE PUTNAM—Long years and successful and happy activity have been the lot of Albert Temple Putnam, well known farmer of Houlton, who is also vice-president of the First National Bank of Houlton. Mr. Putnam lives on the big farm where he was born and is also the owner of another tract of land. His father was one of the incorporators of the First National Bank of Houlton.

Lysander Putnam, father of Albert T. Putnam, was born in Woodstock, New Brunswick, in 1806, while his parents, Aaron and Isa (Patrick) Putnam, were on their way from New Salem, Massachusetts, to Houlton, Maine. They were among the first settlers in this section, and the farm on which Albert Temple Putnam now lives was cleared and reclaimed from the wilderness by Lysander Putnam. The rugged life of the pioneer was his from earliest boyhood, and he early developed the hardihood and the resourcefulness which is the heritage of those who tame the wilderness. Great tracts of timber land yielded to his vigorous axe and to the axes of his later helpers, and he became one of the leading citizens of Houlton. He was one of the incorporators of the First National Bank of Houlton, and one of the large landowners of this section. He was a man of ability and influence to the time of his death, which occurred in 1886. He married Ruth Libby.

Albert Temple Putnam, son of Lysander and Ruth (Libby) Putnam, was born on the farm on which he is now living, in Houlton, in November, 1852, and received his education in the local public schools. From boyhood he became his father's helper on the farm, and when school days were over, at the age of seventeen years, he engaged in farming. Throughout his life he has been so occupied and on the large home farm of one hundred and seventy-five acres he is still directing the operations of his helpers. This homestead is located on North Street, Houlton, where Mr. Putnam has lived all his life, but in addition to these acres he also owns another large tract of land. Politically, Mr. Putnam gives his support to the principles of the Democratic party, but he believes that in local affairs personal fitness for office should be a more important consideration than partisanship, and he votes accordingly. Though he is public-spirited and a loyal supporter of all projects planned for the advancement of the general welfare, he has never been willing to assume public office, preferring to serve in the many ways in which a successful business man may contribute to the general good as a private citizen. He is a member of the Independent Order of Odd Fellows, and his religious affiliation is with the Unitarian church.

Albert Temple Putnam was married to Cordelia Putnam, a descendant of another branch of the Putnam family, daughter of Otis and Temperance (Cone) Putnam. Mr. and Mrs. Putnam became the parents of five children: 1. Fred L., engaged in the hardware business in Houlton; married Alice Pearce, and they have two children: Cordelia and Albert. 2. Arthur O., engaged in the hardware business; married Claire Pearce, and they have five children: Isabel, Hannah, Otis, Melen, and Joseph. 3. Emma, wife of Bernard Archibald. 4. Aaron A., an attorney at law of Houlton; married Maria Louise Hacker of Fort Fairfield, Maine, and they have four children: Elizabeth, Hacker, Maria Louise, and John. 5. Beatrice H., wife of Dr. John O. Willy, an osteopath of Houlton. They have one child, Elizabeth Ann. Mrs. Putnam, the mother of this family, died September 15, 1915.

CLARENCE H. PIERCE—The entire career of Clarence H. Pierce has been identified with the hardware business which operates under the name

Maine—2—7

of the Almon H. Fogg Company, of Houlton. Beginning as a clerk, he has maintained his connection with this concern, and for several years has been its president. He is also president of the First National Bank of Houlton.

Clarence H. Pierce was born in Houlton, February 17, 1848, son of Leonard and Elizabeth (Kendall) Pierce, the first mentioned of whom was born in Roxbury, Massachusetts, in 1793, and the last mentioned of whom was born in New Salem, Massachusetts. He attended the public schools of his birthplace and then completed his training in Houlton Academy. He secured his first position as clerk in the employ of the Almon H. Fogg Company, a concern established in 1858, and was engaged in the general hardware and farmers' supply business. He began his connection with this concern in 1866, and two years later was admitted as a partner. During the sixty-two years which have passed since Mr. Pierce became a clerk in this store, his connection has been continuous and he is still very active, both in the affairs of the Almon H. Fogg Company, of which he has been president for many years, and also in banking affairs. The company at the present time (1928) consists of Clarence H. Pierce, president; G. E. Wilkins, vice-president; L. A. Hawkins, secretary, and H. W. Hughes, treasurer. The concern carries a full line of hardware and farmers' supplies and has long ago established a reputation which is its most valuable business asset. Strict integrity in business dealings, thorough knowledge of the general needs of its patrons, and unfailing courtesy and promptness in service have won for this enterprise the confidence and esteem of a very large patronage, and Mr. Pierce's personal reputation for ability and integrity has greatly strengthened the position of this well known business concern. In addition to his responsibilities in connection with the hardware business Mr. Pierce is also active in banking affairs, and is serving as president of the First National Bank of Houlton, of which he was one of the incorporators, and of which he is the second to serve as chief executive. He has been president of this bank for about twenty-five years, and is known and trusted as a financier of skill and sound judgment. He is president of the Houlton Water Company and president of the Houlton Sewer Company. Throughout his life Mr. Pierce has been a public-spirited citizen, always ready to give generous support to any movement which seemed to him to be wisely planned for the advancement of the general welfare, but he has consistently refused to accept any public offices, except those minor local offices in which the knowledge and skill of a successful business man is of most service. He is known as one of the foremost citizens of Aroostook County, and during the years of his long and active life he has made a host of friends, both among his associates of his own age and among those of the younger generation. His ability, his steady adherence to the highest principles of business and civic ethics, and his personal qualities have greatly endeared him to those who know him best, and to his enterprise the town of Houlton owes much. Fraternally he is identified with Monument Lodge, Free and Accepted Masons, and the Chapter, Royal Arch Masons.

Clarence H. Pierce was married to Frances Madigan who died in 1908, daughter of James C. and Mary A. (Smith) Madigan. Mr. and Mrs. Pierce became the parents of four children: 1. Mary, deceased. 2. Winifred, deceased. 3. Leonard A., who is an attorney in Portland, Maine. 4. James M., a dealer in timber land, living in Houlton.

CHARLES MURRAY FOWLER—As Trial Justice of the Fort Fairfield district, Charles Murray Fowler has performed a valued work in the community of Fort Fairfield, Maine, where he has held this office since 1920. He has been a lawyer in this town since September, 1919. At the last public elections he was a candidate for the office of county attorney. Mr. Fowler is one of the leading citizens of the town, being public spirited by nature, and proving himself constantly to be a participant in whatever movement he believes will tend to better his community or conditions therein.

He was born in Smith's Corner, York County, New Brunswick, Canada, on April 21, 1893, a son of Charles I. and Bertha (Hutchison) Fowler, who came to the United States when he was an infant. The father, who is now deceased, was engaged during his lifetime in the clothing business in Presque Isle; and the mother is still living, in Somerville, Massachusetts. Charles Murray Fowler, as a boy, attended the public schools in

Presque Isle, and later the high school in that town, from which he was graduated in the class of 1913. Then he spent a year in the University of New Brunswick, after which he worked his way through law school by being employed in the mills and in a drug store, and also by joining the State Highway police force. Before he went to law school he studied law in the offices of Jerome B. Clark at Presque Isle, now of Milo. He was admitted to the bar in Maine on September 8, 1919, and the United States District Court June 5, 1923, and immediately opened an office in Fort Fairfield. Politically, he is affiliated with the Republican party, whose principles and candidates he supports, and on whose ticket he was a candidate for the office of county attorney. His valuable services as a lawyer and his adaptability to public work caused him to be chosen for the position of Trial Justice of Fort Fairfield district, a position which he has filled with courage and ability. Mr. Fowler has strong fraternal affiliations, being a member of the Independent Order of Odd Fellows, in which he has been admitted to both Encampment and Canton; the Knights of Pythias; and the Free and Accepted Masons, in which order he is identified with the Blue Lodge in Fort Fairfield, the chapter of Royal Arch Masons in Caribou, the Council in Presque Isle, the Commandery in Houlton, and Anah Temple of the Ancient Arabic Order Nobles of the Mystic Shrine in Bangor. Mr. Fowler is a member of the Phi Alpha Delta National Law Fraternity, the Maine and New Brunswick Country Golf Club, the State and County Bar associations; and is now (1928) chairman of the Republican town committee.

Charles M. Fowler married Elizabeth May Reed, a native of Fort Fairfield, a daughter of the late P. H. Reed, and Maria (Foster) Reed, who is living in Fort Fairfield. Both Mr. Fowler and his wife are members of the Congregational church.

JUDGE ROBERT M. LAWLIS, eminent attorney of Houlton, and justice of the Municipal Court of that city, was born in this community on October 19, 1886, son of Martin and Rose Lawlis, the former of whom is deceased. Martin Lawlis who was born on November 4, 1852, in Houlton, and who died there in 1925 in the seventy-third year of his age, was one of the very well known and highly respected men in this community. It is said of him that "By hard work, honesty and integrity, Mr. Lawlis made a success of his life." He was twice elected to the office of sheriff of Aroostook County, serving thus during 1903, 1904, 1905 and 1906, with honor to himself and much satisfaction to the people. Again, in 1924, after the removal of Sheriff Grant, Governor Baxter selected Mr. Lawlis to fill out the unexpired term. The duties during this year were particularly arduous, but such was the administration of Sheriff Lawlis that the Governor saw fit to commend his work " . . . as the best that a Sheriff ever gave in Maine." For nearly half a century Mr. Lawlis served as a constable and deputy sheriff in Houlton; he was tax collector of the town for many years; and he also served on the building committee for the Houlton High School. He was actively instrumental in the establishment of the Houlton Agricultural Society and he gave liberally of his time and effort during the erection of the present agricultural buildings. Later he served as a member of the board of directors of this society and its ensuing exhibitions. During the period of the World War, this indefatigable man was actively engaged as a special investigator or operator in the Department of Justice of the United States Government. He was long prominent in the social and fraternal world of Houlton, for he held a charter membership in the Houlton Lodge, Benevolent and Protective Order of Elks, and for many years served on the board of trustees of the lodge. His work as chairman of the building committee of the present beautiful Elks' Home in Houlton was notable. He gave willingly of his time in the many details which this beautiful building called for. Every detail of its construction was passed upon by Mr. Lawlis and the building today stands as a monument to the work he did for the order which he loved so well. It is worthy of especial mention, as a mark of the great esteem in which he was held, that, at the time of his funeral, every business house in Houlton closed its doors in observance of the passing of a life-long friend. Martin Lawlis was a man beloved by those who knew him well, and respected by all with whom he came in contact.

Robert M. Lawlis received his early education in the grammar and high schools of Houlton, and later attended Bowdoin College, graduating from

the latter in 1911. He pursued his legal training in the Law School of Harvard University, graduating from there with the class of 1914, when he received the degree of Bachelor of Laws. He returned to Houlton, and after being admitted to practice before the bar of Maine, in 1914, he opened an office of his own, carrying on, with an increasing success, a general practice of the law.

Despite his many professional duties, Mr. Lawlis, like his father before him, has found time in which to take a keen and active interest in the civic affairs of his community. In his political views, he is a supporter of the Republican party, and he served for several years as a member of the Republican Town Committee. He has also served as a member of the Municipal Board. In 1923, he was appointed by State Governor Baxter, Justice of the Municipal Court of Houlton, an office which he has filled with ability and dispatch. He is a director of the Farmers' National Bank of Houlton. Judge Lawlis has also been active in the social life of Houlton, for he is fraternally affiliated with Houlton Lodge, Benevolent and Protective Order of Elks, and Houlton Country Club.

Judge Robert M. Lawlis married Alice F. Madigan, a sister of James C. Madigan, whose biography appears in this volume. Judge and Mrs. Lawlis are the parents of two sons: Robert Madigan and Richard Cottrill. Judge Lawlis and his family maintain their residence in Houlton, where they attend the Catholic church.

LELAND O. LUDWIG, treasurer of the Houlton Savings Bank, one of the most honored and respected citizens of Houlton, has the unique distinction of having been treasurer of that institution for forty years. Born on September 18, 1856, in Waldoboro, Maine, Mr. Ludwig is a son of Gorham and Achsah (Mason) Ludwig, both of whom were natives of Maine. Gorham Ludwig, the father, was a well-known shipbuilder of the North Atlantic coast.

Leland O. Ludwig received his early education in the district schools of the community in which he was born, later attending Lincoln Academy, at Newcastle, Maine. For a short period after the completion of his studies, he lived in Ohio, where he learned telegraphy. Giving up this work, he returned to Maine and went into the insurance business, which he followed for about two years. Not satisfied with this occupation, and desiring to further his ambitions, he entered the Houlton Savings Bank, as a clerk. Here his abilities were soon recognized, and he rose rapidly to higher positions. In 1888 he was made treasurer and a director of the Houlton Savings Bank, and he has held that position since, having been associated with the bank for almost half a century.

Mr. Ludwig has ever found time in which to serve the people of his community in other than a private capacity, and for eight years was treasurer of Aroostook County. In his political preferences he is a supporter of the Republican party. He has been prominent in club and social life and is affiliated with the Benevolent and Protective Order of Elks, and the Independent Order of Odd Fellows.

Leland O. Ludwig married Elloise Bagley, who was born in Presque Isle, Aroostook County, a daughter of John and Jennie (Whidden) Bagley. Mrs. Ludwig's father died while in service during the Civil War. Mr. and Mrs. Ludwig became the parents of three children: 1. Lawrence G., who conducts a farm in Aroostook County; married Tressa Hoyt, and by her became the father of two children, John H. and Elloise. 2. Leland O., Jr., who resides in New Britain, Connecticut. 3. Richard B., engaged in the insurance business in Boston, Massachusetts, as special agent for the John Hancock Company; married Vera Bernice Edwards. Mr. and Mrs. Ludwig maintain their residence in Houlton, in which community they attend the Congregational church.

JAMES C. MADIGAN, prominent attorney of Houlton and a member of the well-known firm of lumber dealers operated by himself and James M. Pierce, was born on December 29, 1890, at Houlton, a son of John Bernard and Lucia Jennette (Rose) Madigan, both of whom are prominent in this State. John Bernard Madigan is also an attorney of note who, in 1916, was appointed a Justice of the Supreme Court of Maine, by Governor Curtis.

James C. Madigan received his early education in the grammar and high schools of the community

in which he was born, and graduated from Georgetown University with the class of 1913. He obtained his legal training at the University of Boston, graduating from there with the class of 1916. After the completion of these courses of study he returned to Houlton, opened an office for himself, and has since carried on a successful general practice in that community. He has also assumed a number of outside interests, among the more important of these being partnership, as above noted, with James M. Pierce, in the lumber business. During the period of the emergency created by the entry of the United States into the World War, Mr. Madigan served in the United States Navy. He enlisted on July 8, 1918, and remained for a full enlistment period of four years.

James C. Madigan married Doris Waterall, of Philadelphia, Pennsylvania, and they have four sons and one daughter: 1. John Bernard, 2d. 2. Mary Anna. 3. James C., 4th. 4. William W. 5. Albert, 2d. Mr. Madigan and his family maintain their residence in Houlton, in which community they attend the Catholic church.

ARTHUR G. LOCKHART—One of the leading bankers of Fort Fairfield, Maine, is Arthur G. Lockhart, who is treasurer of the Frontier Trust Company, of Fort Fairfield, a position which he has held since 1918. For many years prior to his connection with this institution, he was engaged in the banking business in Canada. He takes a prominent part in the civic and social life of his community, and is deeply interested in local church work. He and his family are members of the Baptist church, of which he is treasurer, and of whose Sunday School he is superintendent. Both he and his wife are active in the affairs of the church.

Mr. Lockhart was born in Falmouth, Nova Scotia, on October 7, 1887, a son of the late Charles and Beatrice (Lynch) Lockhart. His ancestors originally came from the United States, but for a time made their homes in Nova Scotia. His parents never came to the United States, and he received his education in Canada, being a graduate of Windsor Academy, in Nova Scotia. When he finished his schooling, Mr. Lockhart became engaged in the lumber business for a year, after which he spent a year and one-half with the postoffice in Windsor. His next work was as book-keeper for the Dominion Textile Company; but finally he gave up this work to go into banking. His first association with financial institutions was with the Union Bank of Halifax, in Parrsboro, a branch of the Halifax bank. Since that time he has continued in banking. When he came to the United States he left a position as manager of the Edmundston, New Brunswick, branch of the Royal Bank of Canada. And since November 13, 1918, he has been the treasurer of the Frontier Trust Company, of Fort Fairfield. His fraternal affiliations are with the Independent Order of Odd Fellows and the Foresters of America and the Free and Accepted Masons, in the last of which orders he is a member of the Blue Lodge, in Fort Fairfield, and of the Caribou Chapter of Royal Arch Masons. He is a member of the Rotary Club, of Fort Fairfield.

Arthur G. Lockhart married Ethel M. Smith, who is a native of Windsor, Nova Scotia. Arthur G. and Ethel M. (Smith) Lockhart are the parents of the following children: Roy, Hugh, Charles, Clare, and Joyce.

PRESTON N. BURLEIGH, United States postmaster at Houlton, and a man who has done a considerable amount of civil engineering, being a graduate in this type of endeavor, was born on February 18, 1866, at Oakfield, in this State. Mr. Burleigh is a son of Albert A. and Lucinda G. (Collins) Burleigh, both of whom were native-born to Maine. Albert A. Burleigh, the father, a civil engineer and railroad man, was for many years the president of the Bangor & Aroostook Railroad.

Preston N. Burleigh received his early education in the public schools of the community in which he was born, and attended Ricker Classical Institute at Houlton. He then studied at Colby College, graduating with the class of 1887, after which he studied for a year at Harvard Law school. After the completion of these studies, he went to Wisconsin, where he remained for more than five years, being engaged there as a civil engineer and also in the lumber business. He then returned to Maine, where he carried on his work as a civil engineer for the railroad and also a

private practice of his own, continuing thus until 1923, when he was appointed United States postmaster at Houlton. This is a second class post-office, having as its assistant, Burns McIntire. There are five regular clerks and one auxiliary, and five regular carriers and an auxiliary who is entirely engaged in handling the parcel post matter at this office. The Houlton postoffice makes deliveries over six rural free delivery routes.

Mr. Burleigh is a staunch supporter of the Republican party, and served one term as a member of the Houlton Board of Selectmen. He holds membership in the Meduxnekeag Club and in Houlton Lodge, Benevolent and Protective Order of Elks.

Preston N. Burleigh married Kate Pearce, a daughter of Joseph and Harriett (Williams) Pearce of Fort Fairfield. Three children have been born to Mr. and Mrs. Burleigh: 1. Albert P., who held the rank of lieutenant in the United States Navy, and who died in the twenty-sixth year of his age. 2. Ralph W., who served with the rank of ensign in the United States Navy; now a teacher in Hollywood High School, Los Angeles, California. 3. Robert, living in Los Angeles, California. Mr. Burleigh and his family maintain their residence in Houlton, in which community they attend the Congregational church.

LEO H. MURPHY—In order to hold the position of superintendent of a town farm, it is necessary to have knowledge of farming, ability to handle unskilled labor, a disposition of kindliness mixed with firmness, and an untiring energy to persevere against many untoward conditions and circumstances. Also, there is great difference from handling an institution for the public and in taking care of one's own possession. Leo H. Murphy, superintendent of the town farm at Presque Isle, Maine, has been a farmer all of his life and is in every way fitted for the position which he so admirably fills and which he has held since July 4, 1915. The average number of people on this farm are seven annually. In order to care for these and to make the farm productive, Mr. Murphy has to be the director of all activities and to watch and arrange for the marketing of the products and to see that the yield is all that can be got from the land. He is the son of George and Mary (Duncan) Murphy, citizens of New Brunswick. His father was born in Ireland in the northern part, and his mother was born in Scotland. Both came to New Brunswick in their early youth and remained there. The father is now retired and lives in Connecticut. His mother died a few years ago.

Leo H. Murphy was born in New Brunswick on December 24, 1890. He had some public school training, but has worked his own way in the rough road of experience since he was twelve years of age, at which time he was thrown on his own resources. He was not satisfied with the little schooling he had and, while working on a farm near Fredericton, New Brunswick, he attended night school in the town. After finishing his school work, he continued to work on a farm as a hired man. In 1902, when still a boy, he came to Presque Isle and continued as a hired hand on a farm for three years. At the end of that time he got himself a job in a paper mill. He worked in the paper mill for four years and then returned to the occupation of farming. He has never owned a farm, but always found work for others, as his ability was such that he never had any difficulty in obtaining employment; and when the time came when someone was needed to take the superintendence of the Town Farm, he was chosen as one who could fill the position and has given proof of the good judgment of those who put him into the position. For twelve years he has given most satisfactory service in the conduct of this institution and continues to hold the esteem and respect of all citizens in this community. Mr. Murphy is a member of the Masonic Order, the Independent Order of Odd Fellows, Rebekah, the Encampment and the Independent Order of Odd Fellows Club.

Leo H. Murphy married Jennie Sarsfield, who was born in New Brunswick. They have three children: Harold Ainsley, Merle Leo, and Mildred Dolores.

GLEN R. CHENEY—Bringing to the automobile business a varied experience in merchandising, and with public utility corporations, Glen R. Cheney started an auto repair business in Washburn, Maine, in 1916, and in 1920 established

the Washburn Motor Company, of which he is president and treasurer. Born at Four Falls, New Brunswick, Canada, September 18, 1892, he was the son of Isaac G. and Mary (Cox) Cheney, who brought him to the United States when he was one year old. Originally a building contractor, the elder Cheney became a minister of the Methodist Episcopal church. He died in December, 1924, and his widow lives in Washburn, Maine.

After being graduated from the Limestone High School, Glen R. Cheney spent a year at the University of Maine, and then found employment as a clerk in Harry Leighton's grocery, in Limestone. From there he went to the Maine & New Brunswick Light & Power Company, where he remained one year, going next to the Washburn Electric Company, where, after four years of service, he started in business for himself. The Washburn Motor Company deals in Ford products, among other things, and employs a staff of eight men. The directors are E. O. Woodman, vice-president and clerk, Woodbury L. Pearce, Harold L. Learned, Milton J. Stairs, and Mr. Cheney. He is a member of Washburn Lodge, Free and Accepted Masons; the Presque Isle Chapter, Royal Arch Masons; and the Council, of Presque Isle. He is a member of the Rotary Club and is a member of the Methodist Episcopal church.

Glen R. Cheney married Eva Ward, daughter of John and Alice (Willey) Ward, and their children are Winifred, Jean and Mary.

HARRY R. O'DONNELL—One of the best known men in Presque Isle and Aroostook County is Harry R. O'Donnell, who is treasurer and general manager of the Aroostook Wholesale Grocery Company, of Presque Isle. This company was the first dealing in wholesale groceries ever organized in the county, and was founded by John H. O'Donnell, father of Harry R. O'Donnell, and pioneer merchant of the vicinity. It was he who made the name O'Donnell respected throughout the county wherever he was known; he died in 1923. Besides Harry R. O'Donnell the other officers of the grocery company are: President, M. S. Donahue; secretary and clerk, Carl A. Weick.

Harry R. O'Donnell was born at Presque Isle, July 22, 1894, son of John H. and Addie (Jackson) O'Donnell, both natives of Presque Isle, the mother now (1928) living, at Presque Isle. Mr. O'Donnell received his early education in the public schools and entered Shaw's Business College, graduating with a thorough comprehension of the theories and routine practices of business. Immediately he joined his father in the grocery business, then handling goods at retail. He was with him when the wholesale company was established, and has been active in its direction from the first. Mr. O'Donnell, like his father before him, is regarded with sincere respect wherever he is known, and has many close and influential acquaintances throughout county and State. He takes part in local political matters, aligning himself under the principles of the Democratic party. His opinions in questions of politics and public welfare, as well as in the direction of political and commercial campaigns are sought after. He is a member of the Presque Isle Merchants' Association, the Rotary Club, and the Mooseleuk Club.

Harry R. O'Donnell married Violet Watson, and they have one child, a son, John H.

MERLE D. STEVENS—The entire active career of Merle D. Stevens has been identified with the Fort Fairfield Light and Power Company, of which he is treasurer and general manager. The business was established by Mr. Stevens' father, but since the death of the father has been operated by the son and the widow.

Hiram Delbert Stevens, father of Mr. Stevens, was born in Fort Fairfield, Maine, November 23, 1863, son of Hiram and Sarah (Whitney) Stevens. He received his education in the local schools of Fort Fairfield and in Ricker Classical Institute, and then for several years was associated with his father in the lumber business and in farming. He was an able and resourceful business man and in later years established the Fort Fairfield Light and Power Company, of which he was head to the time of his death in 1924. He was a Republican in his political faith, and fraternally was identified with the Independent Order of Odd Fellows; and with the Masonic order, in which he held the thirty-second degree. He was a man who commanded in a high degree the respect and esteem of his associates, and his death on September 5, 1924, at the age of sixty years and ten months was a distinct loss to the community. His religious affiliation was with the Congregational church.

Hiram Delbert Stevens was married, January 28, 1888, to Mary G. Haines, daughter of Albert and Mary (Currier) Haines, and they became the parents of four children: 1. Arthur A., received his education in the public schools of Fort Fairfield, and died at the age of twenty-six years. He married Mildred Armstrong, and they had two children, Naomi and Hiram. 2. Merle D., of further mention. 3. Bernice, wife of Preston Boyd, has three children, Robert William, Mary Joan and Marjorie Dawn. 4. Florence K., wife of Morris Downing, lives in Newport, Maine.

Merle D. Stevens, son of Hiram Delbert and Mary G. (Haines) Stevens, was born in Fort Fairfield, Maine, May 2, 1894, and received his education in the public schools of his birthplace. When school days were over he became associated with his father in the Fort Fairfield Light and Power Company, and that association was continued until the death of his father, September 5, 1924. Since that time the business has been continued by Mrs. Hiram Delbert Stevens and other officials of the company, with Merle D. Stevens as treasurer and general manager. The company employs, usually, on an average, four experienced men and one clerk, and is giving to the town of Fort Fairfield and vicinity most excellent service. Mr. Stevens is a supporter of the principles and the candidates of the Republican party, and fraternally is identified with the Knights of Pythias. He is well known in this locality, and is one of the public-spirited citizens of the town. He has a host of friends, and is known not only as a successful business man but also as a congenial associate and a loyal friend. He and his family attend the Congregational church.

Merle D. Stevens is married to May Nickerson, who was born in Nova Scotia, and whose parents always lived in Nova Scotia. Mr. and Mrs. Stevens have two sons: Albert Merle and Gilbert Earle.

THOMAS VINCENT DOHERTY, a prominent lawyer of Houlton, Maine, and long a resident of this community, was born on April 5, 1870, at Woodstock, New Brunswick, a son of James E. and Elizabeth (Smith) Doherty, both of whom resided in Houlton for many years. On the maternal side, members of his family have been natives of Maine for several generations, while the father removed to Houlton in 1871.

Thomas Vincent Doherty received his early education in the public schools of Houlton, and attended the Ricker Classical Institute. He then studied at Bowdoin College, graduating from there with the class of 1895, after which he studied law under the competent preceptorship of two very well known attorneys of Augusta, Williams and Burleigh. Mr. Doherty was formally admitted to the Bar of Maine in 1897, after which he began the practice of his profession in the town of Caribou, in this State. He later spent some time at Butte, Montana, but returned to Maine in 1903, and began practice at Houlton. Although never a seeker of public office, Mr. Doherty has taken a keen interest in the civic and general affairs of his community, being, in his political views, a firm supporter of the Democratic party.

Thomas Vincent Doherty married Lucy F. Tenney, a daughter of Charles P. and Mary S. (Pierce) Tenney, of Houlton. Mr. and Mrs. Doherty maintain their residence in Houlton, in which community Mr. Doherty attends the Catholic church.

EDWIN E. PARKHURST—Making a specialty of seed potatoes, Edwin E. Parkhurst, of Presque Isle, Maine, is associated with his father in operating one of the larger farms in this section. He is the son of Daniel Vincent and Maude (Tompkins) Parkhurst. His mother is now deceased and the elder Mr. Parkhurst continues active with his son.

Edwin E. Parkhurst was born on the farm which he now operates, in December, 1893. He received all of his schooling in Presque Isle and, after completing his school work, became immediately interested in helping his father to carry on the farm. This is one of the large farms on the Parkhurst Road, and has always been known as greatly productive of good crops. It has been brought up to a high state of cultivation both by Mr. Parkhurst and his son and as most of the potatoes raised here are sold for seed purposes

they are an especially selected stock and by great diligence the grade is kept up. The farm is of three hundred and twenty acres and it is enough for the two men to oversee with needed attention for the kind of work they are doing, that is producing high grade seed crops. Mr. Parkhurst, in partnership with Clayton Turner, also owns and operates another farm of one hundred and eighty-seven acres on the Portage Lake Road. Mr. Parkhurst is a member of the Grange; the Mooseleuk Club; and the order of Free and Accepted Masons in which organization he has taken all the degrees leading up to and including the Ancient Arabic Order Nobles of the Mystic Shrine. He is a Republican in politics and a member of the Congregational church.

Edwin E. Parkhurst married Muriel McGowan, a daughter of J. H. McGowan, of Ashland, Maine. They have two children: Marilynn and Carolynn.

JOHN DROST—Many of the finest buildings in Washburn, Maine, were erected by John Drost, who has been a contractor and builder there for many years, and usually employs a force of from twelve to twenty-five workmen.

Born in Carleton County, New Brunswick, Canada, January 24, 1853, he was the son of James and Charlotte (Brown) Drost. His mother's people were Americans, although she was born in the province of New Brunswick, her father having been a veteran of the War of 1812. The elder Drost, who was a lumberman, brought his family to the United States in early manhood, and became an American citizen. John Drost, who had worked in the forests for thirty-six years, acquiring a complete knowledge of lumbering as well as woodcraft, first mastered the carpenter's trade, and then went into business for himself as a contractor and builder.

He has been very successful, and also owns an interest in a general store in New Brunswick with his brother. Mr. Drost is a Republican, and a member of the Baptist church. He is a member of the Independent Order of Odd Fellows, and of the local Rebekah Lodge. He is also an Orangeman.

Mr. Drost has five children: Hattie, Coley, Amanda, Minnie and Lottie

CHARLES FRANKLIN WEST—Among the outstanding and well-known citizens having the welfare and progress of Presque Isle, Aroostook County, as their constant endeavor, is Charles Franklin West, who is part owner, secretary and treasurer and general manager of the Presque Isle "Star-Herald." This journal, which upholds its pages to the highest ethics of journalism, was founded as a weekly the latter half of the nineteenth century. For years it was owned entirely by George H. Collins, until 1910, when a reorganization was effected. In the articles of incorporation Mr. Collins became president of the company and in that capacity continued until 1919, also serving as editor; but in 1919 he relinquished the direction of the paper to Mr. West, still functioning, however, as editor in chief until July 1, 1928. When the company was organized in 1910, Mr. Larrabee and Perley Brown, attorney, were named incorporators with Mr. Collins; now (1928) Mr. Phair is clerk of the company, in which office he has been a number of years, and Mrs. Charlotte H. West, wife of Mr. West and daughter of Mr. Collins, is president and has been since 1925, when her father withdrew from the directorial office. Presque Isle is one of the most charming little cities in Maine. Its population is approximately 5,000; its industries are diversified and profitable, and its railway services complete, as it is cut by three roads. The "Star-Herald" is constantly in the foreground as leader in campaigns for the betterment of the community, and as manager and business director of the paper Mr. West is, therefore, numbered conspicuously among the town's most public-spirited citizens. He has a wide acquaintance in Aroostook County and is president of the Aroostook County Press Association; also, he is an active member of the Maine State Press Association; and in both bodies as well as in his own community he is highly respected as a journalist and man of character.

Charles Franklin West is a native of Canada. He was born at Centerville, Carleton County, New Brunswick, on December 1, 1886, and received his early education in the public schools of Centerville. Then he matriculated in the Provincial Normal School at Fredericton, New Brunswick, where he pursued academic courses of study until he became interested in electrical engineering, when he left the normal school and entered the Hawley School of Engineering, at Boston,

Massachusetts. Upon completion of the engineering courses he entered the employ of the Gould Electrical Company, Presque Isle, and remained there two years, after which he returned to the province of New Brunswick, to act as manager and superintendent of the electric light department in the town of Grand Falls. As manager of the light department and superintendent of the water works he continued for three years, then returned to the United States, to Presque Isle, and purchased an interest in the "Star-Herald." From the first, his management of this journal has been successful. As its business director he has wide and intimate connections with prominent men, and maintains a number of fraternal and social affiliations. He is a member of the Presque Isle Rotary Club, the Merchants' Association, the Independent Order of Odd Fellows, Free and Accepted Masons, being a Knight Templar and member of the Shrine; and a Unitarian. He is liberal in his contributions to charity.

Charles Franklin West married Charlotte H. Collins, of Presque Isle, daughter of Mr. and Mrs. George H. Collins, and they are the parents of two children, a son, George E., and a daughter, Mary Anna. Mrs. West is a member of the Episcopal church.

————

TOM E. HACKER—For three generations the Hacker family has been identified with the business and financial life of Fort Fairfield, Maine, where Tom E. Hacker, while continuing his father's business as a hardware merchant, as treasurer of the Ames & Hacker Company, is president of the Fort Fairfield National Bank.

Although the Hackers are an old Maine family, long settled at Bangor, the first to make their home in Fort Fairfield were Isaac and Violet (Eastman) Hacker, who moved there a few years after their marriage, taking with them their young son, Jerry Frank Hacker. Isaac Hacker established a successful general store and took Jerry Frank Hacker into the business as soon as he completed his schooling. For the rest of his life Jerry Frank Hacker continued a merchant, adding dry goods to his general lines, for a time in partnership with Amos Libby, but after Mr. Libby's death, carrying on the business under his own name. In early life a Republican, he later became associated with the activities of the Democratic party, and filled several local offices creditably. He was a member of the Free and Accepted Masons. Mr. Hacker married (first) Almeda Libby, born in Albion, Maine, daughter of Daniel Libby; and married (second) Elizabeth E. Trafton, daughter of Mark and Maria L. (Libby) Trafton. Five children were born of these two marriages, of whom the two now living are Tom E. Hacker, whose sketch follows, and Maria L. (Hacker) Putnam, wife of Aaron A. Putnam, of Houlton, Maine. The Hackers were members of the Protestant Episcopal church.

Son of Jerry Frank and Elizabeth E. (Trafton) Hacker, Tom E. Hacker was born July 15, 1884, at Fort Fairfield, Maine. He was educated in the Fort Fairfield schools, and at Bowdoin College, where he was graduated in 1907 with the degree of A. B. He then entered his father's and grandfather's business in Fort Fairfield, and soon acquired the reputation for progressiveness and sound judgment which led to his election as president of the Fort Fairfield National Bank in 1920, an institution with which he had been associated since 1910. Mr. Hacker, who is an independent in politics, is now first selectman of Fort Fairfield. He is a member of the Free and Accepted Masons, Fairfield Chapter of the Royal Arch Masons, Caribou Commandery of the Knights Templar of Houlton, and Anah Temple, Ancient Arabic Order Nobles of the Mystic Shrine, of Bangor, Maine. He is a communicant of the Protestant Episcopal church and a vestryman.

Mr. Hacker married Sarah Curry Burns, daughter of Frank W. and Eliza (Slocum) Burns, and their five children are: Jerry, Mary, Tom B., Richard S., and June Hacker.

MYRON L. WILLIAMS—One of the most progressive enterprises in the town of Presque Isle is the steam laundry which was established here many years ago by A. M. Mosier and Howe. After the business became a fixture in the commercial enterprise of the town, it was sold to Mr. Holt who owned and ran it until it was bought by the present owner and proprietor, Myron L. Williams. Mr. Williams has made this one of the up-to-date concerns and by his industrious attitude it is easy to see that it will continue to lead in first

class laundry work as long as he has to do with its management. Mr. Williams is the son of Daniel and Alsade (Rose) Williams, both of whom were born in Maine. In his early life Daniel Williams was a miner and prospector in Colorado and California and after spending many years in this experience, he returned to his native State and settled at Bradford.

Myron L. Williams was born at Bradford, Maine, on December 9, 1881, and received his schooling in the public schools of Bangor, Maine. He was inclined to school work and when only ten years of age he got a position as a clerk in a general store. He kept on in business in the town of Bridgewater where he was clerking until he became old enough to go into railroading and then he became a baggagemaster in Massachusetts, and later became a freight clerk on the New York, New Haven and Hartford Railroad. He was in the railroad business for four years when he was again drawn to his native State, coming to Presque Isle, where he bought the laundry from Mr. Holt. He is a Republican, a member of the Modern Woodmen of America, a Knight of Pythias, and attends the Congregational church.

Myron L. Williams married Lottie Bell Barrett, who was born at Bridgewater, Maine, the daughter of Edward C. and Etta M. (Collins) Barrett. They have two children: 1. Gerald Evan, a student at the United States Military Academy at West Point. 2. Ruth, who is a student of the Presque Isle High School.

FAY F. LARRABEE, M. D.—For the last fifteen years Dr. Fay F. Larrabee has been the health officer of Washburn, Maine, and it goes without saying that he is one of the most widely known and popular physicians in the community. Son of Dr. Charles C. and Annie (Marble) Larrabee, he was born in Brocton, Maine, November 14, 1881. Dr. Charles C. Larrabee is now living at Prospect Harbor, Maine, where he continues the practice of his rofession, although now past eighty years of age. Mrs. Larrabee died in 1907.

Educated in the public schools of Prospect Harbor, and at Westbrook Seminary, he took a preparatory course in medicine at the University of Maine, and then became a student in the Medical Department of the University of Maryland,

Baltimore, Maryland, where he was graduated in the class of 1906. He then returned to Maine, and began the practice of his profession in East Corinth. Dr. Larrabee is a Republican. He attends the Baptist church and is a member of the Free and Accepted Masons, Chapter and Commandery.

Dr. Fay F. Larrabee married Julia Wibby, their two children being Frederick and Willard Larrabee.

REV. JAMES AUGUSTINE HAYES—Since 1915 the rector of the Roman Catholic Church of the Holy Nativity of the Blessed Virgin at Presque Isle, Maine, has been the Rev. James Augustine Hayes, himself a Maine man by birth, and a former chaplain of the United States Navy Yard at Kittery, Maine. Father Hayes' friends and admirers are by no means confined to the faith he serves so loyally.

Born in Portland, Maine, in 1873, he was the son of Mathew J. and Mary E. (Leahy) Hayes, both natives of Ireland, although they were married in Portland. He received his early education in the public and high schools of his native city, and then entered St. Mary's Academy at Van Buren, Maine, where he graduated in the class of 1895. From there he went to the Grand Seminary at Montreal, where he spent two years in the study of philosophy, and the next four years in the study of theology. He was raised to the priesthood in 1900 at the Cathedral of the Immaculate Conception in Portland, by the Rt. Rev. Bishop Healy, and was assigned to St. Michael's Church in South Berwick, Maine, as an assistant, and later transferred to St. John's Church, Bangor. From there he was sent to Winn as administrator, and his next appointment was as chaplain at the Navy Yard, where he served three years.

Father Hayes has twelve hundred souls in his parish, and is also responsible for St. Joseph's Chapel, the mission at Mars Hill, with fifty; and St. Catherine's Chapel, the mission at Washburn, Maine, with eighteen more. He is chaplain of the Presque Isle Council of the Knights of Columbus.

HARRY D. ALLEN—Since 1909 Harry D. Allen, in association with Lewis S. Bean, has operated the Bean and Allen farm, on Houlton

Road, near the village of Presque Isle, Maine. This farm, which is one of the most fertile in the vicinity, is devoted largely to raising seed potatoes, and to the breeding and pasturing of cattle, in both of which pursuits Mr. Allen is widely experienced and thoroughly familiar with the methods calculated to give the best results. He and his partner raise annually many barrels of potatoes, and own at present eighty-five head of registered Holstein cattle, sixty-seven of which are pure bred. Aside from his business Mr. Allen is interested in civic affairs, and heartily supports any movement designed to promote the welfare of the community.

He was born on September 2, 1884, in York County, province of New Brunswick, Canada, the son of George H. and Anna Bell (Christy) Allen, of that place. His father, a farmer, left Canada and came to the United States with his family, finally settling near the village of Presque Isle, Maine. Mr. and Mrs. George H. Allen are now (1928) living in Presque Isle.

Harry D. Allen attended the public schools of his birthplace and when still a boy he left to begin farm work. He came to the United States and at the age of seventeen commenced work on the farm of L. J. Bean, near Presque Isle, Maine. Four years later Mr. Bean died and Mr. Allen assumed the management of the farm, this arrangement continuing until 1909. In that year a partnership was formed between Mr. Allen and L. S. Bean, and they have jointly operated the farm since that time with considerable success. Politically, Mr. Allen is a member of the Republican party. He and his family attend the Free Baptist church.

He married Inez B. Billing, who was born in York County, province of New Brunswick, Canada, the daughter of George and Evangeline (Crabb) Billing, of that place. Mr. and Mrs. Allen are the parents of one child, Pauline.

WILLIE ESTES, a carpenter and farmer at Presque Isle, Maine, where he lived most of his life, and where he died August 7, 1920. He was a self-made man, a good neighbor and friend, and was respected by everybody. When he died he owned a farm of one hundred and sixty acres on the old Houlton Road.

Willie Estes was born at Newry, Maine, February 14, 1860, son of William H. and Rose (Emory) Estes, of whom the mother was the daughter of Judge Emory of Portland. He came to Presque Isle when a boy of six years, and lived the rest of his life in that town and neighborhood. The land was largely uncultivated country when he arrived in the district, but he soon acquired some property of his own, and added to it, cultivating it, while pursuing also his trade of carpenter, erecting buildings for himself as well as for others. He was a Republican in politics, and belonged to the Grange. The farm of a hundred and sixty acres now belongs to the widow of Willie Estes and her son, George, who lives on the farm with his mother.

Willie Estes married Rachel L. Rowse, who was born in King's County, New Brunswick, the daughter of John and Mary (Goggin) Rowse, the father born in New York, while the mother was born in the province of New Brunswick. Mrs. Mary Rowse came to the United States when she was four years old. Children of Mr. and Mrs. Estes: 1. Owen Henry, who died when he was eighteen years old. 2. Elsie L., now the wife of Robert Perry, living at Yakima, Washington. 3. George, residing at home with his mother, married Ruth Elloise Whidden, and they have three children: Amy Evelyn, Christine Jennette, and Doris Elsie. The family attends the Methodist church.

CLARENCE W. FITZPATRICK—Practically the whole of his life has been spent on the farm of which Clarence W. Fitzpatrick, of Presque Isle, Maine, is now manager, his father, who owns it, having retired in 1927. The property consists of one hundred and seventy acres on the State Highway between Presque Isle and Easton, and is highly productive. Born in Woodstock, Carleton County, June 11, 1899, he is the son of John A. and Jennie (Crabb) Fitzpatrick, both of whom were born in New Brunswick, but removed to Maine when their son was three years old.

Educated in the public schools of his home town, Clarence W. Fitzpatrick found congenial employment on the farm under his father's supervision, and for a long time they worked the place on shares.

He is a communicant of the Roman Catholic church, and is active in the affairs of the Knights of Columbus. He is a Democrat.

Clarence W. Fitzpatrick married Rena Parker, who was born in Fort Fairfield, Maine, a daughter of Humphrey Parker.

MEDVILLE B. HAYFORD—One of the finest farms in the Presque Isle section of Maine is owned by Medville (Med) B. Hayford. Some five hundred acres in extent, it is situated on the State Road between Presque Isle and Caribou, and here Mr. Hayford raises potatoes and other general farm produce for sale to local buyers. Mr. Hayford has been active in the civic and fraternal life of his community, and is highly esteemed as a public-spirited citizen. His father, Columbus Hayford, born at Salem, Maine, was a farmer for many years, and died January 7, 1928, at the age of ninety-one years and seven months. He came to Aroostook County when he was only two years old, and eventually bought and cleared the farm where Mr. Hayford now resides. He married Lavinia Pratt, born at Phillips, Maine, and now deceased, and Medville is their son.

Medville B. Hayford was born on June 26, 1870, on the family farm in the town of Presque Isle, Maine. He attended the local public schools and the old Saint John's Seminary, and when he completed his education at the age of nineteen, he took over the management of the farm. When he was twenty-one his father gave him a deed of half interest in the property, and since that time he has continued to raise his crops there, specializing in growing potatoes. Mr. Hayford is thoroughly familiar with the best farming methods and has been very successful in his chosen occupation.

Politically, he is a member of the Republican party. He is affiliated fraternally with the Ancient Free and Accepted Masons, in which organization he has taken the degrees of the Chapter, Council, and Commandery, and is also a member of the Ancient Arabic Order of the Mystic Shrine. He is a members of the Mooseleuk Club at Presque Isle, and of the Natooka Club of Caribou. He and his family attend the local Congregational church.

Medville B. Hayford married Grace Greenlaw,

who was born at Presque Isle, the daughter of Samuel and Mary (Sprague) Greenlaw. Mr. and Mrs. Hayford are the parents of one child, Alicia, who was married to Dr. Forrest S. Walker, a dentist, at Presque Isle. They have one child, Betty.

ELWIN MARION RACKLIFF—Present (1928) owner of a farm that has been in his family since 1847, when his grandfather began the work of clearing and breaking ground, Elwin Marion Rackliff lives on a fertile tract of two hundred and forty acres, situated at the intersection of the Maine State Highway and the old Easton Road, near Presque Isle, in Aroostook County. Though he retired from active work of agriculture many years since, Mr. Rackliff continues to make his residence on the farm, and rents out the fields on shares to neighboring farmers; moreover, he still maintains his interest in affairs of Easton and Presque Isle, and is known for the readiness with which he consents to take part in any kind of project for the promotion of either town.

Elwin Marion Rackliff was born on the farm near Presque Isle on May 9, 1864, son of Francis M. and Frances (Ordway) Rackliff, both of whom were natives of Maine, his father having been born on the Presque Isle farm. This tract was first owned by Alanson Rackliff, grandfather of Elwin. Elwin Rackliff attended school at Presque Isle, under difficulties, for the family was poor, and it was necessary for him, at the age of eight years, to assist in the working of the farm. During the period of cultivation he used to walk behind a plow drawn by three sturdy horses, truly an accomplishment for one of his tender years. During the life of his grandfather most of the farm land had been cleared of trees and brush, and while Elwin Rackliff was a boy and youth he was busily engaged at all possible moments completing the cleaning. Hence, burdened with the occupations of plowing and tree cutting, it was a difficult matter for Mr. Rackliff to find time for classes; but he did manage, somehow, and secured for himself a comprehensive schooling, to which age and experience have added profusely. The first house and granary on the land were constructed by the father and grandfather, of logs hewn with their own hands and by them erected; later, of logs, they

constructed a larger dwelling of one and one-half stories, with more extensive outbuildings and barns; and when Elwin Rackliff assumed charge of the farm he constructed one of the finest houses in the neighborhood, two stories tall, with a fine outlay of structures properly arranged for grain and other produce, and for livestock. He has built and rebuilt, and the farm is now (1928) one of the most pleasing to the eye in Aroostook County. Just as Mr. Rackliff has spent his whole career upon this farm, so is his interest there involved entirely, to the farm and its neighborhood, the county. A member of the Republican party, he is loyal to its principles and supports it constantly. In 1924, when he was sixty years of age, Mr. Rackliff rented the fields of his farm on shares, as heretofore noted, and retired from active work upon it, preferring to spend the eventide of life on the land in a tranquility richly earned.

Mr. Rackliff, like his parents, who were members, attends the Adventist church. Worthy causes in quest of donations are not turned aside by him; his contributions to charity have always been readily forthcoming and substantial. Of him it is said by his neighbors: that he is of high character, honorable in all his dealings, and a good citizen.

JOHN W. ERSKINE—"The Poplars" is one of the most beautiful farms in the Presque Isle-Easton district of Maine, where it is situated on the State Highway between these two cities. This farm, owned by John W. Erskine, a member of an old Maine family, consists of seventy acres on which Mr. Erskine does a general farming business and specializes in potatoes, for which this section is so noted, and which he sells to local buyers. He himself is an active and loyal citizen in this community, being thoroughly interested in all plans for public improvement. He holds memberships in several clubs, organizations and fraternal orders.

Mr. Erskine was born in Bradford, Maine, on April 18, 1870, the son of Roger A. and Elmira H. (Williams) Erskine, both of whom were descended from old Maine families. When he was only four years old he came to Easton with his parents. As a boy he attended the public schools of both Easton and Presque Isle. Then, going on the farm with his father, he helped to pay for the home farm by his work on it and by acting as guide for parties going through this section in the winters. His own first farm he bought from Llewelyn Powers. Since this farm was considerably run down, many local citizens thought that Mr. Erskine was making a mistake in purchasing it; but he, undaunted by their warnings, bought it and paid for it in the first year of his ownership. He operated it for three years, then sold it, and bought a farm of two hundred and ninety acres, which he continued to operate for twenty years. At the end of this period, after Mr. Erskine's health had not been too good for some time, his doctors told him that he must quit active work, whereupon he sold the farm with the idea of retiring. But his many years of farming had made agricultural activity almost a part of his nature, so that he found himself unable to be idle. He then bought his present farm, "The Poplars," on the State Highway between Presque Isle and Easton, a seventy-acre plot, on which he cultivates potatoes and many different farm products. Ever since that time he has devoted most of his attention to this farm, which does not, however, keep him too busy to participate freely in the civic and social life of his community. Mr. Erskine is keenly interested in political matters, especially those affecting Presque Isle, Easton, and this district of Maine, and is identified politically with the Republican party, of which practically all the members of his family have been members. Active in a fraternal way, he is a member of the Independent Order of Odd Fellows, in which order he has gone through all the branches and has served in all the chairs; a Past Captain of Canton, the Canton of which he was Captain having taken in more members during his administration than ever before and having made a record showing for fraternal orders; a member of the Free and Accepted Masons, in which order he has been admitted to the Blue Lodge, the Chapter, and the Council; a member of the Three Link Club; and a member of the Grange.

Mr. Erskine married Elizabeth May Coffey, who was born in Harvey, New Brunswick, Canada, the daughter of James and Elizabeth (Pass) Coffey. Her parents were New Brunswick natives, but came to the United States, where they settled and spent the latter part of their lives in Maine. John W. and Elizabeth May (Coffey) Erskine are the parents of a son, Roger, who is a student in the

high school in Presque Isle, and by a former marriage Mr. Erskine is the father of two daughters: Dorothy A., who was educated in the public schools and high school in Presque Isle and at the Nason Institute in Springvale, Maine, and is now a teacher in the Preque Isle schools, and Mary A., who was educated in the Presque Isle public school and high school, who later became a student at normal school, and now is also teaching in Presque Isle.

John W. Erskine is a trustee of the Methodist Episcopal church, in whose affairs both he and his wife are active.

RUFUS L. WHITTAKER—Specializing in seed and table potatoes, in both of which the quality of his product is recognized as unusually fine, Rufus L. Whittaker operates a farm on his one hundred and ten acres on the State Highway, two miles from Easton and five miles from Presque Isle. He is well known and highly regarded by his fellow-citizens in and near Presque Isle, where he has spent practically all of his life but eight years, during which he was in Southern Port, Maine, and for a short time in California.

He was born on the homestead farm on November 12, 1873, the son of John and Jerusha (Benjamin) Whittaker, both of whom were natives of Aroostook County, the father having been born in Fort Fairfield. John Whittaker was in his day a prominent man in his community, having held the position of county commissioner and many important town offices. The farm which his son, Rufus L., now cultivates on the State Highway, Mr. Whittaker took when it was practically a wilderness. Together with his sons, John Whittaker cleared the ground and established a successful farm. At one time he owned three farms in Presque Isle. John and Jerusha (Benjamin) Whittaker were the parents of twelve children, seven of whom—four boys and three girls—are now living. Rufus L., one of the sons, who now operates the old homestead farm, was educated in the town schools, and as a very young man became a farmer. Practically all his life he has been in Presque Isle, but for eight years which he spent in the southern part of the State and a short time in which he was in California. Keenly interested in the civic and political matters affecting his town, Mr. Whittaker is affiliated with the Republican party, and is a member of the Grange. His religious affiliation, like that of his entire family, is with the Methodist Episcopal church.

Rufus L. Whittaker married Maggie McQuade, a native of Presque Isle, daughter of Thomas and Sarah (Kennedy) McQuade. Rufus L. and Maggie (McQuade) Whittaker are the parents of three children: 1. Leona Avis, the wife of Clowes Seeley, a biography of whom appears in this volume. 2. Elver G., the wife of Maitland Gray. 3. Joseph, who is living at home with his parents.

WARREN B. WHITTAKER—Owning one hundred and five acres of land on the State highway between Easton and Presque Isle, two miles from the former and five miles from the latter, Warren B. Whittaker raises seed and table potatoes and general farm products, which he sells to local buyers. Although his postoffice address is Easton, R. F. D. No. 2, the farm is situated in the town of Presque Isle, and comprises one-half of the Whittaker homestead. Mr. Whittaker takes an active interest in civic and political matters, especially as they affect his community, and is regarded with respect and esteem by the residents of this section.

He was born on the homestead farm in June, 1877, the son of John and Jerusha (Benjamin) Whittaker, both of whom were natives of Aroostook County. His father was born in Fort Fairfield, and was in his day prominent in the district of Maine in and near Presque Isle. He held the position of county commissioner and many other important town offices. He acquired the present farmlands of the Whittakers when they were practically a wilderness, and with the aid of his sons he cleared the ground and established a successful farm. Seven of the twelve children of John and Jerusha (Benjamin) Whittaker—four boys and three girls—are now living. Warren B. Whittaker, one of this family, attended as a boy the town schools; then spent two years in California, where he worked in railroad shops; and one year in Arizona, where he was employed on a cattle ranch. All the rest of his life he has spent on the native farm in this part of Maine. When he first returned from the West, he operated this farm on shares with his brother, Rufus L. Whittaker, whose sketch precedes this, and later bought

it. Like most of the farmers in this section, he has found the cultivation of seed and table potatoes a prosperous occupation. In addition to his agricultural interests, Mr. Whittaker is keenly interested in the public affairs of the community. His political affiliation is with the Republican party. He is a member of the Modern Woodmen of America and of the Grange.

Warren B. Whittaker married Elva Pearl Langley, who was born in Canada, a daughter of James and Ruth (Bunnell) Langley, both of whom were natives of Canada and are now deceased. Her father's occupation was that of blacksmith. Warren B. and Elva Pearl (Langley) Whittaker are the parents of the following children: 1. Jasper V., who was born in 1909 and who is a graduate of the high school in Presque Isle. 2. Madeline, who also is a graduate of the Presque Isle High School. 3. Darrell, a student in the high school. 4. Clarence. 5. Ralph. 6. Lyle. The Whittakers attend the Baptist church, in which Mr. Whittaker holds the position of chairman of the board of trustees.

JAMES ROBINSON THURLOUGH—Owner of two rich farms, one comprising one hundred and sixty acres near the village of Fort Fairfield, where he lives, and the other forty-two acres of woodland near the town of Presque Isle, Aroostook County, James Robinson Thurlough engages intensively in agriculture. While his crops are of a general nature and by him rotated from year to year as best in accord with the market and suitability of the soil, Mr. Thurlough plants annually some fifty acres in good grade potatoes. These he grows in both seed and table varieties, and, complementary to this product operates a potato starch factory in Fort Fairfield, which business is most satisfactorily flourishing and one of those which bring into the village a considerable sum of money regularly, also affording employment to a number of hands, and therefore sustenance to as many families. More than as agriculturist and factory operator, Mr. Thurlough is known equally well as banker. Since 1917 he has been a member of the board of directors of the Fort Fairfield National Bank. Indeed, actively connected with the agricultural, financial and political phases of village and county life, he is eminent among the citizenry, vigorous participant in all enterprises for community welfare.

A native of Maine, James Robinson Thurlough was born on the Thurlough farm near Munroe, Waldo County, March 6, 1846, son of Frederick and Elsie (Whitney) Thurlough. Frederick Thurlough was born in York County and there attended district school. He was, by training and contact, a farmer and a lumberman, and after his establishment on the farm near Munroe he continued in that calling for many years, likewise engaging in business as dealer in lumber, and as proprietor of a sawmill. In all of these pursuits he was attended by fortune, and was accounted for them and because of his participation in public projects, to be one of the community's most representative men. Frederick Thurlough's wife, Elsie Whitney, was born in Penobscot County, of a family old in the history of that county. She was highly esteemed by the people of Munroe and neighborhood during the long residence of her family there, in Waldo County, where with Mr. Thurlough she remained until advancing age overtook them, and they came to Aroostook County, to Fort Fairfield; and here they died. Frederick and Elsie (Whitney) Thurlough were the parents of ten children, of whom only two are now (1928) living: a daughter, Mrs. Charles Morse, whose husband is chief engineer for the Rock Island Railroad, of Chicago; and James Robinson, of whom follows.

James Robinson Thurlough received his education in the public schools of Munroe, Waldo County, and began, at the age of fourteen years, to work with his father in the sawmill and on the farm. When he was twenty-two, in 1868, he had acquired sufficient capital for the purchase of the farm near Fort Fairfield, and has lived here since, in due time purchasing the wood land near Presque Isle, establishing the starch plant, becoming bank director, and, in fine, achieving prosperity for himself and assisting in the achievement of prosperity for village and countryside. Mr. Thurlough is a Republican and loyal to the principles of the party, in which he is prominently identified in Aroostook County political matters. For three years he was a member of the Fort Fairfield Board of Selectmen; for twelve years he was a county commissioner. It was during this period that the Bangor & Aroostook Railroad desired to extend its lines through Fort Fairfield, and Mr. Thurlough was one of those most instrumental in bringing this to pass. He was one of the commission whose signature was affixed to bonds valued at $728,000, which the county took from the railroad as proof of good faith in the venture; and he was of the committee when later the bonds were bought in by the road. Constantly allied with all that is progressive in civic movements, Mr. Thurlough is known as one of the outstanding men in the community. During the World War he served on the various boards and committees prosecuting the war from within this country, and was indefatigable in this work and in the furtherance of the several Liberty Loan drives. He is active in Masonry, having been a Mason since 1867, member of the Fort Fairfield lodge, Free and Accepted Masons, and a communicant of the Baptist church. In matters of charity and kindred worthy appeals he is generous in contributions, giving in a spirit truly humanitarian. He is one of the main supporters of the church.

James Robinson Thurlough married Olive Marshall, and to this union were born children: 1. Agnes, who died at the age of thirteen months. 2. Nellie, wife of James P. Loring, of Yarmouth, Maine, who makes her home on the farm near Fort Fairfield with her father; and she is the mother of one child, James Robinson, 2d, named after her father.

CHARLES H. GOODING—Owner of seventy-seven acres of fertile land on the old Reach Road, later renamed the Sanitorium Road, in Aroostook County, near Presque Isle, Charles H. Gooding is a member of a family old in the history of New England and the State of Maine. Mr. Gooding's grandfather, on the paternal side, was William Gooding, sea captain, who, in his many voyages, circled the world several times, taking with him often his son, Albert William Gooding. William Gooding married Susan P. Merrill, daughter of the Rt. Rev. Stephen Merrill, pastor of the Congregational church.

Albert William Gooding, son of William and Susan P. (Merrill) Gooding, was born at Portland, Maine; married Sarah A. Everett, daughter of Charles H. and Mary (Scott) Everett, her father having been a native of the Province of

New Brunswick, Dominion of Canada, and her mother of Ireland. The family of Scott is of English origin. Albert William Gooding and his wife, Sarah A. (Everett) Gooding, born at Andover, New Brunswick, came to the Presque Isle farm with the earliest of settlers, and cleared the land of trees and rocks. Albert William Gooding was of the serious and hard working type so typical of New England stock and was respected for his good citizenship and for his industry. He lived on the farm for forty-seven years, until his death, September 11, 1926. Buildings which he constructed of logs hewn with his own hands remain on the premises and give testament to his skill and ingenuity. Albert William Gooding and his wife, Sarah A. (Everett) Gooding were the parents of three children, two daughters and a son: 1. Maude, living on a farm. 2. Ina, widow of Reed Lancaster. 3. Charles H., of whom further.

Charles H. Gooding, youngest child and only son of Albert and Sarah (Everett) Gooding, was born on the Presque Isle farm, October 22, 1897. In the public schools of this community he received his education, graduating from high school, after which he engaged immediately in agriculture, under the direction of his father. He is now (1928) thirty-one years of age, and accounted prominent in affairs of the neighborhood. Successful in the direction of the farm, assumed upon the death of his father in 1926, he is well known and favorably in the business houses of Presque Isle. He combines modern methods of farming with crops best suited to his land, and yields are large; these he disposes of in the local markets. He is active in politics, both in town and county, and a member of the Republican party, and upholds in its high respect the name of Gooding, just as did his father and grandfather.

Charles H. Gooding married Bertha Foster, daughter of Harry and Julia (Carter) Foster, her father engaged in agriculture near Presque Isle. Mr. and Mrs. Gooding are members of the Congregational church at Presque Isle and are active in its affairs.

CLARENCE C. BREWER—Starting out in life as a lumberman, Clarence C. Brewer, since his residence here, has become one of the successful farmers and potato dealers of Presque Isle.

His parents, Albert and Esther (Boone) Brewer, were both natives of New Brunswick where they spent all their lives. Albert Brewer was a contractor and bridge builder and for many years was active in that line of construction work.

Clarence C. Brewer was born in Carleton County, New Brunswick, on April 28, 1876. He received his education in the public schools of Woodstock, New Brunswick, where his father was in business. He then started to work in the sawmills and did some work in lumbering, thus becoming familiar with the business from two angles. When he was only a young man of eighteen years of age, he came into Maine and settled at Ashland where he continued to engage in the sawmill and lumbering business. After fifteen years in this line of work and enjoying a certain amount of success from it, he became interested in farming and began the growing of potatoes. He now owns a farm of two hundred acres situated on the Parkhurst Road and also farms at Ashland, on all of which he raises a fine grade of potatoes for the market. He also owns warehouses in several localities from which he ships potatoes. In addition to his farming interests and other business, he is a director in the Washburn Trust Company at Washburn, Maine, and the Ashland Trust Company at Ashland. He is a staunch adherent to the principles of the Republican party and a member of the Masonic Order, of Free and Accepted Masons, having taken many degrees in that body, including a membership in the Ancient Arabic Order Nobles of the Mystic Shrine. He is also a member of the Mooseleuk Club.

Clarence C. Brewer married Leila Rafford, daughter of Warden and Servena (Howe) Rafford, of Ashland, Maine. They have three children: 1. Albert, who is associated with his father in the potato business and who married Helene Plummer; they have three children, Albert, Jr., Terrance, and Juan. 2. Wilfred, a student at Magill Medical College of Montreal, Canada. 3. Burtt, also associated with the father in the potato business; he married Mabel Downing. Mr. Brewer and his family attend the Protestant Episcopal church.

JOSEPH COBURN BUDROW—Prominent in the life of the town of Presque Isle, Maine, Joseph Coburn Budrow is the owner of a farm of one hundred and forty-nine acres, situated on Egypt Road, just off the State Highway between Presque Isle and Easton. He has lived there for the past fifteen years, raising potatoes and other general farm produce which he sells to local buyers. Mr. Budrow is thoroughly familiar with the best farming methods and has been very successful in his chosen occupation. He is active in the civic and fraternal life of his community. His father, George Budrow, born in the Province of New Brunswick, Canada, is a farmer there. His mother, who before her marriage was Zorada Vaudine, was also born in New Brunswick.

Joseph Coburn Budrow was born on September 6, 1889, at Bath, Province of New Brunswick, Canada. He was educated in the local public schools, and when still a boy, began work on a farm. At the age of sixteen he came to the United States, and for six years he worked as a farm hand in Maine. Finally, about 1914, he bought the farm on Egypt Road between Presque Isle and Easton, where he now lives. Since that time he has devoted himself to improving the property and raising his crops, specializing in growing potatoes.

Mr. Budrow is affiliated fraternally with the Independent Order of Odd Fellows, being a member of the Presque Isle Lodge. He is also a member of the Grange, and of the Modern Woodmen of America. He and his family attend the local Baptist church.

Joseph C. Budrow married Vera L. Williams, who was born at Presque Isle, the daughter of Joseph and Fannie (Smith) Williams. Mr. and Mrs. Budrow are the parents of three children: Russell William, Audrey, and Phillys.

WILLIE V. COFFEY—One of the many well-to-do farmers of Presque Isle, Maine, Willie V. Coffey cultivates one hundred and twenty-five acres on the State Highway between Presque Isle and Easton, produces general crops and seed and table potatoes for local buyers.

Born December 9, 1880, at Harvey Station, York County, New Brunswick, Canada, he was the son of James and Elizabeth (Pass) Coffey. Both parents were born there, but when Willie V. Coffey was sixteen years of age, removed to the United

States, and purchased the farm adjoining the one he now occupies. He was educated in the local schools, and until he was twenty-five years old, was his father's assistant on the farm. He then bought the property on which he still resides, and has greatly increased its value by intelligent cultivation. Mr. Coffey is a Republican, and with his wife, is active in the work of the Methodist Episcopal church, of which he is trustee. Both are also members of the Patrons of Husbandry.

His wife was Henrietta Perry, daughter of George W. and Mary (Baird) Perry, of Presque Isle, belonging to a prominent family of Maine farmers. Their children are: 1. Beatrice Elizabeth, who was educated in the local and high schools of Presque Isle and the State Normal School, and is a teacher in Presque Isle. 2. Elsie, who graduated from the high school preparatory to entrance in the Normal School in 1928. 3. Carlton George. 4. Glendon Everett, both in school.

JAMES ARTHUR COFFEY—New England farming is one of the greatest proofs of the endurance of man to wrest from the soil the nourishment for his plants. The long cold winters, the many rocks in the ground, the intensive work that has to be done, year in and year out, has developed a race of sturdy men and women who accept no defeat, but through a most wonderful perseverance and thrift and diligence to duty and industry have made of the seemingly unfertile country one of the most productive farming spots in the country. James Arthur Coffey is one of the sons of New England who have grown up in this section of the country and imbibed that steadiness of habits and frugality of management that has brought a success to his forbears and to himself.

James Arthur Coffey was born at Presque Isle on April 24, 1898. His birthplace was his father's farm, situated at the corner of the State Highway and the old Easton Road. It is the place which is now under his management and belongs to his late father's estate. Mr. Coffey was brought up on this place and while a little boy, he attended the public schools in Presque Isle, and then on into the work of the high school, where he studied for two years only as he began his work on the farm as a regular vocation at a very early age.

Mr. Coffey has never been in any other business than that of farming, except as a side line, he is agent for the American Mill Company. He is interested in the activities of the Grange, of which he is a member, and he is also a member of the Modern Woodmen of America. He and his family are very active members of the Baptist church, in which they take zealous interest. At the time of the death of Mr. Coffey's father, James Arthur Coffey was bequeathed a lifetime lease on the farm which he had so successfully operated for many years. The place belongs to the heirs and comprises one hundred acres, and is under the entire control of Mr. Coffey by the will of his late father. In politics, Mr. Coffey is a Republican.

James Arthur Coffey married Vellora Coffin, who was born at Caribou, Maine, the daughter of Hall and Cora (Ablin) Coffin. Mr. and Mrs. Coffin now live at Presque Isle, where Mr. Coffin is in the trade of carpentering and also runs a farm. Mr. and Mrs. James Arthur Coffey have two children: Lula May and Richard James.

ROLAND SAMUEL HEMPHILL—Owner and operator of one hundred and seventy-five acres of the most productive agricultural land in Aroostook County, Roland Samuel Hemphill was born at Knowlesville, Carleton County, Province of New Brunswick, Dominion of Canada, on July 9, 1885, son of Joseph and Annie (English) Hemphill. Joseph Hemphill brought his family to make their home in the United States, at Presque Isle, and here engaged in farming. At this time Roland Samuel was one and a half years of age. At the present (1928) Joseph Hemphill is retired from farming, and lives in Presque Isle Village; Annie (English) Hemphill died in March, 1924.

Roland Samuel Hemphill attended the public schools of Presque Isle, and after graduating from high school joined his father in the cultivation of the farm. He was thus occupied, until, when yet a young man, he was enabled to purchase the farm of John W. Erskine, situated on the Maine State Highway between Easton and Presque Isle. On these acres he has since engaged in agriculture, to no small success, as he employs the most modern methods of farming and plants only those crops best suited to the land. While he

engages in general agriculture, raising all varieties common to the section, Mr. Hemphill also grows hundreds of bushels of potatoes each year, marketing them, for the most part, in the markets of Presque Isle and Easton, sometimes shipping to distant points. He is well known in the commercial circles of the neighboring towns, where he disposes of produce, and his ability and efficiency as a business man are there recognized. He is a member of the Republican party and takes an interest in politics, but has never assented to the suggestion that he run for office. Fraternally, he is a member of the Grange, to which all of the chief men in the neighborhood interested in husbandry belong; and he attends the Methodist Episcopal church. His donations in the cause of charity are numerous and substantial.

Roland Samuel Hemphill married Almeda Cunningham, born in the Village of Canterbury, New Brunswick, Canada, daughter of Andrew and Eliza Cunningham, who continue to make their home in New Brunswick on a farm. Mr. and Mrs. Hemphill are the parents of three children, two sons and a daughter: Claude, Pauline and Frank.

CHARLES A. JAMIESON—Enterprising as a farmer and potato dealer, Charles A. Jamieson, of Presque Isle, Maine, conducts his farm along business lines in a progressive way that insures him the success so desired by all who cultivate the soil and must depend on seasons and weather for the carrying on of their business. He is the son of Hugh Jamieson, who is a dealer in automobiles, a farmer and a shipper of potatoes. His father was born in Presque Isle on September 2, 1865, and was the son of Hugh and Julia (Dickinson) Jamieson. Hugh Jamieson married Grace Reed, who was born at New Gloucester, Maine, daughter of Levi and Charlotte (Woodbury) Reed.

Charles A. Jamieson was born at Westfield, Maine, on January 20, 1891. He was brougt up in Presque Isle, where he was educated in the public schools and in the high school of this town. After finishing his high school work, he went to work on his father's farm and then came into Presque Isle and carried on a livery and sales stable business for four years. While making a success of this business, he again felt the urge of the soil and finding an opportunity to purchase a good farm, he took advantage of it and bought from A. W. English the farm which he now operates. This farm is located on the Center Line Road and comprises one hundred and twenty-eight acres, all of which is practically under cultivation. While doing some general farming, Mr. Jamieson makes a specialty of his potatoes and brings in a good crop of these every season. He is a member of the Grange, a member of the Order of Free and Accepted Masons, Garfield Chapter, and Aroostook Council. In politics, Mr. Jamieson is a staunch Republican and his religious affiliation is with the Baptist church, which he and his family regularly attend.

Charles A. Jamieson married Annie Crory, who was born at Fort Fairfield, Maine, the daughter of Levi and Mettie (Pryor) Crory. Mr. and Mrs. Jamieson have two children: 1. Catherine. 2. Danoald.

CHARLES FREDERICK AMES is president of an important hardware, plumbing and coal company in Fort Fairfield, Maine. He is also director of a national bank. Before this his business experience was varied, for after he had completed his schooling he worked at farming for a number of years and from that passed to the handling of farming machinery, establishing his own business in company with a friend and associate, and developing it year by year until it comprised also the handling of a great many important side lines.

Charles Frederick Ames was born at Fort Fairfield, Maine, August 11, 1872, son of Stephen W. and Isadora (Haywood) Ames; his father, a farmer, was born at St. Stephens, New Brunswick, and his mother was born at Littleton, Maine. both deceased. Charles Frederick Ames attended the public schools at Fort Fairfield and also a business college at Bangor, Maine. He then took up farming, following the occupation of his parents, and became the holder of a farm in the town of Easton, on which he worked for a period of eight years. At the end of that time he sold his property and returned to Fort Fairfield with his friend and associate, Tom. E. Hacker (q. v.), who has been his partner in business to the present time. He then, with Mr. Hacker, started in to

handle farm machinery, and the business won a considerable degree of prosperity from the beginning, drifting gradually into the handling of hardware and the work of plumbing and handling of plumbing materials. To these were added, in course of time, other side lines, among them Aroostook seed and table potatoes and general farm supplies. The business is known as the firm of Ames & Hacker Company, with Mr. Ames as president, and Mr. Hacker as treasurer. Mr. Ames is director also of the Fort Fairfield National Bank. He is a Republican in politics. He takes considerable interest in public affairs and has been a member of the Board of Selectmen for five years. He is on the Republican committee. He belongs to the Blue Lodge, Free and Accepted Masons, of Fort Fairfield; Caribou Chapter, Royal Arch Masons; the Presque Isle Council of the Royal and Select Masters; the Commandery, at Houlton; and Anah Temple, Ancient Arabic Order Nobles of the Mystic Shrine.

Charles F. Ames married (first) Jennie Waldron, daughter of Charles M. Waldron, now deceased. Children: Adella H., Myria K., and Charles Frederick, Jr. He married (second) Edith M. McCoomb, born at Dexter, Maine. There have been no children to this second marriage. The family attends the Methodist church, of which Mr. Ames is a trustee.

WALTER BURNS LONG—Owning with his sister an estate of two hundred and twenty-five acres on the State Road between Presque Isle and Caribou, Walter Burns Long, who is considered one of the leading citizens of this section of Maine, has been during practically his entire career, a farmer. Although he comes of New Brunswick parentage, Mr. Long was born on the farm which he now operates on the road between Presque Isle and Caribou, on June 21, 1890, the son of John Benjamin and Sarah (Barker) Long, and he was educated in this State and has lived here ever since that time.

His father was born in Kingsclear, New Brunswick, Canada, on the Saint John's River; and his mother was born about one and one-half miles from her husband's birthplace in New Brunswick. Both of the parents are now deceased. When the father was about forty years old the family came to the United States, settling on the farm which Mr. Long and his sister now own. John Benjamin Long did most of the clearing on this farm. When the boy completed his education, he became active in the farm work, his father having died when he was but nine years old. All his life since that time, Walter Burns Long has been a farmer. Interested in political matters, especially those affecting this section of Maine, he is identified with the Republican party, for whose candidates he has cast his vote for many years. He participates freely in the fraternal life of his community, being a member of the Free and Accepted Masons, in which order he has been admitted to the Chapter and the Council. He also belongs to the Grange and to the Mooseleuk Club.

Walter B. Long married Marion Wilkins, who was born in Presque Isle, the daughter of C. H. and Annie (Kempton) Wilkins. Mr. and Mrs. Long are the parents of one child, a daughter: Patricia. The religious affiliation of the family is with the Congregational church, in whose affairs the Longs take an active part.

CHARLES F. PERRY—Owning one hundred and seven acres of land, on which he raises all sorts of crops, specializing in potatoes, Charles F. Perry is considered one of the leading farmers in the community of Presque Isle. This farm is situated on the Center Line Road, and he also has another stretch of land, a wood lot of one hundred and sixty-five acres, in the town of Presque Isle. A native of Maine, he is thoroughly conversant with farming and business conditions here, and has spent practically his whole life in this section.

He was born in Littleton, May 2, 1880, the son of George W. and Mary (Baird) Perry, the former of whom is a native of Littleton, Maine, and the latter a native of Bloomfield, New Brunswick, Canada. The father and mother, on July 10, 1927, celebrated their fiftieth anniversary, and are both well known and highly respected residents of this community. George W. Perry, together with his son, James A., a sketch of whom follows this, conducts a farm, specializing in potatoes and selling to local buyers. Charles F. Perry, of whom this review, who, as has been mentioned above,

owns his own farm of one hundred and seven acres in Presque Isle on the Center Line Road. He has lived all his life in this community, where he attended the public schools as a boy and has been engaged almost continuously in farming ever since boyhood. Keenly interested in the political and civic affairs of his town, Charles F. Perry is affiliated with the Republican party, whose opinions he shares and for whose candidates he casts his vote. He is active in the affairs of the Grange.

Charles F. Perry married Vertie D. Foster, who was born in Presque Isle, a daughter of Dennis and Bertha (Rackliff) Foster, who lived all their lives in Presque Isle, where now, at an advanced age and highly respected in her community, Mrs. Foster continues to reside. Mr. Foster passed on several years ago. Charles F. and Vertie D. (Foster) Perry are the parents of three children: Ralph, Fred, and Lucy. The Perry family's religious affiliation is with the United Baptist church.

JAMES ANDERSON PERRY—Among the enterprising and prosperous farmers of Presque Isle, Maine, is James Anderson Perry, who shares the ownership of a fine tract of one hundred acres on the State Highway from Presque Isle to Mars Hill, on which he produces both seed and table potatoes with his father, and also owns sixty acres of woodland in the same town. Born in Littleton, Maine, March 27, 1886, he is the son of George W. and Mary (Baird) Perry, now of Presque Isle, where they celebrated their golden wedding on July 10, 1927. The elder Perry, born in Littleton, Maine, was always a farmer. His wife was born in Bloomfield, New Brunswick.

James Anderson Perry was nine years old when his father left Littleton for Presque Isle. He had attended the public schools in Littleton and resumed study in Presque Isle, where he attended the high school. From an early age he was his father's assistant on the farm, and he succeeded to the management in 1908. He is a Republican, and attends the Methodist Episcopal church with his family, and is its financial secretary. He is also member of the Grange.

Mr. Perry married Lilla Maud Coffey, daughter of James and Elizabeth (Pass) Coffey. Their children are: Elmer, Woodrow, and Alton James Perry.

PERLEY A. RAMSDELL—Owner of a farm of three hundred and twenty-five acres on the State Road between Presque Isle and Caribou, Perley A. Ramsdell engages in general agriculture, with potatoes a specialty, and disposes of his produce in the markets of Caribou and Presque Isle. Mr. Ramsdell is a native of Presque Isle; he was born there on November 17, 1878, son of William R. and Amy (Elliott) Ramsdell. William Ramsdell was a native of Maine, having been born at New Sharon. With his wife Amy, he came to Presque Isle in 1872, cleared a farm on the Ashland Road, and engaged in agriculture, in which he continued until death. His wife, Amy (Elliott) Ramsdell, is also deceased; both left many friends in Presque Isle and vicinity.

Perley A. Ramsdell received his early education in the public schools of Presque Isle, and after leaving high school attended classes in Shaw's Business Academy, at Houlton. He then spent a year learning the trade of carpenter, in Massachusetts, and decided to make a career of agriculture instead, entering the employ of Henry E. Hutchinson, who owned and conducted the farm now (1928) in the possession of Mr. Ramsdell. He worked for Mr. Hutchinson for several years, and finally bought a half-interest in the farm. In 1918 he purchased the other half, and as sole owner and manager has achieved a very good prosperity. He is well known in business and political circles of Presque Isle and Caribou, a member of the Republican party, and of the Grange. He belongs to the Free Baptist church, and is liberal in his contributions to meritorious causes, charitable and otherwise, sponsored by it.

Perley A. Ramsdell married Lavonia Hutchinson, daughter of Henry E. Hutchinson, formerly owner of the Ramsdell farm, since retired, of Presque Isle, and Ada M. (Hatch) Hutchinson, deceased. Mrs. Ramsdell died in 1927, leaving no children. She had been active in affairs of the Free Baptist church, and was beloved of all who knew her.

———————

HARVEY E. SMITH—Owner and proprietor of sixty acres of the most fertile agricultural land, between Presque Isle and Easton, on the Maine State Highway, Aroostook County, Harvey E. Smith engages in general farming and the growing of potatoes. He raises both seed and table potatoes, chiefly the latter, and disposes of them in the markets of Easton and Presque Isle, where he is known as a business man of sound judgment, as a successful agriculturist, and loyal and public-spirited citizen.

Harvey E. Smith was born at Easton, September 22, 1885, son of Thomas S. and Lizzie A. (Kennedy) Smith, his father being a native of Fort Fairfield, now (1928) in retirement at Easton, and his mother having been a native of Andover, Province of New Brunswick, Dominion of Canada, deceased. Harvey E. Smith received his education in the public schools of Easton, and after completion of studies in high school, until he was twenty-one years of age, worked with his father on the farm. Soon after reaching his majority he decided to make a career of agriculture, and was enabled to purchase forty acres of farm land near Easton. For five years he engaged in the cultivation of this tract, then disposed of it, and for one year rented a farm near Caribou, Aroostook County. The following year he worked as farm hand, and again purchased a tract of land, which he has operated with good success. The methods employed by Mr. Smith in his husbandry are the most scientific of those approved by agricultural specialists in Maine and Washington, District of Columbia. These he adapts to his land with skill, and to such crops as are most suited to growth upon it. The Smith farm was owned by Patrick McDonald for many years, until purchased by Mr. Smith, who has made of it one of the most pleasing to the eye of all the farms abutting on the State Highway. Constantly he is involved in community affairs, including those of the farmside and of Easton and Presque Isle; a member of the Republican party, and loyal to its principles in National questions, he supports as non-partisan those men whom he believes best fitted to fulfil local offices. He is a member of the Independent Order of Odd Fellows, of Easton, and a communicant of the Methodist church; and in affairs of the church he is devout, esteemed highly for his works of good, generous in his contributions to charitable causes.

Harvey E. Smith married Nancy E. Doak, native of Easton, daughter of John and Melvina (Demarchont) Doak; and they are the parents of three children, one daughter and two sons: Agnes, Hartley, and Maxwell.

CLOWES A. SEELEY—As an example of one who appreciates the value of diversified farming, Clowes A. Seeley of Presque Isle, Maine, has carried on a farm and raising livestock for some time with good success in this undertaking. He is the son of George and Hannah (Seeley) Seeley. Although his parents bore the same name, they were in no way related. Both parents were natives of New Brunswick. His father was a farmer who moved to the country in 1908 and settled at Presque Isle where he purchased the farm now owned by Clowes E. Seeley. He was never engaged in any other business than that of farmer, of which he made a success. Both Mr. and Mrs. George Seeley are now deceased.

Clowes E. Seeley was born at Sunbury, New Brunswick, on January 5, 1893, and received his education in the common schools of his native town. He came to Maine with his parents in 1908 and worked on the farm which his father as long as the latter lived. At the time of his father's death, one-half interest in the farm belonged to his uncle, John Seeley, and this interest was purchased by Clowes E. Seeley, and later he inherited from his mother the half that had belonged to his father. The farm as it now stands comprises two hundred and ten acres and is situated on the State Highway between Presque Isle and Easton. Mr. Seeley does general farming making a specialty of table potatoes which he sells to local buyers, and he also keeps five head of horses and two cows, the latter for the use of his own family. He is interested in blooded racing stock and owns the race horse Virginia Dare, which has made a very good record. As a rule, Mr. Seeley does much of the farm work himself with the help of one man, but during the busy season he employs three or more men as the need may be. He is a Republican in his political affiliations and a member of the Free Baptist church.

Clowes E. Seeley married Leona Avis Whittaker, daughter of Rufus L. Whittaker (q. v.). They have one child, Orin.

ADELBERT G. STAIRS—Among the self-made men in this section, there is none more outstanding than Adelbert G. Stairs, who is one of the successful potato growers with a well established business of over twenty years standing. He is the son of William and Mary (Elkins) Stairs. His father was a native of New Brunswick and his mother a native of Maine. Both parents are now deceased.

Adelbert G. Stairs was born on June 8, 1872, at Moro, Maine. He came to Presque Isle when a lad of fifteen years of age, with little education and not a cent to his name. He worked as a farm hand for Elisha E. Parkhurst, and by diligence and thrift he was able to take a half interest in the farm on which he worked. After twelve years, he bought the farm outright. He carried on the cultivation with increasing success and put up all the buildings which are now on the place. At first the farm comprised one hundred and sixty acres and is well located on the State Highway between Presque Isle and Easton, but as time went on and Mr. Stairs has learned to make the most of an acre of ground, he found that he did not need such a large place and sold off ninety acres. He now cultivates his seventy acres by doing some general farming but makes a specialty of seed potatoes and some table potatoes. With his seed potatoes he has been most successful and for twenty-two years he has sold them to A. E. Waddell of New Bedford, Massachusetts. He ships some of his table potatoes, but sells most of them to local dealers. In addition to his crops, he raises all of his own horses and has disposed of a number of horses by selling them at different prices which have amounted to about five thousand dollars. He attends personally to much of his business and to his farm and enjoys the reward of being a diligent and enterprising farmer. He is a Republican in politics but has never held any public office. Both Mr. Stairs and his wife are active members of the Congregational church.

Adelbert G. Stairs married Clara B. Tompkins, a native of New Brunswick, daughter of Albert Tompkins. They had one child, Mildred, now deceased.

CLARENCE A. POWERS—One of Maine's distinguished sons, Clarence A. Powers, of Fort Fairfield, ranks high in the commercial and financial world, as well as being a prominent member of the Republican party and serving his State and community in various positions for a number of years. Mr. Powers operates with his son-in-law,

Edward Edmunds, Jr., as partner, the important firm of C. A. Powers and Company, potato shippers and dealers in fertilizer, and has been vice-president of the Fort Fairfield National Bank for thirty years, and in addition is a controlling factor in many other business and financial institutions throughout the State. He was born in Fort Fairfield, in February, 1868, son of Roderic Powers of Maine, and Elizabeth (Hodgdon) Powers, of New Hampshire. Roderic Powers was a highly respected resident of his community, being engaged in the agriculture and carpenter trades.

Clarence A. Powers received his education in the public schools of Easton, after which he began his career in farming. Due to his energy and thorough attention to details, he was successful from the start and gradually advanced until he was one of the leading producers and shippers in the county. Continuing in his original policy, he turned his attention to other fields, and through his great business ability, soon became one of the leaders in the commercial life of the State. At the present time, he is president of the John Watson Company, dealers in hardware and farm machinery, operating stores in Houlton and Fort Fairfield; vice-president of The Aspinwall Company of Houlton; director of the Bangor and Aroostook Railroad; director of the Northern Telegraph Company; vice-president of the Aroostook Telephone Company and director of the Danforth Trust Company, together with interests in a number of other corporations. Although his success as a business man attests to his close attention to his affairs, he has always found time to take an interest in the life of the community and its progress, and for a number of years served as selectman of the town. For two years he served on the council of Governor Milliken, and also two years on the council of Governor Baxter. He was elected as a member of the Legislature and filled this post during the years 1917 and 1918. While engaged in his duties at the State capital, he gained an enviable record as a statesman of sterling character and brilliant ability, and his community can well be proud of his achievements. Mr. Powers is an active figure in fraternal circles and is a member of the Free and Accepted Masons, being connected with the Blue Lodge of Fort Fairfield, Caribou Chapter, Presque Isle Council and Houlton Commandery. He is a member of Anah Temple, Ancient Arabic Order Nobles of the Mystic Shrine, Bangor, and of the local Rotary Club.

Clarence A. Powers married Ida F. Grant, daughter of Francis Grant, and they have one daughter, Helen, who married Edward Edmunds, Jr., and they have five children: Jean Elizabeth, Patricia Helen, Clarence and Edward Perrin (twins), and Phyllis Sylvia.

MERLE ROY SMITH—After finishing his common school education and a course in a business College, Merle Roy Smith took up the work of farming, and combining his business training with his knowledge of agriculture has carried on successfully the operation of a farm near here for many years. He is the son of Frank B. and Elizabeth (Currier) Smith. His father was born at Richmond, Maine, and his mother at Winthrop, Maine. They came to live in Presque Isle many years ago where Mr. Smith was well known as a carpenter by trade and a farmer. Both Mr. and Mrs. Smith are now deceased.

Merle Roy Smith was born in Presque Isle, Maine, on August 7, 1882. He covered the entire course of public school work from the elementary grades through the high school and then went to Portland, Maine, and took a course in Shaw's Business College. With a background of schooling and technical business training, he worked on his mother's farm where he studied diligently the needs for carrying on a first class farm as a business enterprise and then he later bought his own place, which is located on the Parkhurst Road and comprises one hundred and twenty acres of arable land and which Mr. Smith puts into general crops and some potatoes. He is not a shipper but sells his potatoes to the local dealers in Presque Isle. He has never operated any other farm and, having concentrated all of his energy to making this productive, he has succeeded well in his undertaking. He is a member of the Grange and the Congregational church, and in politics Mr. Smith is a Republican.

Merle Roy Smith married Blanch Kitchen, daughter of William Kitchen. They have four children: Irving Kitchen, Roger Williams, Lawrence Purrington and Mary Elizabeth.

HAROLD O. WEBBER—As a business man and a farmer, Harold Orville Webber, who owns a farm near Easton, Maine, evidences the success of diversified interests. In addition to his general farming, he has a wood and ice business, thus keeping himself independent of seasons for his commercial activity. He is the son of George and Nettie E. (Hartley) Webber. His father is a farmer who lives at Presque Isle. His mother is deceased.

Harold O. Webber was born at Bridgewater, Maine, September 2, 1885. He went to the town school until he was thirteen years of age and then gave all of his time to farming. However, he did not remain on the home place, but hired himself out at the age of fourteen years and continued as a hired hand until he was thirty-four years old. He then purchased from E. A. Ross, a farm of one hundred and sixty acres on the State Highway about one and one-half miles from Easton and five and one-half miles from Presque Isle. Here he raises seed and table potatoes. He sells his produce to local dealers and conducts his wood and ice business in the town of Easton, making deliveries in that town and vicinity. He is a member of the Independent Order of Odd Fellows at Easton. In politics, Mr. Webber is an independent voter with an inclination to socialism.

Harold O. Webber married Anna M. Branch, who was born at Central City, Colorado, a daughter of George and Mary A. (Walters) Branch, both of whom were natives of Devonshire, England, who on coming to this country settled first in Claremont, New Hampshire, and later came to Maine and then settled in Colorado. Mr. and Mrs. Webber have one child, a daughter, Ruth Alice, who was educated at the Easton High School and the Normal School at Presque Isle and is now a teacher at Wakefield, Massachusetts.

LEON EDGAR SUTTER—Always engaged in the business of farming, and living on the home farm where he was born, Leon Edgar Sutter is one of the steady reliable producers of farm products that can always be found interested in the affairs of the community and the progress of agriculture. He is the son of William and Lydia (Scott) Sutter, both of whom were born in New Brunswick, coming here to this country when small children and spending most of their lives here where Mr. Sutter was a farmer.

Leon Edgar Sutter was born on June 28, 1880, the youngest of four children. His birthplace was the farm where he was brought up and from where he attended school through the lower grades and the high school. He remained with his father on the home farm until he was twenty-five years of age, which he then purchased, and has continued to remain here and to cultivate it. It is located on the old Reach Road and comprises one hundred and twelve acres of tillable land. Mr. Sutter also owns a wood lot of one hundred and sixty acres near the town of Chatham, Maine. His products are those of general farming and a good crop of potatoes which he sells to local buyers and in this way is relieved of the business of shipping. Mr. Sutter is a member of the Blue Lodge, Free and Accepted Masons; the Knights of Pythias; the Grange and the Mooseleuk Club. In politics he is a Republican and he is a member of the Congregational church.

Leon Edgar Sutter married Edith Hamilton who was born at Patten, Maine. They had eight children: Amber, Dorothy (deceased), Phillip, Mildred and Madeline (twins), James and Jean (twins, both deceased), and Roger.

GEORGE W. TURNER—Farmer, owner, and proprietor of some five hundred and fifteen acres of rich agricultural land, George W. Turner is one of the substantial men in the community of the village of Mapleton, near which he lives, and engages in general agriculture, specializing in the growing of seed and table potatoes, marketing his produce through the Fruit Growers' Association, and by them retained as representative agent in this locality with authority to purchase produce throughout the county.

George W. Turner was born in Carleton County, Province of New Brunswick, Dominion of Canada, on January 27, 1870, son of John B. and Hannah (Craig) Turner, farmers, who came to the United States and settled on a farm near Mars Hill when George W. Turner was thirteen years of age. The following year they came to the farm in Mapleton, and here died, the father having been for many years a millwright, in connection with his farming. George W. Turner received his elementary education in the public schools in Carleton County, New Brunswick. He engaged immediately in farming, at which he has continued during the succeeding years. Not only has he become one of the most successful and substantial farmers of the neighborhood, but he has participated extensively in public affairs, having constantly as his interest the progress and welfare of Mapleton and the countryside. A Republican, he is loyal to the principles of government upheld by that party, and is possessed of a considerable influence in political matters locally. Among the offices of a public character which he has held are those of selectman, of the Board of Selectmen of the village of Mapleton, and commissioner of roads. In the exercise of each of these positions he served faithfully and with intelligence. Fraternally Mr. Turner is active as a member of the Modern Woodmen of America. With his family he attends the Methodist church; of large heart, his contributions to charitable and other worthy causes are substantial and readily forthcoming. During the World War, and upon the entrance into it of the United States, Mr. Turner took part on various boards and committees having in charge works for the prosecution of the conflict from this country, and in the several Liberty Loan drives he was most actively engaged. Of him it is said that in every way he is a good and true citizen.

George W. Turner married Margaret Waddell, native of Mapleton, daughter of Matthew and Sarah (Stewart) Waddell, an honorable house that has for long figured in the history of this part of the State. To this union have been born five children, all of whom have reached maturity: 1. Colby, married Helen Wilcox. 2. Mark, married Emily Cyr. 3. Katie, wife of William Relyea. 4. Matthew, married Doris Dudley. 5. Marguerite, wife of Orin Winslow.

MAURICE. S. RUSSELL—Well known among the successful farmers of Woodland, Maine, is Maurice S. Russell, who owns two farms and raises a good grade of potatoes, which he sells to the local market. He has been a member of the Board of Directors of the Washburn Trust Company since it was organized, and is active in local affairs. He has been a resident of Woodland since he was seventeen years of age.

Maurice S. Russell was born in Brighton, Somerset County, Maine, August 29, 1870, son of Sullivan, a farmer who came to the town of Washburn about 1887, and of Irene (Willard) Russell, both of whom are now deceased. As a boy Mr. Russell attended the local public schools, helping his father on the farm during the summer seasons, and attending school in the winter months, but when he was seventeen years of age his parents removed from Brighton to Washburn, and he came with them. He began his active life as a farm hand, but later purchased what he now calls his back farm, containing about one hundred and thirty acres. Later, he purchased what is known as the Buzzel farm on the Perham Road, and on this last farm he is now living (1928). This farm contains one hundred and fifty acres and is fully equipped, with good buildings which Mr. Russell himself erected, and modern machinery for the efficient management of the farm work. He specializes in the raising of a good grade of potatoes, which he sells locally. Long years of experience have made him an expert in this branch of agriculture, and his crops are of the first quality. In addition to the management of his potato farm, Mr. Russell has also been a member of the Board of Directors of the Washburn Trust Company since its organization. He is an able and a resourceful business man, keen, far-seeing, and just in his dealings, and he has long possessed the confidence and esteem of his fellow-farmers and of those with whom he is associated in other connections. He gives his support to the Republican party, as do most of his neighbors, and he has borne a full share of the burdens of local public office, serving as road commissioner, as a member of the school board, and on various committees. Fraternally, he is identified with the Blue Lodge, Free and Accepted Masons, of Washburn; with Washburn Chapter, Royal Arch Masons; and with Caribou Council, Royal and Select Masters, of Presque Isle; also with the Independent Order of Odd Fellows, of Washburn. His religious membership and that of his family is with the Universalist church.

Maurice S. Russell was married to Elianore Tuttle, who was born in Washburn, Maine, daughter of Leander and Margaret (Tuttle) Tuttle. Mr. and Mrs. Russell have had ten children: 1. Edna, wife of Eugene Pike. 2. Elroy, who lives at home. 3. Henry, who is engaged in the grocery business in Washburn. 4. Ernest, who died in the fall of 1927. 5. Otis, lives at home. 6. Mahala, wife of Reed Price. 7. Lillian, lives at home. 8. Earl, died at the age of five years. 9. Merle. 10. Pearl, died at the age of fifteen years.

WALTER H. MERRITT—One of the successful potato growers of the Fort Fairfield section of the county is Walter H. Merritt, owner of Brookmead Farm, located on the road from Presque Isle to Fort Fairfield. Mr. Merritt has a farm of two hundred and forty acres on which he raises general crops, but he specializes in potatoes and grows seed which he sells to the local market.

Walter H. Merritt was born in New Brunswick, Canada, October 20, 1871, son of Joshua and Leta (Jamieson) Merritt. The parents removed from New Brunswick to the States when Mr. Merritt was twenty years of age and settled on the farm which he now owns and operates. Both are deceased. Mr. Merritt received his education in the common schools of New Brunswick and accompanied his parents to Maine when he was twenty years of age. He was associated with his father in the work of the farm until the death of the latter, when he took over the big farm, which he has since operated. This farm is known locally as the Daggett Farm, having been formerly owned by the father of Charles F. Daggett. Mr. Merritt has demonstrated his ability as an agriculturist and though he does not devote all of his acres to the growing of potatoes, he makes a speciality of growing seed for the local market and in addition raises general farm crops. Mr. Merritt gives his support to the candidates and the principles of the Republican party and has himself been active in local public office, serving as tax collector for a period of two years and as deputy sheriff for four years. He has won in a high degree the confidence and esteem of his associates and is well known both in Presque Isle and in Fort Fairfield. Fraternally, he is identified with the Blue Lodge, Free and Accepted Masons, of Presque Isle; and with the Independent Order of Odd Fellows, in which

order he has passed through all the chairs, and he is a member of the Encampment and of the Canton. He also holds membership in the Order of the Rebekahs, and in the Three Links Club.

Walter H. Merritt married Lottie Annis, who was born in Easton, Maine, daughter of Moses and Mary (Dudley) Annis. Moses Annis was a millwright and a veteran of the Civil War. Mr. and Mrs. Merritt are the parents of three children: 1. Ralph, who graduated from high school in June, 1927, and has spent one year at the University of Maine. 2. Ruth, who graduated in June, 1928, from the high school in Presque Isle. 3. Avis, who is also a student in Presque Isle High School. The family are attendants of the Methodist church, and both Mr. and Mrs. Merritt are active in the work of the church. Both are highly respected in the community and have many friends.

WILLIAM HENRY MacALLISTER—A man whose work in many different lines of endeavor stood out prominently during his life, most of which was spent in Maine, was William Henry MacAllister, who was born in Milltown, New Brunswick, Canada, and who died in Houlton, on May 13, 1914. His daughter, Elizabeth MacAllister, who resides in Houlton, is now owner of the farm that belonged to her father, which is three hundred acres in area and is situated in Orient, Aroostook County, Maine. She also owns the Snell House, in Houlton, one of the best known hotels in Northern Maine, now under the management of A. J. Needham, a practical hotel man. This hostelry is well equipped, having sixty guest rooms and rooms in suite, mostly all having running hot and cold water, and a dining room with a seating capacity of seventy persons. Mr. MacAllister's parents were Ellis William and Ann (Ames) MacAllister, members of old families.

William Henry MacAllister, who came to be one of the best known and most loved residents of this section of Maine, and whose business judgment and ability and foresight were recognized by all those who knew him, was born of poor parents, and by his own efforts reached the position of prominence in the community which he attained. He came to Maine from his native town, Milltown, New Brunswick, when he was eighteen years old, and as a boy started to work in the woods. After that time he spent most of his life in farming and lumbering. He has often been praised for his foresight, which has been of considerable benefit to his family. Seeing what a future there would be for Maine timberlands, Mr. MacAllister many years ago bought timberland for fifty cents an acre, acquiring many thousands of acres. The same land today is worth from $12 to $15 an acre, and his family is prospering through the ownership of lands which his vision prompted him to buy and through the profits which have accrued from these properties. As he lived in Orient, Aroostook County, Maine, whither he came from Canada, he became increasingly popular with the passing years, so that he was chosen to fill many positions and offices of trust in the town. Always active in the town's public affairs, Mr. MacAllister for two years represented Orient in the lower house of the State Legislature; and for two years was the town treasurer, and held numerous other town offices. Keenly interested at all times in the civic and political matters affecting the development of his community, he was affiliated with the Republican party, for whose candidates he cast his vote. Also active in the fraternal life of the town, he was a member of the Independent Order of Odd Fellows and of the Benevolent and Protective Order of Elks.

Mr. MacAllister married Almeda Brackett, a native of Weston, Maine, and a daughter of William and Lucinda (Durbin) Brackett. Mr. and Mrs. MacAllister became the parents of two children: 1. Elizabeth, who now owns the homestead farm in Orient consisting of three hundred acres, as well as the Snell House, an important hotel in Houlton. 2. Ellis William, a jewelry manufacturer of Providence, Rhode Island, who married Grace Buckland, by which marriage there is one daughter, Lucille. Mr. MacAllister was a member of the Congregational church, while his wife's religious affiliation is with the Baptist church.

HERBERT W. COFFIN—Practically the entire career of Herbert W. Coffin, to the present time (1928) has been identified with the lumber and general merchandise business in Fort Kent, Maine. The little town of Fort Kent is not far

from the St. John River, has a well-built railroad station, and ministers to a large section of surrounding country in the matter of stores, mail, and other general service. Mr. Coffin was a partner of George H. Page in the general store and lumber business for some years, but since 1925 has been engaged in the lumber business alone, the two departments of the earlier business having been separated. He has his office in the old store, but Mr. Page has the general store business.

The Coffin family is of old New England ancestry, tracing back to the celebrated Tristram Coffin, who was one of the early settlers of Nantucket Island. Whitman Henry Coffin, father of Mr. Coffin, was born in China, Maine, and is still living (1928) at the age of ninety-four years. He was a joiner by trade and during the early years of his life followed that occupation. For some years he was associated with his brother in the contracting business in Massachusetts, but later he returned to Maine, where he was the owner of mills and was engaged in the feed, grain, flour, and lumber business, in China, Maine. He married Jemimah Willey, who is now deceased, and they became the parents of five children, among whom is Herbert W., of further mention.

Herbert W. Coffin was born in Newton Center, Massachusetts, May 6, 1872, and received his education in the public schools, including the high school, of Patten, Maine. When his high school course was completed he came to Fort Kent, Maine, where he entered the employ of B. W. Mallett and Company, as clerk. Later he entered the employ of I. H. Page, and upon the death of Mr. Page, Mr. Coffin remained in the employ of the son, George H. Page. Later he became a partner of Mr. Page in the lumber business, under the name of Page and Coffin, and this partnership was continued until 1925, when the partnership was dissolved, Mr. Coffin taking over the lumber business for his own, and Mr. Page retaining the general merchandise business as his possesion. This arrangement has continued to the present time. Mr. Coffin has his office in the old store and is developing a thriving lumber business, while Mr. Page is steadily maintaining and building up the general store business. Mr. Coffin is a Republican in his political affiliations, and fraternally he is identified with the Blue Lodge, Free and Accepted Masons, of Fort Kent; with Caribou Chapter, Royal Arch Masons; and with the Modern Woodmen of America. His religious affiliation and that of his family is with the Presbyterian church. Mr. Coffin is one of the highly-respected citizens of the community, and both he and his wife have many friends in this locality. Herbert W. Coffin is married to Alice I. Howard, who was born in Grand Falls, New Brunswick, Canada, daughter of Fred and Ruth Howard. In addition to the conduct of his lumber business, Mr. Coffin is also a potato grower.

JOHN ALLEN CHURCHILL—Certified seed potatoes and general farm crops are the products of the big two hundred acre farm owned by John Allen Churchill. The farm is located just outside the village of Washburn on the Caribou Road.

John Allen Churchill was born in Washburn, Maine, February 20, 1857, son of Job and Ann (Crouse) Churchill, the first mentioned of whom was a native of Maine and the last mentioned of whom was born in New Brunswick. Mr. Churchill attended the local public schools, living the usual life of the boy on the farm, going into the woods at an early age, his first work in the woods being done when he was fourteen years old. When school days were over, he continued as a farm hand and as a chopper in the woods, but about 1880 he purchased a farm of his own, and since that time he has devoted his time and his energy to farming. His certified seed potatoes are of the best to be had, and he sells to the local market. Politically, he supports the principles and the candidates of the Republican party, and he has been very active in local affairs. He was road commissioner for twenty years, a member of the Board of Selectmen for several years, and has always been a progressive and public-spirited citizen. He is a member of the Independent Order of Odd Fellows, of Washburn; and of the Blue Lodge, Free and Accepted Masons, of Washburn, and is well known in this locality. He and his family are attendants of the Baptist church.

John Allen Churchill married (first) Lizzie A. Dyer, who died April, 1890, and he married (second), November 29, 1893, Edna E. Tuttle. She died January 16, 1896, and Mr. Churchill married (third), December 25, 1898, Addie U. Bugbee. To

the first marriage were born five children: 1. Lewis F. 2. Laura, wife of George R. Russell. 3. Harry A., married Pearl Hanson. 4. Coley, married Ethel Burchel. 5. Guy, married Pearl Gordon. To the third marriage Mary was born, and she married Herman W. Walker.

JESSE P. CHURCHILL—Numbered among the prominent and substantial agriculturalists of Crouseville, Aroostook County, is Jesse P. Churchill, owner of one hundred and ninety acres of fertile land in Washburn Township, and of a second farm comprising eighty acres distributed on either side of the line in Washburn and Mapleton townships; and it is upon this latter farm that he makes his home. He engages in general agriculture, with a specialty of seed and table potatoes, and disposes of the produce both in Crouseville and nearby markets. His home is situated on the State Road between Crouseville and Presque Isle, just across the river from the place where he was born, December 13, 1859. Jesse P. Churchill is a son of Job and Ann (Crouse) Churchill, his father having been a native of Washburn and his mother of the Province of New Brunswick, Canada.

Mr. Churchill attended the common school at Crouseville, and at the age of eight years began to work upon his father's farm, attending classes in winter time only. It was his habit, insisted upon by him, to pay to his parents a small sum of money each week for board, room and clothing; and although when he was nineteen he moved away, for a time, he continued to pay the weekly fee without interruption. After having worked with his father for a number of years, more or less continuously, he went to Wisconsin, and there engaged as woodsman for some six years. When he returned to the farm at the close of this period, he purchased the land from his father. In husbandry he has met with good success, employing the latest of scientific methods of farming. A Republican, Mr. Churchill is loyal to the principles of government for which the party stands and wields a considerable influence in matters political. With his family he attends the First Adventist Church, and is generous in contributions to charitable and other kindred causes of like worthy character.

Jesse P. Churchill married (first) Louise Crouse, deceased. To this marriage were born three children: Christie·Ann, Sherman, and Louise. Then he married (second) Florence Kitchen, native of Providence; and they are the parents of six children: Murray, Caroline, Dorothy, Donald, Pauline, and Maurice.

HERSCHEL P. BUGBEE—The farm which Herschel P. Bugbee, of Washburn, owns and operates has been in the Bugbee family since the town of Washburn was settled. Mr. Bugbee's father and grandfather before him tilled the fertile acres of this farm on which general crops and an excellent grade of potatoes are now being raised, and Mr. Bugbee has spent his life here.

Herschel P. Bugbee was born on the homestead farm on the edge of the village of Washburn, Maine, January 29, 1877, son of Alfred C. and Mary S. (Smith) Bugbee. He attended the local public schools until he was thirteen years old, helping on the farm and in the woods even as a boy, and his entire life to the present time (1928) has been spent on the farm and in the woods. He owns the homestead farm of one hundred acres, and is known as a successful farmer and a skilled potato grower. In his political faith Mr. Bugbee is a Republican, and fraternally he is identified with the Independent Order of Odd Fellows and with the Modern Woodmen of America. His religious affiliations and that of his family is with the Baptist church.

Herschel P. Bugbee was married (first) to Eliza McUbrey. She died, leaving two children: Rubie E. and Ceola A. Mr. Bugbee married (second) Gertrude (Dickinson) Pearce, widow of William Pearce. There are no children of the second marriage.

BENJAMIN FRANKLIN GIBERSON— One prominent in the affairs of Presque Isle and Caribou, Aroostook County, is Benjamin Franklin Giberson, who owns two hundred and forty-five acres of the most fertile farming land in the Aroostook Valley, situated on the Maine State Highway between Caribou and Presque Isle. Here he raises potatoes extensively and disposes of his produce in the local market, and by rail to points more distant; he has been in business as operator in potatoes since 1915, with very sound success; and is admired for his commercial ability and respected for his high character wherever he is known.

Benjamin Franklin Giberson was born in New Brunswick, Dominion of Canada, not far distant from Fort Fairfield, Maine, on February 2, 1872, son of George Washington and Calise (Trambelay) Giberson, his father having been a native of the Province of New Brunswick, and his mother of Quebec, Canada, both deceased. Benjamin Franklin Giberson came to Fort Fairfield with his parents when he was about ten years of age. Here the father engaged in his trade as shoemaker, and took an interested part in community matters. At Fort Fairfield Benjamin Giberson received the balance of his education, and when he left school went to work in the town shingle mill. His next employment was under a dealer in potatoes, until, after a period of experience, he engaged in business for himself, as shipper of potatoes. In this capacity he continued for eight years, and in 1915 purchased the farm since occupied, which he at once incorporated with the potato shipping business, already well organized, at Presque Isle. Mr. Giberson is not only prominent in the commercial life of Presque Isle and Caribou, but plays a part in politics. He has never accepted the suggestion that he run for office, but holds a considerable influence in the Republican circles of both communities. At present he is a deputy sheriff, and serves to the evident satisfaction of all concerned. He is a member of the Knights of Pythias, and attends the Baptist church.

Benjamin Franklin Giberson married Georgia Ann Everett, born at Fort Fairfield, daughter of Samuel and Anna (Grass) Everett, the former a native of England and the latter of Canada. Mr. and Mrs. Giberson are the parents of one son, Donald Everett, member of the graduating class of 1929, in the Presque Isle High School.

CHARLES B. GIBERSON—Owning one hundred acres of land in the neighborhood of Mapleton and Castle Hill, Charles B. Giberson is one of the leading agricultural men of this community of Maine, specializing in the cultivation of potatoes, for which this country is noted. The Giberson farmlands are situated on the State Highway, thirty of the one hundred acres being in the town of Mapleton and the other seventy in Castle Hill. While potatoes are Mr. Giberson's specialty, he also does a general farming business, selling his product locally to the people whom he has known practically all his life. For although he is a native of New Brunswick, he came to the United States with his parents when he was only two years of age.

Mr. Giberson was born in Aroostook Falls, in the Province of New Brunswick, Canada, a son of George Washington and Calise (Trambelay) Giberson. Both of his parents were Canadians, his father having been a native of New Brunswick, and his mother of Quebec. Both of them are now deceased. When he was two years old, Charles B. Giberson was brought to the United States by his parents, who settled in Maine. Mr. Giberson, as a boy, had little opportunity to receive a wide education, for he had been attending the public schools for only a short time when he was forced, because of the death of his parents, to find work for himself. He was fourteen years old when he found it necessary to do small jobs—chores and farm work; but the early experience which he received in farming, as well as the rigorous life which he was compelled to lead, placed him in a splendid position to acquire facility in the labors that have brought him large profits since that time. For the appearance of his farm today and of the crops that it yields are ample testimony of his ability in agricultural matters. Mr. Giberson always has been deeply interested in the public life of his community, and ready to lend his support to whatever movements he believes are designed to improve conditions among the farmers of this section. He and his family are members of the Methodist Episcopal church.

He married Louise Witham, who was born in Fort Fairfield, Maine, a daughter of Otis and Orintha (True) Witham. Charles B. and Louise (Witham) Giberson are the parents of seven children: 1. Helen, who is the wife of Willard Waddell. 2. Frank. 3. Esther. 4. Darrel. 5. Pauline. 6. Betty. 7. Margaret.

ANDREW JACKSON BECK—Since 1920 Andrew Jackson Beck has been president of the Washburn Trust Company, of Washburn, Maine. He is also manager of the American Fruit Growers, Incorporated, of Maine, and is active in various fraternal, financial, and civic organizations. Mr. Beck was engaged in legal practice from 1913 to 1923, but is no longer engaged in general practice, devoting his time to his business connections, and using his legal knowledge for his own business transactions.

Andrew Jackson Beck was born at Deer Isle, Maine, September 17, 1891, and is a son of Fred W. Beck, who was a sea-faring man during his early life, but later was engaged in business as proprietor of a prosperous meat and grocery business, and of Minnie R. (Lufkin) Beck, both of whom are living. He received his education in the public schools, including the high school, of Deer Isle, and then took a post-graduate course in Westbrook Seminary, in order to prepare himself for college. He then matriculated in the law school of the University of Maine, at Orono, Maine, where he completed his course with graduation in 1913. He successfully passed the required examinations for admission to the bar at Rockland, Knox County, appearing before Justice Phillbrook, in 1913, and at once came to Washburn, Maine, in order that he might look the place over. This was a case in which to see was to remain, and Mr. Beck decided to locate permanently here. He opened his law office and after the usual period of waiting for clients to appear succeeded in building up a practice which has steadily grown through the years. From 1913 to 1923 he fully demonstrated his ability as a practitioner, but in 1920 he was elected president of the Washburn Trust Company, and since that time he has devoted an increasingly large proportion of his time and attention to the business of the trust company. In 1923 he retired from legal practice and since that time has given all of his attention to his business enterprises. As has already been stated he is manager of the American Fruit Growers, Incorporated, of Maine, and in both connections his business acumen and his sound judgment have been important factors in building up the organizations. He is president of the Rotary Club of Washburn, and is very active in local public affairs, giving his support to the Republican party. He has served as town treasurer for a period of one year, and has been a member of the school board and tax collector for the same period of time. He is also serving as town moderator. Fraternally, he is identified with Washburn Lodge, Free and Accepted Masons, of which he is a Past Master; with Caribou Chapter, Royal Arch Masons; Houlton Commandery, Knights Templar; and Anah Temple, Ancient Arabic Order Nobles of the Mystic Shrine, of Bangor.

Andrew Jackson Beck was married to Evelyn Thompson, daughter of Melvin and Cora (Scott) Thompson, and they are the parents of one son, Fred Nelson. Mr. and Mrs. Beck are members of the Congregational church, but they are attendants of the Baptist church, at Washburn.

CHARLES E. WILLEY—After fifteen years of farming in the employ of another, Charles E. Willey purchased Clover Hill Farm, located on the State Road between Fort Fairfield and Limestone. Here he is engaged in general farming, including among his crops a good grade of potatoes, which he sells to local buyers. He is a member of the Board of Directors of the Limestone Trust Company, and has served as a member of the Board of Selectmen of Limestone.

Born in New Hampshire, February 28, 1888, Charles E. Willey is a son of John and Ellen (Forrest) Willey, both natives of New Hampshire, now deceased. Mr. Willey began his school training in his birthplace, but his parents removed to Limestone when he was nine years of age and engaged in farming here. Consequently, the boy attended the schools of Limestone, and was a student in the Limestone High School for two years. He had early become his father's helper on the farm, and when school days were over he became a farm hand in the employ of John Ward, with whom he remained for a period of fifteen years. He was an able farmer and thrifty and after fifteen years of experience he purchased the farm of one hundred and fifty-nine acres located on the State Road between Fort Fairfield and Limestone, in the town of Limestone, known as Clover Hill Farm. This fine farm he has since been successfully operating, raising general crops and also a good grade of potatoes, but he does not specialize in the last mentioned crop as do so many of

the farmers of this region. He sells to local buyers and is content to divide his attention among the several crops which he raises, rather than trust his whole return to the staple crop of the locality. Being a man of excellent business ability his opinion is much sought by his fellows, and he is rendering valuable service as a member of the Board of Directors of the Limestone Trust Company. He gives his support to the Republican party, and is one of the public-spirited men of the town. His religious affiliation and that of his family is with the Methodist church.

Charles E. Willey married Maud Fitzimmons, who was born in Limestone, Maine, daughter of James and Phœbe (Cox) Fitzimmons, farmers, who came to Limestone from New Brunswick, Canada. Mr. and Mrs. Willey have five children: 1. Bedford, who was educated in the local public schools, including the high school; married Violet Gallagher, and resides in Limestone. They have two children, Emeline and Gloria Lavelle. 2. Vera, received her education in the local schools and in the high school of Presque Isle, also in Presque Isle Normal School and in Presque Isle Business College, and also spent one year in the New England Conservatory of Music at Boston. 3. John, a graduate of the local high school. 4. Loomis, at home. 5. Buell, at home.

GEORGE WILLEY—Dealing in a fine grade of potatoes, George Willey has specialized for many years in this branch of farming in the Limestone district. He owns what is known as the Sunny Side Farm, consisting of one hundred and sixty acres on the West Limestone Road. In addition to his potato growing, Mr. Willey also does a general farming business, and acts as buyer for the S. Cohen Company, a position which he has held for a number of years. He has lived in this section of Maine practically all his life, his family having come here from New Hampshire as early as 1879. He now is deputy sheriff of Aroostook County, and has served his town as selectman. He is ready at all times to take part in movements that he believes will be beneficial to the community, especially to the farming interests, with which he has so long been closely identified.

He was born in Colebrook, New Hampshire, in

June, 1873, a son of Isaac and Sarah Jane (Forrest) Willey, both of whom are now deceased. They were natives of New Hampshire, but in 1879 they removed to Maine, and spent the rest of their lives as farmers in Limestone. As a boy, George Willey attended the public schools of his native town and those of Limestone, but while he was still very young he went to work on the farm with his father. He and his brother, Arthur Willey (q. v.), bought the home farm from their father, and proceeded for a time to operate it jointly; but at length he sold his interest to his brother, who continues to operate it. It was known for years as the Charles Howett farm. Finally George Willey bought the farm which he now conducts on the West Limestone Road, and decided to specialize in potatoes, a commodity that has proven lucrative to many agriculturists in this part of Maine. Actively interested in public affairs, he takes a prominent part in political matters, being affiliated with the Republican party, in whose principles he is a firm believer. On the Republican ticket, he was elected twice to the office of town selectman in Limestone, and he is now deputy sheriff. He and his family are members of the Adventist church, of Limestone. He is a member of the Free and Accepted Masons, being a Master Mason; the Knights of Pythias, in which he is affiliated with the Limestone lodge; and the Grange.

George Willey married Dora B. Turner, who was born in Four Falls, Victoria County, New Brunswick, Canada, a daughter of Holden and Belle (Hamilton) Turner, who removed to Limestone when Mrs. Willey was only six months old and continued to live here for the rest of their lives as farmers. George and Dora B. (Turner) Willey are the parents of the following children: 1. Lula A., who is the wife of Dennis Getchell, who lives in Limestone and is a farmer. 2. Turner, who is living at home with his parents. 3. Mildred B., who is the wife of B. R. Mitchel, by which marriage there is one son, George Walter.

ARTHUR WILLEY—As owner and proprietor of the Balm of Gilead Farm, situated on the old Caribou Road in the town of Limestone,

Arthur Willey does a general farming business, specializing in the cultivation of a fine grade of table potatoes, which he sells to local buyers. He also is a director and a member of the Executive Board of the Limestone Trust Company, one of the leading banking institutions of this section of Maine. Although he was born in New Hampshire, he has spent practically all of his life in Maine on the farm which he now owns and operates, and therefore is thoroughly conversant with local agricultural conditions and has a wide acquaintance among the people of this district.

He is a son of Isaac and Sarah Jane (Forrest) Willey, both of whom are now deceased. They were natives of New Hampshire, having lived for many years in Colebrook, New Hampshire, in which town Arthur Willey was born on January 10, 1872; but in 1879 they removed to Maine, settling in Limestone, where they spent the rest of their lives as farmers. Arthur Willey, who was eight years old when he arrived in Maine, attended the Limestone public schools, and then went on the farm with his father for three years. Three brothers, George (q. v.), Isaac, and Arthur, purchased the home farm from their father, and continued for some years to operate it jointly. Finally Arthur Willey bought the interests of his brothers in the farm, and continued to conduct it for himself. This farm, one of the choicest plots of ground in this part of Maine, was cleared by the father, Isaac Willey, with the help of his sons. Here the Willey family spent its early days; and here Isaac Willey built the buildings, cleared the ground, and made the spot fit for farming. Since that time, Arthur Willey has remodeled the buildings, and has done everything in his power to bring about a general improvement of the land. Actively interested in the civic and social development of his community, Mr. Willey takes part in those movements which he believes will prove helpful to the public welfare, and is a highly respected, public-spirited citizen. He and his family attend the Adventist church.

He married Gertrude Blaisdell, a native of Auburn, but lived in Fort Fairfield, Maine, a daughter of Hiram and Sarah (Thompson) Blaisdell. Arthur and Gertrude (Blaisdell) Willey are the parents of one son, Jasper, who was educated in the public schools of Limestone; attended the high school, from which he was graduated; took a business course in Boston; married Fern Noyes; and now owns and operates a truck garden, a very successful enterprise, in Scarboro, Maine.

DELMONT EMERSON—For many years Delmont Emerson has been prominent in the life of Island Falls, Maine. He is treasurer of the Northern Woodenware Company and of the Emerson Lumber Company, and in association with his brother, Harold L. (q. v.), he assisted in the organization of the Island Light Company, which recently passed into other hands. Mr. Emerson has served as town treasurer, and is highly esteemed in his community as a public-spirited citizen. He is active in the social and fraternal affairs of the town. His father, Martin L. Emerson, born at Norridgewock, Somerset County, Maine, was a farmer and lumber man, and engaged in this work until his death. His mother, who before her marriage was Isabel G. Carr, was born at Bowdoinham, Maine, but lived for the most part at Lewiston.

Delmont Emerson was born April 20, 1864, at Island Falls, Maine. He attended the local public schools, and when he completed his education, became associated with his father in the management of the farm, the lumber business, and a general store. About 1904, he and his brother, Harold Emerson, organized the Island Lighting Company, whose business they carried on until 1927, when they sold to other interests. Meanwhile Mr. Emerson has become treasurer of the Northern Woodenware Company and the Emerson Lumber Company, and a director of the Houlton Trust Company, positions which he still holds. In all his business connections his unusual energy and ability have made him of extreme value to his companies. Politically, Mr. Emerson is a member of the Republican party, and for three years he served as town treasurer at Island Falls; two terms as member of the House and two terms in the Senate. He is affiliated fraternally with the Ancient Free and Accepted Masons, being a member of the Island Falls Lodge, and of the Chapter and Commandery at Houlton. Both he and his wife are very active in church work, being members of the local Congregational church, of which Mr. Emerson is a trustee.

He married Myra H. Morrison, who was born at Sherman, Maine, the daughter of Alonzo and Abbie (Washburn) Morrison. Mr. and Mrs. Emerson are the parents of one child, Rosewell, who was educated at the Island Falls public schools and at Bowdoin College, and is now associated in business with his father. He married Bertha Campbell Whitney and they are the parents of three children: Delmont Whitney, Frank LeRoy, and Patricia Marie.

HAROLD LaFOREST EMERSON—Merchant, lumberman, one of the pioneers in the development of the electrical system in Island Falls, Harold LaForest Emerson, who died March 7, 1911, was justly regarded as one of the most progressive and successful business men of Aroostook County, Maine.

Born March 24, 1872, at Island Falls, he was the son of Martin L. and Isabel G. (Carr) Emerson, and a brother of Delmont Emerson (q. v.) and Ralph Waldo Emerson. The elder Emerson was a highly-respected farmer and lumberman of Island Falls, a native of Norridgewock, Somerset County, and his wife was born at Bowdoin, but had lived at Lewiston for some years prior to her marriage. Educated in the public schools, Harold LaForest Emerson joined his father and brothers in the development of a general store, and of the Emerson Lumber Company, both of which prospered, and the latter is still active, and controlled by the family. The organization of the Island Lighting Company, although it eventually passed to the control of others, was among the most important of the Emerson local enterprises.

Apart from his business activities, Harold LaForest Emerson always found time for any worthwhile civic activity, and was a devoted member of the Congregational church. He was less interested in fraternal organizations than his brother Delmont, and his charities, while numerous, were unostentatious. But as a lifelong resident of the community, he had a wide circle of friends and business acquaintances, who remember him as a genial and wholly trustworthy man, possessing lofty ideals and wide vision.

Mr. Emerson married Geneva Walker, daughter of Joseph and Clara (Dyer) Walker, who was born in Island Falls, after her parents had moved there from Searsport, Maine. Two children were born of this union: 1. Raymond LaForest, educated at the University of Maine, spent two years in the service of the United States Navy during World War, and was discharged with the rank of first-class fireman. He was then for two years with the Northern Woodenware Company as manager of camps; three years in hardware business in Island Falls; now with Emerson Brothers. He married Doris Pride, and their son is Joseph Walker. 2. Ralph, educated at the University of Maine and at Yale University, four years with the Northern Woodenware Company; later joined Emerson Brothers. He married Leah Crabtree, and their children are: Harold L. and Ralph Eugene.

DWIGHT W. DORSEY is a well-known funeral director in Fort Fairfield, Maine. He was a licensed embalmer, with considerable practical experience before he entered the undertaking business on his own responsibility, and thus buttressed by graduated courses in schools of embalming and anatomy. Mr. Dorsey has discontinued the livery business which he inherited from his father, and is devoting his entire time to farming and the mortuary business. Mr. Dorsey takes an active interest also in public affairs and has held public office.

Dwight W. Dorsey was born at Fort Fairfield, Maine, May 12, 1892, son of Edward J. and Alice Maude (Webb) Dorsey, the father in the livery business in Fort Fairfield, both parents were born in Fort Fairfield of families long there resident and both are now deceased. Dwight W. Dorsey was educated in the public and high schools of Fort Fairfield, and after that went with his father in the livery business, and remained in that business until his father died. He became administrator of his estate. Later on he went to work for K. C. Haycock, an undertaker of Fort Fairfield, and worked for him during a period of twelve years. He bought the business in October, 1925. Mr. Dorsey acquired his practical experience with K. C. Haycock, but he also took courses at the N. E. Institute of Anatomy, Sanitary Science, and Embalming, graduating in 1923. He has made his business very modern and up-to-date, and has a fine new funeral car and all the other appurtenances. Mr. Dorsey is an independent Democrat. He was

deputy sheriff for two years and is now town constable. He belongs to the Free and Accepted Masons, Blue Lodge of Fort Fairfield; Royal Arch Chapter at Caribou; Commandery at Houlton, and a charter member of Anah Temple, Bangor, and the Masonic Club at Fort Fairfield; the Knights of Pythias Lodge, and the Rotary Club; and also the Merchants' Association of Fort Fairfield.

Mr. Dorsey married Phebe M. Boulier. Children: Edward J., and Phillip D. Mrs. Dorsey is a Catholic, while Mr. Dorsey attends the Episcopal church.

CHARLES O. AUSTIN—One of the leading business men of the Washburn section of Maine is Charles O. Austin, president and general manager of the Washburn Electric Company. He has held this position since 1919, and before that time was engaged in electrical work in other cities. Mr. Austin's experience has been unusually broad. For two years he studied in New York, and acquired there his first experience in the type of work that he has made his vocation ever since. He is deeply interested in the civic and social life of his community, and is an astute student of business and industrial conditions. His fraternal affiliations are both strong and extensive, and he is generally considered as one of the really substantial men of Washburn and of this part of Maine.

He was born in Norridgewalk, Somerset County, Maine, March 19, 1875, a son of Norman I. and Amanda (Fuller) Austin, both of whom are now deceased. His father, whose first work was in the machinists' trade, subsequently became a farmer. As a boy, Charles O. Austin attended the public school of his native town, and later went to Kent's Hill Academy with the intention of preparing himself for college. But conditions were such that he was unable to attend college, so he went to New York, where he worked for two years, learning the details of electrical work and acquiring knowledge of all the many phases of electricity. While he was in New York, he attended night school, complementing the education which he already had received in Maine. Then, from 1900 until 1909, he worked for the firm that is now known as the Bangor Hyro-Electric Company, of Bangor, Maine;

from 1909 until 1911, he was city engineer of Bangor; and in 1911 he came to Presque Isle, where he accepted a position as superintendent of the Gould Electric Company, which he retained until his health failed and forced him to spend a year in Montreal, Province of Quebec, Canada. There he recuperated, and later returned to this section of Maine, where he bought an interest in the Washburn Electric Company. Subsequently he bought the company outright. This business was established by E. M. Hines in 1911, and since 1919 Charles O. Austin has been its president and general manager. Keenly interested in the political affairs of the town, State, and Nation, Mr. Austin is affiliated with the Republican party, of whose principles he is a staunch supporter. He is a member of the Ancient Free and Accepted Masons, in which he has gone through all the York rites and has taken eighteen degrees of the Scottish Rite, and is affiliated with Anah Temple of the Ancient Arabic Order Nobles of the Mystic Shrine, in Bangor.

Charles O. Austin married Bertha McAlpine, who was born in Pembrook, Maine, and who was the widow of Henry Simmons. Both Mr. Austin and his wife attend the Methodist Episcopal church, in whose affairs they are active.

NED W. DOWNING—As a contractor and builder, Ned W. Downing, one of the foremost citizens of Presque Isle, has erected or helped to erect many outstanding buildings in this town and the surrounding community. The size of his business may be estimated from the fact that he employs one hundred and eighty-five men, and from the fact that he is now working on the construction of two business blocks and a high school in Caribou, the training school and grade school in Presque Isle, and an addition to the Court House in Houlton.

He was born in Patten, Maine, April 1, 1883, the son of Samuel and Emma (Sutherland) Downing, both of whom are now deceased. His father's occupation was that of carpenter. Ned W. Downing was educated in the public schools and high school in Easton, into which town his parents moved when he was only eleven years old. When he had reached the age of seventeen years, he be-

gan to learn the carpenter's trade, in which he has continued ever since that time. He worked in Presque Isle until 1907, as a journeyman in this trade; then he established his present business. He is keenly interested in civic and political matters, but remains unaffiliated with either of the two large political parties, preferring to follow an independent political course, voting for those candidates whom he thinks will be most capable of filling their offices. He is a member of the Knights of Pythias; the Modern Woodmen of America; the Merchants' Association, in which he is one of the trustees; and the Mooseleuk Club.

Mr. Downing married Lillian Pelletier, and they became the parents of the following children: 1. Mabel, who is the wife of Bert Brewer. 2. Dorothy. 3. Doris, who was a twin with Dorothy, but who died at the age of seven years. 4. Mildred. 5. Harold. 6. Margaret. Mr. and Mrs. Downing and their family attend the Roman Catholic church, although Mr. Downing's people were Baptists.

THOMAS E. HOUGHTON—One of the well-known large scale farmers of this part of the State of Maine is Thomas E. Houghton, who, with his mother, owns four farms in the town of Fort Fairfield, and a half interest in four more farms in Piscataquis County, this State. Mr. Houghton raises general crops, but he specializes in certified seed potatoes, which he ships and also handles some in the local market. He is a member of the Board of Directors of the Fort Fairfield National Bank, and is also the third selectman of the town of Fort Fairfield.

Thomas E. Houghton is a son of Emmons William and Cora A. (Haines) Houghton, and a grandson of William and Dolphus Houghton. On the maternal side he is a grandson of Albert L. and Mary L. (Currier) Haines. He is one of three children, both of the others now deceased: Ervin A., who died at the age of twenty-one years; and Verna May, who died at the age of seven years. Mr. Houghton attended the public schools of Fort Fairfield, and after completing his course in the high school continued study for two years in the University of Maine, at Orono. Upon the death of his brother he left college to become his mother's assistant on the farm, and he has continued as a farmer to the present time (1928), operating four farms in Fort Fairfield, and holding, with his mother, a half interest in four more farms in Piscataquis County, Maine. Mr. Houghton has added extensively to the original holdings of which he took charge for his mother at the time of the death of his brother, and he is widely known as a skilled agriculturist and as a very successful business man. In addition to the raising of general crops, he specializes in the staple crop of the county, certified seed potatoes, which he sells both locally and by shipment to other sections of the country. As a member of the Board of Directors of the Fort Fairfield National Bank he is closely identified with the financial interests of the place, and with all his activities he finds time for local public service, being now (1928) third selectman of the town of Fort Fairfield. Mr. Houghton has also served in the State Legislature, 1921-23, and is an earnest supporter of the Republican party. His religious affiliation is with the Congregational church, and his mother is active in the church work in general and in all of its various societies.

Thomas E. Houghton is married to Asenath Watt, who was born in Fort Fairfield, daughter of John and Jennie (Good) Watt, and they are the parents of four children: 1. Thomas E., Jr. 2. Mary Priscilla. 3. John William. 4. Frances Louise.

GEORGE H. CHURCHILL—Specializing in the cultivation of potatoes, George H. Churchill conducts a general farming business on a plot of one hundred and thirty acres on Forest Avenue, in Fort Fairfield, Maine, although he maintains a winter home on Main Street, in Fort Fairfield. He is a director of the Frontier Trust Company of this town, of which institution he is one of the charter stockholders. He is active in the public life of his community, having served for three years as a selectman, and having participated freely at all times in the work of different fraternal societies and organizations in Fort Fairfield and vicinity.

Mr. Churchill was born in Jacksontown, New Brunswick, Canada, August 3, 1865, a son of Wil-

liam and Jane (Good) Churchill, both of whom are now deceased, the father having died when the son was only four years of age. Although the father never came to the United States, the mother has lived in the States for the last several years. As a boy, George H. Churchill attended the public schools of his native town, Jacksontown, New Brunswick, but left school at the age of twelve years. After he had left school, he remained at home until he was twenty-one years old, helping his family; but when he was twenty-two years of age he married. Even after his marriage, however, he worked one-half of the home farm in New Brunswick until, in 1892, he came to the United States. Having saved $1,500, he bought a farm on the Presque Isle Road, which he continued to operate for fourteen years, at the end of which period he sold it and bought his present farm. In his political attitude, he is closely identified with the Republican party, of whose principles and candidates he has been practically all his life a staunch supporter. He was elected a selectman in Fort Fairfield on the Republican ticket, and for three years served in this capacity. He has been a stockholder of the Frontier Trust Company, one of the leading banking institutions of this section of Maine, since its foundation, and is now a director of the company. Active at all times in the work of the Free and Accepted Masons, Mr. Churchill is affiliated with the Blue Lodge in Fort Fairfield, the Chapter of Royal Arch Masons in Caribou, the Council in Presque Isle, the Commandery in Houlton, and Anah Temple of the Ancient Arabic Order Nobles of the Mystic Shrine in Bangor. He and his family are members of the Congregational church.

Mr. Churchill married Ella B. Kimball, who was born in Jacksontown, New Brunswick, Canada, his own native town, a daughter of Henry and Hannah (Pennington) Kimball, the former of whom was a clergyman in the Free Baptist Church. George H. and Ella B. (Kimball) Churchill are the parents of one child, a daughter, Bulah, who is the wife of A. Wade Marshall. Mr. and Mrs. A. Wade Marshall, who live in Fort Fairfield, where Mr. Marshall is a farmer, have four children, grandchildren of Mr. Churchill: Winston Churchill Marshall, Thomas Lowell Marshall, Shirley Blanche Marshall, and George Kempton Marshall.

BENJAMIN FRANKLIN CLEAVES—As an agriculturist, Benjamin Franklin Cleaves, of Presque Isle, who owns a farm of one hundred and ninety acres on the Cleaves Road, serves both the market and the potato grower by supplying seed potatoes and marketable potatoes of the highest grade. He is the son of James R. and Mary Jane (Argent) Cleaves. His father was born in York County, Maine, and his mother at Fort Fairfield, Maine. His father was one of the early settlers in this part of the country, coming here before the Civil War and spent his entire life on the farm which his son continues to cultivate. His mother is still living in Presque Isle at the age of eighty-two years.

Benjamin Franklin Cleaves was born on his father's farm October 20, 1873. He started his education in the town schools and later went to the Easton High School for a short time. His inclination was to be a farmer and while still quite young he stopped his school work and became active with his father in the farm work. This farm, situated just off the State Highway, has been his one interest and by concentrating all his energy to its cultivation and maintenance, Mr. Cleaves has brought it up to a high state of cultivation and a profitable yield of crops. Since it has been in his possession, he has added many improvements in the way of new and modern buildings and general equipment. Mr. Cleaves is a Republican and takes an interest in all that pertains to the party although his busy life on the farm has occupied all of his time so that he has had no desire for public office, but his interest in public affairs is sincere. He is first and last a farmer and sells his products to local dealers. He is a member of the Order of Free and Accepted Masons, the Order of the Eastern Star and the Grange; also of the Mooseleuk Club.

Benjamin Franklin Cleaves married Theresa P. Doe, daughter of William C. and Emma (Goss) Doe. Mrs. Cleaves was born at Mapleton, Maine. They have no children.

GROVER W. CLEAVES—A resident of the village of Westfield, Grover W. Cleaves owns a farm of one hundred and seven acres on the corner of the Houlton and Westfield roads. Here he does a general farming business, growing potatoes on an extensive scale and selling his products to local buyers. Deeply interested in the civic and social life of Westfield and the surrounding community, Mr. Cleaves is active in political matters and in the affairs of the Grange, and is affiliated with local fraternal orders. He is regarded by his fellow citizens as one of the really substantial members of this district, in which he has lived for so many years.

He was born in Presque Isle, December 14, 1866, a son of James R. and Mary Jane (Argent) Cleaves. His father was born in York County, Maine, and his mother at Fort Fairfield, Maine. James R. Cleaves was one of the early settlers in this part of Maine, coming to this section before the Civil War and proceeding to spend his entire life on the farm which his son, Benjamin Franklin Cleaves, now operates. The mother, Mary Jane (Argent) Cleaves, who was born in 1845, still resides in Presque Isle. Grover W. Cleaves, who now owns a farm in Westfield, attended, as a boy, the common schools of his home town; and after he completed his education he became interested in agricultural work. He has spent practically all his life in farming, and is thoroughly conversant with the problems of his occupation and with local conditions, with the result that he has one of the most beautiful farms in this part of Maine. He is interested in civic and political matters, being a member of the Republican party, for whose candidates he casts his vote. He is a member of the Pomona Grange, of which he is a Past Master; and of the Independent Order of Odd Fellows, in which organization he is affiliated with the Easton Lodge. At all times he has been a close follower of the works of Robert Ingersoll, and is keenly interested in reading the books of the world's great thinkers.

Mr. Cleaves married Emma Dyer, a daughter of Sumner and Ellen (Harmon) Dyer, of Dover, and Foxcroft, Maine. Mrs. Cleaves was born in Presque Isle and died December 17, 1927. Grover W. and Emma (Dyer) Cleaves were the parents of several children: 1. Effie, who is the wife of Elmer Lovely. 2. Benjamin, who is living at home. 3. Bessie, also living at home. 4. Helen. 5. Thomas Paine.

SAMUEL ROSS—There is still opportunity in the older States for the pioneer farmer, as Samuel Ross, of Monticello, Maine, has shown in the course of a highly successful career, provided, of course, that the farmer knows his business, and combines energy with thrift.

Born in Rockland, Carson County, New Brunswick, February 26, 1859, son of Daniel and Martha (Foster) Ross, both natives of that Canadian Province, Samuel Ross attended the public schools of New Brunswick up to his thirteenth year, and then went to work as a farm boy. For a time he was employed near Lincoln, then at Danforth, and at Kingston, Maine, on various farms, and also picked up a practical knowledge of woodcraft and the tanning industry, but his real vocation was the land, and when he had attained the age of twenty-four he purchased some unimproved land at Monticello, on the Lake Road, and having cleared it for agricultural purposes, began its cultivation before he had even erected the first of the necessary farm buildings. There he lived and worked until a few years ago, when the opportunity came for him to buy the 100-acre tract he now occupies across the road from the original farm. This he obtained from the Edward Gould heirs, and repeated his former program of bringing the property to the highest point of productiveness. He and most of his family attend the Baptist church. He is a Republican, but has been too busy to take a very deep interest in politics.

Mr. Ross married Euphemia Lauders, daughter of Charles and Ann (London) Lauders, of Bridgewater, Maine, and they have six children, the eldest son, Guy, living on the first of the two farms Mr. Ross developed, and which he gave him: 1. Maud, wife of Wellington Beaulya; they have one daughter, Muriel. 2. Guy, married Myra Dorsey, and their children are: Irene, Marion, Virginia, Morris, Laura, and Alston. 3. William, married Thelma Dillon, by whom he had one daughter, Madeline; he is now a carpenter in Boston. 4. Elbridge, married Ada Tausch, and is a farmer; their children: Della, Mafine, and Phyllis. 5. Velma, married (first) Ralph Murphy, their children were Ruth and Dorothy; she married (second) George Washington Nason, a farmer of Monticello; their children: J. M. and Alston. 6. Miles, married Mary Porter and their children are: Garfield, Audrey, Ruth, and Clara. Miles is associated in farming with his father.

JOHN FRANK AVERILL is a prominent business man of Fort Fairfield, Maine. He is a general trader who buys and sells all sorts of property, but who in the main is a cattle dealer and operator in farming real estate. He has for many years bought and sold stock, such as horses and cattle, and he has bought and sold a great number of farms. He is in addition director of a bank. It will thus be seen that he is a successful all round merchant with many varieties of experience in business behind him.

John Frank Averill was born at Fort Fairfield, Maine, October 3, 1877, son of Stephen L. and Lucy (Currier) Averill, of whom the father was a farmer, and both were natives of Fort Fairfield, and both now deceased. The father married twice, his second wife being Mrs. Eva Hall. John Frank Averill attended the public school and spent two terms also in high school. He then worked on his father's farm until he was twenty-five years old. Then he worked for a year as hired hand on another farm, later purchasing a farm of his own in the town of Easton, and worked on it, but after that he made a practice of buying farms and selling them. His method being to develop them and put them into good shape and then sell them at a profit. He has thus owned a great number of farms in different localities, but finally he returned to Fort Fairfield, where he owned and operated two farms. Recently, however, he has been more or less in retirement as regards farming, but he continues his trading, buying and selling horses and cattle and other property. Mr. Averill is a Republican, but has not accepted and has not sought any sort of political office. He belongs to the Knights of Pythias of Fort Fairfield; the Blue Lodge, Free and Accepted Masons; Fort Fairfield Chapter, Caribou, Royal Arch Masons; and some other organizations.

Mr. Averill married Verna L. Jameson, born at Fort Fairfield, daughter of Silas and Phoebe (Lunn) Jameson. Children: Anna L. and John Frank, Jr. Mr. and Mrs. Averill are both active in connection with the Methodist church, he being on the finance committee and the board of trustees.

EDWARD MELVIN HINES—Numbered outstandingly among public spirited and substantial men of Washburn, Aroostook County, Maine, was Edward Melvin Hines, who devoted the whole of his active career to the progress of this community and to the welfare of the nearby towns of Presque Isle and Caribou. Edward Melvin Hines was born at Presque Isle, March 9, 1861, son of Joseph and Marcella (Hall) Hines, deceased, and there received his education in the public schools.

In early life, Mr. Hines taught school at rural posts, but abandoned the profession soon after attaining his majority to establish himself in business in Washburn. He founded a hardware and machinery house under his own name, as sole proprietor, but after a period took into association a partner, W. R. Smith, of Caribou, and with him expanded the enterprise, enlarging the business in Washburn and opening a trading unit at Caribou. Messrs. Hines and Smith speedily achieved prosperity in the proprietorship of their joint affairs, and Mr. Hines found occasion to extend his activities, under his own right, to further interests of an independent character. It was he who established the Washburn Electrical Company, and of this organization, he was president until his death. When the proposal was first made that the Aroostook Valley Railroad Company might extend its lines through Washburn, Mr. Hines was most influential in its support. He was for a number of years a personal and intimate friend of Senator Gould, who, upon occasion, remarked that chiefly through Mr. Hines' effort was the railroad venture a success. He was not alone most instrumental in the bringing of the road to Washburn, but also in contributing to its freight and express patronage after its installation had been effected, thus insuring life to it during the first difficult years. Moreover, Mr. Hines stood firmly in support of the new school building for Washburn, when the building was proposed, and to him is accorded much of the credit for voting of necessary bonds. He served on the building committee of the school after the bonds had been voted, and for a number of years was an interested member of the Washburn School Board; for, since the years when he was interested in teaching professionally he had always maintained an unflagging devotion to the science of education. He was a charter member of the local Blue Lodge of the Free and Accepted Masons, and an active participant in all matters of Masonry, was its secretary for twenty years. He was a member of the Royal Arch Masons and Royal and Select Masons at Caribou, Knights Templar at Houl-

ton, and of Kora Temple, Ancient Arabic Order Nobles of the Mystic Shrine at Lewiston. To Mr. Hines is universally given the credit for having brought to Washburn the local chapter of the Order of the Easter Star, called Coldvale Chapter, of which Mrs. Hines was first Worthy Matron. It is said of Mr. Hines that he was a leading citizen, foremost in the affairs of Washburn, benefactor of the community, contributed generously to its progress; and when he died, at his Washburn home, on August 11, 1921, in his sixty-first year, his loss was mourned sincerely in the hearts of his many friends of Washburn, Presque Isle, Caribou and Houlton, and in the circles of which he was member throughout the county of Aroostook. Funeral services were conducted by the Masons and the Eastern Star, jointly, and were attended by the large numbers of whom he was beloved.

Edward Melvin Hines married Nellie Elmira Annas, native of Presque Isle, daughter of Alfred and Elmira (Wilson) Annas. Mrs. Hines was for a number of years a teacher in rural schools, and after marriage, as first Worthy Matron of the Eastern Star and member of many other societies, was prominent in women's affairs of Washburn. Her demise, on May 28, 1911, was poignantly felt by her family and by associates among whom she was accustomed to move; she was possessed of a most refined character and a personality that endeared her to her numerous friends. Edward Melvin and Nellie Elmira (Annas) Hines were the parents of one child, a daughter, Marcella Mildred.

Marcella Mildred Hines received her early education in the schools of Washburn, and upon completion of studies in high school matriculated in Bates College, at Lewiston, Maine, whence she graduated with the class of 1911, in the spring when occurred the death of her mother. When, after this sad loss, Miss Hines had recovered sufficiently she took a position as teacher of English at Washburn High School, and as such distinguished herself most creditably. She became the wife of Earl M. Gibson, now (1928) manager of the cinema at Washburn, who was born in Washburn, graduated from Washburn High School and Ricker Classical Institute at Houlton. As Mrs. Gibson, she has assumed a conspicuous rôle in affairs of the social circles of the community; like her mother, Mrs. Gibson is Past Worthy Matron of the Order of the Eastern Star, and in addition is Past District Deputy Grand Matron of the Eastern Star of Aroostook County. She is also Past Grand of the Rebekah Lodge of Washburn. Mr. Gibson is the son of Manning S. and Myra (Reiley) Gibson. He is a member of the Washburn Lodge, Free and Accepted Masons, also Washburn Rotary Club, and Washburn Independent Order of Odd Fellows.

Baptist church, Mr. Ross contributes liberally to causes sponsored by it.

Thaddeus D. Ross married Hattie Belyea, daughter of James and Elizabeth Belyea, both of whom were natives of Maine, though they spent the later years of life in Boston. Mr. and Mrs. Ross are the parents of six children: Inez, Alice, Leland, Clyde, Olie, and Grace.

THADDEUS D. ROSS—One of the prominent and well to do landowners of Monticello is Thaddeus D. Ross, who is proprietor of two large farms in this neighborhood, one of seventy acres and the other of one hundred and sixty, both bordering on the Lake Road. Mr. Ross engages in general agriculture, rotating his crops from year to year, and specializing in the growing of potatoes. For the storage of this valuable crop he maintains a capacious cellar, on the quarter section, and in town possesses a warehouse for storage of potatoes and other agricultural produce.

Thaddeus D. Ross was born near Lake Road on September 5, 1879, son of Ludlow and Nanney (Belyea) Ross, both of whom were natives of New Brunswick, Dominion of Canada, former deceased. Ludlow and Nanney (Belyea) Ross were married in Maine, and spent the balance of their lives in Monticello, save for four years in residence at Kingman, Maine. They were the parents of seven children, of whom Thaddeus D. was the only son, and he received his education in the common schools of Monticello. At the age of sixteen years he went to work as woodsman and farmer, doing this for seven years, engaging himself as woodsman in the winter and as farmer in the summer. At the age of twenty-three years he purchased his first farm land, a tract of seventy acres, which he cultivated with success until 1925, when he purchased the quarter section from Guy Fletcher. Mr. Ross employs the soundest of business methods in the conduct of these lands, and is regarded highly by the business men of Monticello with whom he has commercial dealings. He takes an active part in the political life of the community and is affiliated with the Republican party. His opinion on matters of a political character is often sought after, and when given, is received with appreciation. A member of the

WILLIAM GILBERT CHAMBERLAIN, M. D.—Prominent in the ranks of physicians of the community in and near Fort Fairfield, Maine, William Gilbert Chamberlain, M. D., has done more than the usual work of a member of his profession, having served as health officer of this town for twelve years. Interested in the growth and development of Fort Fairfield, he has shown himself ready at all times to support movements that he thought would benefit the town and improve conditions among the people; has taken an active part in the social and fraternal life of the community; and has rendered valued service as a member of the school board. Dr. Chamberlain is held in high esteem by his fellow citizens, and his opinions on matters relating to the welfare of the town are respected and sought by those who have had proof of the soundness of his judgments.

He was born in Queens County, New Brunswick, Canada, May 28, 1870, a son of Cornelius and Elizabeth (Hetherington) Chamberlain, both of whom were natives of New Brunswick and who never came to the United States. His father was a harness maker in New Brunswick. As a boy, William Gilbert Chamberlain attended the public schools of his native town; then he became a student at the Provincial Normal School until he left this institution to become a school teacher for four years; and finally he went to the Chicago Homeopathic Medical College, from which institution he was graduated in the class of 1897 with the degree of Doctor of Medicine. On August 16, 1897, he was admitted to the practice of the medical profession in Maine, practicing first in Masardis, Maine, for a few months, and then coming to Fort Fairfield, where he has maintained his offices ever since 1898. He is now a member of the Board of Registration of Medicine in Maine, an office to which he was appointed by Governor

Baxter. He was a member of the school board of Fort Fairfield for twenty-one years; and for twelve years was health officer of the town. In his political convictions he is affiliated with the Democratic party, of whose principles and candidates he is a staunch supporter. Active in the organizations of his profession, he is a member of the American Medical Association, the Maine State Medical Society, and the National Homeopathic Association. Dr. Chamberlain holds memberships in different branches of the Free and Accepted Masons, in which order he is affiliated with the Blue Lodge in Fort Fairfield, the chapter of Royal Arch Masons in Caribou, the Council in Presque Isle, the Commandery in Houlton, and Anah Temple of the Ancient Arabic Order Nobles of the Mystic Shrine in Bangor. He and the members of his family attend the Congregational church of Fort Fairfield.

Dr. Chamberlain married Maud D. Glendenning, who was born at Harvey Station, New Brunswick. They are the parents of the following children: 1. Ethel, who is the wife of M. P. Roberts, whose biography appears elsewhere in this work. 2. Judson, who is living in West Medford, Massachusetts, being a graduate of the Fort Fairfield High School, and having married Doris Parker, by which marriage there is one child, William Gilbert, Jr. 3. Edna, who was educated in the high school at Fort Fairfield and at Colby College, and is now a teacher of English in the junior high school in Los Angeles, California. 4. Glenn, who teaches science in the Presque Isle High School, and who is a graduate of Bowdoin College. 5. Dolly, who now is a student in the high school in Fort Fairfield, Maine.

FRANK L. STITHAM—Owning three hundred acres of land in and near Littleton, Frank L. Stitham has been for many years one of the prominent farmers of this section of Maine. Doing a general farming business but specializing in potato raising, he has built for himself here a lucrative trade, selling to local buyers. Having spent most of his life in this part of Maine, where he has participated freely in the public affairs of his community and has shown himself to be actively interested in its welfare, he is well known by the local citizens and is thoroughly conversant with conditions. He served his town for some years as a member of the school board.

Mr. Stitham was born in East Winn, the son of Thaddeus and Frances Lillian (White) Stitham, an old and prominent family in this section. His father passed on May 8, 1928, but his mother still lives on the old homestead, not far from Littleton, which consists of a hundred-acre farm. Mr. Stitham now works this farm himself, in addition to his two hundred acres on the Stitham and Gentle Road in Littleton. Mr. Stitham is one of the five children of Thaddeus and Frances Lillian (White) Stitham: 1. Frank L., of whom further. 2. Mabel, deceased. 3. Sadie, wife of William H. Anderson, a sketch of whom appears in this volume. 4. Gus, now deceased. 5. Ella, wife of Edson Briggs.

The eldest of these children, Frank L., received his education in the public schools, and since he finished his schooling he has been engaged practically all of his life on the home farm. The farm on the Stitham and Gentle Road he bought in 1905 from Peter Travers. Mr. Stitham is actively interested in the affairs of his town, especially from a political viewpoint, being a member of the Republican party. For some years he served as a member of the school board. His religious affiliation is with the Baptist church, in which both he and his wife are active and in which he holds the office of deacon.

Frank L. Stitham married Susie A. London, a daughter of James W. and Bessie (Crandlemire) London, farmers who reside in Monticello. They are now the parents of four children: 1. Ralph E., who was born in 1903, and is now on the old homestead of his grandfather; he married Laura Hersey, by which marriage there is one child, Marcella. 2. Hazel, the wife of Lloyd Newman, who lives with Frank L. Stitham. 3. Dorothy, who is a student at the Ricker Classical Institute. 4. Maxine, who is at home.

MELVIN P. ROBERTS—Since the close of the World War, Melvin P. Roberts has been engaged in legal practice in Fort Fairfield, Maine. He is a graduate of Colby College and of Harvard Law School, and during the World War served on the draft board in the local office at Fort Fairfield. Mr. Roberts is a member of the law firm of Trafton and Roberts.

Melvin P. Roberts was born in Caribou, Maine, November 22, 1891, son of C. Blake and Annie (Trafton) Roberts, and received his early education in the public schools of Caribou. When his course in the Caribou High School was completed he became a student in Colby College, at Waterville, Maine, from which he was graduated with the class of 1913, receiving at that time the degree of Bachelor of Arts. As he had chosen the legal profession as his future field of activity, he then entered Harvard Law School, where he was graduated in 1918 with the degree of Bachelor of Laws. He then served as a member of the draft board in the local office at Fort Fairfield, continuing in that capacity until the close of the war. In the spring of 1919 he became associated with Herbert W. Trafton, who is a member of the board of public utilities, with office at Augusta, and that connection has continued to the present time (1928). Mr. Roberts looks after the local office and Mr. Trafton attends to the Augusta office. Politically, Mr. Roberts supports the principles and the candidates of the Democratic party. He is a member of the Caribou Lodge, Free and Accepted Masons; and of Garfield Chapter, at Caribou, Royal Arch Masons; and his religious membership and that of his family is with the Episcopal church.

Melvin P. Roberts is married to Ethel Chamberlain, daughter of Dr. W. G. Chamberlain, a physician of Fort Fairfield (q. v.). Mr. and Mrs. Roberts have three children: Sarah, Philip, and David.

EDWARD P. TITCOMB—Of an old Maine family, and a highly successful farmer, Edward P. Titcomb, of Littleton and Houlton, is also a Maine man by choice, for he spent two years in California in early manhood, on a ranch, returned home long enough to be married, and then went to California, where he remained twelve years, being in charge of a ranch most of that time. But he had owned a farm in Littleton, and eventually he returned to cultivate it himself.

Born in Littleton, Maine, January 28, 1862, he was the son of Benjamin and Mary (Crosby) Titcomb. His father was born in Durham, his mother in Houlton, Maine. The father was killed in the Civil War and the mother lived to be sixty-six years old. Edward P. Titcomb was educated in the Littleton public schools, and had acquired a practical knowledge of farming on his father's farm before going to California.

On his return to Maine, Mr. Titcomb took an active part in all local civic affairs. His Littleton farm, on which he resides, consists of two hundred acres, and his Houlton farm of one hundred acres. Both are on the North Road, and besides general farming, he grows potatoes on both places, and owns his own warehouse at Hill's siding for convenience in shipping. A Republican, he served as selectman, and was chairman of the board for twelve years. He is a member of the Independent Order of Odd Fellows, and a member of the Baptist church. He comes of a family which has always responded to calls for public duty, his father having volunteered during the Civil War, and died in his country's service.

Mr. Titcomb married Mary A. Bubar, of a family long settled in Maine. Their children are: 1. Orie Nevers (see a following biography). 2. Alton, who is in the ice business in Houlton, Maine. 3. Mabel. 4. Newel, who married Helen Bliss, and has a farm on the North Road, in Littleton. They have two children. 5. Byron E., who lives in Presque Isle.

ORIE NEVERS TITCOMB—For more than one hundred years the Titcomb farm on the Ridge Road out from Monticello, Maine, has been in the same family. The present owner, Orie Nevers Titcomb, inherited the place from his father who had inherited it from his father before him, and so the family have been engaged in farming for generations, and continue to lead in that line of occupation.

Orie Nevers Titcomb was born on his father's farm near Monticello and Littleton, Maine, September 14, 1887. He is the son of Edward P. and Mary A. (Bubar) Titcomb, who live in the town of Littleton (see a preceding biography). He was educated in the schools of Littleton supplemented by eight months training in a business school in Houlton, Maine. He has always followed the occupation of a farmer and now handles the two hundred acres that his father and grandfather farmed before him. In addition to growing his crops, Mr. Titcomb is a potato shipper and operates a warehouse in association with James A. Stone under the firm name of Stone and Titcomb. He was chairman of the Board of Selectmen on two different occasions, and is a member of the Grange and of the Baptist church, where he and his family are very active. He is also a member of the Order of Free and Accepted Masons and is a Past Master of his lodge.

Orie Nevers Titcomb married Gladys Brown, of Presque Isle, Maine, daughter of John D. and Carrie (Higgins) Brown. They have four children: Florence, Edward Payson, John, and Ralph Malcolm.

ALBERT F. COOK—Barrister, engaged in the legal profession in Fort Fairfield, Aroostook County, Maine, since the month of April, 1919, Albert F. Cook was born at Bangor, Maine, on October 6, 1889, son of Albert and Mary E. (Lombard) Cook.

Albert Cook, the father, was for a number of years in business as meat merchant in Bangor, and enjoyed the highest reputation in the mercantile circles of the city as one who paid his obligations promptly and who guided the course of his enterprise successfully. Both he and his wife, Mary E. (Lombard) Cook, resided in Bangor until the end of their days.

Albert F. Cook, the son, received his early education in the elementary schools of Bangor, and graduated from high school there in 1907, at the age of eighteen. He matriculated in the fall of that year in the University of Maine, and for two years pursued a general curriculum in that institution. Meanwhile was apparent within himself a growing interest in the law, and when, after the completion of two years of academic work, he found himself with requirements for entrance into law school fulfilled, he entered the Law School of the University of Maine, and applied himself diligently to legal studies for three years, graduating with the degree of Bachelor of Law in 1912. He had passed all courses with distinction, both in college and in law school, and it was without real difficulty that he passed the examinations permitting him to practice before any bar in the State of Maine. At once he began to practice, in the fall of 1912, at Bangor, and continued in this practice, which always has been of a general character, until the United States entered the World War in 1917. Able-bodied and loyal to his country, Mr. Cook discontinued his profession to enlist in the Connecticut Infantry. He was stationed at Camp Upton and Camp Raritan with the rank of drill sergeant, and was mustered out in the month of April, 1919. That same month he came to Fort Fairfield, and here began practice anew. During the years that have succeeded his practice has grown, and his station in the legal fraternity of village and county has kept pace. He is not only apt in preparation and argument of cases before justice but is, moreover, active in affairs of the village, constantly allied with enterprises for its development. He is a Republican, and in the party exercises a considerable power; for two years, 1921-22, he served on the Board of Selectmen. Fraternally, his interests are extensive, including membership in the Fort Fairfield Blue Lodge of the Free and Accepted Masons; the Benevolent and Protective Order of Elks at Bangor, and the Independent Order of Odd Fellows, at Fort Fairfield. Mr. Cook's family attends the Congregational church, is devout in its service, and generous in contributions to charitable and other worthy causes, regardless of race or creed involved, giving in a spirit truly humanitarian. Of him it is said that he is a skillful solicitor of unimpeachable ethics, a valuable citizen of his community, and an upright and honorable man in all his dealings.

Albert F. Cook married Olive Thomas, daughter of Oscar and Ella (Fowler) Thomas; and to this union has been born one child, a daughter, Norma P.

BENNETT E. RAMSEY—Among the Maine farmers who have profited largely through the production of potatoes as a money crop, is Bennett E. Ramsey, owner of a two hundred acre farm on the North Road of the town of Monticello.

He was born at White Cove, Grand Lake, New Brunswick, August 3, 1862, the son of Robert Orchard. On the early death of his parents he was adopted by George and Sarah (Briggs) Ramsey, and took their name. In 1866, the family removed to the United States from Canada, and lived at Littleton, then at Blaine, and finally settled in Monticello, in 1876. George Ramsey was a harness maker. Bennett Ramsey was educated in the public schools of Monticello. At the age of seventeen he obtained work in a shingle mill, where he remained ten years, and then entered the service of the Bangor and Augusta Railroad Company as a roadman, employed in locating and constructing buildings. Four years later he returned to Monticello and for the next four years plied his father's craft of harness making. Then he made his start as a farmer, in which he was to find his real life's work and best reward.

On July 2, 1898, he purchased the property he now occupies, on which, however, he had been living for several years. He is a member of the Free and Accepted Masons, Monumental Lodge, Aroostook Royal Arch Chapter, Presque Isle Council, Houlton Commandery, and Kora Temple of the Mystic Shrine at Lewiston. He is also a member of the Grange. He is a Republican.

Mr. Ramsey married (first) Birdie L. Howe, whose one child, Charles, died at the age of eight, the mother following some years later. He married (second) Anna A. Robertson, who was born in Monticello, Maine. He and his wife are both active in the affairs of the Methodist Episcopal church, where he is chairman of the board of trustees.

LEWIS F. CHURCHILL—Successor to his father, who retired in 1915, Lewis F. Churchill has since that date served on the road commission of the town of Washburn, Aroostook County, Maine, and has charge of both State and community roads. His father was for many years, until retirement, a road commissioner; and both father and son have established for themselves meritorious records in the service of the public. Lewis F. Churchill is also interested in agriculture: he owns a fertile tract of one hundred acres on the Taber Road; and this farm is conducted by his sons, under his direction, engaging in general agriculture, disposing of the produce in the local markets.

Lewis F. Churchill was born at Washburn on March 10, 1881, son of J. Allen and Lizzie (Dyer) Churchill. Lizzie (Dyer) Churchill is deceased.

J. Allen Washburn was for many years a farmer and dealer in lumber, active in the affairs of Washburn and vicinity, and respected by all who had business with him; and now (1928) he devotes the greater part of his time to community matters in which he is invited to participate, having put behind him the absorbing cares of business. He is considered one of the most public-spirited citizens of the town. A Republican, loyal to the principles of government upheld by the party, he has always exercised a wide influence in politics, and in public office has served conscientiously, not alone as commissioner of roads but in other capacities as well. The name of Churchill has long been an honored one in Washburn and Aroostook County.

Lewis F. Churchill attended the public schools of the place of his birth, and upon completion of studies went into association with his father, on the farm. Here he continued until he had reached his majority of years, then launched out for himself in the career of agriculture. He purchased eighty acres in Dunn Township, managed them with good profit for six years, and disposed of the farm; he bought a second holding, and conducted it with like favorable results for the next five years; then, in 1915, he purchased the one hundred acres on the Taber Road, which he has owned since. This farm is known as the Mel Greenleaf farm and is admired widely over the countryside. Mr. Churchill causes the latest and most scientific methods of agriculture as approved by State and National Departments of Agriculture to be applied in care of the hundred; and under his direction and the industrious application of his sons, yields are large indeed. Like his father, Mr. Churchill is a member of the Republican party, and possessed of a considerable influence in political matters of town and county. Fraternally he is a member of the Modern Woodmen of America. He is a member of the Baptist church, is devout in its service, and generous in his contributions to charitable and kindred causes of worthy appeal. It is said of him that he is one of the most substantial citizens of the community, sincerely interested in its development.

Lewis F. Churchill married Lela Sears, of Limestone, who died in July, 1927. To this union were born five children: 1. Basil, graduate of high school, married Lela Gould. 2. Wallace, student in the high school. 3. Evelyn, also a student in the high school. 4. Amos. 5. Roy.

WILLIS P. BRIDGHAM—Born in Ashland, Maine, May 1, 1860, the son of Zebulon and Hannah (Walker) Bridgham, he was educated in the public schools of Ashland, Coburn Classical Institute, Waterville, Maine, and Augusta Business College. At the early age of sixteen he started out to learn the cheesemaking business, at which occupation he was employed at Ashland, Maine; Little Falls, New York; and Presque Isle, Maine; after which time he purchased the factory at Ashland and successfully operated it for several years. He was counted as one of the best cheesemakers of that time.

In 1888 he purchased the residence and store formerly owned and occupied by the late D. N. Rogers. Restocking the store with general merchandise, and by strict attention to business and honest and square dealing he built up a large and prosperous business. Mr. Bridgham was always interested in anything that would advance the interests of the community in which he lived. Although never seeking public office, he served his town many years as first selectman, also as town clerk. He was postmaster under President Cleveland. A director of the Merchants Trust and Banking Company of Presque Isle, Maine. He was influential in organizing the Ashland Trust Company at Ashland, Maine, and was its first president, which position he held until his death, January 3, 1922. He held the confidence and esteem of the community in which he lived, and is remembered by a large circle of friends and business acquaintances as a financier of ability and good judgment, a merchant of strictest probity; devoted to his family and a faithful servant of the community in which his activities formed so important a part.

In October, 1888, Mr. Bridgham married Clara E. Drummond, of Waterville, Maine, their children being: 1. Florence M., now Mrs. Harvey L. Alieff, of Ashland, Maine. 2. Mildred R., now Mrs. Bernard G. Blake, of Freeport, Maine. 3. Hadley D. Bridgham, living at Freeport, and Ashland, Maine.

HERBERT T. POWERS—Banker, barrister, Herbert T. Powers was born at Pittsfield, Maine, November 13, 1870, son of Hannibal Hamlin and Abbie (Neal) Powers, and since the month of November, in the year 1892, has practiced the pro-

fession of law in Aroostook County, locating first in the town of Blaine for one year, and in 1893 in Fort Fairfield, where he now (1928) resides, a principal member of the community, respected by all who know him.

Mr. Powers received his early education in the public schools of Pittsfield, then entered Maine Central Institute. Upon graduation from the latter institution he matriculated in Bowdoin College, and upon leaving the college began to read law in the offices of J. W. Manson, of Pittsfield. He applied himself industriously and intelligently to the case books, discussing troublesome points with Mr. Manson, fitting himself in every way for the prosperous general practice that he later enjoyed. Mr. Powers advanced rapidly in study of the law, and when only twenty-one years of age, in the month of September, 1892, took the examinations which permitted him to practice his profession before any bar in the State of Maine. He was elected to the House of Representatives in 1898 at the age of twenty-seven. Here he served very creditably until 1901 and gave ample proof of his quality of mind in discussion, support of and opposition to measures coming up for consideration. In Fort Fairfield Mr. Powers has taken an active part in all enterprises for community development, in political life and commercial affairs. He is one of the foresighted body of citizens who founded the Frontier Trust Company, and was, because of his legal training and generally sound judgment in business, as well as because of his high character, chosen by them to be president of the organization and in this important office he has continued, to the complete satisfaction of associates, through succeeding years. Known widely for his public-spirited interest in Fort Fairfield and for his talent in the law, Mr. Powers is possessed of a considerable influence in the public voice. When he became candidate for the post of county attorney, he was elected by a good majority of votes, and during the four years of his term distinguished the office with integrity to justice and a tireless devotion to duty in all ways commendable. When this office became vacant in 1924, through the resignation of the then incumbent, Mr. Powers was asked to fill the unexpired portion of the term by the Governor of the State. Fraternally he has strong and extensive connections, including membership in the Blue Lodge at Fort Fairfield of the Free and Accepted Masons,

Royal Arch Masons at Caribou, Royal and Select Masters at Presque Isle; and the Benevolent and Protective Order of Elks at Houlton. During the World War, after the United States joined the allies in Europe, Mr. Powers worked indefatigably on the various boards and committees prosecuting the war from within this country, and was instrumental in securing many investments in the several Liberty Loan campaigns. He served wherever there was opportunity to serve. He is a Protestant, and is generous in contributions to charity and other causes of like worthy nature.

Herbert T. Powers married Una Lincoln Neal, and to this union were born two children: 1. Neal, educated in the schools of Fort Fairfield and in Boston University, engaged in the insurance business at Fort Fairfield. 2. Alice M., graduate of the Wheaton School, instructor in the public schools for three years, and at present (1928) doing secretarial work in Boston. Mrs. Powers died in 1912 and Mr. Powers married (second) Etta B. Haynes, of Bangor.

HENRY W. PERRY—As postmaster of Fort Fairfield, Henry W. Perry has displayed an excellent executive ability, and has performed in an efficient and creditable manner the duties of his office, to which he was appointed in 1924 by President Calvin Coolidge. The Fort Fairfield Postoffice is what is known as a second class office, having three regular clerks, one substitute clerk, one regular carrier, and one substitute carrier, and covering four rural routes. Mr. Perry, who always has taken a keen interest in public affairs and has shown himself ready to support any movement which he has believed would improve conditions in the community, is affiliated politically with the Republican party, in whose principles he is a steadfast believer and whose candidates he sanctions by his vote.

Mr. Perry was born in Mars Hill, Maine, April 27, 1866, a son of Henry O. and Martha (Preble) Perry, both of whom are now deceased. For many years his father was Collector of Customs, and in later years established what is today known as the H. O. Perry insurance business. Henry W. Perry, as a boy, was educated in the public schools; and, after he completed his education, he went into the customs office with his father. Afterward he was a clerk in a hardware store, and for twenty years conducted a hardware store on his own account. Finally he sold the hardware business, and for a time operated a variety store. Then, in 1924, he was made postmaster of Fort Fairfield. Active in fraternal work, Mr. Perry is a member of the Free and Accepted Masons, in which order he is affiliated with the Blue Lodge; and a member of the Knights of Pythias. He and his family attend the Congregational church.

Henry W. Perry married Mora C. Knight, who was born in Houlton, Maine, a daughter of Herman and Abbie (Hadley) Knight, and they are the parents of three children: 1. Wellman L., who is assistant manager of the United Drug Store, in Boston, and who married Adelaide Stilphen, by which marriage there are five children: Constance, Dorothy, Stilphen, Margaret, and Beyrl. 2. Ellen Beyrl, who is the wife of Louis Fowler, the manager of the Atlantic and Pacific Tea Store in Dover Foxcroft, Maine. 3. Margaret, who is a student at the State Normal School, in Presque Isle.

CYRUS H. ALLEN—Owner and operator of a fertile tract of one hundred and twenty-five acres on the Shorey Road in Westfield Township near the village of Westfield (formerly a plantation), Cyrus H. Allen engages in general agriculture and specializes in the production of table potatoes, of which product and other produce he disposes in the local market. He is now (1928) second member of the Westfield Board of Selectmen, in which position he has served since 1921; for one year he was commissioner of roads for Aroostook County. Cyrus H. Allen was born in Westfield Township on July 21, 1889, son of Edwin and Kate (Chase) Allen, both of whom make their homes at Westfield, his father having engaged in farming for a number of years before his retirement.

Edwin Allen was born at Presque Isle, Aroostook County, August 9, 1862, son of Moses and Melissa J. (Buck) Allen. The family of Allen has resided in Westfield Township for many years, the homestead having been in its possession since 1847. Edwin Allen has constantly been active in the affairs of the community here, and his wife,

Kate (Chase) Allen, is a native of Westfield, daughter of Cyrus and Abbie (Hinckley) Chase. Both are highly regarded by all who know them. They are the parents of three sons: Moses, Cyrus H., and Clarence L.

Cyrus H. Allen received his education in the public schools of the Westfield district, and upon completion of his studies assisted his father in the management of the family acres. In this he continued until he was twenty-two years of age, when he purchased the farm from his father and conducted it independently. Mr. Allen employs the most modern of methods of agriculture recommended by State and National Departments of Agriculture, rotating crops according to plan, and adapting seeding and cultivation best to fit his own special soil, of which he constantly makes a study. Under his husbandry the land yields large return, and in Westfield village and commercial centers outlying he is favorably regarded for the intelligence with which he directs his business operations. A Republican, he is loyal to the principles of government upheld by that party and strong in Republican ranks of village, township and county, possessed of a considerable influence in local elections. During the World War he served tirelessly on the various boards and committees of war work, and participated in the campaigns for sale of Liberty Loan bonds. He is a member of the Independent Order of Odd Fellows and of the Modern Woodmen of America, and with his family attends the Baptist church. In contributions to charitable and other causes of like worthy character Mr. Allen is generous, giving in a spirit truly humanitarian.

Cyrus H. Allen married Mary Baird, native of the Province of New Brunswick, Dominion of Canada, daughter of Samuel and Annie (Lawrence) Baird; and to this union have been born five children: Phyllis, Kathleen, Edwin, Madeline, and Lawrence.

LESLIE ARLINGTON CURTIS—Starting with the practical experience he gained on his father's farm, added to that obtained in the service of other farmers, Leslie Arlington Curtis rented a small farm for a time, purchased it, was the owner of more than sixty acres while still in his twenties, and now has one hundred and sixty acres of land on the Lake Road in the town of Monticello.

Son of William F. and Arelda (Rodgers) Curtis, he was born in New Brunswick, Canada, January 7, 1865. His parents were Americans, who removed from Plymouth, Maine, to Canada, in the sixties, and as there were nine children, the youngsters' all had to work at an early age. Leslie Arlington Curtis decided to try his fortunes in the United States, and became a farm hand in Maine at the age of eighteen. He and his family are members of the Baptist church, in which he is a deacon. He is an Orangeman, and a Knight of the Maccabees.

Mr. Curtis married Clara Bell Crutcher, daughter of Liberty Benjamin and Alice (Tarbell) Crutcher. She was born in England, where her parents continued to reside. Their one son is Francis Leslie Curtis, born in 1899, and educated in the schools of Monticello, who is his father's assistant on the farm.

IRA D. CURTIS—An excellent example of the prosperous and reliable citizens who have attained a competence largely as a result of their own industry is Ira D. Curtis, who owns two one hundred acre tracts in the town of Monticello, Maine, on one of which he has specialized successfully in growing potatoes.

Son of William F. and Arelda (Rodgers) Curtis, he was born in Marineashee, New Brunswick, May 29, 1877, but of American parentage, his father being a native of Plymouth, Maine, who removed to Canada in the sixties. Being one of a family of nine children, five boys and four girls, Ira D. Curtis was obliged to leave school at the age of fifteen, and found work on a farm, where he remained several years, and until he was able to buy the one hundred acre property on the Lake Road, on which he still resides, from Burt Madigan. He has developed this land until it has become one of the finest farms in the town, and practically built all the farm buildings himself. His second tract of one hundred acres is still in timber.

Mr. Curtis married Mary E. Kent, who was born in Deer Island, New Brunswick, and they have one son, Ira D. Curtis, Jr. The Curtis family are members of the Primitive Baptist Church, and belong to the Republican party. Local buyers take practically their entire crops.

HARRY A. GREENWOOD—In the field of finance and insurance in Aroostook County, Harry A. Greenwood is one of the most prominent figures of this section of Maine. For over a quarter of a century he has been associated with the public and community life of Ashland, ever to the fore in all projects for the advancement of the citizens and the section in general.

Mr. Greenwood was born in Greene, August 9, 1864, the son of Septimus B. and Rachel (Lowell) Greenwood, both natives of Maine, who had lived all their lives in Androscoggin County. Following his early education in the public schools of his native town, Mr. Greenwood took courses at the Litchfield Academy and at the Farmington Normal School. When his scholastic career was ended, Mr. Greenwood taught schools in Maine and New Hampshire for about ten years, at the end of which time he went to Boston, Massachusetts, where he was clerk in a grocery store for about five years. He came to Ashland in 1900 and became associated with Willis P. Bridgham in a general merchandise business. He was appointed postmaster of Ashland by President Wilson and officiated in that capacity for about nine years. Before coming to Ashland he was superintendent of schools in the town of Wales, in Androscoggin County, prior to the union of the schools of the district. He has served Ashland as school committee and town treasurer, and is one of the Board of Selectmen, and he is also president of the Ashland Trust Company, one of Aroostook's thriving banks. He is a member of the Episcopal church and is affiliated with Lewistown Lodge, No. 25, Independent Order of Odd Fellows.

Mr. Greenwood married Mary Eva Bridgham, daughter of Zebulon and Hannah (Walker) Bridgham, the former a prominent farmer of Aroostook County. Mr. and Mrs. Greenwood are the parents of one child, a son, George B., who received his education in the public and high schools of Ashland, later graduating from Dean Academy. He then took a course at the Bliss Electrical College at Washington, D. C., and is now with the Westinghouse & Duquesne Light and Power Company, of Pittsburgh, Pennsylvania.

OWEN KINGSLEY STORY—One of Maine's most distinguished sons, Owen Kingsley Story, of Washburn, is a leader in commercial circles as well

Maine—2—10

as being a prominent member of the Republican party, actively engaged in serving his town and State faithfully and commendably for many years in various offices. Mr. Story was a member of the State Legislature two terms, 1921-22 and 1923-24, and his terms were characterized by his earnest and sincere endeavors to serve the best interests of the commonwealth and its people. He was one of the men who framed and put through the bill for a uniform poll tax, and also was a member of the group which organized the Federal Farm Loan Association, of which he has been president since its inauguration.

Mr. Story was born in Washburn, May 3, 1872, son of James Munroe Story, of Vermont, and Mary Harriett (Harris) Story, of Sebago, both of whom are deceased. James Munroe Story came to Washburn about 1859 or 1860, and at the outbreak of the Civil War, heeding the call to service, enlisted in the Fifteenth Maine Infantry, of which he was a member for five years. After his honorable discharge from the army, he returned and was occupied for the remainder of his life in agriculture and mercantile business, serving as postmaster of the town for twenty years, during which time he gained an enviable reputation for efficiency and ability.

Owen Kingsley Story received his education in the local public schools, and after high school, engaged in farming which has always been one of his greatest interests. Energetic and ambitious, and with great ability to see ahead, he steadily progressed until he is today president of the O. K. Story Company, one of the important enterprises of the vicinity. This concern, organized in 1920, operates an important general hardware and farm machinery business and are also leading factors in the potato industry in addition to producing other crops on their two large farms, one of 125 acres in this town and the other 200 acres on Gardner Creek in the town of Wade, specializing in seed and table stock. The officers of this company are, in addition to Mr. Story: H. E. Umphrey, treasurer, and William Gardine, secretary. All his life, Mr. Story has taken a deep interest in civic affairs and has always had some official connection with the political life of the town or State. For eight years he served as deputy sheriff and for six years of this time he served as tax collector of the town. During the latter term he collected and turned in to the treasurer before the

10th of January each year, excepting one, and that year it was in February. This is a record seldom if ever equalled by any collector in any part of Maine. He has also performed the duties of town treasurer for six years. For twenty-five years he has been a member of the Republican Town Committee, acting as its chairman. His whole-hearted interest has always been enlisted in the support of all projects for community welfare and progress, and recognition of this fact by his fellow-citizens is expressed by his having been elected to represent them in the State Legislature. Popular in fraternal circles, Mr. Story is a member of the Blue Lodge of Washburn, Free and Accepted Masons, Caribou Chapter, Presque Isle Council and Houlton Commandery. He is a prominent member of Anah Temple, Bangor, Ancient Arabic Order Nobles of the Mystic Shrine, and has been a member of the local Grange for fifteen years. For twenty years he acted as financial secretary of the Independent Order of Odd Fellows, and in the local Rotary Club he takes an active interest. With his family, he attends the Baptist church.

Owen Kingsley Story married (first) Mary Anderson, of New Brunswick, who is deceased. To this union were born two children: 1. Archie, married Florence Durgin, and they have two sons, Robert and Ralph. 2. Sadie, who was educated in Washburn and in business college at Boston, and is now a stenographer with the Standard Oil Company. Mr. Story married (second) Alanda Boyd, widow of Parker Smith.

JOHN A. STORY—Filling a number of important posts in the civic departments of his town and State and taking an active interest in the progress and welfare of his community at all times, John A. Story, of Washburn, is one of the State's outstanding citizens, who for twenty years occupied a prominent place in the government service with the United States Bureau of Fisheries. For a number of years, Mr. Story was superintendent of Fish Hatcheries at Green Lake, Maine.

Mr. Story was born in Washburn, April 8, 1874, son of James Munroe and Mary Harriett (Harris) Story, of Sebago, both of whom are deceased. He received his education in the local public schools, and after high school, entered the service of the

State in connection with the Bureau of Fisheries. He advanced steadily by reason of his thorough knowledge and ability and later became associated with the United States Bureau of Fisheries, where he remained for twenty years. At that time, his mother, who was in poor health, desired him to return home to live with her, and to grant her wish, he resigned his position and returned to gladden her last days. Since his mother's death, he has lived practically retired. Mr. Story has always been prominent in civil affairs and serves his town as first selectman, being energetic and sincere in his desire to further the interests of his community. He owns a large farm of ninety acres, which he rents to a local farmer. In politics, Mr. Story has always followed the principles of the Republican party. Prominent in fraternal circles, he is a member of Washburn Blue Lodge, Free and Accepted Masons, and of Caribou Chapter; of the Independent Order of Odd Fellows of Washburn. His religious affiliation is with the Baptist church.

John A. Story married Ada E. Thompson, who was born in Caribou, daughter of Pearce and Mary A. (Richards) Thompson, and they have one adopted son, Walter Raynor, who was educated in the local public schools, graduating from high school.

———

RAYMOND R. JOHNSTON is a prominent business man of Fort Fairfield, Maine. He is head of an important furniture company bearing his name. He is a director also of an important trust company. In addition to this he is a general trader, dealing in different kinds of property and goods. And he is head also of a second large furniture company at Calais, Maine. The furniture business is the gradual outgrowth of a general store owned by the father of Mr. Johnston. It has been greatly developed by Mr. Johnston, who has shown great ability in developing several different lines of buying and selling.

Mr. Johnston was born at Fort Fairfield, Maine, August 11, 1878, son of Charles W. and Adelaide (Small) Johnston, both of whom are now deceased. Raymond R. Johnston received his education in the local schools, and also spent three years at Dartmouth College. After leaving school he became associated with his father in his general store business. After father and son became associated the business gradually widened, and in the course of time began to make a specialty of general house furnishings. The business is now known as the Johnston Furniture Company and employs five clerks. An important sideline is the buying and selling of potatoes. Mr. Johnston is also president of the furniture company, known as the F. L. Stewart Company at Calais, Maine. He is a director also of the Frontier Trust Company, of Fort Fairfield. He is a Republican in politics. Among organizations he belongs to the Free and Accepted Masons, Blue Lodge, and the Rotary Club.

Mr. Johnston married Alice Conant, born at Fort Fairfield, daughter of Stephen R. and Harriett (Dolly) Conant. Children: 1. Carl, educated in the local schools, having spent also one year in a private school in Boston, and another year in a business college, and now associated with his father in business. 2. William S., a student at Bowdoin. 3. Harriett, a student at Colby. 4. Raymond R., Jr. The family attends the Congregational church, where Mrs. Johnston is choir director, and where both Mr. and Mrs. Johnston are active in church work.

———

FREDERICK E. PETERSON is a prominent automobile dealer at Fort Fairfield, Maine. His specialty is the auto bus and he deals also in accessories. He is in addition a director of the Fort Fairfield Bank. Mr. Peterson's automobile business is now over ten years old, but all his life he has been associated with Fort Fairfield where he was born and reared, and where he has passed from one field of work to another and from one business to another until he has built up his present valuable interest.

Mr. Peterson was born at Fort Fairfield, April 3, 1885, son of Julius and Hannah (Simonson) Peterson, both of whom were natives of Denmark, and both of whom crossed to New Denmark, Canada, and then to the United States, settling at Fort Fairfield, the father pursuing the trade of blacksmith. Frederick E. Peterson attended the local schools, graduating from high school in 1904. After that he worked with his father, following the blacksmith trade until 1917. Then he became connected with the automobile business, finally

establishing his auto bus business. Mr. Peterson specializes in Hudson and Essex cars. His side lines include general supplies and auto accessories, and he employs from a dozen to fifteen men. He established the business in 1917. He is a director of the Fort Fairfield National Bank. He is a Republican in politics, and he belongs to the Free and Accepted Masons, Blue Lodge, and the Rotary Club.

Mr. Peterson married Kathleen Conant, born at Fort Fairfield, daughter of Stephen and Harriett (Dolly) Conant. Children: Edwina Alice, Ida Muriel, and Gilbert Chamberlain. The family attends the Congregational church, but Mr. Peterson is an Episcopalian, while his wife is a Unitarian.

———

GEORGE H. PAGE—One of the progressive and successful merchants and manufacturers of Fort Kent, Maine, is George H. Page who owns and operates a general store and factory for making potato starch. He also takes a prominent and active part in civic affairs and has held and does now hold public office. He is the son of Isaac H. and Abbie (Philbrick) Page. Isaac H. Page came to Fort Kent when a boy with his father, Colonel David Page, in 1847, and later he worked in a store in Houlton as a clerk for Rufus Mansur and afterwards for Patrick Collins. He then came back to Fort Kent where he was a clerk for Hon. Isaac Hacker for two years and later took charge of the store that Mr. Hacker owned at Vanburen, where he remained for a year and a half, when for two years he was employed at Presque Isle by C. F. A. Johnson. In 1864, he was appointed clerk in the quartermaster's department of the army in Virginia where he served for one year. In 1865, he returned to Fort Kent, where he was employed by his brother-in-law, George Seely. In 1866, he became Seely's partner and the firm was known as Seely and Page. After Mr. Seely's death, which occurred in 1874, after which time Mr. Page carried on the business with the same firm name until two years later, when he bought out the Seely interest and ran the business alone until 1880, when he formed a partnership with Mr. Mallett and the firm was known as Page and Mallett. In 1888, Mr. Page sold out his part to Mr. Mallett and in 1889 Mr. Page was appointed deputy collector of customs at Fort Kent.

George H. Page was born at Fort Kent, Maine, October 16, 1879. He began his education in the common schools here and finished at the Ricker Classical Institute at Houlton, Maine. When he finished his school work, he became associated with his father in business and has always continued in business here. He is a member of the Blue Lodge, Free and Accepted Masons; the Houlton Commandery, Knights Templar; the Bangor Temple, Ancient Arabic Order Nobles of the Mystic Shrine. In politics Mr. Page is a Republican.

George H. Page married Laura Bolton, daughter of James and Anna (Burgoyne) Bolton. They had two children: James and David. Mrs. Page died in 1914.

LESLIE H. HUGGARD, M. D.—Specializing in pediatrics, Leslie H. Huggard, M. D., is one of the leading physicians of Limestone, Maine, where he has been practicing since 1905. Since he started his practice here, he has made a special effort to follow new developments in his profession, taking post-graduate courses every two years. Ready and willing to devote his energies freely to the work of caring for the sick of the community, Dr. Huggard has won a deserved reputation for skill in his profession; for he possesses all those qualities that go into the making of a competent physician. His practice extends all over Aroostook County, in which he is known as a public-spirited citizen, always eager to participate in whatever enterprise will tend to improve conditions in one way or another.

Dr. Huggard was born at Henderson Corner, Queens County, Province of New Brunswick, Canada, April 18, 1875, and received his early education in the public schools of his native district. Then, desiring a broader education, he became a student at the Provincial Normal School, in New Brunswick, from which he was graduated in the class of 1894. His next venture in the academic world was that of becoming a student at the University of Vermont, where he attended the medical school, from which he was graduated in the class of 1905 with the degree of Doctor of Medicine. For some time after the completion of his course at the University of Vermont, he served as an interne at the Boston City Hospital, where he acquired a practical knowledge of his profession. And although he has had offices in Limestone, Maine, since 1905, he has taken considerable post-graduate work at regular intervals. In 1908 he took a special course in medicine in New York City, and since that year he has taken post-graduate work every two years. Becoming interested in the diseases of infants and children, Dr. Huggard decided to specialize in pediatrics, with the result that he now has a large and lucrative practice in his special field of medicine. People come to him from many miles around Limestone for his expert advice and treatment of the diseases of their children. Taking an active interest in political matters, Dr. Huggard is identified with the Republican party, of whose principles and candidates he is a firm supporter. He and his family attend the Protestant Episcopal church.

He comes from a New Brunswick family, being a son of John and Elizabeth (Barnes) Huggard, who are New Brunswick farmers and who never came to the United States. Dr. Leslie H. Huggard has been in the United States since he came here to study medicine. His wife is Elizabeth Phair, who is a native of Limestone, Maine, a daughter of George A. and Annie (Kelley) Phair.

ALFRED L. NOYES—Like his father before him, and with equal success, Alfred L. Noyes, of Limestone, Maine, combines general farming with the ownership and management of lumber and starch mills, selling his farm products to local buyers.

Born September 11, 1879, he was the son of Josiah M. and Sybil B. (Davis) Noyes, both of Maine families, and now deceased. Educated in the public schools of Limestone, Alfred F. Noyes was associated with his father in his various enterprises, a farm, a lumber mill and a starch factory, until he was twenty-five years old, when he started in business for himself along the same lines. He attends the Methodist Episcopal church, and while not actively concerned with politics, is a Republican. He is a member of Limestone Lodge, Free and Accepted Masons, Caribou Chapter, and the Council, of Presque Isle. He is also a member of the Modern Woodmen of America, and of the Patrons of Husbandry.

Mr. Noyes married Ethel M. Long, daughter of Warren and Nellie (Chase) Long, who was born on her father's farm in Limestone. Both parents are now dead. Their children are: 1. Warren M., proprietor of a hardware and farm machinery store, and town clerk of Limestone, married Marion Watson, and they have a son, Stewart Noyes. 2. Linwood, a farmer, who married Marshie Finnemore, and their three children are: Clayton, Preston, and Marjorie. 3. Josiah M., a farmer, who married Muriel Beckwith; their two children are: Barbara and Richard. 4. Dora E., a student at Andover Academy. 5. Phillip B., now a student in the high school. 6. Gerald G., a schoolboy.

DENSMORE J. GRASS—Among the farmers of Maine who have prospered through the cultivation of potatoes as their main crop is Densmore J. Grass, who owns a highly-cultivated farm of one hundred and sixty acres on the Lake Road in the town of Monticello.

Born in Carleton County, New Brunswick, in 1860, he was a prosperous farmer there until at the age of twenty-six he was ruined by a bank failure, and came to the United States. His parents, George and Annie (Everett) Grass, were both natives of New Brunswick, and lived and died there. Settling in the town of Monticello, he worked as a hired hand until he was able to accumulate enough capital to purchase his present farm from the Wellington estate. It was well provided with farm buildings, but again Mr. Grass was overtaken by misfortune, this time a fire, which destroyed his home and most of the outbuildings. All have been replaced, and the Grass farm now includes some of the finest buildings in the town.

Mr. Grass became a citizen soon after his arrival in Maine, and since then has been a member of the Republican party. He has served on the school board, and is a member of the Black Knights, of the Orangemen, and was admitted to the Free and Accepted Masons in Houlton.

He married (first) Ella V. Bowser, born in New Brunswick. Their one son, Norman Benson Grass, married Miss Drake, and lives in the State of Washington, their children being Ella, Iona, and Norman. Mr. Grass married (second) Alma P. Grant, daughter of John and Lydia (De Long) Grant, farmers of Carleton County, New Brunswick, Canada. Of the second union were born Elva, deceased, who married Miles Prosser; Edna, who married Colby Foster, farmer of Houlton, whose five children are: Elva, Iva, Doris, Alma, and Phyllis; George, who married Viola Crouse, and is a farmer in Littleton, their children being Iona, Ruth, Leota, Mafine, and Densmore; John, who married Lona De Long, and is a farmer in Littleton; Eben, who owns the garage and the bus line to Houlton; Gladys, who married Ora Estabrook, also of the garage and Houlton bus line; Frank Woodruff, student in the normal school at Presque Isle; Ralph, who is in the army at Fort Williams; and Lydia. The family makes a genuinely patriarchal appearance at the Baptist church and elsewhere upon the occasion of reunions.

WALTER E. FRANK—The present treasurer of the Washburn Trust Company and also treasurer of the town of Washburn, is a native of Maine, the son of Luther and Carrie (Hawkes) Frank, both of whom were born in the State of Maine and now live in Westbrook, where Mr. Luther Frank is engaged in the business of building and contracting.

Walter E. Frank was born at Westbrook, Maine, July 17, 1887. He had a complete public school education, which was finished by his graduating from the Westbrook High School in 1906. Equipped with an education, he went to work for the S. D. Warren Paper Company, where he remained for some time, then took a job in the United States Postal Department. After this, he made a connection with the Fidelity Trust Company of Portland, Maine, where his talent for banking and financing began to show itself and he was promoted steadily from one position to another, being at one time in the collection department and then as teller. After learning the inside working of a financial house, he sold stocks and bonds and was quite successful in this line when he decided to return to the paper business and went back to his old company; the S. D. Warren Paper Company. He then established and ran a business in Westbrook, which he sold out at the end of two years and again returned to the S. D. Warren Paper Company. While he was working in this concern he took a course in commercial law, economics, and accounting at the Portland University, Portland, Maine, and after finishing that, he came to Washburn Trust Company and for the past six years he has been treasurer of this organization. For one year he acted as town treasurer and four years ago he was elected to that office, which he continues to fill. For the past four years he has been treasurer of the local chapter of the Red Cross, and also treasurer of the Washburn Chautauqua Association. Mr. Frank is a member of the Blue Lodge of Westbrook, Free and Accepted Masons; and is a Past Master of the Warren Phillips Lodge, No. 186, a member of the Chapter and Council of Westbrook, a Knight Templar of the Houlton Commandery. He is a member of Anah Temple, Bangor, Maine, Ancient Arabic Order Nobles of the Mystic Shrine; member of the Order of the Eastern Star at Cumberland Mills, Maine. He is a member of the American Legion of Washburn, is a Past Commander, and has been for the last five years finance officer of this organization; he is treasurer of the Washburn Rotary Club, and also a member of the Aroostook Valley Fish and Game Club. During the World War, Mr. Frank went to Boston and enlisted in the United States Navy as a first-class yeoman. He had a record of service of six years in the National Guard previous to this time. He has always been one to respond to preparedness in the defense of the country. He is a Republican in his politics and a member of the Baptist church.

Walter E. Frank married Ida B. Butter, who was born in Casco, Maine. They have two children: Wilma C. and Phyllis B.

ORVILLE V. JENKINS—Active in town and county offices and also conducting a farm, Orville V. Jenkins, of Littleton, Maine, is one of the most energetic citizens of his community. He is the son of Robert and Persis (McGuire) Jenkins, both natives of Maine and now deceased. They had a family of ten children, five of whom survive them.

Orville V. Jenkins was born at Glenwood, Maine,

on May 21, 1872. After a common school education, and some work on his farm, he became active in civic affairs and has been prominent in the public eye ever since. He is at present State Highway Supervisor, which position he has held for twelve years. He is also treasurer for the town of Littleton and has served as selectman and town clerk and on the road commission. Mrs. Jenkins is also interested in civic activity and is now town clerk. Mr. Jenkins has always been a Democrat in politics and is a member of the Grange. He and his family attend and are active members in the Baptist church.

Orville V. Jenkins married Maude A. Dougherty, of Littleton, daughter of Bernard and Alice (Pike) Dougherty. Mrs. Jenkins' father is a veteran of the Civil War and is still living (1928) at the age of eighty-eight. Mr. and Mrs. Jenkins have four children: 1. Vinal P., who was educated at the common schools of Littleton with two years at high school; he is now associated with his father in farming. 2. Halsted H., a student at Ricker Classical Institue for one year and now (1928) a sophmore at Colby College. 3 and 4. (Twins) Paul R. and Phillip E., both students at Ricker Classical Institute.

F. N. VOSE—It has been said by persons conversant with such things, that wood-working is the prettiest work in the world; certain it is that the utility of it is beyond question, for its influence is felt in every phase of human endeavor. F. N. Vose, owner and proprietor of the Houlton Planing Mill, has had ample opportunity to demonstrate the value of good mill work, and has furnished the material for numerous construction jobs that will stand for many years after he is gone.

Mr. Vose was born at Unity, Waldo County, Maine, son of Charles S. and Eliza Ellen (Foster) Vose, both natives of Maine and progressive farmers and stock growers of this section. He received his education at the public schools of Waldo County and in 1885 graduated from Freedom Academy, after which he received a flattering offer to take charge of the Plummer Farm School at Salem, Massachusetts. He made a splendid record at this institution and it was with great reluctance that his pupils bade him good-bye as he departed to accept the position of superintendent of the

Truant Department of the City of Cambridge, Massachusetts. He had not been in this new position long, however, when he became convinced that merchandising was more nearly in line with his talents, so he opened a general store at Thorndike, Maine, and at the same time acted as agent of the American Express Company at this place. He was next called to the position of deputy sheriff of Waldo, his native county in Maine. Then he went to Stockholm as a bookkeeper for the Stockholm Lumber Company, which position he filled satisfactorily for six years. Next he traveled through Aroostook County as a salesman for the Tapley Shoe Company, and finally removed to Houlton, where he established himself with the Houlton Planing Mill, which had been established in 1902. In 1915 he bought the business from I. H. Davis; now employs fourteen hands, and conducts a general planing mill concern. They are making wood novelties and small furniture and building a very satisfactory business. He is also a partner in the McClusky Coal & Wood Company, and is sole owner of the Peabody Potato Carrier Company, both concerns having done well ever since his influence in their management began to make itself felt.

Mr. Vose is a consistent member of the Republican party; he takes great interest in local and State elections, but has never offered his name for high office. He served as selectman and three years as town clerk at Thorndike. For the same length of time he was secretary of the Houlton Agricultural Society, in the work of which he is regarded as an authority.

Mr. Vose married (first) Jennie Johnson, who died in 1904, leaving five children: Rena J., Ruby E., Louise F., Vivian C. and Frederick B. Vose. He married (second) Mattie Johnson, sister of his first wife, his wives having been daughters of David B. and Fannie (Giles) Johnson. A son, Edwin D., is the offspring of the second marriage. Mr. Vose attends the Baptist church of Houlton and contributes liberally to its many activities in the realm of religion and charity.

FRANK L. JEWELL—Prominent in the farming and general civic activities of Monticello, Frank L. Jewell has always resided here, maintaining his agricultural interests on his well-conducted farm, and sharing in town government matters as a valued official and clerk. He was born in Monticello February 4, 1881, a son of Granville E. Jewell, a farmer, now deceased, who was also a native of this town, and Arrilla (Scudder) Jewell, who was born in the northern part of Maine, and survives her husband.

Mr. Jewell, one of seven children, attended the Monticello public schools, and then at once began work on the farm, where he continues to the present as the owner of one hundred and sixty acres on the West Road, where he raises potatoes and grain for his own use.

In the political field, Mr. Jewell is a Democrat, but his vote is cast for the candidate whom he believes is best fitted for the responsibilities of public office. He is the third selectman of the town of Monticello, and since 1915 he has officiated as clerk of the election board. Fraternally, Mr. Jewell is affiliated with the Loyal Order of Orangemen, Independent Order of Foresters, and the local Grange of the Patrons of Husbandry. With his family he attends the Methodist Episcopal church.

Frank L. Jewell married, September 27, 1911, Rena Hogan, a native of Monticello, daughter of Michael Hogan, born in New Brunswick, Canada, and now deceased, and Frances Hogan, born in Monticello, and survives her husband. Mr. and Mrs. Jewell have one daughter, Beatrice, a graduate at Monticello High School, and now (1928) a student at Ricker Classical Institute.

LUCENE A. HILL—For nearly three score and ten years Lucene A. Hill, of Littleton, Maine, has lived on the same farm on which he was born, lately in prosperous retirement, after many years of intelligent and unremitting effort. He is one of the men who realized that Maine could produce the finest potatoes in the country, and the warehouse he built on Hill's siding for shipping purposes is still evidence of his industry in the earlier days.

Grandson of Joshua Hill, one of the pioneers of York County, Maine, and son of Ivory and Abiah H. (Knight) Hill, he was born February 22, 1859, one of seven children, and the only one now living. He was educated in the public schools, and became his father's assistant on the farm at an early age.

He combined farm work for a time with lumbering, and in 1886 erected a mill where he produced lumber in long and short lengths, and continued to operate it for the next sixteen years. Always ready to aid in promoting the welfare of the community in which was born, he has been a liberal contributor to all the Protestant churches, and has been active in Republican politics, serving as selectman and school supervisor. Since his retirement some years ago, Mr. Hill has rented both the farm and warehouse, retaining, however, the old home on the one hundred acre farm which he had done so much to render highly productive.

Lucene A. Hill married Eliza J. Hare, daughter of Henry and Mary Ann (Gentle) Hare. She was born in Monticello, Maine, one of nine children. Both of her parents were English, but they had come to the United States in early life, and Mr. Hare, who was an accountant for many years, eventually became a farmer.

WILLIAM HAYWARD ADAIR—One of the most prosperous farmers in the town of Littleton, Maine, is William Hayward Adair. For over fifteen years he has been the owner of a hundred acres of land situated along the Ridge Road, where he raises potatoes and general farm produce for sale to local brokers. Mr. Adair's energy and his thorough knowledge of farming methods have made him very successful in this field. He is one of the most respected citizens in his community.

His father, James A. Adair, was born in the Province of New Brunswick, Canada, but he came to the United States and for thirty-six years he lived in the towns of Houlton and Littleton, Maine. He was a farmer and engaged in this work until his death. He married Mary A. MacDonald, also born in New Brunswick, who is living now with her son.

William Hayward Adair was born on March 14, 1892, at Houlton, Maine. He attended the local public schools, and when he completed his education began work on a farm. For a number of years he was employed by various farmers in the neighborhood, until in 1912 his father purchased the farm along the Ridge Road, where Mr. Adair now lives. Soon afterwards he arranged to take over this farm from his father, and about a year

thereafter the elder Mr. Adair died. Since that time Mr. Adair has continued to run the farm, raising potatoes and other general produce which he markets to local brokers.

Politically he supports the principles and candidates of the Republican party. He is a member of the Grange and of the United Baptist church.

OSCAR CRANE—One of the substantial men of Littleton and the owner of several tracts of land comprising three hundred and twelve acres in Littleton and one hundred and five acres in Ludlow, Oscar Crane, who is now retired from active business life, is a public-spirited citizen and always has participated freely in the affairs of his town and community. He is the descendant of a family that has lived in Maine for several generations, and his father was born in this State. The name Crane is an old one, doubtless of Norman origin, and one that appeared in America in the early days of the white settlers on this continent.

The name appeared in England in 1272, when there was a William de Crane. The cognomen is derived from the town of Crannes, in Maine, an ancient province of Northern France. Crannes, or Craon, has for its root the Gaelic cran, meaning water, and the bird of that name doubtless received its appellation from its trait of frequenting watery places. The Cranes were without doubt Normans who came to England with the Conqueror, who is said to have started from Crannes, on the River Oudin. Cranae was an island of Laconia in the Mediterranean. Cranus was a town of Caria, in Asia Minor, and there was a king of Athens who bore the name. Cranea was a small country in Greece on the Ionian Sea, and Craneus was the first king of Macedonia. Crania was the ancient name of Tarrius in Cilicia, and Crane a city of Arcadia, in Greece. In the successive migrations of peoples from the east and south to the north and west, it is probable that they carried with them the names of their local geography. The English home of the Cranes was in Suffolk. In 1382 William Crane, of Stowmarket, married Margaret, daughter and co-heir of Sir Andrew Butler, by which marriage he came into possession of Chilton in the Hundred of Stowe, which remained in the family longer than three hundred years, through twelve generations of aristocratic landholders. Henry Crane, the American forefather of this race, was born in England in 1621, and came to this country and settled in Milton, Massachusetts, in 1667. Later generations of Cranes were actively engaged in the War of the Revolution, in which they performed distinguished service.

The father of Oscar Crane, who was a native of Maine, was David Crane, a farmer, a shoemaker, and a digger of wells, who married Matilda Briggs, by which marriage there were three children: 1. Oscar. 2. Clara, the wife of John Mc-Keever, who lives in Garland, Maine. 3. Steven E., a farmer in Littleton. Matilda (Briggs) Crane who, like her husband, is now deceased, was a native of Grand Lake, New Brunswick. Oscar Crane, the eldest child of this family, who was born on April 24, 1865, in Hodgdon, Maine, and attended the public schools of his native town, came later to Littleton, where he now owns much land and where he has lived for many years on the North Road. For seven years he conducted a store in Littleton, which he sold in 1927. Since the sale of his store he has been living retired. In his political opinions he maintains a course independent of the existing political parties, but at all times has been actively interested in the welfare and the civic progress of his town and the community near it. He has served on the school board and on building committees, and is now a justice of the peace.

He married Nellie C. Robison, who was born in the Province of New Brunswick, Canada, the daughter of Robert and Margaret (Lorren) Robison, who came to the United States when she was a young woman. Oscar and Nellie C. (Robison) Crane are the parents of the following children: 1. May, who was educated in the Littleton public schools and is now the wife of Lawrence Hannon, a Littleton farmer. 2. Daisy, also educated in Littleton schools, who lives at home with her family. The Crane family's religious affiliation is with the Baptist church.

DAVID A. NASON—The senior member of the firm of Nason, Nason and Peabody, of Monticello, Maine, is the founder of his business in which

he has continued active for about forty years. He is the son of John and Abigail (Grass) Nason, of New Brunswick, and who always lived in New Brunswick.

David A. Nason was born in Trey's Station, Sunbury County, New Brunswick. He was educated in the schools of Hartford, New Brunswick, and as he became interested in business, he moved to Monticello, Maine, where he followed the trade of carpenter and later became interested in establishing a lumber mill. Out of this enterprise grew a contracting and building business and as Mr. Nason's sons came to maturity, he took them into the business with him. He is now practically retired from active work, but never has let go his interest in the affairs of the business, although his sons are now carrying the big load of responsibility, yet not without the council of their father, who, having grown up in and with the business, knows every phase of it, and any problem that might arise. Mr. Nason is a Prohibitionist in politics, an Orangeman and a member of the Baptist church. He has been in active business for more than forty years, and during that time built for himself and his family a permanent means of livelihood that stands as a monument to his talents and ability as a good business man.

David A. Nason married Henrietta Grass, of Woodstock, New Brunswick. They have had six children: 1. Wilmot, a farmer and woodsman. 2. Alfred M., farmer and mill owner. 3. Laura May, wife of William Coppertight. 4. Norris F., whose biography follows. 5. John, associated with his father. 6. Edith (deceased) was the wife of Guy McLaughlin.

NORRIS F. NASON—Doing a general farming business and raising potatoes, Norris F. Nason who, for the greater part of his life has been a resident of Maine, owns one hundred and sixty acres of land on the North Road in the town of Monticello. Although he was born in New Brunswick, Canada, he was brought to the United States when he was less than a year old, so that he is thoroughly conversant with conditions in this section and is well known by the people of the community.

Mr. Nason was born in Hartford, New Brunswick, Canada, the son of David A. Nason, a native of Hartford, New Brunswick, and of Henrietta (Grass) Nason, of Woodstock, New Brunswick; and the grandson of John Nason, who always lived in New Brunswick. David A. Nason, the father of Norris F. Nason, was educated in the Hartford, New Brunswick, schools; came to Monticello, Maine, when he became interested in business; established here a lumber mill, which later became a contracting business, into which he took his sons as they reached maturity, so that he now has practically retired from active work. A Prohibitionist in politics, an Orangeman, and a member of the Baptist church, the elder Mr. Nason always has taken an active interest in public affairs. He and Henrietta (Grass) Nason became the parents of six children, who are listed in connection with the biography of David A. Nason, which appears preceding this.

Norris F. Nason, one of these children, who was born in Hartford, New Brunswick, on March 11, 1886, was brought to the United States by his family when he was only ten months old. Since that time he has grown up, reached maturity and farmed in this section. He attended the public schools of Monticello, of which town he became one of the prosperous men when he engaged in a general farming business. He specializes in potatoes, which he cultivates extensively, and has his own warehouse on Sharp's Siding, in Monticello.

He married Mary E. Carmichael, a native of New Brunswick who has lived in this section of Maine since her childhood. Although Mr. and Mrs. Nason have no children of their own, they are rearing and educating a niece and a nephew, Helen and Burley McLaughlin, children of Mr. Nason's sister, who died. The Nason family's religious affiliation is with the Baptist church.

HON. ELISHA E. PARKHURST, one of the foremost and oldest residents of North Aroostook, Aroostook County, who has not only done much for his community and made his lasting mark in the public affairs of this section of the State, has an additional claim to fame because of the fact that it was from his idea that the spraying machine for potatoes was invented. In proof of this latter statement Mr. Parkhurst has a letter to that effect, which he received from the United States Department of Agriculture.

The career of Mr. Parkhurst is a wonderful story of perseverance and determination, culminating in achievement and success. He was born in the town of Dresden, Lincoln County, January 26, 1834, the son of Elisha and Lucy (Emery) Parkhurst, the former a native of Vermont and the latter of Fort Fairfield, Aroostook County. Mr. Parkhurst was descended from old Revolutionary stock, the family having a record of his grandfather and the latter's three brothers having fought on the side of the American Colonists in the Revolutionary War.

When he was ten years old the parents of Mr. Parkhurst moved to Unity, Waldo County, where he obtained his education in the public schools of that town. After leaving school he worked on his father's farm and in various capacities around his nighborhood and then, when but twenty years of age, he married the daughter of one of his neighbors. For about two or three years he continued to reside in Unity, and then removed to North Aroostook. He had no capital but the bountiful ambition of youth, and the fore-knowledge that success awaited him. He started in a very humble way as a vendor of tinware to the wives of the farmers of the vicinity, taking in exchange for his wares sheep pelts, furs and hides. Noticing that the locality was rich in deep loam, Mr. Parkhurst decided to make North Aroostook his habitat. He made a bargain with the late Augustus Allen for what is now known as the Ferguson farm, a tract of about one hundred and sixty acres. He erected a frame house and to the five acres of cleared land on the property he added another five acres which he cleared himself. He remained on this farm until 1865, when he sold it to advantage and bought the homestead where his grandson, Edwin E. Parkhurst, now resides. When he bought this second farm there were six acres of cleared ground, with growing crops of two acres of wheat, three acres of oats and one of potatoes. He built a house there and resided in it for about nine years. With the fiancial backing of Joseph Hines he managed to clear about twenty acres more, and, later added to this another ten acres. He was now fairly started on his career as an agriculturist, being, indeed, one of the leading farmers of Aroostook at that time. He sold his crops to the Woodstock Agricultural Society, and teamed to Bangor, bringing back on his return trip a load of hardware for Walter Bean, who ran the leading store for those goods on North Main Street, Presque Isle. He built a barn on his property, hewing the timber himself for the frame, as his schedule called for the clearing of ten acres per year.

One of the most interesting episodes of Mr. Parkhurst's career, and one which was to be of great benefit to his community, was his experiment with alsike clover in 1868. He had heard of the success attending the experiments in this grass in New Brunswick and he purchased from a Woodstock dealer ten pounds of the seed, which had been imported from England. This he distributed to the Aroostook farmers and in a very short time a market for this clover was established in Bangor and in Portland. This was the start of the cultivation of alsike clover in New England.

In 1873 Mr. Parkhurst took up the breeding of thoroughbred cattle, choosing shorthorns for his experiment. He continued in this until 1883, at which time he went extensively into the raising of potatoes, during which period he conceived the idea of the spraying machine, previously mentioned. The manufacture of starch then attracted his attention and in 1886 he built a starch factory at Parkhurst, which was in successful operation for ten years. The raising of potatoes again captured his thoughts and he became prominent as one of the most successful and prominent men in that line, operating a number of farms and raising and shipping large quantities to Southern markets. He also took an interest in the raising of fruit on the Pacific Coast and was deeply interested in a number of farms out there.

In spite of his many and varied business interests, Mr. Parkhurst found time to make his mark in public and community affairs in his town and county. From 1871 to 1873 he was an active member of the State Board of Agriculture; State Representative, 1877 to 1878, and a member of the State Senate from 1883 to 1885. For four years he was a trustee of the Maine State College of Agriculture, and was very active in the Grange, being Chaplain of his local Grange from 1878 to 1881 and the first Master of the Pomona Grange of Aroostook. He also acted as trustee of the Northern Aroostook Agricultural Society from 1870 to 1896.

Hon. Elisha E. Parkhurst married, in 1854, Sarah C. Small, a native of Unity and daughter of Alanson and Polly (Chase) Small. To Mr. and Mrs. Parkhurst were born three children, as follows: Idella M., Daniel V., and Percy E., the latter deceased.

JESSE PHILLIP TRACY—As an active citizen in his community, Jesse Phillip Tracy, of Littleton, Maine, also takes an interest in all that pertains to farming and the advancement of agriculture in the State of Maine. He is the son of Isaac and Lucy (Miller) Tracy, natives of New Brunswick who came to Maine in 1881 and remained here the balance of their lives. They owned the farm of seventy-five acres on which Mr. Tracy now lives and also another farm of fifty acres to the north of this one. Both are now deceased. They had four children, all of whom are living: Mrs. J. F. Leavitt, William J., Mrs. McCordick, and Jesse Phillip, of whom further.

Jesse Phillip Tracy was born in Centerville, New Brunswick, on June 11, 1878. He came to the State of Maine with his parents when only three years of age and grew up on the farm and was educated in the schools at Littleton, Maine. After he finished school he continued to live on the farm with his father with whom he became associated in carrying on the farm business, and at the death of his father he inherited the place which he still cultivates. He does some general farming, but makes a specialty of raising potatoes for which there is always a good market. In politics, Mr. Tracy is a Republican and has been first and second selectman of the town of Littleton and also tax collector. He is active as a member of the Grange and is deacon in the Baptist Church, where he and his wife are earnest workers.

Jesse Phillip Tracy married Margaret Jane Elliott, who was born in New Brunswick, the daughter of Charles and Jane (Hunter) Elliott, who came to Littleton, Maine, from New Brunswick, where they continue to reside. Mr. and Mrs. Tracy had five children: 1. Ellwood, who was educated at Littleton and Houlton and later at Ricker Classical Institute and Farmington Normal School and now teaches school at Shelburne. 2. Edith, deceased. 3. Merl, who is a student at Ricker Classical Institute, and twins, who died in infancy.

GEORGE A. GORHAM—A well-known attorney, and a man who holds a prominent position in several of the leading industries of Houlton, is George A. Gorham, born June 2, 1869, at Eastport, Maine.

Mr. Gorham moved with his parents to Houlton while he was a child. He received his preparatory education in the public schools of that community, later attending Ricker Classical Institute, from which he graduated in 1887. He then entered Colby College, and graduated from there with the class of 1891. Upon the completion of these courses of study, Mr. Gorham began his practical legal training, and for a time he read law under the competent preceptorship of the members of the firm of Powers & Powers, at Houlton. He was admitted to the Maine bar in 1893, and immediately thereafter he began the practice of his profession in Houlton. For approximately thirty years he has carried on this work, meeting with ever increasing success. He is now one of the most esteemed citizens of that community, and he is known among the members of his profession for his excellent attainments. Mr. Gorham is also vice-president of the Houlton Trust Company, a director of the Summit Lumber Company, and clerk and director of the Northern Woodenware Company, of Island Falls, Maine.

Despite the many varied and exacting duties of his profession, Mr. Gorham has nevertheless found time in which to take a keen and active interest in the welfare of the community, although he has never consented to hold an office of any kind. In his political preferences he is a strong supporter of the Republican party. He has been active in club and social life and he is fraternally affiliated with the Houlton Lodge, Free and Accepted Masons, of which he is Past Master.

George A. Gorham married Belle P. Pearce, who was born in Fort Fairfield, Maine, a daughter of Joseph and Harriett E. (Williams) Pearce. Mr. and Mrs. Gorham are the parents of two children, a son and a daughter: 1. Joseph P., a student in Harvard Law School. 2. Helen K., a student in the Houlton High School. Mr. Gorham and his family maintain their residence in Houlton, in which community they attend the Unitarian church.

LEO C. GOOD—Pursuing the varied activities of the practical farmer throughout his business career, Leo C. Good has a leading place among the successful potato growers in the Monticello neighborhood, his repute being based upon his exact knowledge of the requirements of this feature of agriculture, its shipping and its marketing. He is also up-to-date in general farming, and as a dealer in farming implements.

Leo C. Good was born September 25, 1884, in Monticello, a son of Charles Frederick Good, a farmer and potato shipper, born in Monticello, and Susie (Cheney) Good, a native of New Brunswick, both parents now deceased. After attending the common schools of Monticello, Mr. Good entered upon his career as a farmer, and he now owns ninety acres on the Fletcher Road with his residence in the village of Monticello; he also deals in farming implements, and he has a filling station on the North Road, near his residence.

In politics a Republican, Mr. Good is a member of the school board, and served as a member of the Board of Selectmen four years. He is a local preacher of the Methodist Episcopal church.

Leo C. Good married, June 26, 1907, Lula Rideout, who was born in Blaine, daughter of Wallace and Hannah (Harris) Rideout. Their children: Herschel, a graduate at Ricker Classical Institute; Lawrence, a student at Ricker Classical Institute; Ruth, in the Monticello High School; Garth, in the grade schools; and Audrey.

WILLIAM McCLUSKEY—His perseverance, enterprise and skill in farming matters have combined to place William McCluskey among the leaders in potato-raising in Monticello and this agricultural section of the State. His father was a pioneer in this neighborhood, and Mr. McCluskey has followed in his footsteps in his successful efforts to make potato-farming pay; and with three good farms under cultivation, and one of the most commodious warehouses hereabouts, he has earned his repute as one of the very able men in his line.

William McCluskey was born in January, 1877, in Albert County, New Brunswick, a son of David McCluskey and Bertie (Fullerton) McCluskey, both of whom came from New Brunswick to Maine in 1880, and now reside in Houlton, and the parents of five sons and two daughters. Mr. McCluskey, Sr., came here and bought and cleared his own farm, built his farm buildings, and raised his family to become successful in agricultural industry. William McCluskey attended the Monticello public schools and immediately gave his attention to farming matters, and gradually became one of the foremost of the potato-growers in this place, besides raising grain for his own use. He is the owner of two farms on the Fletcher Road, one of two hundred and ten acres, and another comprising one hundred and twelve acres, and the third of about one hundred acres, cultivating potatoes and grain, and shipping potatoes from the large warehouse that he has but recently erected at Monticello Station, and that is accounted one of the most up-to-date in the county. He is assisted by his son George in all his work.

Mr. McCluskey gives his political allegiance to the Republican party; and he is a member of the Free and Accepted Masons, as a Past Master of his lodge; and of the local Grange, of the Patrons of Husbandry. He is a self-made man, prominent in all the affairs of the town; and with his family he attends the Baptist church.

William McCluskey married, January 29, 1901, Effie Jewett, who was born in Carleton County, New Brunswick, daughter of Joel and Alice (Allerton) Jewett, of New Brunswick, and they have one son, George Herbert McCluskey, who was born in Monticello, attended the public schools here, and is associated with his father in business, and there was also a daughter, Vesta Fay, who died at the age of sixteen.

J. M. FOSTER—As an agriculturist, and later a dealer in farm products, J. M. Foster, of Monticello, Maine, stands among those of his State as one of the stable citizens who have by steady perseverance helped to advance the welfare of his community. His parents, Alonzo and Hannah (Gerow) Foster, were natives of Canada, coming to Maine as children and spending most of their lives at Newbury, Maine. His father has a military record of service in the Civil War and is a Civil War veteran.

J. M. Foster was born at Monticello, Maine, on March 9, 1876. He was educated first at the town schools and later at the Ricker Classical Institute. After completing his work at the Ricker Classical Institute he taught for one year. At the end of this time he took up the business of farming, which he has continued to pursue and has added to this other lines of kindred interest. He carries on quite an extensive business of dealing in potatoes, hay and straw, and also does a real estate business, principally handling the buying and selling of farm lands. He is a Republican in politics and has served as selectman of the town and also on the school board, in the village of Monticello, where he makes his home. He is a member of Monument Lodge, Free and Accepted Masons.

J. M. Foster married Zelma F. Good, daughter of Fred and Susie (Cheney) Good, natives of Canada. Mr. and Mrs. J. M. Foster have two children: 1. Maxine S., a student at Colby. 2. Frederick Good, third year student at high school.

ALBERT W. BRIGGS—A farmer, business man and representative in the State Legislature, Albert W. Briggs, of Monticello, Maine, is a man of affairs whose interests are not confined to any one line. He is the son of James Elisha and Sarah (Farley) Briggs, natives of New Brunswick but who have lived in Bridgewater since they were children. They had a family of thirteen children, six of whom are living. Both parents are now deceased.

Albert W. Briggs was born at Bridgewater, October 11, 1857. He was educated in the common schools and high school of Bridgewater and attended school during winter months until he was twenty-one years of age. In summer, he worked on the farm and in the woods. When he became of age he went out West to Michigan, Wisconsin, and Minnesota, where he was a woodsman for three years, then returned to his native State and bought a farm which he worked for a number of years. He purchased another farm of one hundred and fifty acres on the road between Monticello and Mars Hill, and after owning it for twenty years, he moved on it in 1911. He is also associated with his brother, W. O. Briggs, who deals extensively in potatoes and has a large warehouse in Littleton, Maine, and in the last session of the

Legislature, he represented his district in that body. He is a Republican in politics and has held most of the town offices. For twenty years he was selectman, fifteen of which he was chairman of the board. He has been collector of taxes and a member of the school board. He is a member of the Independent Order of Odd Fellows and of the Grange. He is a member of the Baptist church.

Albert W. Briggs married Maude Ketchum, daughter of James and Louise (Smith) Ketchum of Bridgewater. They have eleven children: 1. Nina M., a graduate of Ricker Classical Institute and Presque Isle Normal School, now postmistress at Edgewater, Florida. 2. Harvey C., educated at town schools. 3. Birdie, a graduate of Ricker Classical Institute. taught school several years; now the wife of L. C. Cory of Blaine, Maine. 4. Arthur, educated at Ricker Classical Institute. 5. Nettie, educated at Ricker Classical Institute and at Colby, trained as a nurse in Massachusetts and is now in the Memorial Hospital, Chicago, Illinois. 6. Velma, educated at Ricker Classical Institute and at Colby, taught school at Carmel, Maine; is now the wife of Thet Moore. 7. Helen, educated at Ricker Classical Institute, is the wife of Ralph Bither. 8. Mildred, educated at Ricker Classical Institute, the wife of Ervin Dewett, now living in Florida. 9. Alice, educated at Ricker Classical Institute. 10. Albert W., educated at Ricker Classical Institute, now living at home. 11. Dora, a graduate of Ricker Classical Institute in 1927.

PERLEY E. BUBAR—The farming interests of the Monticello section and, indeed, a considerable portion of the State of which Monticello is a flourishing centre, have always been championed along the most progressive lines by Perley E. Bubar, a Granger known and esteemed throughout the State for his prominence in that order, a farmer of practical, present-day methods. The Wadlia Farm that he has cultivated for years is one of the leading and model farms in this part of the State; and besides his agricultural activities, Mr. Bubar is a thoroughly capable holder of public office, and a highly respected and useful citizen.

Perley E. Bubar was born January 12, 1877, at Littleton, Maine, son of Henry J. Bubar, a farmer, now deceased, and Amanda (Abernathy) Bubar, who survives her husband, both parents natives of New Brunswick, Canada, but who had spent practically their entire lives in Maine. Mr. Bubar attended the common schools in Littleton, and then entered upon his career as a farmer, at first with his father until he married at the age of twenty-three years, when he became owner of a farm in his own right for some ten years. Mr. Bubar then purchased of his father-in-law the farming property of one hundred and sixty acres that he now owns, the well-known Wadlia Farm, where he raises potatoes and grain for his own use.

A Republican in political matters, Mr. Bubar holds the office of second selectman of Monticello; he has been a member of the board ten years, and held its chairmanship six years; and he has also been a member of the school board. Grange matters have always greatly interested Mr. Bubar; he was formerly Master of Monticello Grange, Patrons of Husbandry, No. 338, and since 1924 he has been Master of Aroostook and Penobscot Union Grange; and he is a member of the Independent Order of Foresters. His religious faith is that of the Methodist Episcopal church.

Perley E. Bubar married Vesta Wadlia, who was born on the farm on which the family reside, a daughter of Coleman L. Wadlia, who also was born on this farm, as his ancestors were for a century, and Elizabeth (Morrison) Wadlia. Mr. and Mrs. Bubar have three children: 1. Margaret, graduate of Ricker Classical Institute, teacher for six years, now a student at Castine. 2. Henry C., also educated at Ricker Classical Institute. 3. Lawrence, a student.

JAMES KIDD PLUMMER—Connected for many years with the Houlton Trust Company, of Houlton, James Kidd Plummer won the respect and admiration of his community. He was born on November 4, 1863, in Richmond, New Brunswick, Canada, six miles from Houlton, Maine, and died on January 8, 1925, at Winter Park, Florida.

Mr. Plummer was the son of Silas Taber and Catherine R. (McKenzie) Plummer, the father a native of Albion, Maine, the mother of Richmond, New Brunswick. As a boy he attended the Ricker

Classical Institute, and later became a student in Colby College with the class of 1886. In his early life he did not enjoy robust health and after leaving college spent several years in the Maine woods. He became interested early in life in the subject of law, which he studied. Later he was admitted to the bar of Maine, but never actually engaged in practice, merely using his legal knowledge in his own financial and business enterprises. He was the principal organizer of the Houlton Trust Company and served that institution as its first president, then as vice-president. Mr. Plummer adopted the practice of spending his winters in the South, but continued active in Houlton, where he always spent several months of the year. Interested at all times in political matters, he was a Republican. He was a member of the Free and Accepted Masons.

In Santa Anna, California, on February 21, 1906, Mr. Plummer married Adelaide Hewes, daughter of Benjamin Warren and Cora (Tupper) Hewes. Her father was a native of Plymouth, Massachusetts, while the mother was a native of Maine. Mr. and Mrs. James Kidd Plummer became the parents of one son, Silas Hewes, who died at the age of five years.

ARNOLD A. DAY—Service both in the United States Army and in the Customs Department of the United States Government is the outstanding record of the active career of Arnold A. Day, customs deputy collector at Station Monticello at the Port of Houlton, where he resides and officiates in other and as important public offices, and has the merited esteem of his associates and the general public.

Arnold A. Day was born January 28, 1895, at Wesley, in Washington County, a son of Corrin Day, a farmer, and Carrie (Guptill) Day, both natives of this State and lifelong residents of Washington County. There Mr. Day attended the grammar and normal schools, and after graduating at Shaw's Business College, he taught school for a year, when he enlisted for the World War.

At the close of the War, Mr. Day was principal of the Junior High School at Monticello for a number of years; and in 1925 he was appointed by Governor Milliken to his present office as cus-

toms deputy collector for the Port of Houlton, Monticello Station, on the Bloomfield Road, his duties including those of customs and immigrant official. Mr. Day is a Republican in politics, and he has also held the office of chairman of the Monticello Board of Selectmen, and of the Monticello School Board.

Enlisting at Calais in the United States Army Infantry in the World War, Mr. Day received his discharge with the rank of corporal at Camp Devens, Ayer, Massachusetts, and he is commander of the Monticello Post of the American Legion. His religious faith is that of the Methodist Episcopal church, and he is a member of the board of trustees of that church in Monticello.

Arnold A. Day married, December 24, 1920, Claire Curtis, who was born in Monticello, daughter of George C. and Nora (Hogan) Curtis, her father a carpenter; and they have one child, Shirley. Mr. Day is a member of Monument Lodge, Free and Accepted Masons.

HARRY D. HARTT—To the mercantile progress of Monticello, Harry D. Hartt has added his own enterprising methods, his general store, with its central location, its thorough equipment, and its increasing patronage fully meeting the needs of an appreciative community. Here Mr. Hartt began his business career, and as a town official and an associate in the general advancement of Monticello, he is respected and esteemed in his citizenship.

Harry D. Hartt was born April 12, 1888, in the Province of New Brunswick, Canada, a son of Rev. Henry Hartt, a Baptist clergyman, born in London, England, and Lucy (Tapley) Hartt, born in New Brunswick, both of whom spent the last thirty years of their life in Maine, and both now deceased. Mr. Hartt attended the grammar schools and then went to work in a general store at Monticello as a clerk, and afterwards, for several years, he was employed by the Dunn Furniture Company at Houlton. Mr. Hartt established himself in his present business as general storekeeper at Monticello, in 1915, where he employs two clerks.

A Republican in his political views, Mr. Hartt both as a voter and in office supports the principles of that party, having represented his town as selectman for three years. Fraternally, he is affiliated with Monument Lodge, Free and Accepted Masons; and he attends the Methodist Episcopal church, and is its treasurer.

Harry D. Hartt married, October 20, 1910, Julia M. Jewett, who was born in New Brunswick, a daughter of Edward J. and Marie Jewett; and they have three children: Dorothy Linton, Greeda and Gloria.

DON C. SYLVESTER is the owner of six farms in Maine. He is an extensive potato grower, specializing in certified seed stock. He has been in the various lines of agriculture all his life, and he has purchased farms as he went along.

Don C. Sylvester was born at Mars Hill, Maine, May 31, 1884, son of Alden and Rachel (Blackden) Sylvester, of whom the father, who was a farmer, is retired and resides at Mars Hill, while the mother is deceased. Mr. Sylvester was educated in the public schools and then engaged in farming, working at first on his father's farm, then starting in a small way for himself, and then gradually enlarging his property and extending his activities, watching out for farms in the neighborhood that came on the market, and buying pieces of land and houses and other farms. He at present owns six farms in the town of Westfield and one in Mars Hill. He first started in the potato business with his brother, Arthur, and his brother-in-law, Clinton E. Richardson, under the firm name of Sylvester & Richardson. They continued in partnership for five years, at the end of which Mr. Sylvester bought the business for himself. Mr. Sylvester is a Republican. He belongs to the Modern Woodmen of America, Independent Order of Odd Fellows, No. 148, and Grange.

Mr. Sylvester married Hazel Beals, born at Blaine, Maine, daughter of William and Charlotte (Noble) Beals. Six children have been born to the marriage, including two sets of twins: Kenneth; Merton; Edna and Edwin; Carroll and Kathlyn. The family attends the Baptist church.

J. WALTER TAPLEY, who now owns a jewelry store at Presque Isle, Maine, has behind him a considerable business experience in various lines. He was for many years a school teacher,

and was also for a number of years connected with the railroads. For a time he was in the banking business and was acting treasurer to a trust and banking company. He has taken much interest in public affairs also and has been town clerk for a number of years.

J. Walter Tapley was born at Bridgewater, Maine, November 20, 1879, son of William and Ada (Parsons) Tapley, the father born in Canada and brought to the United States when he was two years old, becoming a farmer and engaging in farming all his life. The mother was a Kennebec Yankee. Mr. Tapley received the usual education in the public schools, and attended also the high school at Bridgewater and the Ricker Classical Institute at Houlton. On leaving school he attached himself to the teaching profession and was a school teacher for eight years. Then he went into the railroad business and became an employee of the Bangor & Aroostook Railroad, and he continued at this work for a period of six years. In 1910 he went to work for the Merchants' Trust & Banking Company at Presque Isle and became its acting treasurer. He resigned in 1922 and bought the jewelry business of E. J. Waddell, and this business he has developed and regularly employs two watchmakers. He looks after the other work along with Mrs. Tapley. He has been town clerk since 1922, and is a Republican in politics. He belongs to the Free and Accepted Masons, and has been through the various degrees, including the Ancient Arabic Order Nobles of the Mystic Shrine; a member of the Order of the Eastern Star; the Independent Order of Odd Fellows, Encampment and Canton, and the Rebekahs. He is a member of the Merchants' Association and the Mooseleuk Club.

J. Walter Tapley married Mrs. Maude (McGuire) Webb, daughter of Alonzo and Harriett (Jamieson) McGuire, and widow of Frederick Webb. Mrs. Tapley has by her first marriage a daughter, Alice, now a student of Boston University. Mr. and Mrs. Tapley attend the Congregational church.

BERT G. WRIGHT—Buying and shipping potatoes and dealing in fertilizer and farm machinery have proven to be profitable enterprises for Bert G. Wright, who has had his headquarters in

Limestone for many years. Participating in several different phases of the town's business and industrial activity, Mr. Wright is a member of the Executive Board of the Limestone Trust Company, and is also interested in real estate, having one thousand acres of land in the town of Ashland, Maine, which he plans to develop. He has taken a prominent part in the public and social life of the town, having served both as tax collector and selectman.

Mr. Wright, who is a son of James S. and Mary (Whitnect) Wright, was born in Caribou, Maine, September 25, 1882. His father, who is a farmer and is living in Caribou, is a native of Canada: while his mother, who died in 1904, is a native of Maine. As a boy, Bert G. Wright attended the public schools of Caribou, but left school early in life to become associated with Carl C. King and P. H. Gould, potato dealers; and for five years he worked for them in the winters, and farmed in the summers with his father. Then he bought a farm in Fort Fairfield, which he continued to operate for two years, at the end of which period he came to Limestone, where he was employed by F. W. Gibbons and Company, a Boston potato firm. After he had remained for some years with this firm, he became associated with M. J. McCarthy, who also conducts a potato business in Boston. Since 1917 Mr. Wright's headquarters have been situated in Limestone, and he gradually has disposed of his interests in Fort Fairfield and elsewhere to devote his whole time to his business in Limestone. He sold his Fort Fairfield farm; then, leaving M. J. McCarthy, he established his own business as a potato buyer and shipper, and in connection with it he has transacted a considerable business in farm machinery and fertilizer. Mr. Wright's enterprise is looked upon in his community as one of the really essential business interests, and the people have come to regard him with high respect and esteem for his sound judgment and ability and his willingness at all times to deal fairly with them. In his political convictions, he is a Republican of the independent sort, having a preference for the principles of the Republican party, but wishing always to align himself on the side of sound and efficient government. Actively interested in the civic and social affairs of his town, Mr. Wright has been chosen at different times by his fellow-citizens

to serve in important public positions. For one year he was tax collector of the town, and for three years he was a selectman. His fraternal affiliation is with the Knights of Pythias; and he and his family are communicants of the Roman Catholic church.

Mr. Wright married Rose Anna Fontain, who was born in Jackman, Maine, a daughter of Louis Fontain. Bert G. and Rose Anna (Fontain) Wright are the parents of the following four children: Mildred A., Patricia Ann, James S., and Colene Eugenia.

CARROLL D. WILDER—A believer in scientific agriculture, and an example himself of the advantages which a thorough training affords, Carroll D. Wilder, of Washburn, Maine, was for a year a teacher of the newer farm methods at the Caribou High School, and then, forming a partnership with his father, proceeded to carry his theories into execution. The firm was known as V. E. Wilder & Son, and specialized in Irish cobbler seed potatoes.

Born in Washburn, Maine, February 27, 1898, son of Vernum E. and Victoria P. (Smith) Wilder, Mr. Wilder comes of a long line of Maine farmers. His father, a farmer all his life, was a native of Washburn, where he died August 23, 1926. His mother was born in Castle Hill, Maine. After being graduated from the Washburn High School, Carroll D. Wilder spent two years at the University of Maine studying agriculture, and after his engagement as a teacher ended, he and his father undertook the development of two farms of one hundred acres each, one of which Carroll D. Wilder subsequently purchased. After his father's death he also purchased the homestead farm and now operates both. The venture proved in all respects a success. Mr. Wilder is a director in the Merchants Trust & Banking Company, of Presque Isle, has been for five years a director in the Northern Maine Fair Association, and has been for three years a member of the School Board. He is active in Republican politics. He attends the Baptist church, and is a member of the Free and Accepted Masons, of the Washburn Royal Arch Masons, Caribou Commandery, Knights Templar of Houlton, etc. He is also a member of the Patrons of Husbandry.

Carroll D. Wilder married Bessie Lacey, of Lawrence, Massachusetts, and they have two children, Caroline and Harold Wilder.

GEORGE F. WASHBURN—First selectman of the Board of Selectmen of Presque Isle, Aroostook County, and a member of that board since 1919, George F. Washburn figures prominently in the public life of the town and is accounted one of the most interested in the welfare of the community. Under his supervision Presque Isle, population approximately 5,000, disbursed a sum of $55,-000 for work on the streets in 1927. Since 1923 Mr. Washburn has been president of a company operating a store doing a retail trade, and is secretary and treasurer of the Presque Isle Starch Company, which office he assumed in 1919. The starch industry is one of those principally represented in Presque Isle, and the Presque Isle Starch Company is one of the largest here. Mr. Washburn is a member of the Board of Directors of the Northern Main State Fair Association. He is connected indirectly with several business enterprises, and himself is interested in the sale of fertilizers.

George F. Washburn is a native of Maine, born at Masardis, on August 8, 1878, son of Ruben and Elsie J. (Leavitt) Washburn, his father having devoted his life to agriculture, born in the Province of New Brunswick, Dominion of Canada, and his mother born in Maine. George F. Washburn received his early education in the grade schools of Masardis, and for three years attended high school there. For the next twenty years he engaged in farming, at first under his father and later as proprietor of his own lands, near Presque Isle. At present, and many years since (1928), he is retired from the very active work connected with agriculture, and devotes the whole of his time to service in business and to public office. He has many friends in private, political, commercial and fraternal life, and is a member of the Blue Lodge of the Free and Accepted Masons, the Independent Order of Odd Fellows, and the Presque Isle Rotary Club. With his family he attends the Congregational church, and contributes generously to those charitable causes sponsored by it.

George F. Washburn married Blanche L. Porter, born at Mapleton, Maine, daughter of Lemuel and Hester (Smith) Porter. Mr. and Mrs. Washburn are the parents of three children: 1. Marie Evelyn, wife of Frank Lyman Higgins, of Presque Isle; she is a graduate of Presque Isle High School and Lasalle Seminary at Boston, also Chandler Business College, Boston. 2. Mamie Arline, educated in the Presque Isle High School and normal school, and member of the class of '29 in the University of Maine, post-graduate student of Columbia University, New York, and University of Southern California; a school teacher. 3. George Franklin, Jr.

ALONZO S. JEWELL is a farmer of Westfield, Maine, and owns what is known as the Brookdale Farm. This comprises seventy-five acres on the Houlton Road and he owns in addition fifty-nine acres on the back road. He engages in general farming and plants about twenty acres of potatoes, and sells to local buyers. He keeps about seven head of cattle and four horses. He is representative of the successful pioneers in Maine, who went into the rough country, and as farmers and lumber men, cultivated it and won prosperity out of it.

Alonzo S. Jewell was born at Calais, Maine, October 20, 1860, son of David and Annie (Small) Jewell, both of whom were natives of Maine, who spent most of their lives in Farmington, Maine. They came to Westfield when Mr. Jewell was ten years old and died there. The father settled his farm in the region when it was a wilderness and cleared it. The boy was educated in the public schools, and took charge of the farm when he was nineteen years old. It was then all covered with woods and he cleared the entire place, built all the buildings, built the fences, and laid out the fields. During his early life he farmed in summer and worked in the woods in winter. He is a Republican in politics and has been tax collector for years.

Mr. Jewell married Carrie McNally, born in Ashland, Maine, daughter of William McNally. There were no children to the marriage, but Mr. and Mrs. Jewell have adopted four, three boys and one girl, giving them every advantage in education. The children are: 1. Chester, who attended the high school at Westfield and went also to school in Boston, now employed with the Produce Company at Boston. 2. Elbridge, who is superintendent of a machine factory at Oakland, Maine. 3. Omar, now in the garage business in California. 4. Lula, wife of Rufus Snow, living at Bangor. Mr. and Mrs. Jewell attend the Baptist church.

JOHN KNOWLEN—In October, 1924, John Knowlen was appointed postmaster of Westfield, Maine, by Postmaster-General New. Since July of that year he had served as acting postmaster, and for many years before that he was a teacher in the Maine schools. Mr. Knowlen is very prominent in Westfield life, being a member of several fraternal organizations, and at one time or another he has been chosen by the people to fill almost every office of the town government. To the position which he now holds he has devoted himself with his customary energy and ability, discharging all the duties of the office in a highly efficient manner. Mr. Knowlen was born May 4, 1872, at Sheridan Plantation, now a part of Ashland, Maine, the son of Roswell and Maria (Metcalf) Knowlen, both now deceased. His father was a farmer and engaged in this work until his death.

John Knowlen entered the public schools of Presque Isle, Maine, and later attended the Maine State Normal School at Farmington. When he completed his academic education, he began to teach in the Maine schools, and he continued in this profession for twenty-five years, until he became postmaster at Westfield. On July 1, 1924, he took over the duties of acting postmaster, and on October 1, 1924, he was regularly appointed by Postmaster-General New, and has remained in the position since that time. The Westfield Post Office is one of the fourth class, having one rural route. Politically, Mr. Knowlen is a member of the Republican party, and he has filled almost all of the town offices very capably. He is affiliated fraternally with the Ancient Free and Accepted Masons, in which organization he is a member of the Blue Lodge. He is also a member of the Independent Order of Odd Fellows, Encampment and Canton.

Mr. Knowlen married Annie Nickerson, who was born at Bloomfield, Province of New Brunswick, Canada, the daughter of Charles and Bathsheba Nickerson, of that place. Mrs. Knowlen, like her husband, has been a teacher in the Westfield schools for twenty-five years, and is now town treasurer. They are the parents of one child, Harry, who is a member of the class of 1928 at the Maine State Normal School, at Farmington. Mrs. Knowlen supports the faith and tenets of the Seventh Day Adventist Church. Mr. Knowlen inclines toward the Methodist Episcopal church.

GUY HILLMAN MILLER—A man of considerable prominence in the town of Monticello, Maine, is Guy Hillman Miller. At various times he has owned several different farms in Aroostook County, and he is now the proprietor of one hundred and ten acres of land, situated along the Lake Road in the town of Monticello, where he raises potatoes and other general farm produce for sale to local buyers. Mr. Miller is well acquainted with the best farming methods, and has been very successful in his chosen occupation. He is active in local church work and highly esteemed in his community as a public-spirited citizen. He was born at Littleton, Maine, the son of Edmund H. and Sarah (Wright) Miller. Both of his parents were born in the Province of New Brunswick, Canada, and came to the United States while still very young. His father was a carpenter by trade, but later became the owner of a farm, which he operated.

Guy Hillman Miller attended the public schools of Littleton, but when he left to begin farm work, his education did not stop. Constant reading of the best literature has broadened his culture and kept him thoroughly informed. When his father was totally disabled by shock, Mr. Miller took complete charge of the home and farm, and after the death of his parents, he continued this occupation. He has owned several farms in Aroostook County, improving each one, and then selling and buying another. With the exception of three years which he spent in Cambridge, Massachusetts, as an employee in the assembly department of the Ford Motor Company, he has devoted his life to farming work, specializing chiefly in the raising of potatoes. Patents have been granted Mr. Miller on two inventions, a derrick and a special wrench. Politically, he supports the principles and candidates of the Republican party. He attends the local Baptist church, and has always taken an active part in church work, serving as deacon, and as a member of the financial committee.

Mr. Miller married Lillian M. Harris, who was born at Cambridge, Massachusetts, the daughter of George Harris.

JAMES HENRY BURKE—A farmer and a horse dealer, James Henry Burke owns a home and a farm in the village of Fort Fairfield, Maine, where the total area of his lands amounts to one hundred and ten acres. Each year he brings about ten carloads of horses from the West; and, in his own farm work, he makes a specialty of cultivating potatoes, which he sells locally in Fort Fairfield and vicinity. He also produces hay and grain for his own use. Taking an active part in the public life of his community, Mr. Burke has strong fraternal affiliations, and is keenly interested in civic and social matters and ready at all times to devote his time and energies to whatever movements he believes will tend toward the improvement of conditions in his town, State and Nation.

Mr. Burke was born in the Province of New Brunswick, Canada, April 5, 1855, a son of Edward and Delia (Baltdridge) Burke, who removed to the United States when he was a nine-year-old boy, and settled in Fort Fairfield. The father was a farmer by occupation, and is now deceased. The mother is living in Fort Fairfield. James Henry Burke was educated in the public schools, but while he was still very young he left school to work on a farm as a hired hand. When he was about twenty years old, he started to farm for himself, buying land in Fort Fairfield. Later he sold this first farm, and bought his present plot of one hundred and ten acres, which is known as the Haines farm. Always having been interested in horses, he began to bring in horses from the West and to sell them, doing an increasing business of this sort as time went on. He is active in the work of the Free and Accepted Masons, in which order he is a member of the Blue Lodge in Fort Fairfield; the Chapter of Royal Arch Masons in Caribou; the Council in Presque Isle; the Commandery in Houlton, and Kora Temple, of the Ancient Arabic Order Nobles of the Mystic Shrine in Lewiston.

Mr. Burke married Phebe Brown, who was born in Andover, New Brunswick, Canada, a daughter of Hugh Brown. James Henry and Phebe (Brown) Burke became the parents of the following children: 1. Ralph, who is a student in the University of Maine. 2. Helen, a student in Bates College. 3. Adelaide, a student in high school. 4. Isabelle, a student in high school. 5. Ruth, in grammar school.

Mrs. Brown, who was deeply loved as a member of the community in and near Fort Fairfield, died in February, 1917, and the loss of her was greatly mourned in this section of Maine. She was an active member of the Methodist Episcopal church, and at all times took a leading part in the work of this congregation. Mr. Burke, who also is a member of this church, is represented on its finance committee and its board of trustees.

JAMES D. ROSS—Deputy Sheriff James D. Ross, throughout a very active career in business and civic matters, has always allied himself with Littleton's progress, and he has been instrumental both as a public official in many offices and as a farmer who has specialized in potato culture and the raising of fine cattle, in adding to the excellent status of township affairs, as well as to its citizenship of enterprise and ability.

James D. Ross was born March 8, 1856, on the Mashwaak Road, in New Brunswick, a son of James and Jane (MacDonald) Ross, both natives of New Brunswick, but who had resided at Littleton for many years, where they died. James Ross, a veteran of the Civil War, who served three years in the Union Army, was always in poor health as a result of his experiences; he was the father of nine children, but three of whom are living: Rev. Theodore Ross, a clergyman at Lincoln; Dr. Frederick C. Ross, of Boston, Massachusetts; and James D. Ross, of whom further.

After attending the public and high schools of Littleton, Mr. Ross entered upon his career as a farmer, at first assisting his father, and afterwards coming into possession of his one-hundred acre farm on Ridge Road, this having been the homestead which, after his father's death, he purchased of the other heirs. Here he established a dairy, and specialized in the raising of Holstein cattle, as well as in general farming and potato growing, and he built the first potato house on the Bangor and Aroostook Railroad north of Houlton. Since 1918, Mr. Ross, who is a Republican in his political views, has served this section of the State as a deputy sheriff. He is also health officer, and has from time to time been elected to all the principal town offices. Fraternally, he is affiliated with the Independent Order of Odd Fellows, of which he has been a member since 1897.

James D. Ross married Octavia Nelson, who was born in Bridgewater, daughter of John K. and Elinore (Tobey) Nelson. Their children: 1. Linwood L., attended Ricker Institute and Colby College, and resides in Springfield, Massachusetts, where he is employed by the New England Telegraph and Telephone Company; he married Jennie Brown, and they have two children: James and Elinore. 2. Ervin, attended Littleton public schools, and Bangor Business College, and resides at Needham, Massachusetts, and is a member of the firm of H. A. Johnson and Company, of Boston; he married Florence Crossman, and they have two children: Ervin J. and Ernestine. 3. Mildred, educated at Ricker Classical Institute, was a stenographer in the office of H. P. Wood and Company, in Boston, for twenty-one years; married J. F. Whitcomb, and they live in Waltham, Massachusetts. 4. Ada, was graduated at Ricker Classical Institute, and is a teacher in the public schools.

LEWIS ELMON BERCE—The greater part of the active life of the late Lewis Elmon Berce, of Woodland, Maine, was spent in this locality, and for many years he was known as the owner of the big two hundred and seventy acre farm which is now owned by his widow and operated by his youngest son. Mr. Berce was one of the prominent men of the town of Woodland and his life was one of useful activity and of kindly and helpful association with his neighbors. Greatly loved and respected by all who were closely connected with him, he had the respect and the high esteem of all with whom he was associated, either in business or in social dealings, and his passing at the age of sixty-five years, lacking one month, was a

distinct loss to the community in which he had so long been one of the familiar figures.

Lewis Elmon Berce was born in Sebec, Piscataquis County, Maine, August 14, 1855, and died at his home in Woodland, Maine, July 15, 1920, son of Isaac Elmon and Emeline (Annis) Berce, both of old Maine families, and highly respected among their associates. He received the education which the common schools of his day afforded, and as a boy worked on the farm and in the woods. When he reached his majority he followed the example of so many young men of his time and went West, where he worked as lumberman in the woods along the Red River. When he returned East he settled in Woodland, Maine, where he became the owner of a two hundred and seventy acre farm, and where he also operated a saw-mill in which he manufactured shingles in addition to the regular saw-mill work. A good citizen and a good neighbor, he was always ready to lend a helping hand when there was need, and his general kindliness of spirit found full expression in his family life. Necessity had deprived him of the opportunity for an extended education, but he was determined that his children should receive the advantages which he had missed, and spared no effort to give them the best possible education. A man of public spirit, always ready to serve his fellows, Mr. Berce never sought or desired public office. He did consent to serve in some minor offices, and was always a member of the town Republican Committee, but his preference was to serve as a private citizen. He and his family were members of the Baptist church.

Lewis Elmon Berce was married (first) to Julia Carlton, daughter of Charles and Emma (Morse) Carlton, both representatives of old Maine families, their daughter Julia being the first girl born in Woodland. She died and Mr. Berce married (second) Mary D. Carlton, a sister of his first wife. To the first marriage one daughter was born, Edith, who married David McElwain, and has two children, Marion and Ralph. To the second marriage three children were born: 1. Woodbury L. (see a following biography). 2. Blanche, who was educated in Caribou High School; in Presque Isle Normal School, and in Gray's Business College, and is now (1928) employed as an accountant in Los Angeles, California. 3. Hudson C., a graduate of Ricker Classical Institute and attended the

University of Maine for three and a half years, lives on the home farm and operates it for his mother, who owns it. He married Bernice Bolster, and they have one child, Lewis Charles.

WOODBURY L. BERCE—For many years the Berce family have been known in this section of Maine as progressive farmers and potato growers. Woodbury L. Berce, who owns one and operates two farms near Washburn, Maine, was born at Woodland, Maine, in Aroostook County, September 22, 1892, son of Lewis Elmon (see a preceding biography) and Mary D. (Carlton) Berce. Mr. Berce owns one of the most highly cultivated farms in this part of the county. It comprises one hundred and seventy-five acres, situated on the edge of the village of Washburn, and also he rents other potato lands. On these farms he does some general farming, but specializes in a brand of potatoes for seed of such high quality as to be known as certified seed potatoes. Mr. Berce was educated in the public schools of Caribou, Maine. And, after finishing his high school work, he entered the University of Maine, where he was a student for two years. He then went over into New York State and was manager of a potato farm for a year, after which time he returned to Maine. He was at first associated with his father in farming during the summer months and during the winter months he was busy with shipping potatoes which had been stored in the warehouse. In 1916, when he was at the age of twenty-three years, he decided to start out for himself and rented a farm near Caribou, which he operated profitably and was soon in position to take advantage of an opportunity to purchase his own farm. This farm was taken from the State by Oliver Stoddard and had become known as the Stoddard Farm when Mr. Berce purchased it from Mr. Stoddard and it continues to be called by that name, although Mr. Berce has owned it for many years. Mr. Berce is a Republican in political activity and has held several public offices. He served the town as selectman for two terms. He is a member of the Blue Lodge and Chapter of Free and Accepted Masons at Caribou; the Council at Presque Isle and the Commandry of Knights Templar at Houlton. He and family are members of the Baptist church.

Woodbury L. Berce married Eva Norbeck, of Woodland, Maine, daughter of George and Ada (Johnson) Norbeck. They have two children: Woodbury L., Jr., and Pauline.

HAROLD G. BROWN—Local manager of the Aroostook County Telephone and Telegraph Company since 1919, at Presque Isle, Harold G. Brown had his first experience with that company as repairman, later was cashier at Caribou, and in a short time was promoted to the office which he now (1928) ably fills. Mr. Brown is counted among the outstanding men of the Presque Isle community and constantly gives his support to enterprises calculated for its welfare and betterment.

Harold G. Brown was born at Hartland, New Brunswick, Dominion of Canada, July 15, 1889, son of S. J. and Helen (Nichols) Brown. S. J. Brown was for many years engaged in the making of harness in New England, at Mars Hill, Maine, and was there well liked and respected as a man of high character. Harold G. Brown received his grade school education and part of his high school training at Hartland, and at the age of fifteen years left school to go to work. He worked at various trades until he became connected with the telephone company at the Smyrna Mills, Maine, offices, and with this organization (the Katahdin Telephone Company) remained for a number of years. He was nineteen when he went to Caribou as company cashier. Mr. Brown believes in the principles of the Independent party, and casts his vote accordingly. He is a member of the Knights of Pythias and the Methodist church. His heart is warm toward charitable causes, and those sponsored by the church or brought to his attention elsewhere are not denied.

Harold G. Brown married June Clark, born at Smyrna Mills, daughter of Lowell and Mrs. Clark; and they are the parents of seven children: Gerald, Nadine, Phillip, Arthur, Richard, Betty, and Marylin.

FREDERICK L. HAMILTON—As a job printer in Presque Isle, Frederick L. Hamilton has won a favorable reputation in the community as a business man, and is highly respected by his business associates. He obtained his first experience in this type of work in a newspaper office, which he entered almost immediately after his graduation from the high school in Presque Isle. He was born in Patten, Maine, on August 9, 1885, the son of George S. and Luna (Hamilton) Hamilton. His father, who was a farmer and carpenter, is now deceased; while his mother, who although her maiden name was Hamilton was unrelated to Mr. Hamilton before her marriage, is still living. Frederick L. Hamilton as a boy attended the public schools of Patten, his birthplace, and later was graduated from the high school in Presque Isle. After he completed his schooling, he worked for a time with George H. Collins in the office of the "Star Herald"; then attended Bates College for a year, doing work for a newspaper while he was a student; and then worked again for the "Star Herald." Deciding that he was in need of outdoor work, he became engaged in the postal service, driving a rural route for about eight years in Fort Kent, Maine. Then he returned to Presque Isle, where he worked in the printing plant of C. A. Gammon, and in 1923 he bought this plant from Mr. Gammon.

Mr. Hamilton, who is keenly interested in the civic and social affairs of Presque Isle and the surrounding community, as well as in business and industrial developments, is affiliated politically with the Republican party. He is a member of the Free and Accepted Masons; he also holds a membership in the Merchants' Association and the Mooseleuk Club, and attends the Congregational church.

CHARLES F. DAGGETT—Sometimes a man's achievements are so easily the result of natural talents that he is not conscious of being of any particular value to his community. Such is the case with Charles F. Daggett of Presque Isle, Maine. Mr. Daggett is one of those modest men who never like to sound their own trumpets of glorification and find that in the day's work there occur many things that are valued by others, but being done without undue exertion or effort on the part of the doer are considered insignificant by him. But however modest Mr. Daggett might be with regard to what he thinks of his acts in commercial and civic life, they are not considered without appreciation by his fellow-citizens. Mr. Daggett is well known both as a lawyer and a banker and an authority on both subjects.

Charles F. Daggett is the son of Orin and Mary (Perkins) Daggett. He was born September 9, 1856, at New Sharon, Maine, and after receiving a common school education he was graduated at Wilbraham Academy, then went to New York City, where he read law in the offices of Nelson, Cook and Thorn. Subsequently he studied with the law firm of Powers and Powers at Houlton, and was admitted to the bar in the State of Maine in 1878. For two years he practiced law in Fort Fairfield, Maine, and then moved to the town of Presque Isle in the fall of 1880, where he has since made his home. Not confining himself alone to law in his interest in public affairs, Mr. Daggett took an active interest in the Presque Isle National Bank and for thirty-four years was the president of that institution, retiring in January, 1928. To have rendered such valuable service to both stockholders and depositors is in itself a service highly appreciated by all business men in the community and those in private life who have enjoyed the privileges of the bank. In politics, Mr. Daggett is a Republican and for several years was county attorney. He was also on the Governor's staff during the administrations of Henry Cleaves, William T. Cobb and Governor Fernald.

Charles F. Daggett married Alifair Dyer. They have one child, Helen A.

GRANVILLE C. GRAY—Lawyer, banker, World War veteran and public servant, Granville C. Gray, of Presque Isle, Maine, has had a wider experience and observation of men and events than falls to the lot of most men under forty, all of which will be useful in the responsible position he now occupies in the business community as vice-president and treasurer of the Merchants' Trust and Banking Company.

Mr. Gray was born in Baring, Maine, March 25, 1895, the son of Charles W. and Elizabeth (Harmon) Gray. His father, who is still living, was for many years engaged in the furniture business in Brewer, Maine, and Granville C. Gray received his early training in the public schools of

168 MAINE—A HISTORY

Baring, Machias, and was graduated from the high school at Brewer in 1912. He then entered Maine University, and was graduated in the class of 1916 with the degree of Bachelor of Arts, and had made progress in his legal studies when he was ordered to the Mexican border in 1916 as a member of the National Guard. On being released from the service, he returned to Maine, passed the bar examination in the spring of 1917, but on the entry of the United States into the World War, he enlisted at Bangor with Company G, 2d Infantry, Maine National Guard, in which he was made a sergeant, and was sent to camp at Plattsburg, and then to Camp Devens, where he was commissioned as first lieutenant, seven months later was assigned to the University of West Virginia as instructor, and received his honorable discharge on December 22, 1917. Again home in Maine, he went to Bangor as adjustor for the Travelers' Insurance Company, and in 1922 settled in Presque Isle as assistant treasurer of the Merchants' Trust and Banking Company. On July 1, 1924, he was promoted to treasurer and vice-president. A Republican in politics, Mr. Gray served two terms as solicitor for the city of Brewer, resigning that office to go to Presque Isle. He is a member of the Free and Accepted Masons, and of the Blue Lodge of that order; of the Knights of Pythias, the Merchants' Association, the Rotary Club, and the Penobscot Bar Association. He attends the Congregational church.

Mr. Gray married Annie E. Wright, daughter of Everett and Elizabeth (Holmes) Wright, of Machiasport. Their children are: Nanabelle E. and Everett W.

RICHARD ALEXANDER GRAVES, M. D. —His practice interrupted for a time by the World War, during which he served with distinction in V. R. 76, the French Military Hospital, operated by an American unit under Dr. Blake, and attained the rank of first lieutenant, Dr. Richard Alexander Graves returned to Presque Isle, Maine, where he is one of the most popular, as well as one of the most respected physicians.

Born in Presque Isle, October 21, 1889, he was the son of Richard and Bessie (Fraser) Graves. He attended the Presque Isle public schools, was

graduated from the high school, and then entered the medical department of the University of Pennsylvania, where he was graduated in the class of 1912, with the degree of Doctor of Medicine. He then spent a year as interne in the Eastern Maine General Hospital, and had established himself in general practice in his home town when the opportunity came for him to be of service to the Allied cause.

Dr. Graves is a member of the Free and Accepted Masons, Chapter, Council, and Commandery, and a member of the Order of the Eastern Star. He also belongs to the Mooseleuk Club, the Rotary Club, and the Knights of Pythias. He attends the Congregational church with his family. In politics he is an Independent. He is a member of the County, State, and American Medical associations.

Dr. Richard A. Graves married Mildred Doane, daughter of Frank and Gertrude (Allingham) Doane, of Lincoln, Maine. Their one son is Richard Alexander Graves, Jr., born May 2, 1918.

FRED P. STEVENS—A young man who has stuck by his home town and progressed with it, is Fred P. Stevens, of Presque Isle, Maine. Mr. Stevens is one whose authority on the correct styles for men is without question, for in the business of which he is president and treasurer, he sees to it that the very latest modes of gentlemen's furnishings are placed within buying reach of the men of Presque Isle. It is his pleasant manner in being able to help those who need his goods to find exactly what they want that has kept this business in the lead in this line of merchandise. Mr. Stevens is the son of D. A. and Annie (Black) Stevens. His father established the business which has since been incorporated under the name of Fred P. Stevens Company, in 1886.

Fred P. Stevens was born at Houlton, Maine, January 12, 1881. He was four years of age when his father opened the store at Presque Isle, and after he had gone through all the grades of the public school and graduated from the Presque Isle High School, he went into the store with his father and learned the business from behind the counter, where he soon acquired that ability to sense the desires of a customer and to build for himself a trade that has continued to grow. He has never known nor been interested in any other line of business and when the time came to incorporate, it was perfectly natural that he should be the president and treasurer of the corporation for he knows so well how to manage every department of it. Although Presque Isle is not a metropolis, yet, the volume of business done regularly by the Fred P. Stevens Company in their retail store requires the assistance of two clerks who are kept on throughout the year. Mr. Stevens is a Republican in his political affiliations and was at one time president of the Rotary Club of Presque Isle. He is a Free and Accepted Mason, member of the Blue Lodge, the Council, the Consistory, and of the Ancient Arabic Order Nobles of the Mystic Shrine.

Fred P. Stevens married Isadora Harmon, of Florida, daughter of the Rev. L. L. Harmon, a minister of the Free Baptist Church. Mrs. Stevens is organist in the Union Baptist Church of Presque Isle.

RALPH K. WOOD—Among the younger members of the Maine bar who seemed destined to future leadership in the profession is Ralph K. Wood, of Presque Isle, who has identified himself to a large extent with the civic activities of his adopted community.

Born in Randolph, Vermont, June 29, 1892, son of R. R. and Clara (Edson) Wood, both of pioneer Vermont families, he was educated in the public and high schools of Randolph, and at the University of Maine, where he was graduated from the Law School in the class of 1914, and admitted to practice in the same year. He opened an office in Fort Fairfield, but a few months later, began the practice of his profession in Presque Isle, where he has built up a large clientele among the business men and the institutions they represent.

Mr. Wood is a member of the Free and Accepted Masons, Chapter and Council; and of the Mooseleuk Club. He is a communicant of the Protestant Episcopal church, and is active in the councils of the local Democratic organizations.

Ralph K. Wood married Edna Crosskill, daughter of Henry C. and Susan (Oxner) Crosskill, of Bangor, Maine. They have one child, Margaret Wood, born June 21, 1916.

WILLIAM RICHARD ROIX—Since 1915 William Richard Roix has engaged in the general practice of law in Presque Isle, Aroostook County, and is here regarded as one of the most prominent and outstanding members of the community. He enjoys a wide and favorable reputation as a leader in the Republican party, and has served that political organization in elevated capacities on various occasions. He began the practice of law at the age of twenty-five years, at Limestone, where he remained for three years, next removing to Ashland, Maine, and practicing there for a period of four and a half years, until 1915, when he located at Presque Isle.

William Richard Roix was born at Bangor, Maine, on July 7, 1882, son of William A. and Luella (Mahoney) Roix, he having been born at Belfast, Maine, and she at Northport. William A. Roix was for many years captain of a steamboat plying between Bangor and Boston, Massachusetts, for the Eastern Steamship Company. William Richard Roix received his early education in the public schools of Bangor and Boston, and after completion of courses in high school matriculated in the Eastern Maine Conference Seminary, at Bucksport. From the seminary he was admitted to the University of Maine, to the Department of Law, and there he graduated with the degree of Bachelor of Laws, in 1906, and passed the bar examination entitling him to practice in the State of Maine in October of that year. He began practice at Limestone, and in 1909 went to the State House of Representatives as assistant clerk. In 1913, while located at Ashland, he was elected to the office of chief clerk, House of Representatives, and served in that capacity until 1919, meanwhile changing residence to Presque Isle. In 1919 he was elected State Attorney for Aroostook County, and as such served for four years. His political engagements were even more extensive than this: In 1917 he was chosen Secretary of Maine State Electoral College; in 1921, President of the State Electoral College, and in the same year Messenger to Washington, District of Columbia, carrying the State electoral vote. Mr. Roix has built up an extensive general law practice in Presque Isle; clients appreciate the able manner in which he prepares cases and defends them. He is constantly aligned with those of the town who strive for its welfare and progress. Mr. Roix has a number of fraternal affiliations, including membership in the Blue Lodge of the Free and Accepted Masons, the Knights of Pythias, Modern Woodmen of America, and the Order of the Eastern Star.

William Richard Roix married, and is the father of three children: 1. Luella, wife of Henry Pendergast, of Waterville, Maine. 2. Marjorie Louise. 3. William Richard, Jr.

HARVEY F. McGLAUFLIN—Since 1922 Harvey F. McGlauflin has been general secretary of the Grange Insurance Companies. There are three of these companies, the Aroostook County Patrons Mutual Fire Insurance Company, the Northern Maine's Patrons Mutural Fire Insurance Company, and the Aroostook Mutual Fire Insurance Company, and all of them are benefited in no small degree by the considerable energy and ability of Mr. McGlauflin, and the thorough knowledge of his position which he gained in the years in which he acted as assistant secretary. Mr. McGlauflin is also the owner of some two hundred acres of land at Presque Isle, where he raises potatoes and other general farm produce for local buyers. He has been active in the civic and fraternal life of his community.

His father, Ernest T. McGlauflin, held the position of secretary of the Grange Insurance Companies for many years and it was after his death, on January 26, 1922, that Mr. McGlauflin succeeded him. His mother, who before her marriage was Eva A. Griffin, is still living.

Harvey F. McGlauflin was born at Presque Isle, Maine. He attended the local schools, including a three-year term in the high school, and when he completed his education, began work on a farm, where he remained for three years. At the end of that time he became employed by the Bangor & Aroostook Railroad, but after three years there, returned to farm work. Mr. McGlauflin continued in this occupation until he entered the insurance business as assistant secretary of the Grange Companies, his father being secretary, and this arrangement continued until his father's death on January 26, 1922. On February 1, 1922, he succeeded to the position of secretary of the Grange Companies, in which place he has remained since that time. Mr. McGlauflin is also the owner of a two hundred acre farm, and specializes in the raising of potatoes. He is thoroughly familiar with the best farming methods and has been very successful in this field.

Politically, he is a member of the Republican party. He is affiliated, fraternally, with the Ancient Free and Accepted Masons, and is also a member of the Independent Order of Odd Fellows, the Modern Woodmen of America, and the Grange.

Harvey F. McGlauflin married Georgia E. Wray, born at Jacksontown, Province of New Brunswick, Canada, the daughter of Elmer E. and Elsie E. (Good) Wray. Her father was born in New York State, but later moved to New Brunswick, where he married Elsie E. Good, who was born in New Brunswick. A farmer by occupation, he came to Presque Isle and purchased a farm on the Houlton Road. Mr. and Mrs. McGlauflin are the parents of the following children: 1. Irene D. 2. Dana E. 3. Earl G. 4. Mearl H. The last two are twins.

FREDERICK P. WHITNEY—A lifelong association with the affairs of Presque Isle, civic and professional, has secured for Frederick P. Whitney a place of leadership in his profession as an attorney-at-law and as court recorder, and he has held other responsible and town offices with a thorough understanding and intelligence that have been of direct benefit and influence to the community and its institutions. Mr. Whitney possesses the unfailing regard and respect of all with whom he is associated in office or in the course of the practice of his profession.

Frederick P. Whitney was born June 20, 1868, at Presque Isle, a son of James F. Whitney, a merchant, and Sophronia (Nason) Whitney, both natives of Presque Isle. After attending the Presque Isle common schools, he was then graduated at the classical school conducted by St. John's Episcopal Church; and preparing for his profession with a two years' course at Bowdoin College, and in the law office of Judge George H. Smith, he was admitted to the bar in 1896. In that year he opened his office at Presque Isle, where he has continued to practice since. He has held the office of court recorder for the Presque Isle Municipal Court since its establishment in 1917, now serving his third term therein. He held a commission as trial justice for over twenty years, and also was a disclosure commissioner for more than thirty years. He is a Republican in political matters, and for twenty years was town auditor. He is affiliated with the Knights of Pythias, and is a member of the Episcopal church. His family attends the Roman Catholic church.

Frederick P. Whitney married, in 1909, Mildred Amelia Willett, who was born at Presque Isle, daughter of John B. and Ozite (Beauleau) Willett; and they have three sons: Sumner F., John Franklin, and George William.

RICHARD FOSTER CROCKER—For a period of fourteen years Richard Foster Crocker has been associated with the Madawaska Training School, and since 1925 he has been principal of the school. Mr. Crocker is a graduate of the University of Maine, and for a short time after his graduation was engaged in landscape gardening.

Richard Foster Crocker was born in Stockton Springs, Maine, September 4, 1891, son of Edwin M. and Estelle (Mudgett) Crocker. He was brought to Belfast, Maine, by his parents when he was one and a half years of age and, after attending the public schools of Belfast, became a student in the University of Maine, at Orono, where he was graduated with the degree of Bachelor of Science. For a short time after completing his course in the University he was engaged in landscape gardening, but in 1914 he came to Fort Kent and took a position as teacher in the Madawaska Training School. Here he has remained during the fourteen years which have passed since that time, and in 1925, he was made principal of the school, which position he is still holding (1928). He has brought to his work fine preparation and excellent ability, and has served faithfully and well both as teacher and as principal. He is a Republican in his political sympathies and is actively interested in the general welfare, taking especial interest, of course, in educational matters, in the interest of which he has served as chairman of the school committee for a period of six years, and is now (1928) president of the Aroostook County Teachers' Association. He is a member of the Blue Lodge, Free and Accepted Masons, of Fort Kent, and a member of the Board of Directors of the local Rotary Club. His

religious interest is with the Congregational church, of which he and his family are attendants.

Richard Foster Crocker is married to Matilda Weed Moholland, who was born in Veazie, Maine, daughter of James H. and Annie E. (Page) Moholland. Mr. and Mrs. Crocker are the parents of four children: 1. Richard F., Jr. 2. Barbara Ellen. 3 and 4. Anne Maria and Hope Mavis (twins).

WILLIAM RUFUS PIPES—A determination to succeed in the face of adversity has characterized the career of William Rufus Pipes, who with his son, Harry R. Pipes, owns and operates the large dry goods and furnishings business under the name of W. R. Pipes and Sons, Incorporated. In the early years of his business, everything he had was completely lost in a disastrous fire, but undaunted, he set to work courageously to reorganize. The wholesale dealers made a proposition that if he could rebuild, they would furnish all the merchandise necessary to restock the store. He managed to finance the erection of a new building, in which he resumed business, continuing in that location for forty years.

Mr. Pipes was born in Albert County, New Brunswick, April 30, 1851, son of Rufus Pipes and Jane (Brewster) Pipes, both of New Brunswick. They came to the United States when Mr. Pipes was a child and spent the remainder of their lives in Houlton and are buried at New Limerick. Rufus Pipes was an educator of great ability and taught school for many years.

William Rufus Pipes was educated in the public schools of Houlton, and at the age of fifteen years, entered business as clerk in the store of C. E. Goodnow and Company, later known as E. C. Goodnow and Company. In that business he remained for eleven years, when he came to Presque Isle to assume charge of the store of Johnson and Phair, which he successfully managed for three years. He then established his own independent business at its present location, at first renting the property and purchasing it after the first year. For four years he carried on a prosperous business, acquiring a reputation for the highest dependability and integrity, when the fire occurred which totally ruined his entire business. He refused to allow this setback to discourage him, and with the trust and

confidence of his dealers, soon erected a new building where he resumed his merchandise trade and
operated continually in that location for forty
years. On February 18, 1924, his business was
totally destroyed by fire for the second time, and
in June of that year he built a modern brick building containing three stores on the street floor and
seven offices above, and the business of W. R. Pipes
and Sons, Incorporated, now occupies one of these
stores. In 1925, his son was taken into the firm as
treasurer, and together they conduct one of the
most reliable and best known mercantile houses in
the vicinity, employing from five to ten people. Mr.
Pipes is the oldest established merchant in the town
and has always been a leader in all projects for
community welfare, besides being a factor in its
progressive business development. In fraternal
circles he is prominent in the Free and Accepted
Masons, having attained his thirty-second degree in
the Ancient Accepted Scottish Rite; is Knight
Templar, Past Commander; and Shriner. In politics Mr. Pipes follows the principles of the Republican party, and his religious affiliations are with
Unitarian church, of which he is a trustee.

William Rufus Pipes married Sarah Graham, of
Woodstock, New Brunswick, daughter of Hugh
and Anna (Evans) Graham, and their son is Harry
R., mentioned before.

A. HOWARD SMITH—Part owner and treasurer of the A. M. Smith Company, dealing in
hardware, finished lumber and building materials,
A. Howard Smith is counted as prominent among
the public-spirited citizens of Presque Isle, Aroostook County. The business was founded in 1880,
by Aubrey M. Smith, father of A. Howard Smith;
and in 1917 was incorporated. Aubrey Smith died
on June 12, 1926, and at present his widow,
mother of A. Howard Smith, resident in the State
of California, is president of the company. The
third director and member of the controlling body
is Otis R. Smith, brother of A. Howard Smith,
son of Evie (Howard) Smith. A. Howard Smith
was born at Presque Isle on July 2, 1890, son of
Aubrey M. and Evie (Howard) Smith, and
throughout his residence in this city, which has
been continuous, has resided in the house where
he was born.

A. Howard Smith received his early education
in the public schools of Presque Isle, then for one
year attended classes in the Worcester Academy.
Upon graduation from the academy, in order to
better to fit himself for the commercial life, which
he had decided to follow, he studied in the Bryant
and Stratton Business College, and went immediately into association with his father in the hardware, lumber and building supplies business. Mr.
Smith assumed personal direction of the company
in 1921, when his father and mother removed to
California, and at the death of his father five years
later became its manager in permanence. Constantly he has engaged actively in community enterprises; a loyal supporter of the Republican party,
he has several times been urged to run for public
office. During the World War he served on various
local boards and committees having as their purpose the raising of funds and other means of
prosecution of the war, also serving with distinction on the labor board. He is active fraternally,
affiliated with the Free and Accepted Masons, Blue
Lodge of Presque Isle, Royal Arch Masons, Royal
and Select Masters, Knights Templar, and Ancient
Arabic Order Nobles of the Mystic Shrine; and
a member of the Presque Isle Merchants' Association, in this organization having served on the
first Speculative Committee. With his family he
attends the Unitarian church. He is a member and
one of the board of trustees of the church, and
gives liberally to charitable causes sponsored by
it, as well as to those cases which come to his attention otherwise.

A. Howard Smith married Louise Jacques, who
was born in New Brunswick, Canada, daughter of
Howe and Isadore (Ganong) Jacques; and they
are the parents of one child, a daughter, Lura
Louisa.

EDWARD I. WADDELL—One of the prominent men in the public affairs in Presque Isle, is
Edward I. Waddell, the present postmaster, who
has held this office since his appointment by President Harding. Mr. Waddell has always been particularly active in Republican politics and was
one of the leading merchants of the town until
January 1, 1923, when he entered the government
service in his present position. For twenty-eight
years he carried on a successful jewelry business

founded by himself, and built up a reputation for dependable products and expert workmanship.

Mr. Waddell was born at Castle Hill, October 19, 1872, son of John Waddell, who is deceased, and Hannah (McGlauflin) Waddell, who is still living. John Waddell was engaged in farming for the greater part of his life.

Edward I. Waddell attended the public schools at Castle Hill and high school at Mapleton. After the completion of his formal education, he learned the jeweler's trade with the late H. H. Robinson, of Presque Isle. In 1895, he engaged in this business independently and soon became one of the leaders of this craft, as evidenced by the fact that he was chosen secretary-treasurer of the Maine Retail Jewelers' Association. In the mercantile life of the town, he has been particularly active and assisted in the formation of the local Merchants' Association, of which he was chosen as its first secretary, remaining in that position for five years. As postmaster of Presque Isle, Mr. Waddell heads a postoffice of the second class and has for his assistant Llewelyn F. Pellelier. The force of employees consists of four regular clerks, three regular and one substitute city carriers, and four rural routes with one substitute. There is much modern equipment and a parcel post truck to care for the large amount of business. With his courtesy and efficiency, Mr. Waddell is continuing the excellent reputation for public service which he established in his long political career, when he served for four years as chairman of the Republican Town Committee, fourteen years as town clerk, and four years as chairman of the Republican County Committee. In religion, Mr. Waddell attends the Unitarian church.

Edward I. Waddell married (first) Rosella Humphries, who is deceased, daughter of Charles and Mary (Sproul) Humphries, and their daughter is Marjorie, a graduate of Aroostook State Normal School. Mr. Waddell married (second) Ivah Woodbury, of Patten, daughter of Dr. Benjamin Collins and Matilda Albina (Knowles) Woodbury. She was educated at Patten Academy and studied music at the Faelten Pianoforte School of Boston. An exceptionally accomplished musician, Mrs. Waddell is at present a teacher of the piano in this town.

MALCOLM S. W. DINGWALL—In the business of general insurance and land surveying, Malcolm S. W. Dingwall, of Presque Isle, Maine, holds the esteem and high respect of the entire community. Mr. Dingwall is a native of Canada, the Province of Ontario, and was brought up in that country until he reached manhood. His birthplace was Port Hope, Ontario, and his early education was in the schools there. When he had reached the collegiate age, he intended entering the Military College but circumstances prevented the fulfillment of this ambition and he went into business instead. However, he did master his first year in mathematics and continued to study at night, making the best of every minute offered for self improvement. His first position was with the Canadian Pacific Railway in the government work department, where he was employed from 1904 to 1909 as an engineer. This practical experience and training gave him a start as an engineer and in July, 1909, he accepted a position with the Aroostook Valley Railroad Company and came into Maine. He practically built the Aroostook Valley Railroad and finding this country a good place to settle, he finally made his home in Presque Isle, Maine, where he opened an office as a land surveyor. As this country was then beginning a new development on account of the new railroad bringing it closer to other communities, Mr. Dingwall soon had a flourishing business and added to that a general insurance line which has grown until at this time he has one of the largest insurance and land surveyor's offices in this section. He maintains four agents and a fully equipped office with adequate force to take care of his constantly growing customers. He is a staunch Republican in his political proclivities, a member of the Order of Free and Accepted Masons; a member of the Ancient Arabic Order Nobles of the Mystic Shrine; secretary and treasurer of the Merchants' Association; was president of the Mooseleuk Club; and is major of the First Battalion, 152d Field Artillery, Maine National Guard. He and his family are members of the Methodist church.

Malcolm S. W. Dingwall married Maude A. Reiley, who was born at Priceville, Ontario. They have four children: 1. Dorothy. 2. Deborah. 3. Douglas. 4. Dana.

STORER W. BOONE, M. D.—One of the younger but none the less prominent physicians of the progressive community of Presque Isle, Aroostook County, is Storer W. Boone, native of Presque Isle, born there on March 29, 1894, son of Dr. Sherman and Elizabeth (Bird) Boone, his father likewise actively engaged in the practice of medicine at Presque Isle, located in the same building where are the offices of Storer W. Boone. Dr. Sherman Boone is well known throughout Aroostook County, and in point of view of service, is one of the county's oldest practicing physicians. Dr. Sherman Boone is the son of Richard and Anna Skidmore (Shirley) Boone; and Richard Boone is now (1928) living, aged ninety-four years.

After receiving his early academic instruction in the public schools of Presque Isle, Storer W. Boone matriculated in the McGill Medical School at Montreal, Dominion of Canada, where his father before him had prepared for the great humanitarian profession; and at the termination of the prescribed courses, in which his work was distinguished by its general excellence, graduated, with the degree of Doctor of Medicine, in the class of 1919. For more than a year Dr. Boone served as interne in the Montreal Maternity Hospital and the Montreal General Hospital, both in Montreal, specializing particularly in obstetrics and diseases of women, with an extensive training in urology. In 1921, he began the practice of his profession at Presque Isle, and was appointed to serve under Dr. Coombs in the diagnosis and treatment of venereal disease, having under their charge northern Aroostook County. In the years since 1921, Dr. Boone, like his father, Dr. Sherman Boone, has achieved prominence in the medical profession, and already is well known in the county for the unimpeachable ethical viewpoint in which he holds a position of important responsibility. In the spring of 1928 he took a course in the study of nose and throat in New York. The name of Boone, for several decades connected honorably with the practice of medicine in Presque Isle, has become of double significance, possessed by two such worthy practitioners, father and son. Dr. Storer W. Boone belongs to the Aroostook County Medical Society, the Maine State Medical Society, and the American Medical Association, as well as to the Canadian Medical Society, to which he was admitted after graduation from the McGill Med-

ical School. He is highly regarded by physicians of community and State and upholds a place in public activities constantly increasing in magnitude; known first as physician he is known second as a public-spirited citizen. He is active in the Free and Accepted Masons, Royal Arch Masons, at Presque Isle, Royal and Select Masters, Knights Templar, Ancient Arabic Order Nobles of the Mystic Shrine; a member of the Mooseleuk Club, and of the college fraternity Alpha Kappa Kappa. He is a communicant of the Church of England, loyal and devout in its support, and generous in his contributions to charitable and other causes sponsored by it.

Dr. Storer W. Boone married Phebe McGregor, of Vancouver, British Columbia, Canada, graduate of McGill University. Before marriage Mrs. Boone attended the Baptist church.

NATHAN P. COOK—After four years spent in Florida in boat building and orange growing, Nathan P. Cook returned to his old home in Presque Isle, Maine, and opened a shoe store on Main Street, where he has prospered ever since. It is an up-to-date place, founded in 1893, with polite clerks and a varied stock, showing a knowledge of both merchandising and display on the part of its proprietor.

Born in Presque Isle, in March, 1866, son of Sidney and Harriett F. (Perry) Cook, he comes of pioneer Maine stock. His father was a builder and the grist and sawmills of the town still testify as to his skill. Both parents are now dead.

Educated in the public schools of Presque Isle, Nathan P. Cook took a business course in Boston before going to Florida. Since his establishment in business after his return, he has taken a lively interest in the affairs of the community, and has served several terms as selectman, about eight years in all, and is prominent in Republican circles. He has also served on the school board and is a member of the Rotary Club and the Merchants' Association. He is a member of the Free and Accepted Masons, and of the Blue Lodge, and also belongs to the Independent Order of Odd Fellows. He is a Unitarian.

Nathan P. Cook married Eudora L. McGuire, daughter of Alonzo and Amelia (Jamison) Mc-

Guire. Their children are: 1. Sidney F., who manages a service station for automobiles in Presque Isle, and who married Edna Guin. 2. Harriett A. 3. Charles S.

JUDGE CARL A. WEICK—Justice of the Municipal Court of Presque Isle, Aroostook County, since 1917, Carl A. Weick has served with dignity, honor and distinction. Variously involved in the affairs of the town, Judge Weick, in 1928, at the age of thirty-four years, was elected president of the Presque Isle National Bank, succeeding in that office the Hon. Charles F. Daggett, who retired after a continuous service of thirty-three years. In addition to the duties of these offices Judge Weick carries on a law practice that is busy and exacting.

Judge Carl A. Weick was born at Springfield, Maine, on May 7, 1893, son of Charles F. and Mary H. (Budge) Weick. He is the youngest of a family of six children. His father, who fought for the Union in the Civil War, died while Judge Weick was in school and he was thereby left largely to his own resources at an early age. He received his education in the public schools of Springfield, in the University of Maine College of Law, where he graduated with honors and a degree of Bachelor of Laws, in 1914, and Bowdoin College. Graduating from Bowdoin with the Bachelor of Arts degree in 1916, he married soon thereafter and came to Presque Isle to commence the practice of law in the same year. Judge Weick is a member of the Republican party and actively concerned in the principal movements of that organization locally and in Aroostook County. He belongs to several local clubs, the Rotary Club, Three Link Club, and Mooseleuk Club, and is affiliated with the Free and Accepted Masons and Independent Order of Odd Fellows. He is a Past Master of the Blue Lodge of Presque Isle and a member of other Masonic bodies. He is a member of the Board of Trustees of the Presque Isle Public Library and attends the Congregational church. He is also a member of Delta Kappa Epsilon at Bowdoin, and of Phi Alpha Delta and Phi Kappa Phi at the University of Maine.

Judge Carl A. Weick married Harriet J. Scrib-

ner, born in Springfield, daughter of Ralph and Minnie (Burr) Scribner, and they are the parents of two children, daughters, Marjorie L. and Barbara L.

BURDAN H. KIMBALL—A man of great philanthropy, which he exercised regardless of creed or color, Burdan H. Kimball, late of Fort Fairfield, whose death occurred October 29, 1919, was one of the most distinguished sons of this great commonwealth, a leader in the affairs of his community, giving especially of his energy and material assistance to his own church and all the other churches of this vicinity, regardless of denomination. A man possessing the splendid qualities which were inherent in Mr. Kimball is not found in every community, and the residents of this town were proud to call him friend and to number him among the foremost citizens of Fort Fairfield. He was an active factor in the agricultural industry, specializing in potato raising and earning the esteem and acclaim of all his buyers for the superior quality of his product and the fairness and consideration with which all business dealings were conducted. Mr. Kimball was born in Carleton County, New Brunswick, Canada, in 1863, son of Jedediah and Eliza (Murphy) Kimball, both of whom were born in Carleton County. Jedediah Kimball was a prominent farmer in his native county and took an active part in all affairs of his vicinity.

Burdan H. Kimball was educated in the common or public schools of New Brunswick, and after the completion of his formal education, engaged in the agricultural industry in that country. After his marriage, he came to Fort Fairfield and bought a farm on Center Limestone Road, and proceeded to engage in raising potatoes. So successful was he in this enterprise that he was enabled to secure several large farms which he operated to advantage, being a leader in the output of potatoes from this locality, all of which he disposed of to local buyers, his crops being famous for their superior excellence and absolute dependability. Although his political principles were those of the Republican party, Mr. Kimball never took an active part in politics nor sought public office, although with his splendid views on public affairs and his zeal for civic betterment, he would have been an ideal office-holder. He was a member of the Free Baptist church in Canada, but attended the Union church after coming to Fort Fairfield for nineteen years being active and extremely liberal in all work connected with this church, while he was impartial in his charities and help to all church organizations, as aforementioned. His fraternal connection was with the Foresters' Lodge.

Burdan H. Kimball married, December 19, 1888, Minnie Savage, who was born in Carleton County, New Brunswick, Canada, daughter of William and Jane (Harneth) Savage, her father being a farmer of that province. To this union were born two daughters: 1. Gaynell, married Rev. Guy Wilson, an evangelist of the Methodist church, residing at Brookline, Massachusetts. 2. Kathleen, married Fred S. Kilburn, whose sketch follows this.

FRED S. KILBURN—His father's successor as cashier of the Fort Fairfield, Maine, National Bank, Fred S. Kilburn bids fair to rival him in usefulness to the community, in whose affairs he is taking an active part.

Born March 4, 1897, at Fort Fairfield, Maine, the son of Hiram B. and Mary E. (Dayton) Kilburn, he attended the local public schools, and was graduated from the high school in 1915. He then went to Boston, Massachusetts, where he entered Bryant & Stratton Business College, and on receiving his diploma returned to Fort Fairfield and found work in the bank in a clerical capacity. As he demonstrated his fitness, promotion was rapid. He was finally made assistant cashier, and on his father's resignation in 1925, was elected to succeed him. Soon afterwards his parents removed to California, where they are enjoying a well earned life of ease and tranquility. The elder Kilburn had been cashier for thirty years.

Fred S. Kilburn is a member of the Free and Accepted Masons; of Garfield Chapter, Royal Arch Masons; Caribou Commandery of the Knights Templar, of Houlton, Maine, and Anah Temple, Ancient Arabic Order Nobles of the Mystic Shrine, of Bangor, Maine. He attends the Congregational church, and is its organist. He is also treasurer of the Fort Fairfield Rotary Club.

Mr. Kilburn married Kathleen Kimball, daughter of Burdan H. and Minnie (Savage) Kimball,

whose biographical sketch precedes this. Mrs. Kilburn is a graduate of the Boston Conservatory of Music and is now organist at the St. Paul's Episcopal Church at Fort Fairfield.

CYRUS HENRY DICKEY, born at Gardiner, Maine, on April 25, 1850, died September 8, 1927, was the son of the late Major William Dickey. His attractive home on the bank of the Fish River, was directly opposite the Hotel Dickey, which was for many years the home of his father. During the Aroostook War the officers' quarters were located on this site, which is not far from the old time Block House, Mr. Dickey taking a deep interest in the preservation of this historic structure.

Mr. Dickey received his education in the schools of Portland and at Colby College. His first work in the way of business was that of a clerk in a shoe store in Portland, where he remained for several years. He then started in a business of his own in association with a partner, whose name was Eaton, the business being established at Frenchville, Maine, the firm being known as Eaton and Dickey. After several years he severed his interest from those of Mr. Eaton and started a lumber business by buying and shipping shingles. Mr. Dickey operated this lumber business on the St. John's River a long distance above Fort Kent. He lived at Frenchville until about 1895, when he moved to Fort Kent and remained here the rest of his life. He became prominent in Fort Kent through his different business interests and undertakings. Mr. Dickey served as Deputy Collector of Customs at Fort Kent, having held this position since February 9, 1904, his territory reaching from Frenchville on the St. John's River below Fort Kent to one hundred and twenty miles northwest of Fort Kent. He was one of the organizers of the Fort Kent Trust Company, and at the time of his death was serving this organization as president; his office as Collector of Customs also being in the bank building.

In the days before the automobile came into favor, Mr. Dickey was known as a lover of good horses and owned and drove the best stock. He was a man of liberal views in matters of religion and politics; in his religious belief he was a Universalist, but with his wife, he attended the Congregational church. In his youth he was a Democrat in his political affiliations, but as years came on and he thought more for himself, he became an adherent to the principles of the Republican party and was enumerated as one of that group.

On January 10, 1899, Cyrus Henry Dickey married Leanna Mallett, who was born at Saint Francis, Maine, on April 6, 1859, the daughter of Bartlett Welch and Isabell (Willey) Mallett. Mr. and Mrs. Dickey had no children. Mr. Dickey's sudden death occurred in Fort Kent, Maine, on September 8, 1927. In his passing the town and county lost a very valuable citizen who was held in the highest respect and great esteem by the entire community.

PAUL DUDLEY SARGENT—The life of Paul Dudley Sargent has been of unusual variety and interest, replete of progress, and he is today numbered prominently among the foremost citizens of Augusta, Maine. Meanwhile his activities have carried him far afield. For a period he worked in Washington, District of Columbia. His operations during the length of his career—extending over more than thirty years as this is written (1928)—have centered in several communities, but for the most part, and, indeed, always, save for the time spent in Washington, have confined themselves to the State of Maine, of which he is a native son. He is known widely through this commonwealth in engineering circles, wherein his reputation bids fair to be national in scope, and in affairs of business. He is now vice-president of the New England Metal Culvert Company, whose plants are at Palmer, Massachusetts, Portland, Maine, and Boston, Massachusetts.

Mr. Sargent was born at Machias, Maine, May 8, 1873, son of Ignatius Manlius and Helen Maria (Campbell) Sargent, his father having been a prosperous merchant of that community. From Machias High School he took his diploma in 1892, and in the fall of that year matriculated in the University of Maine, from it taking the degree of Bachelor of Civil Engineering in 1896. Thirty years later, 1926, in recognition of the value of his works as engineer, Mr. Sargent received from his *alma mater* the degree of Doctor of Engineering. This followed long years of constructive enterprise.

In 1897, following graduation from university, Mr. Sargent went to work as assistant engineer connected with construction of the Washington County branch of the Maine Central Railroad. At this he was engaged more than a year, and did so well that from 1899 to 1903 he was engineer in charge of maintenance of way for the railroad corporation. Altogether he served it seven years, and left the road only to assume office as register of deeds, Washington County, which office, elective, he retained until June 1, 1905. A Republican, he received a good majority of votes, and filled the post with a conscientiousness which justified election. Always since the year of his majority, incidentally, he has supported the principles of the party, and is a valued member at the present time, of wide and constructive influence. In 1905 Mr. Sargent became State Highway commissioner, holding this charge six years, until 1911; and on February 15, 1911, became assistant director in the Bureau of Public Roads, United States Department of Agriculture, at Washington, where he had offices until August 15, 1913—thirty months of service to the Nation's highway program. This brought him in close touch with leading men throughout the Nation. On August 15, 1913, he became chief engineer of the State Highway Commission, Maine; and for this service he is best known at the present time, as he held the position more than fourteen years, until December 31, 1927. As State highways engineer he was enabled to perform works of permanent benefit to his native State. On January 1, 1928, Mr. Sargent became vice-president of the New England Metal Culvert Company, and since then has given the whole of his professional and financial direction to this corporation.

Member of the National Guard from 1896 to 1900, Mr. Sargent was of assistance to the country during its participation in the World War as supporter of the several patriotic campaigns, notably those of the Liberty Loan. He is endowed largely with the qualities which beget friendship, has legion friends, and is active fraternally on a wide scale. He is a member of the Free and Accepted Masons, in which he belongs to the Chapter, Royal Arch Masons; the Commandery, Knights Templar; and the Temple, Ancient Arabic Order Nobles of the Mystic Shrine; and is a member also of the American Society of Civil Engineers, American

Society of Testing Materials, the Massachusetts Highway Association, the Maine Association of Engineers, American Road Builders' Association, the Permanent International Association of Road Congresses, and the American Association of State Highway Officials, of which he was president in 1919. He served continuously as a member of the executive committee until his resignation from State highway work in 1927. Mr. Sargent was appointed by President Coolidge as a delegate to represent the United States at the fifth congress of the association at Milan, Italy, in September, 1926, and attended as one of five delegates from the United States. He belongs to the Augusta Country Club, of Augusta; the Quaboag Country Club, of Monson, Massachusetts; and is a communicant of the Congregational church.

Mr. Sargent married, June 6, 1900, at Calais, Maine, Sarah Sawyer McAllister, daughter of Weston and Sarah (Collins) McAllister.

ARTHUR W. CROUSE—One of the respected citizens of the community in and near Crouseville and Washburn, Maine, Arthur W. Crouse is now a retired farmer. He has lived in this section of the State for the greater part of his life, although at one time he spent four or five years in Wisconsin. Mr. Crouse was born September 5, 1859, in the town of Washington, Maine, a son of Abraham and Caroline (Christie) Crouse, both natives of Casswick, Province of New Brunswick, Canada. The father, who was a lumberman and a farmer by occupation, was twice married, first to Caroline Christie, who is the mother of Arthur W. Crouse; and second to Bethiah Clark. By the first marriage there were two children, and by the second marriage there was a large family of children.

Arthur W. Crouse, one of the two children of Abraham and Caroline (Christie) Crouse, who came to the United States in 1870, attended as a boy the common schools of Crouseville, but left school at the age of thirteen years. First, he worked in the woods in Maine, and then proceeded to Wisconsin, where he worked in the woods for five years. At the end of that period he returned to Maine. He is a Republican in politics and he and his family are members of the First Adventist church, of which he is one of the board of trustees.

His wife is active at all times in the work of the church.

Arthur W. Crouse married Serena M. Corliss, a native of Milltown, Maine, a daughter of Rev. Moses W. and Octavia (Haynes) Corliss. By this marriage there were several children: 1. Abraham, who is now cultivating the home farm, and who married Ona Haynes, by which marriage there are two children, Opal and Crystal. 2. Octavia, who is the wife of Robert Scott, a farmer of Presque Isle, Maine, by which marriage there is one child, Wilburne. 3. Arline, who is the wife of the Rev. John Holman, a minister in the First Christian Adventist church, who resided in Massachusetts, where they have one child, Margaret. 4. Lloyd A., who is employed by the Aroostook Valley Railroad. 5. Arvard, who is a student in the high school of Washburn. 6. Moses, who also is a student in the high school.

HENRY HAVELOCK BARTLEY is a successful farmer of Westfield, Maine. He owns nearly two hundred acres and cultivates them with the skill and experience of a lifetime devoted to farming, for he began to work as a boy and has been at it ever since. He is both a farmer and a distributing merchant, for he specializes in potato raising, and he sells his potatoes to local buyers.

Mr. Bartley was born in Carleton County, New Brunswick, February 23, 1871, son of John and Abigail (Fulton) Bartley, of whom the father was born in Nova Scotia, while the mother was born in New Brunswick. Mr. Bartley came to the United States in 1904 and settled on a farm in the town of Westfield, and at the end of three years, namely in 1907, purchased the farm which he has since developed. He is a Republican in politics. He was an assessor six years, and was on the road commission four years. His farm is situated on Houlton Road. He belongs to the Independent Order of Odd Fellows, No. 148, and the Grange.

Mr. Bartley married Ethel M. Kennedy, born in New Brunswick, daughter of Thomas and Jane (Blake) Kennedy, of whom the father was born in Ireland and the mother in New Brunswick. Children: 1. Henry Earl. 2. Ashton. 3. Willis. 4. Hale, now deceased. 5. Lavinia. 6. Raymond. 7. Norval. 8. Curtis. 9. Vernon. 10. Ruth. The family attends the Free Baptist church.

ADAM PHILLIPS LEIGHTON, JR., M.D.
—Dr. Leighton was born in Portland, January 23, 1887, a son of Adam Phillips Leighton and Mary Isadore (Butler) Leighton. His father at one time was mayor of Portland, and was a well-known figure in the State. For over fifty years he was in the railroad news and scenic post-card business, an owner of Curtis and Son Company, chewing gum manufacturers and vice-president of the Sen-Sen, Chiclet and American Chicle Company of New York. Dr. Leighton received his education at Phillips Exeter Academy and at the Holbrook School, New York, and his medical degree at Bowdoin Medical School this State. He served as house physician at the Maine General Hospital in Portland in 1910 and 1911 directly after his graduation, and then went abroad to take up post-graduate work. He entered the Rotunda Hospital at Dublin and, after working there for two years, received the degree of L. M. from the University of Dublin. In 1912, he did further student work in Vienna at the Schauta Klinik. After this experience he returned to Portland and opened his own private hospital, the first maternity hospital in either Maine, New Hampshire or Vermont. Dr. Leighton has successfully conducted this institution for sixteen years and has been in active practice outside of the hospital demands during that time, specializing in obstetrics and gynecology and surgery pertaining to these branches of medical work. In spite of his manifold activities in his chosen profession, Dr. Leighton has found time to give attention to civic concerns and has taken, from time to time, office in the affairs of government. A member of the Common Council in 1916 and 1918, president of that body, alderman in 1919 and secretary of the Maine Board of Medical Registration of which he has been a member for fourteen years, he may be said to have done his share in the interests of good citizenship. In the financial world of Portland the benefit of his keen judgment has been appreciated and he serves on the Board of Directors of the Chapman National Bank and on that of the United States Trust Company, and the Cumberland County Loan and Building Association.

During the World War Dr. Leighton ranked as a lieutenant in the Medical Corps of the United States Navy and is still a member of the Medical Reserve Corps. Dr. Leighton is a member of the American Legion; the Kiwanis Club, of which he has been president; the Cumberland Club; Portland Club, Economic Club, Portland Country Club; Purpooduck Country Club; the Chamber of Commerce; and the Parish Club of the State Street Church. He and his family are members of the Congregational Williston Church of the City. He also belongs to the Bramhall League and to the United States Naval Reserve Association, and to the medical college fraternity, the Alpha Kappa Kappa. Dr. Leighton is fraternally connected with Masonry, being a member of the Atlantic Lodge of Free and Accepted Masons, the Greenleaf Chapter of Royal Arch Masons, Portland Council of Royal and Select Masters and Portland Commandery Knights Templar. He is a Past Potentate of Kora Temple of the Ancient Arabic Order Nobles of the Mystic Shrine, and is of the 32d Degree of the Ancient Accepted Scottish Rite. Dr. Leighton is connected, too, with the Benevolent Order of Elks and with the Knights of Pythias.

Dr. Leighton belongs to the American and to the Maine Medical associations, the Cumberland County Medical Society and the Portland Medical Club. A member of the New Hampshire Surgical Society and a Fellow of the American Association of Obstetrics, Gynecologists and Abdominal Surgeons, and president of the Aegis Medical Club.

Dr. Adam Phillips Leighton, Jr., married, October 29, 1924, in Portland, Anna Leahy, of Worcester, Massachusetts, daughter of Mr. and Mrs. Thomas Leahy. Dr. Leighton has a daughter by a former marriage, Eleanor Francesca, born February 2, 1913.

FRANK L. WHITE—The establishment of the hospital in Presque Isle, Aroostook County, can be justly attributed to the strenuous efforts and untiring zeal of the late Frank L. White, who was one of the leading attorneys of that section until failing health forced him to abandon his extensive practice. Mr. White realized the need of a hospital in Presque Isle and the history of the institution is a lengthy story of almost unaided effort on his part. It is generally admitted that but for Mr. White's faith, self-sacrifice and personal work the project would never have materialized.

Mr. White was born in Winthrop, Kennebec County, October 19, 1859, the son of Charles W. and Mary (Keezer) White. His early education was received at the local public school, followed by a course at the old Presque Isle Academy, which at that time stood on the site of what is now the training school. He then entered the Albany, New York, Law School, graduating with the degree of Bachelor of Laws in 1889. He was admitted to the bar and started in the practice of his profession in Presque Isle. For a short time he was in practice alone, later taking into partnership the late Orin J. Smith. When the partnership was dissolved a few years later Mr. White continued alone until, in May, 1907, he was forced to give up practice on account of failing health. He then took up farming, having been advised that an outdoor life was best suited to him, and this he continued up to the time of his death. During the last years of his life Mr. White was affiliated with the Church of Christ, Scientist.

On December 25, 1886, Mr. White married Myrtle L. Todd, the daughter of Israel J. and Martha Jane (Parsons) Todd, of Caribou, Aroostook County. Mrs. White was educated in the public schools of Presque Isle and the high school of Caribou, followed by courses at the academy of Fort Fairfield, Aroostook County, Farmington Normal School and the State Normal School at Aroostook. She was a teacher in the schools of Aroostook County for several years and was appointed to the post of superintendent of schools in Presque Isle for thirteen years. She then substituted as teacher at the Normal School, not desiring to take up a steady position. Mrs. White was president of the Maine Federation of Women's Clubs from 1918 to 1920, inclusive, and was active in the Unitarian Church of Presque Isle. Her busy and fruitful life ended June 6, 1928.

On March 8, 1924, Mr. White died at his home in Presque Isle. The funeral service, which was largely attended, was conducted by Rev. J. B. Ranger, pastor of the United Brethren church, and services were also held at the hospital, which owed so much to the efforts of Mr. White, and conducted by Rev. William Snow, of the local Methodist church. The interment was in Maysville Cemetery. The passing of Mr. White was deeply mourned by the community which recognized fully that it had lost a public-spirited citizen

who was ever willing and ready to aid in every way in any project which would be of benefit to his fellowmen.

HENRY KING BRADBURY—During nearly a quarter of a century of authority as treasurer of the Vanburen Trust Company, of Vanburen, Maine, Henry King Bradbury, who was one of the organizers of the institution, won the esteem of his fellow citizens by the uprightness of his character and the efficient manner in which he carried out his obligations to the public. He was a man of fine presence and attractive personality, a maker of friends and a public-spirited citizen of the highest character, whose passing was a blow to a wide circle of business and social acquaintances and a real loss to the community in which he had risen to prominence.

Born in Houlton, Maine, in 1865, he was a son of Henry C. and Julia A. (Keaton) Bradbury, and acquired his education in the academy there, now known as the Ricker Classical Institute. Upon completion of these courses he became associated with his father, who was for many years the manager of the Shaw interests, remaining in that association until he was twenty years of age, when he accepted a position as bookkeeper with the Titcomb lumber enterprise. Leaving this after a time, he engaged independently for two years as a furniture dealer, but withdrew from this and came to Vanburen, where he took the positions of bookkeeper and manager for Allen E. Hammond and the Vanburen Mercantile Company, later serving as bookkeeper for the Vanburen Lumber Company. He remained in these occupations until 1905, when, in association with others, he organized the Vanburen Trust Company and was made treasurer, a post which he administered until his death. In his political faith he adhered to the principles of the Republican party and was affiliated with the Masonic body, having membership in St. Aldemar Lodge, No. 17, Free and Accepted Masons; was a Past Commander of the Knights Templar and a member of the Temple, Ancient Arabic Order Nobles of the Mystic Shrine. His death occurred April 11, 1928.

Henry King Bradbury married Jennie E. Abbett, of Houlton, Maine, daughter of James Abbett.

Their children are: 1. Hilda (twin), a graduate of Colby College, later a teacher of French in the Classical High School of Lynn, Massachusetts. 2. Ralph (twin), also a graduate of Colby College, later associated with the Amoskeag Manufacturing Company, of Manchester, New Hampshire. He married Mildred Crocket and they are the parents of Robert Bradbury. 3. Richard, married Eva Smith and resides with his wife in Vanburen.

Henry King Bradbury had in his nature the fine combination of keen business acumen and attractive friendliness. He was devoted to the interests of the people in a degree only second to that which he took in his home and family, was faithful to trust and a conscientious citizen of unblemished integrity.

ALEXANDER H. CHRISTIE—Growing and shipping potatoes is the specialty which Alexander H. Christie has chosen in connection with his agricultural work in the village of Mapleton, Maine, where he owns two hundred acres of land. His farm is situated on the State Highway one-half mile from Mapleton, and is one of the finest tracts of land in this section of the State. Mr. Christie, who removed to the United States from New Brunswick, Canada, when he was thirty-five years old, is regarded as one of the leading citizens of this district, where he has spent much of his life and where he is well known and highly respected by the members of the community. He was born in York County, the Province of New Brunswick, Canada, on February 22, 1865, a son of John T. and Catherine (McFarland) Christie, who were natives of New Brunswick. They never came to the United States, but remained on the family farm in Canada, where John T. Christie had been a farmer all his life and at the time of his death was cultivating the soil on the same farm on which he was born.

Alexander H. Christie, as a boy, attended the public schools in his native district of New Brunswick. His first work was that of farming. Eventually both he and his brother, Walter R. Christie, a sketch of whom follows, came to the United States, Alexander H. then being at the age of thirty-five years, and settled in Maine, working for five years as a hired hand on a farm owned by Lewis S. Bean. Later he took one-half interest in Mr. Bean's farm, which was located in Creasy Ridge. Finally he bought the Bean acres, but subsequently traded this land for his present farm just outside of Mapleton, giving $18,000 cash bonus at the time of the trading. Mr. Christie always has been active in the civic and social matters of interest to his community, and has been a staunch Republican in his political convictions. The religious affiliation of the Christie family is with the Methodist Episcopal church.

Alexander H. Christie has been twice married; (first) to Jennie Brewer, who is now deceased; and (second) to Gertrude Hammond. By his marriage to Miss Brewer, he is the father of several children: 1. Ralph, who married Mattie Fisher. 2. Alice, who is the wife of Hugh McPhee. 3. Harold, who married Mary Smith, by which marriage there is one son, Harold, Jr. Alexander H. and Gertrude (Hammond) Christie are the parents of one son, Lewis, who is living at home with his family.

WALTER R. CHRISTIE—Perhaps no man in this vicinity has had more publicity as to his accomplishments than has Walter R. Christie of Presque Isle, Maine. Mr. Christie is not a native of the States but came to this country from New Brunswick. He is the son of John T. and Catherine (McFarland) Christie, who were both natives of New Brunswick and who never came over into the States but always remained on the farm where John T. Christie had carried on the cultivation of the soil for many years, never having any other business than that of a farmer and living unto the end of his life on the same farm where he was born. Both parents are now deceased.

Walter R. Christie was born in York County, New Brunswick, on September 6, 1871. When a lad, he went to the common schools of his native town and continued as he grew up to alternate his schooling with his work on the farm with his father until he was seventeen years of age. He then decided that in order to learn more of the industry of farming that he would go to other places and so hired out as a farm hand for two years in New Brunswick. Being then tempted to try for parts unknown, he crossed the border into

Maine and soon found work as a hired man on farms in this section. After three years, when he was about twenty-two years of age, he purchased his first farm and by care and industry he succeeded so well in its operation that he now owns many farms and is now considered one of the largest potato growers in Aroostook County. He is a Republican in politics and takes a keen interest in the affairs of his party. He also belongs to the Blue Lodge, Free and Accepted Masons; the Rotary Club and the Mooseleuk Club. Mr. Christie is a member of the Baptist church.

Walter R. Christie married Zellah K. Kitchen, who was born in New Brunswick, in Carleton County, the daughter of William and Mary (Estey) Kitchen. They had two children: 1. Thelma Fay, who was educated at the Presque Isle High School and at Timmons College, and is now the wife of Ivan L. Craig, manager of the Bell Telephone Company at Harrisburg, Pennsylvania. 2. Phillip Arnold, a student at the Presque Isle High School. Mrs. Christie passed away April 30, 1927.

FREDERICK HOLLAND TAYLOR— Prominent in the civic affairs of the town of Ludlow, and for the past three years a member of its Board of Selectmen, also a veteran of the World War, is Frederick Holland Taylor, who owns and is proprietor of sixty fertile acres of farm land in Ludlow neighborhood. Mr. Taylor was born on the farm now (1928) occupied by him, August 8, 1890, son of Holland and Rachel (Adams) Taylor. Holland Taylor was born in New Brunswick, Dominion of Canada, and came to the United States with his parents when six years of age. Before roadways were even begun in the Ludlow vicinity he bought and cleared of trees the farm of sixty acres. Holland Taylor was a Republican, and outstanding in the early development, both political and commercial, of Ludlow. The name of Taylor is here held in highest respect. Rachel (Adams) Taylor, wife of Holland Taylor, is a native of Maine, born at Littleton; and since the death of Holland Taylor has made her home at Houlton, near Ludlow.

Frederick Holland Taylor received his early education in the grade schools of Ludlow, then attended and graduated from the high school at

Houlton. Love of the soil that had been his father's was inherited by the son, and immediately upon his graduation Mr. Taylor returned to the farm, where he remained for two years in farm work. At that time he went to Boston and secured employment on the elevated railway; and with this corporation he continued until the United States entered the World War in 1917, when he enlisted in the army, at Camp Devens. As a private in the ranks, he went overseas with the 82d Division of the American Expeditionary Forces; when mustered out on his return to the United States, January 1, 1920, after a distinguished record in Europe, he held the rank of second lieutenant. He was twice wounded, at St. Mihiel and in the Argonne Forest. Later, he enlisted in the Reserves, of which he has since been a member, at present (1928) with the rank of captain, commanding Company A, 386th Infantry, at Caribou, Maine. For a time after his overseas experience, Mr. Taylor worked in his erstwhile capacity with the Boston elevated railway, then purchased the farm on which he was born, which meanwhile had left the proprietorship of the family. On the farm he makes his home, and is well known in Ludlow and Houlton as an agriculturist of ability and as an astute man of business. He engages in general farming and markets the produce at both centers. As a member of the Republican party, like his father before him, Mr. Taylor is active in political matters, and because of his courageous record in war and admirable conduct of affairs in peace is widely popular, and exerts considerable influence in questions of public policy. He is a member of the Blue Lodge at Houlton of the Free and Accepted Masons, and Royal Arch Masons; and with his family attends the Free Baptist church, whose causes in the name of charity he answers generously.

Frederick Holland Taylor married Daisy Hall, daughter of Franklin and Matilda (Blaney) Hall, and they are the parents of four children: Holland Frederick, Arline Iris, Freeman Frederick, and Russell Frederick.

JOEL WELLINGTON—Monticello and all its activities, business and civic, have always had a vital interest for Joel Wellington, native, lifelong resident, and prosperous agriculturist in this section of the State, his share in the growth and progress of this community being distinguished for his personal encouragement of its enterprise and every movement in behalf of its general welfare. Joel Wellington was born December 1, 1866, at Monticello, son of James C. Wellington, who was born in Kennebec, and Jeannette (Bubar) Wellington, who was born at Blaine; his paternal grandfather was Joel Wellington, his maternal grandfather, Joseph Bubar. James C. Wellington, his father, was engaged in the real estate interests, and was also a farmer.

Joel Wellington attended the Monticello public schools and attended a school of dentistry in Indiana for two years, but he never engaged in the practice of that profession, preferring to spend his entire life in the farming business. He has been a resident of Monticello since 1888, owner of two hundred and fifty acres, also of wild wood land. He has always been prominent in the affairs of the township, is a Republican in his political views, has served as a member of the school committee, declining other town offices; but was at one time a candidate to represent his town in the State Legislature.

Fraternally, Mr. Wellington is affiliated with the Benevolent and Protective Order of Elks; and the Free and Accepted Masons, in all the bodies including the Ancient Accepted Scottish Rite, and the Ancient Arabic Order Nobles of the Mystic Shrine. His family attends the Methodist church.

Joel Wellington married, June 29, 1887, Florence May Goodell, who was born at Grand Lake, New Brunswick, daughter of Solomon Goodell, a native of Maine. Their children: 1. Elbridge C., who is buyer of and has charge of the potatoes for the Atlantic and Pacific stores; he married Lottie Williams, and they have three daughters, Jean S., Betina D., and Ethel C., who have all taken honor parts in the public schools. 2. Lorina Hazel Wellington, who married Fred Z. Mills, a farmer, and they reside at Monticello; they have four sons: Gerard Wellington Mills, Joel Frederick, Spencer LeClair, and Gregory Delmont.

THOMAS W. HUGGARD—The general business life of Houlton is brought to the fore by manufacturers and merchants of the enterprise of Thomas W. Huggard, who, with his brother, Robert L. Huggard, is actively engaged in the production of pungs, as well as general automobile repairing, their Aroostook pungs being their specialty and securing their well-won repute. Mr. Huggard is one of the foremost of Houlton's citizens, and an associate in its fraternal and its business activities, highly regarded in all his dealings.

Thomas W. Huggard was born November 14, 1871, at Norton, New Brunswick, a son of Joseph Huggard, a carpenter, and Margaret (Kierstead) Huggard, both parents now deceased. The family removed to Houlton when their son Thomas was eight years old, and he here attended the public schools. He began to learn the business of carriage-making, and he followed along that line with success to 1905, when he joined with his brother, Robert L., in the manufacture of Aroostook pungs and in the expert repair of top-coverings and side-curtains for automobiles, and incorporating their concern in 1907, they now employ six men.

In his political convictions a Republican, Mr. Huggard with his vote and influence supports the principles of that party. Fraternally, he is affiliated with the Loyal Order of Orangemen; the Free and Accepted Masons, as Past Master of Monument Lodge; as Past High Priest of Aroostook Chapter, Royal Arch Masons; member of Council and Commandery, also, as well as the Order of the Eastern Star; and his business affiliations are those of the Houlton Chamber of Commerce, and the Business Men's Association. With his family he attends the Baptist church.

Thomas W. Huggard married Irene Saunders, who was born in New Brunswick, but removed with her parents to Houlton in early years. They have one daughter, Mildred, who married Louis Merrithew, and they are the parents of Irene Merrithew.

ARTHUR C. PERRY—One of the best known merchants and lumber dealers of Presque Isle, Maine, was Arthur C. Perry, the son of Nathan and Ann (Goodale) Perry. His father was in business in Presque Isle in the early days, having come to Presque Isle from Bangor, Maine, in 1863, and engaging in a business which he carried on until the time of his death in 1878.

Arthur C. Perry was born at Bangor, Maine, on

August 7, 1851. His early boyhood days were spent in Bangor, where he attended school up to the time his family moved to Presque Isle, when he was about twelve years old, and he then finished his schooling here and immediately afterwards went into business with his father and continued in that association until the time of his father's death. After that event, he associated himself with his two brothers, Charles G. and E. Sumner Perry, in the lumber and mercantile business and he was connected with this line of work when President Harrison appointed him to the position of postmaster, which place he held for the term of four years. After finishing his postmastership, he went into the insurance business and here made a splendid success. He was especially fitted by talent and disposition to fill this place in the community, for in serving as agent for some of the best insurance companies he built for himself an enviable reputation for fairness which was most satisfactory to both his customers and to those companies which he represented. He was especially successful in the line of fire insurance and held the confidence of the entire community. As a business man he was exact, with the most methodical habits and was noted as one who was scrupulous in the discharge of his obligations of whatever nature. As a citizen, he was noted for his faith in the progress of his town and was always most proud to note any matter that indicated prosperity. His pride in the town was more than of personal interest for in its development he put his very heart. Coming here as he did in 1863, when the place was a small village, he had seen it grow under his very eyes, for with the exception of two years spent at Washburn, he was a familiar figure to all inhabitants for the period of fifty-one years and by reason of his distinctive traits of character and unusual personality, he was one who would be noted in any community and especially in this locality. His keen interest in promoting various enterprises and his long residence in Presque Isle made his judgment of great value and it was sought by all who desired to have his influence in furthering a project. He was one of the most useful citizens in that he never was unwilling to serve in the interest of the town, and ability and capability made his services in constant demand. He was a most ardent Republican and in all political matters was earnest in his support of the principles of his party. For many years he was

a director in the Presque Isle National Bank and a member of the Unitarian Society of the village of which he was an active supporter. Mr. Perry died on August 6, 1914, and his insurance business, which he so splendidly established, is now carried on by his two sons, Nathan F. Perry and George W. Perry.

On February 14, 1884, Arthur C. Perry married Nellie Freeman, daughter of Dr. George Howard and Martha Ann (Lovering) Freeman. They had two children: 1. Nathan F. 2. George W., whose biographies respectively follow that of their father.

NATHAN F. PERRY—Well known in the business life of Presque Isle, Nathan F. Perry is equally prominent in social and civic affairs. He is president of the Arthur C. Perry Company, an insurance firm, and of the Perry Company, wholesale and retail dealers in finished lumber and coal. He is also a director of several corporations, including the Bangor and Aroostook Railroad. Mr. Perry's business acumen and initiative have made him of great value to the various companies with which he is connected. He has served as a member of the Presque Isle Board of Selectmen and of the school board. His father, Arthur C. Perry, now deceased, a review of whom precedes this, established the insurance company which bears his name, about 1880. His mother, who before her marriage was Nellie Freeman, is still living.

Nathan F. Perry was born on June 11, 1888, at Presque Isle, Maine. He entered the local public schools and later attended business college. When he completed his education, he entered the employ of the G. H. Freeman Hardware Company, which was established by his mother's family, and with whom he remained for one year. At the end of that time he became associated with his father in the insurance business with which he has since been connected, becoming president of the company after his father's death. In this firm Mr. Perry employs an office manager, two salesmen and a number of clerks. He is also president of the Perry Company, dealers in finished lumber and coal, which was formed in 1927 by the consolidation of the Aroostook Moulding Company and the Perry Coal Company. He is a director of the Presque Isle National Bank, of the Bangor nad Aroostook Railroad Company and all its subsidiaries, of the local telegraph company and of the Van Buren Bridge Company.

Politically, Mr. Perry is a member of the Republican party, and for a number of years he served as a member of the Presque Isle Board of Selectmen, and of the school board. During the World War he served as vice-chairman of the United States Fuel Administration for the State of Maine. He is affiliated fraternally with the Ancient Free and Accepted Masons, being a member of all bodies of the York and Scottish Rites, and of the Mystic Shrine. He is also a member of the Presque Isle Rotary Club and Merchants' Association, and of the Moosleuk Club.

Nathan F. Perry married Edna Lindow, who was born at Woodstock, Province of New Brunswick, Canada, the daughter of Frederick and Minnie (Hayden) Lindow. Mr. and Mrs. Perry attend the Congregationalist church.

GEORGE W. PERRY—A prominent business man of Presque Isle is George W. Perry. He is treasurer of the Perry Company, dealers in finished lumber and coal, both wholesale and retail, and vice-president of the Arthur C. Perry Company, an insurance firm, in which positions he has been very successful. He is also the owner of a farm, one hundred and thirty acres in extent, situated along Parkes Road, on which he has placed a tenant. Mr. Perry specializes in raising potatoes, shipping from 5,000 to 6,000 barrels annually to the large city markets. He takes an active part in the social and fraternal life of his community.

George W. Perry was born August 27, 1896, at Presque Isle, Maine, the son of Arthur C. Perry, whose sketch precedes this review, and who established the Perry Insurance Company about 1880, and of Nellie (Freeman) Perry. He attended the local public schools and when he completed his education, he entered his father's insurance business. His position there occupied his time until after the establishment of the Aroostook Moulding Company, about 1915, which traded in finished lumber. In 1919 the Perry Coal Company was founded, and in 1927 these two companies were consolidated, under the firm name of The Perry Company, Mr. Perry becoming treasurer of the resulting firm. After the death of his father he also became vice-

president of the Arthur C. Perry Insurance Company, which position he still holds. In addition to these connections Mr. Perry supervises the raising of potatoes on his farm, and their shipment to city buyers.

Politically, he supports the principles and candidates of the Republican party. He is affiliated fraternally with the Ancient Free and Accepted Masons, in which organization he has taken the degrees of the York Rite, and is Past Master of Trinity Lodge at Presque Isle. He is also a member of the Ancient Arabic Order Nobles of the Mystic Shrine; a member of the Presque Isle Rotary Club and Merchants' Association, and of the Moosleuk Club. He and his family attend the Unitarian church.

George W. Perry married Mary H. Hilton, who was born at Castle Mills, Maine, the daughter of Elmer E. and Carmelia (Belyea) Hilton. Mr. and Mrs. Perry are the parents of two children, Doris Ann and George Arthur.

HERBERT F. KALLOCH, M. D.—With the exception of one year spent in Waterville, Maine, Dr. Herbert F. Kalloch has spent his entire professional career in Fort Fairfield, Maine, where he has built up a large general practice. For twenty-eight years he has been ministering to the needs of the people of this town and vicinity, and he is known as one of the skilled and faithful physicians of this part of the State. Dr. Kalloch is active in local affairs and is now (1928) serving as health officer of Fort Fairfield.

Henry F. Kalloch, father of Dr. Kalloch, is a native of this State, and during the early years of his life he was engaged in business as a ship carpenter. Later, he gave up that strenuous occupation for the less arduous one of the proprietor of a general store in St. George, which he is still operating. He married Amanda Gilchrist, now deceased, and both were highly esteemed in the communities in which they lived. In St. George Henry F. Kalloch is widely known, and has made a reputation for honest business dealing.

Dr. Herbert F. Kalloch, son of Henry F. and Amanda (Gilchrist) Kalloch, was born in St. George, Maine, May 12, 1868, and after attending the local public schools, continued study in Coburn

Classical Institute, from which he was graduated with the class of 1888. For three years after his graduation he was engaged in teaching, and at the end of that time he began professional study in the Medical College of Bellevue Hospital, New York City, and in the Medical Toxicological Chemistry Department, completing his course in the last mentioned school in 1896, and in Bellevue Medical College in 1898. July 20, 1898, he successfully passed the required examinations of the medical board, and he served his internship in the Lying-in Hospital in New York City. He began practice in Fort Fairfield, and has been located here throughout his active career, with the exception of one year spent in Waterville. Dr. Kalloch is a member of the Aroostook County Medical Society, the Maine State Medical Society, and the American Medical Association. Along with his professional responsibilities he finds time for a considerable amount of local public service. He casts his vote independently, regarding personal fitness for the discharge of the duties of office as of more importance than party affiliations, and he has served on the school committee, and as superintendent of schools during the period prior to the union of the various local schools. In his present position as health officer he is rendering efficient service, and he is active in club and fraternal circles, being a member of the Blue Lodge, Free and Accepted Masons, of Fort Fairfield; of Caribou Chapter, Royal Arch Masons; and of Presque Isle Council, Royal and Select Masters.

Dr. Herbert F. Kalloch married Jessie Bartlett, who was born in Andover, New Brunswick, daughter of Caleb and Georgiana (Sloat) Bartlett. Dr. and Mrs. Kalloch were the parents of one son, Colby Bartlett, who after attending the Fort Fairfield schools and graduating from high school became a student in and a graduate of Colby College, in 1920, at Waterville, Maine. He is now a contractor and builder in Jersey City, New Jersey, under the name of the L. M. Steele Company. He married Leonie Butt, of Brooklyn, New York. Mrs. Herbert F. Kalloch died in 1912.

FRED J. PARENT—One of the most important citizens of Vanburen and the founder of Parent Brothers, a general store dealing in farm implements, hardware, and a large variety of mer-

chandise, was Fred J. Parent, who was born in Hamlin Plantation on September 8, 1867, and who died on November 29, 1925. Very successful in the business which he established in 1903, he built a foundation upon which his sons might work in future years. The three sons, two of whom are now married, are living in Vanburen, where their mother, Margaret (Smith) Parent, also resides.

The father, Fred J. Parent, was successful as a farmer and as a business man, and was one of the best known and most highly respected men in the community in and near Vanburen. He had few educational opportunities as a boy, and when he was very young he started to work. Making an important place for himself in his community by his own relentless effort and the use of his native talents, he started life as a farmer, became one of the founders of the First National Bank of Vanburen, and then in 1903 established the Parent Brothers store, which his sons now own and control. In addition to handling hardware and farm implements and general merchandise, this store also has connected with it several farms which Fred J. Parent started many years ago. In 1926 these farms produced 17,000 barrels of potatoes, which is an indication of their annual output. They provide employment for fifteen persons. Fred J. Parent married Margaret Smith, who also was born in Hamlin Plantation, and they became the parents of three children: 1. Dr. J. Wilfrid Parent, who studied medicine at the Jefferson Medical College, from which he was graduated in the class of 1924. Since that time he has practised his profession in Vanburen. He has served in the United States Naval Hospital, having been a member of the Regular Staff in Panama in 1925. He married Mary Brodie, and they have one daughter, Mary, born in 1928. Dr. Parent is a member of the Knights of Columbus, the American Medical Association, and the Aroostook County Medical Society. 2. Lorn F., who was educated in Vanburen in the public schools, and who later attended Saint Mary's College, as well as Saint John's Preparatory School, in Danvers, Massachusetts. Since he completed his education, he has been engaged in the Parent Brothers Store in Vanburen. He is a director of the Vanburen Trust Company, and is a member of the Knights of Columbus. He married Yvonne Guerrette, and they have one daughter, Ruth, born in 1928. 3. Percy P., who was educated in the public schools of Vanburen and at Saint Mary's College, and is now associated with his brothers in business.

HAROLD G. MICHAUD—One of the younger but none the less prominent men of the prosperous community of Presque Isle, Aroostook County, is Harold G. Michaud, owner and proprietor of a garage, maintaining an agency for the Graham-Paige motor cars and, with a staff of several men, carrying on a general repairs service; and who, during the World War, made for himself a distinguished record in the air service overseas, in the service of his country.

Harold G. Michaud was born in Presque Isle, June 16, 1895, son of William and Edith (Martin) Michaud, both of the parents natives of the Dominion of Canada, Province of New Brunswick, the father, as the name signifies, of French extraction. The elder Michaud came to the United States early in life, and during later life conducted an automobile and public auto hire service in Presque Isle, until his death, July 5, 1927. Edith (Martin) Michaud is now (1928) living, resident in Presque Isle. Harold G. Michaud received his education in the public schools of this community, and after his graduation from the high school drove a public service automobile, until the United States entered the war. He enlisted, and went to Fort Slocum, and served four months there in the air service. Overseas he was in the service for sixteen months, and when mustered out upon his return to the United States held the rank of first-class sergeant. Mr. Michaud at once joined with his father in the automobile business, and continued with him in it until January, 1925, when he purchased his interest and has since been sole owner and proprietor.

Mr. Michaud is favorably known in commercial circles of Presque Isle as a man in whom confidence is not misplaced; honest and industrious, his career has been most honorable. He is a member of the Republican party, and is loyal to its principles of National government, though he usually is non-partisan in local matters. Already his name has been mentioned for public office. He is popular, and an active participant in the affairs of the American Legion and the organization of soldiers who saw service overseas, Société 40 Hommes et 8 Chevaux, commonly called the "Forty and Eight." The society took its name from railway cars used in troop transportation in France, which were so labelled, indicating that each car would hold forty men and eight horses.

DONALD WATT—Among the younger business men of Fort Fairfield one of the most successful and prominent is Donald Watt, who is a partner in the Fort Fairfield Lumber Company and also in the firm of Watt and Gouiou, which holds the agency for Dodge automobiles.

Donald Watt was born in Fort Fairfield, Maine, July 14, 1897, son of John H. and Jenny (Good) Watt, the first mentioned of whom was engaged in business as a harness maker, and both of whom are now deceased. Mr. Watt attended the local schools and after leaving Fort Fairfield High School obtained a position as clerk in a clothing store in the employ of the Lawrey Clothing Company. Upon the death of Mr. Watt's father the harness business which he had conducted for many years was reorganized as an auto agency, under the firm name of Watt and Gouiou, handling Dodge automobiles. Later Mr. Watt became a partner in the Fort Fairfield Lumber Company and there is every prospect that his business career will be a very successful one. Mr. Watt is a Republican in his political faith and is a public-spirited citizen, but as yet he has held no public office. He is a member of the Blue Lodge, Free and Accepted Masons, of Fort Fairfield; of Caribou Chapter, Royal Arch Masons; Houlton Commandery, Knights Templar; and of Anah Temple, Ancient Arabic Order Nobles of the Mystic Shrine, of Bangor. He is also a member of the Rotary Club.

Donald Watt was married to Mildred Graves, who was born in Presque Isle, daughter of Richard and Bessie (Frasier) Graves. Mr. and Mrs. Watt have two children: James and Martha. They are members of the Congregational church.

DAVID L. DUNCAN—The little town of Washburn, Maine, is fortunate in having for its postmaster a man who is thorough and eager to see that all is handled in a businesslike manner. David L. Duncan, who has been in the office of postmaster since 1922 was appointed by President Warren G. Harding and reappointed by President Calvin Coolidge. This is what is known as a third-class office, maintaining a regular clerk, a special clerk and one rural free delivery route. Mr. Duncan is a native of Scotland and a naturalized American citizen. He has lived in the State of Maine for many years and is as much a part of the citizenry of this State as many of her native sons. His interests have always been with the best interest of the State and he is actively aggressive in promoting her welfare.

David L. Duncan was born in Scotland, September 28, 1860. He came out to New Brunswick when he was twelve years old and lived there for a number of years until he decided to come over in the United States. He came first to Washburn and was in the employ of Johnson & Phair as a woodsman. He remained in the employ of Johnson & Phair for a period of thirty-four years. During this time he was a woodsman and then was put in charge of saw mills. In this work he was most proficient and proving his ability to handle a factory was also put in charge of starch factories and then he was given the management of the general store. With this general and special experience, he was well equipped to carry on almost any kind of business, but on leaving the Johnson & Phair Company, he became connected with the Pitcher Starch Company, of Caribou, Maine. His ability for organization was so marked that this company sent him to Michigan to build for them a starch factory there. After finishing and putting into operation that plant, he returned to Maine and settled permanently in Washburn, where he has been ever since. While Mr. Duncan had some school education, he is a self-educated man, and taking advantage of opportunities offered through his business experience has placed himself within the list of those who are well informed on general topics and accurately informed on many special topics, particularly the lines of business in which he has been engaged. He is a staunch Republican in his political principles and has taken an active interest in the affairs of the party since his naturalization as a citizen in 1891. He is a member of the Blue Lodge, Free and Accepted Masons, and of the Order of the Eastern Star; for forty-three years he has been a member of different encampments and cantons and been through all chairs of the Independent Order of Odd Fellows. He and his wife are active members of the Methodist church, in which organization he has been a member of the Board of Trustees since the church was organized here.

David L. Duncan married Catherine Chapman, from Scotland. They have six children: Annie, Mary, Bessie, Harry, Mildred, and David Otis.

—————————

REV. JOHN J. FINN is pastor of the Catholic Church of St. Dennis at Fort Fairfield, Maine. The parish is not a large one, consisting of about a thousand souls, but it is nevertheless large in comparison with the civic population. Father Finn has just passed his fortieth year and has been a priest seventeen years. He has been assistant pastor and pastor at several churches in Maine, and has had the advantage also of an education in Canada.

John J. Finn was born at Biddeford, Maine, April 1, 1886, son of Cornelius and Margaret (Lombard) Finn, of whom the father is deceased, while the mother resides with Father Finn. He received his preliminary education in the Catholic public schools at Biddeford and then went to St. Mary's College at Vanburen, Maine. He graduated from that college in 1904, and then went to Montreal to study for the priesthood, graduating from the seminary there in 1910. He was ordained at Portland, Maine, by Bishop Louis S. Walsh, and his first charge was as assistant pastor at the Church of the Sacred Heart at Waterville, Maine, where he was stationed for one year. After that he was assistant pastor at St. Mary's Church, Biddeford, and he continued there for a period of four years. He then went to St. James' Church at Kingman, Maine, having been promoted pastor, and he remained there for four years. Finally he was appointed pastor at Fort Fairfield. Father Finn is chaplain of the council of the Knights of Columbus at Fort Fairfield, and is himself also a fourth degree Knight of Columbus. He is one of three children, of whom the other two are James Finn, the youngest, and Mrs. Patrick Coakley, of Boston, the eldest.

THOMAS MERLE HOYT—A leader in the farming and farm products industries at Presque Isle, Maine, Thomas Merle Hoyt is now the owner of many valuable properties, and president of the Hoyt Seed Company, Inc., growers and dealers in potatoes, handling especially high grade seed potatoes; he is also president of the Higgins Fertilizer Company, Inc. Farm management occupies the greater part of his time, but his opinion in business matters is highly regarded, and he acts as a director of the Merchants' Bank and Trust Company, of Presque Isle.

Mr. Hoyt was born in Easton, Maine, on October 26, 1873, a son of John F. and Julia A. (Weymouth) Hoyt, both descended from old and distinguished agricultural families, and both now deceased. John F. Hoyt was born in New Vineyard, Maine, while his wife was a native of Newport.

Thomas Merle Hoyt attended the Easton public schools, and was graduated from the high school there, after which he undertook the course of study in business school at Houlton, Maine. At the age of nineteen he purchased his first farm in Aroostook County, although he continued to spend most of his time on the home farm until he was twenty-four. Mr. Hoyt has been interested not only in all kinds of farming, but has also bought and sold stock extensively, and dealt in fertilizers. Gradually, however, he has concentrated on potato raising and farm management, his fine energy and ability bringing him merited success. Associated with him in the Hoyt Seed Company, Inc., are F. C. Wheeler, who acts as treasurer, and D. W. Cory, who is a director. Mr. Hoyt is now the owner of twelve farm properties of the best type, six of which are located in Presque Isle, four in Easton, and two in Westfield, Maine. Politically an independent voter, Mr. Hoyt has always been interested in the problems of government and the civic welfare, contributing liberally to many worthy enterprises. He is affiliated fraternally with the Free and Accepted Masons, and is also a member of the Independent Order of Odd Fellows, the Mooseleuk Club, and the local merchants' association. He and his wife worship in the faith of the Baptist church.

On November 19, 1897, Thomas Merle Hoyt married Effie Blanche Smith, daughter of Daniel and Charlotte (Smith) Smith, both of Presque Isle, and both now deceased. Mr. Smith, until his death in 1918, was also a farmer at Presque Isle.

JOHN BLAKE ROBERTS—To the maintenance of the high standards of the judiciary of the Caribou section of the State, as well as its old-established banking institutions, President John Blake Roberts, of the Caribou National Bank, has devoted his increasingly valuable gifts in behalf of a community where he has spent his entire life, and in whose progress he is a decided factor. Whether as attorney or financier, Mr. Roberts has demonstrated his capabilities as a public servant, always zealous for the public good, an intelligent and painstaking associate in all matters pertaining to community advancement.

John Blake Roberts was born February 14, 1880, at Caribou, a son of Calvin Blake Roberts, a native of Hartland, and Annie Staples (Trafton) Roberts, who was born at Fort Fairfield, Calvin Blake Roberts having been a prominent lawyer. Laying the foundation of his successful career in the public and high schools at Fort Fairfield, Mr. Roberts continued in the well-known Maine institutions, Hebron Academy, where he was graduated in 1900, and at Colby College, where he was graduated in 1904 with the degree Bachelor of Arts. Making his special preparation for his profession at the Law School of Harvard University, he was graduated there in 1907 with the degree Bachelor of Laws, and upon his admission to the bar in that year, he came to Caribou, where he established himself in his profession as an attorney-at-law, and in which he has continued to the present as a counsellor in law matters, having also served up to October, 1923, as judge of the Municipal Court.

Since 1913, Mr. Roberts has been associated with the immediate business interests of the Caribou National Bank, as a member of the Board of directors, as vice-president, and now as president of the bank, having resigned his judgeship in the local court in order the more thoroughly to perform his banking duties. In the political field, he adheres to the principles of the Republican party.

He was appointed, December 29, 1927, by Governor Brewster, Judge of Probate, to fill an unexpired term of Judge Fessenden, deceased. He received the nomination of the Republican party in June Primaries, 1928, for Judge of Probate for Aroostook County.

John Blake Roberts married, September 4, 1907, Blanch L. Lamb, of Sangerville, daughter of Nathan J. and Nellie (Carr) Lamb; and they have two children: Mildred A., a student at Colby College; and John B., Jr., a student in Caribou schools. The family are communicants of the Protestant Episcopal church.

CHARLES L. STODDARD—Though the greater part of the active career of Charles L. Stoddard was devoted to farming and to cattle raising in various sections of the country, he also had considerable experience in mercantile business and in the livery business. He is now (1928) salesman for the Washburn Auto Company, and special agent and claim adjuster for the Aroostook Valley Railroad Company.

Charles L. Stoddard was born in Washburn, Maine, February 22, 1849, son of Charles O. and Sarah (Wilder) Stoddard, both natives of Pembroke, Washington County, Maine, engaged in farming, and both now deceased. He attended the local public schools beginning, even as a boy, his work on the farm, and when school days were over he remained with his father on the farm for some years. Later he entered the employ of other farmers and continued as a farm hand until he was thirty years of age. He then went out West, where he had charge of a cattle ranch in Northern Texas, after having served for five years as a cowboy. Later he went to Kansas, where for some time he had charge of a stock farm. Finally, however, he returned to the East and purchased a livery business in Washburn, which he successfully conducted for a period of three years. At the end of that time he sold the business and went to Perham, Maine, where he became a clerk in a general store. That position he held for five years, serving not only as clerk, but as a scaler of lumber for the same firm. After having gained sufficient experience in the business of managing a general store he engaged in that line of business for himself in Washburn, where he successfully conducted a general store for fifteen years. At the end of that time he sold his store and associated himself with the Aroostook Valley Railroad Company, as agent at Washburn. That connection he maintained for only two years, when he became salesman for the Washburn Auto Company and special agent and claim adjuster for the Aroostook Valley Railroad Company.

Politically, Mr. Stoddard gives his support to the

principles and the candidates of the Republican party. He is active in local public affairs, has served as selectman and in minor offices, and in 1893 was elected to represent his district in the State Legislature. He is a member of the Board of Directors of the Washburn Building and Loan Association and is known as a very able business man. Fraternally, he is identified with the Independent Order of Odd Fellows, with the Order of Rebekahs, with the Masonic Order, and the Order of the Eastern Star; and he is an active and interested member of the local Grange, also of Pomona Grange, and of the State Grange. His religious affiliation is with the Methodist church, which he has served as a member of the Board of Trustees for several years.

Charles L. Stoddard was married to Lucy M. Smith, who was born in Washburn, Maine, daughter of William and Sarah A. (Finney) Smith.

WILLIAM FREDERICK BUZZELL, who was one of the most prominent and respected citizens of Houlton, Maine, was a man whose integrity in business and loyalty to his friends were very marked. Born on October 30, 1865, in Houlton, Maine, Mr. Buzzell was a son of William David and Louisa Bickford (Howe) Buzzell, both of whom are now deceased. William David Buzzell, the father, was born at Grand Lake, Maine. The mother, Louisa Bickford (Howe) Buzzell, was a native of Ludlow, Maine.

Their son received his preliminary education in the public schools of Houlton, later attending the old Houlton Academy, which is now known as the Ricker Classical Institute. When a young man, Mr. Buzzell journeyed to Minneapolis, Minnesota, where he became engaged in construction work. Later he returned East to Fells, Massachusetts, where he worked as a carpenter for some time. He then removed to Concord, Massachusetts, where he once more became engaged in contracting and building. In a short time Mr. Buzzell became interested in the building of boats and yachts, establishing his business at Monument Beach, Massachusetts. Here he had the misfortune of having his entire plant wiped out by fire. About this time his brother, who was the proprietor of the Exchange Hotel at Houlton, Maine, died and Mr. Buzzell and another brother together took charge of the enterprise. At the end of two years Mr. Buzzell sold his share of the business and took over a furniture and undertaking business, now known as the Houlton Furniture Company, which he conducted until the time of his death on November 3, 1918. Mr. Buzzell was an energetic and successful executive. In his business life he was loyal and faithful to his obligations, generous of soul, and merited the confidence and esteem of the community in which he lived.

Despite the many business activities in which he was engaged, Mr. Buzzell, nevertheless, found time in which to take a keen interest in the improvement of his community, and at the time of his death was chairman of the Building Committee for the new Masonic Temple. In his political preferences he was a strong supporter of the Republican party. He was fraternally affiliated with Monument Lodge, Free and Accepted Masons; Royal Arch Chapter; St. Aldemar Commandery; Ancient Arabic Order Nobles of the Mystic Shrine, and the Fidelity Chapter of Order Eastern Star. He was also a charter member of the Benevolent and Protective Order of Elks. He was an attendant and supporter of Court Street Baptist Church.

William Frederick Buzzell married, in 1888, Sarah F. Newcomb, who was born in Dennis, Massachusetts, a daughter of Isaiah F. and Jane A. (Chase) Newcomb, both of whom were descendants of old Puritan stock. Mr. and Mrs. Buzzell became the parents of four children, one son and three daughters: 1. Louise, who graduated from Ricker Classical Institute and Colby College and is now a teacher and talented musician. 2. William Olin, who received his education at the Ricker Classical Institute and Colby College, and who is now in Seattle, Washington. 3. Helen Thomas, graduate of Houlton High School and Sargent School of Physical Training, is the wife of Wilfred Schaffner, and now resides in Marion, Ohio. 4. Marion Eustis, who was educated at Ricker Classical Institute and Colby College, is the wife of Frederick E. Hyde, of Connecticut, now associated with the Houlton Furniture Company.

JAMES D. HOGAN—Owner of three hundred and ten acres of land near the town of North Limerick, James D. Hogan is accounted one of the influential citizens of his community. The acres are divided into two farms, one, a quarter section, being homestead land in the family of Hogan for two generations; the other, comprising one hundred and thirty acres, is uncultivated and given over to timber and natural deposits. James D. Hogan was one of twelve children born on the old family homestead, on the Bangor State Road, on March 31, 1863, son of John and Margaret (Conologue) Hogan. John Hogan was the first of the family to settle near North Limerick, on the homestead property. Here he erected with his own hands a cabin of logs, of timber cut from his land, and engaged in farming. John Hogan was born in Maine, at Houlton, of Irish stock; Margaret (Conologue) Hogan was born in Ireland. At the death of John Hogan, the property was apportioned among the widow and the children, of whom seven, five sons and two daughters, are now (1927) living.

James D. Hogan received his education in the schools of North Limerick, and with some difficulty, for the family was poor and the children obliged to work at odd jobs in order to supplement the income of the father. But Mr. Hogan contrived to obtain a very creditable schooling withal, for he was industrious and intelligent, and made the most of his opportunities when they occurred. After his education had been completed he went to work on the farm with his father, engaging in cultivation and harvesting in the summers and in woodcutting in the winters. As the children reached maturity the economic problem of the family was made less difficult, for several removed to positions in Limerick and other towns; and in due time the income from the farm was more than sufficient for the needs of those remaining. Under the terms of the father's, John Hogan's, last will and testament, the homestead passed first to the widow, and at her death reverted to the children; and when Mrs. Hogan died, James D. Hogan was able to purchase the farm from the heirs. This he did, and later bought the one hundred and thirty acres of wild land on the Bangor State Road, which, with the original quarter section, makes him the owner of one of the largest of acreages in this part of the State of Maine. On the homestead farm he engages in general agriculture, specializing in the raising of potatoes; these crops he disposes of in the Limerick markets and at Houlton. Mr. Hogan is one of the representative men of his neighborhood in agricultural and political matters. He is a Democrat, as his father was before him, and exerts a considerable influence in local elections. His activity in public matters has led, several times, to requests that he run for town and county offices; indeed, offers made by the local Democratic organization have been most attractive, with election practically assured, but always Mr. Hogan has refused. He is a member, with his family, of the Catholic church, and generous in his contributions to charity and other deserving causes.

James D. Hogan married Mary Harrigan, like him, of Irish stock. They were the parents of three children: 1. Lewis, who lives at home, educated at Houlton and Nova Scotia, and graduated from University of Maine. 2. Roy, educated in the public schools of Houlton, also lives at home on the farm. 3. Abbie, wife of William O'Donnell, manager of the Atlantic and Pacific store at Houlton, and by him is the mother of one child, a daughter. Mary (Harrigan) Hogan, wife of James D. Hogan, is dead; her memory is warm in the hearts of her many friends, and her loss felt keenly by Mr. Hogan and the children.

REV. JOSEPH ARTHUR NORMAND, who is the pastor of Saint Louis Roman Catholic Church at Fort Kent, Maine, has been located here in charge of this parish since September, 1925. The parish comprises about thirty-five hundred members and a school with over six hundred pupils and a convent of twenty-four nuns of the Order of the Little Franciscan Sisters of Mary. The Mother Superior of this convent is the Reverend Mother Saint Michel. Father Normand has one assistant, Father Origine Bouchard.

Father Joseph Arthur Normand was born in Quebec, Canada, December 2, 1886. He is the son of Phillip and Caroline (Thibault) Normand, both natives of Quebec. They had a family of six children, one· of whom became a nun with the name of Sister Bibianne, and is· now deceased. In 1893, the family moved to Westbrook, Maine, where Father Normand was brought up, but his education carried him back to Canada, where he attended Montreal College, graduating from there in the class of 1909. He then went to Baltimore, Maryland, and graduated from the college there in 1913. He was ordained by Bishop Corrigan in March, 1913, and sent as assistant to Saint Mary's parish, Lewiston, Maine. He was later sent to Fort Kent as assistant and, after one year, he was sent to Notre Dame Church at Waterville, Maine, as assistant. He was here for one year when he was sent to Saint Andrew's parish, Biddeford, Maine, where he remained for two years, when he was made pastor at Saint Francis, Maine, and remained there for three years. At the end of this time, he was made pastor of Grand Isle, Maine, where he stayed for two and one-half years, when he was made pastor of his present charge at Fort Kent, Maine. He is a fourth degree Knight of Columbus and Chaplain of the Fort Bend Council, Knights of Columbus.

JOHN HERBERT CHASE—Presque Isle, Aroostook County, lost one of its most prominent and progressive citizens with the death of John Herbert Chase. It is not too much to say that he was liked by everybody and he ever had a cheerful word and kindly smile for all he met. He was a loving husband, a good neighbor and an indulgent father. He was noted throughout the State and country as a lover of good horses; not as a racing man, but as an owner. Only three years before his death he had purchased the fine racing mare, Northern Lilly. He never raced her, but raised two fine colts by her.

Mr. Chase was born in Fort Fairfield, Aroostook County, January 20, 1871, the son of William and Leora (McGuire) Chase. He was brought to Presque Isle by his parents while but a small boy and obtained his education in the public schools of the locality. Upon the completion of his scholastic courses he went to work on one of the local farms, doing that work in the summers and in the winters working in the logging camps. He was finally enabled to purchase a farm of two hundred and twenty-five acres just outside of the village of Presque Isle, which he successfully cultivated, at the same time being enabled to give free rein to his love for horses. In politics he was a Republican and was affiliated with the Grange and with the Modern Woodmen of America. He was an attendant at the local Baptist church.

John H. Chase married Effie W. Hatch, a native of Gardiner, Kennebec County, the daughter of Albion and Harriet (Willey) Hatch, the former a veteran of the Civil War. Mr. and Mrs. Chase were the parents of eight children, as follows: 1. Allena; married to Walter Wray. 2. Milford. 3. Eunice; married to Raymond Knight. 4. Allen. 5. Pauline. 6. John. 7. Wallace. 8. Linwood.

FAYETTE L. BLACKSTONE—One of the progressive Maine farmers who specializes in the production of potatoes, Fayette L. Blackstone, of Perham, Maine, owns four hundred and fifty acres of land, of which one hundred and fifty acres are in cultivation, the rest in wood.

Born on the farm he now occupies, April 3, 1873, he was the son of Bowdoin R. and Amelia L. (Story) Blackstone. His father, who was born in New Sharon, Maine, was brought to Perham by his family, and helped to clear the land on which he spent the whole of his life. His mother was born in St. Albans, Vermont. Hartson Blackstone, grandfather of Mr. Blackstone, like most pioneers, not only believed in general farming, but was forced to practice it. Maine's reputation as a potato producing State was to come later. With profits realized from this yielding crop, Fayette L. Blackstone has erected the substantial farm buildings with which the place is now amply supplied, and invested part of the surplus in bank and other stocks. He was associated as a shareholder with the Washburn Trust Company from its foundation, and was elected a member of the Board of Directors in 1924.

Always a Republican, Mr. Blackstone has served the community as constable and as a member of the school board. His family attends the Baptist church, for which he is collector.

Mr. Blackstone married Mary I. Austin, daughter of Samuel W. and Emma (Holmes) Austin, who have a farm in Perham. Their children are: 1. Hartson, who married Kate Hughes, their children: Phyllis, Richard, Ruth and Hartson. 2. Milford H., a contractor and builder, who married

Rubena Long, and has a daughter, Barbara. 3. Read W., who works with his father on the farm, and married Addie Fox. Their children: Clayton and Donald. 4. Carroll, also associated in farm work with his father, who married Glenna Estey, and has one child, Wendall.

IRA CLAYTON—The story of the success of Ira Clayton, general farmer and potato grower, of Washburn, Maine, is one of clear purpose, energy, and thrift. Beginning with a capital of only two hundred dollars, but a few years ago, he is now (1928) the owner of a two hundred and forty acre farm on the Tabor Road, and is well known for his ability and skill as an agriculturist.

Ira F. Clayton, father of Mr. Clayton, was in early life engaged in the lumber business, operating saw mills and cutting timber from the woods. He married Delia Robison, and she is now living in the village of Washburn. Mr. Clayton died in the spring of 1928, and both he and his wife were very highly esteemed in this locality with a host of friends.

Ira Clayton, son of Ira F. and Delia (Robison) Clayton, was born on Garfield Plantation, October 3, 1881, and received his education in the common schools of Ashland, Maine. When his course in school was completed he worked as a lumberman in the woods and as a stream driver until he had succeeded in saving the sum of two hundred dollars. With this modest capital he decided to become his own master and purchased a farm from Elisha E. Parkhurst, paying one hundred dollars down. That left him one hundred dollars of free capital, and with this small amount he set to work carrying on general farming operations and growing potatoes. He is a hard worker and with his muscle he mixes brains and a love of his work. As time passed success came to him in abundant measure, and through the years thrift and prudence have enabled him to carry his various projects to success. The little farm purchased with one hundred dollars down represents now but a fragment of his land, for about four years ago he purchased of the Armour Fertilizer Company the big John Doherty farm, consisting of about two hundred and forty acres. He still raises general crops to some extent, but he specializes in the staple crop of

Aroostook County, potatoes, and deals some in certified seed, selling to local buyers. Mr. Clayton owes his success to the magic of hard work and steady purpose and added to sound judgment and business acumen, and his prosperity is well earned. He is a supporter of the Republican party, and is well known in local fraternal organizations, being a member of the Blue Lodge, Free and Accepted Masons; and of the Maccabees; also of the local Grange, Patrons of Husbandry. Mr. Clayton and his family are attendants of the Methodist church.

Ira Clayton is married to Jessie Sloat, who was born in Washburn, Maine, daughter of Joseph and Martha (Burcher) Sloat, farmers of Washburn. Mr. and Mrs. Clayton have two children: Athil Ira and Pauline Arline.

WILLIAM C. CROUSE—With a warehouse in the village of Crouseville which is capable of storing 19,000 barrels of potatoes, William C. Crouse has more than the usual facilities for cultivating and shipping this product on an extensive scale. Although he carries on a general farming business on his one hundred and twenty acres of land, Mr. Crouse specializes in the growing of potatoes, for which this section of Maine is so well noted. He is deeply interested in the public affairs of his community, both civic and social, and takes an active part in the political matters of Crouseville and Washburn. Both he and his wife are active in the work of the First Adventist church, in which he is an usher and in which Mrs. Crouse is a teacher in the Sunday school.

He was born in the village of Crouseville on April 1, 1897, a son of J. Wilmot and Mary L. (Clark) Crouse, the former of whom was born in Crouseville and the latter in Washburn. The father, J. Wilmot Crouse, is a cattle and meat dealer, and both he and his wife now reside in Crouseville. As a boy, William C. Crouse attended the common schools of Crouseville, but left school at the age of thirteen years to work on the farm with his father. He remained on the farm until he was twenty-one years old, tilling the soil in the summers and driving a meat cart in the winters. When he was twenty-one years old, he became engaged in farming on his own account, first buying eighty acres of land from his father,

and later buying the other forty acres that he now possesses. All of this land was originally his father's. Mr. Crouse is now one of the highly respected citizens of his community, a prosperous and substantial farmer who owes his success to his own native talents and ability and hard work. He is keenly interested in the public life of Crouseville and Washburn, and is especially active in political matters, being affiliated with the Republican party, for whose candidates he casts his vote.

He married Alice Pearl Flewelling, who was born in this section of Maine, a daughter of Edwick J. and Annie (Brewer) Flewelling, both of whom are farmers.

CHARLES ALCOCK SMITH died at Westfield, Maine, in the prime of life, having just passed his thirty-fifth year. He was at the time making a great success of his life, and his death was a loss to the town, for he was respected by everybody and was a good husband and father. He had traveled much and had had a varied business career, but at the time of his death he was settled in Westfield, managing the general store of the town which his mother had purchased for her two sons, and taking an active part in civic affairs. Few men were more generally popular and his passing was a loss felt by everybody.

Charles Alcock Smith was born at Bridgewater, Maine, May 4, 1885, and died January 18, 1920, at Westfield, Maine. He was educated in the public schools of Bridgewater and at the Ricker Classical Institute, graduating in the class of 1906. He was in the Colby class of 1908. He was on the Colby football team and was going to leave college, but he stayed for another season to help the team at the solicitation of the other students, and was an outstanding all around athlete. After leaving college he went to California with his uncle, George Briggs, and worked on a ranch in that State. After that he became engaged in the oil business. Some time afterwards his mother purchased the general store at Westfield for her two sons, Charles A. and Malcolm D. (q. v.). Mrs. Smith now conducts the store, Malcolm D. Smith being occupied with other interests. Charles A. Smith was a Republican and took a keen interest in the affairs of the town. He was town clerk and was also assistant postmaster. He belonged to the Independent Order of Odd Fellows, No. 148, Grange, Three Link of Presque Isle, and Delta Upsilon Greek letter fraternity.

Mr. Smith married, October 8, 1909, at Portland, Maine, Ethel Walker, born at Nordhoff, California, daughter of John and Minnie (Gibson) Walker. Children: 1. Mary Eleanor, a graduate in the Westfield High School, now (1928) attending the New England Conservatory of Music at Boston. 2. Gladys Evelyn, a junior in the high school. 3. Charles Gibson. 4. Wendell Walker. The family attends the Baptist church.

MALCOLM D. SMITH—First member of the Board of Selectmen of the village of Westfield, Westfield Township, Aroostook County, Malcolm D. Smith has served on the board since 1924, and for two years was tax collector. He owns and is proprietor of a fertile farm tract of ninety-four acres, near the village, on which he raises seed potatoes, chiefly certified; these he ships to outlying points or sells in the local market. He is accounted one of the substantial men of the community, interested in all movements designated for the welfare and advancement of the community. Mr. Smith was born at Bridgewater, Maine, July 31, 1884, son of Charles and Mary A. (Teague) Smith, his father a native of the Province of New Brunswick and his mother of the State of Maine.

Malcolm D. Smith received his elementary and high school education in the public schools of the Westfield district, and entered the Ricker Classical Institute at Houlton, Aroostook County, Maine; thence he matriculated in Colby College, at Waterville, Maine, and graduated with the class of 1908. For several years thereafter he accepted teaching charges, and was also employed by the American Thread Company; but at the conclusion of this period of professorial and first commercial experience he entered into association with his brother, Charles A. Smith (q. v.), in the proprietorship of a general store at the village where he has since resided. In due time, however, Malcolm Smith severed the partnership with his brother, and retired from the retail establishment to the ninety-four acre farm nearby. Here he has prospered as husbandman; under his able direction the acres have yielded largely. He employs the most modern and approved methods of scientific farming, adapting the methods best to suit his particular soil. Both as farmer in the production of high grade seed potatoes and as business man in their disposal he is acknowledged to exercise equal ability, and is as highly regarded for his sound judgments in business as he is respected for his character as a man. Mr. Smith is a Republican, staunch in support of the Republican principles of government, and strong in political ranks of village and county, possessed of wide influence in local elections. In public office his service has been conscientious and above criticism. He is a member of Lodge No. 148, of the Independent Order of Odd Fellows, and a communicant of the Baptist church, generous in contributions to charity. During the World War he served on various boards and committees of the village in the prosecution of the war from this country, and was a participant and leader in the several Liberty Loan campaigns, with results commensurate with the endeavor exercised.

Malcolm D. Smith married Lila B. Sylvester; and to this union have been born six children: Doris, Mortimer, Maxine, Audrey, Mary, and Rachel. Mrs. Smith is interested in affairs of the Baptist church.

MARSHALL B. CROUSE—Cultivating a high grade of potatoes, Marshall B. Crouse is one of the leading farmers of that section of Maine in and near Washburn. Together with his mother, he owns the Crouse homestead farm in the village of Crouseville, town of Washburn, Maine; and he also owns eighty acres of his own in the same town and the same village. The whole area, which consists of connected farmland of a fine and fertile variety, comprises two hundred acres. More interested in dairy farming than in the other branches of his work, Mr. Crouse keeps twenty-eight head of registered Holsteins and markets his products in Presque Isle and Caribou. He devotes considerable attention to fine seed potatoes.

Mr. Crouse was born in the town of Washburn, August 20, 1892, a son of Jesse and Florence A. (Clark) Crouse. The father, Jesse Crouse, died April 22, 1920. He was a native of Zealand, New

Brunswick, Canada, and came to the United States, where he settled in Maine and became engaged in the lumber and farming business. The mother, Florence A. (Clark) Crouse, now lives with her son, Marshall B. Crouse, who came with his parents to the United States when he was only twelve years old, attended as a boy the grammar school in Crouseville and later the high school in Washburn, and then went on the farm with his father. Since that time Mr. Crouse has devoted his life to farming, and, with his many years of experience and his wide acquaintance with the people and the conditions of his community, he is well fitted for the agricultural endeavor in which he is now engaged. The beauty of his farmlands and the high quality of the products that he sells are ample testimony to his ability and judgment as a farmer. Always actively interested in political matters, he is affiliated with the Republican party, for whose candidates he casts his vote. He is a prominent member of the Grange, and participates freely in the work of this organization.

Mr. Crouse married Albina W. Flewelling, who was born in Cardigan, in the province of New Brunswick, Canada, a daughter of Fred D. and Miriam (Boone) Flewelling. Her parents never came to the United States, but Mrs. Crouse is an active woman of the Washburn section of Maine, especially in church work. Both Mr. and Mrs. Crouse are members of the Adventist church, in which he was superintendent of the Sunday school for a period of five years, and is now a member of the official board of the church, as well as of the official board of camp meetings.

Marshall B. and Albina W. (Flewelling) Crouse are the parents of several children: 1. Jessie W. 2. Arthur LeRoy. 3. Frederick Marshal. 4. Miriam Alberta. 5. Ivan Havelock.

FRED E. WOODMAN—After thirty-eight years of successful farming, Fred E. Woodman has retired and is enjoying his well earned years of leisure in the village of Washburn. Mr. Woodman began his independent career as a farm hand, working upon the farm which his son now (1928) owns. He is one of the highly respected citizens of this locality and has many friends here.

Fred E. Woodman was born in Plymouth, Maine, February 6, 1865, son of Nathaniel and Emily (Buzzell) Woodman, both natives of Plymouth and both now deceased. The parents were in very modest circumstances and the boy was able to receive only the meagre educational advantages which could be secured by attending the local rural school during the winter months. As soon as the spring work began on the farm he was obliged to help, and when school days were over he remained with his father until he was twenty-one years of age. For two years after attaining his majority he worked as a farm hand on the farm which his son now owns, but during this time he gave the money he earned to his father as the family needed his help. When he was about twenty-four years of age he rented a farm in Washburn and operated it for two years. At the end of that time he purchased his own farm, which he continued to successfully operate for a period of thirty-six years, at the end of which time he sold out and came to the village of Washburn to live. He is a Republican and is serving as a member of the Board of Selectmen of the town of Washburn. Fraternally, he is identified with the Blue Lodge, Free and Accepted Masons, of Washburn; with the local Grange, Patrons of Husbandry; and with the Modern Woodmen of America. Mr. Woodman and his family attend the Advent Church, which he has served as a member of the board of deacons for many years.

Fred E. Woodman was married to Bertha Dickison, who was born in Washburn, Maine, daughter of Samuel and Melvina (Stoddard) Dickison, who are engaged in farming in this town. Mr. and Mrs. Woodman have four children: 1. Wallace E., owner and proprietor of Sunny Brook Seed Farm, married Bertha Crouse. 2. Mona, wife of Charles Carlton. 3. Gladys, wife of Earl Graham. 4. Bernice, a student in the high school, preparing for teaching.

DAVID E. SUTTER—The oldest resident on the Parsons Road of Presque Isle is David E. Sutter, who owns a one hundred acre farm on which he has lived since his birth. He has seen the old settlers of this neighborhood live on their farms and has seen them carried to their burial places and still he has remained on the old farm.

He has a host of friends in this part of the county, and has for many years been known as an expert agriculturist.

David E. Sutter was born on the homestead farm, in the part of Presque Isle which was formerly known as the town of Maysville, October 7, 1863, son of Stephen and Grace (Dunn) Sutter, both natives of Mirimuche, New Brunswick, and both now deceased. The father was a farmer and a lumber dealer and the owner of the farm on which Mr. Sutter is now living, having inherited it from his father, Byron Sutter. The farm has been in the family for more than a hundred years, and was operated for many years as a source of lumber supply. Mr. Sutter began to work in the woods with his father at an early age, first cutting for lumber as had been done for years before. His father, however, began to clear the tract for farming purposes and the boy assisted with this work. As the years passed he remained on the home farm, becoming its owner, and steadily year by year increasing the acreage under cultivation. The farm is located on the Parsons Road and its one hundred acres have been developed into fine farming land. Politically, Mr. Sutter gives his support to the Republican party. He is a member of the Independent Order of Odd Fellows, of Presque Isle; also of the Mooseleuk Club; and of the local Grange, Patrons of Husbandry.

David E. Sutter was married to Clara Kempton, who was born in Presque Isle, daughter of Ivory and Olive (Bennett) Kempton. Mr. and Mrs. Sutter became the parents of three children: 1. Harry, a farmer, who married Fay Plummer, and has one son, Richard, a student of the Presque Isle High School. 2. Susie, wife of Leewood Lister, who is manager of the Beverly Farms Trust Company of Beverly, Massachusetts. They have one child, Barbara Ann. 3. Evelyn, a graduate of Presque Isle High School, who lives at home. The family are attendants of the Congregational church.

ORRIN PELKEY—One of the State's important producers of food staples, Orrin Pelkey is one of the leading growers of potatoes on the large farm, owned by himself and his sister, on the Fort Fairfield Road. His career as one of the leading agriculturists of the county has been characterized by thorough honesty and industry, and as one of Fort Fairfield's most esteemed citizens, he has always taken a constructive interest in all civic affairs and has ably supported all projects that were directed toward its welfare and progress.

Mr. Pelkey was born in his present home, July 20, 1881, son of Joseph E. Pelkey of New Brunswick, and Sarah L. (Bump) Pelkey of Rangeley. Joseph E. Pelkey came to the United States when he was ten years old, and was a highly respected resident of this section all his life. He and his wife, who are now both deceased, had two children: 1. Victoria, married George W. Scott, and 2. Orrin, of whom later.

Orrin Pelkey received his education in the public schools of Presque Isle and after leaving high school, engaged in agriculture on his present farm and has ever since continued to operate it, specializing in potatoes of high quality which are sold to the local buyers. By his energy and ability, he has built up a large and successful trade, acquiring a reputation for high grade products of thorough dependability. Mr. Pelkey follows the principles of the Republican party in his political affiliations, and although he has never sought public office, he has always displayed a keen interest in all issues due to his earnest desire for community advancement and improvement. With his family, he attends the Methodist church. In fraternal circles, he is a member of the local encampment, Independent Order of Odd Fellows, and the Three Link Club.

Orrin Pelkey married Cordelia R. Ryder, who was born in New Brunswick, daughter of Richard and Lavina (Lockhart) Ryder, both natives of New Brunswick who later came to the United States, spending the rest of their lives here. To this union were born three children: 1. Elsie L., married Donald McIver and they have two children, Richard and Lois. 2. Rodney. 3. Kilburn.

ALEXANDER McPHERSON—Owner of two hundred and ten acres of rich farm land on the Bangor State Road near Presque Isle, Aroostook County, where he has lived for a number of years, and where he is highly regarded by all who know him, Alexander McPherson here engages in general agricultural pursuits and specializes in the growing of potatoes. He sells the produce in Presque Isle markets and in that community plays an important part in furtherance of civic programs for improvement, in matters of a political character, and in commerce, as operator in farm products. For a number of years he was resident in Presque Isle, retired from his first farm; consequently he is well acquainted in the village. The farm which he now (1928) owns he purchased in 1925 as a gift to one of his sons; but the son's health was poorly, and the result has been the return of the father to active participation in his lifetime career. Alexander McPherson was born in the province of New Brunswick, Dominion of Canada, June 26, 1867, son of Alexander and Margaret (Reid) McPherson.

Both Alexander and Margaret (Reid) McpPherson were natives of New Brunswick, and lived there until they died. The family is of Scotch origin (the name was originally MacPherson), and was founded in America, Canada, New Brunswick, by the first bearer of the Christian name Alexander, who was one of the early settlers in the province, father of Alexander who married Margaret Reid and grandfather of Alexander who owns the farm near Presque Isle.

Alexander McPherson, 3d, attended the public schools in the district of his birth in New Brunswick, and upon completion of studies, at the age of seventeen years, made his first trip south into the United States. He remained in Maine for two years, and returned to Canada with the firm intention of one day establishing residence permanently in the United States. An opportunity came more quickly than he hoped; when he was twenty-one he received an offer of employment on a farm in this State, and as farm hand he worked during the next five years. At this time he perceived another opportunity to purchase a farm for himself and to become farm proprietor in his own right. The tract which he bought was located on Buzzell Road and was plentifully covered with trees. These he cleared off, and in a few years had the soil in good and workable condition, meanwhile having constructed a home and outbuildings for the greater comfort of life. Upon this first farm Mr. McPherson attained to some prosperity, and in due time saw fit to retire from its care; he sold the land to his eldest son, Reid, and moved into Presque Isle with the intention of spending

the eventide of life in tranquillity and at ease; but, when his second son, Ralph, took unto himself a wife and expressed a desire to operate a farm, Mr. McPherson did not refuse, and purchased for him the land on the Bangor State Road. When the health of Ralph made it impossible for him longer to continue full direction of the farm, Mr. McPherson abandoned leisure and donned his working clothes. Now (1928) at the age of sixty years, he arouses the admiration of his acquaintances by the vigor with which he meets resumption of his career. Mr. McPherson is a member of the Grange, and is one of those most alive to the interests of that organization; he is a Republican, loyal to the party principles of government, something of a leader in local politics. His contributions to charitable and kindred causes of worthy appeal are substantial. It is said of him that he is a good and active citizen, interested keenly in the welfare of village and countryside, and most honorable in the conduct of his affairs.

Alexander McPherson married Hattie M. Savage, daughter of David and Rachel (Skillings) Savage, the family of Savage having long been resident on the Kennebec and old in the history of New England. Both David and Rachel (Skillings) Savage are deceased. Mr. and Mrs. McPherson are the parents of four and the grandparents of three children: 1. Reid, married Iris Smith, and they have three children, Hilda, George Alexander, and David Reid. 2. Ralph, married Marie Banks, died in fall of 1927. 3. Cluny, married Amy Beckwith. 4. Rachel. The members of the family attend the Congregational church.

———

JASON SAMUEL KEMPTON—The Elm Brook dairy farm, near Presque Isle, is one of the delightful spots in this section of Maine, being unusually well kept and consisting of three hundred and eighty acres of beautiful lands, one hundred and fifty acres of which are tillable. This farm is cultivated by Jason Samuel Kempton, who has a lease on what is known as the Parsons farm, where he has conducted a general farming business and a dairy since 1900. He takes a lease on this property for five to ten years at a time, and the present lease is scheduled to expire in 1931. Mr. Kempton keeps thirty head of fine cattle, as well as seven horses, and markets his general farming and dairy products in Presque Isle and the surrounding community. He employs regularly two hands. A man whose own native talents and diligent effort have brought him the success that is his, Mr. Kempton is now one of the really prosperous and substantial men of this section of Maine, where the people have high regard for his opinions, especially on matters relating to local agricultural problems.

Mr. Kempton was born in Woodland, Maine, in February, 1867, a son of Ivory B. and Olive (Bennett) Kempton, and as a boy he attended the public schools. When he completed his education, he became engaged in farming, which since that time he has made his life's work. He performed different sorts of farming work for many years, during which he became thoroughly conversant with conditions in this section, and finally, in 1900, took a lease on the Parsons farm, where he has conducted the farm and dairy business ever since that time. A prominent man in his community, Mr. Kempton is deeply interested in public affairs, and is ready always to support whatever movements he believes will tend to improve Presque Isle and vicinity civically or industrially. In matters of politics, his convictions have aligned him with the Democratic party, for whose candidates he casts his vote.

He married Maria Bennett, who was born in Fort Fairfield, a daughter of Robert and Mary (Read) Bennett. Jason Samuel and Maria (Bennett) Kempton are the parents of the following children: 1. Ralph J., an automobile salesman of Presque Isle, who married Hazel Irving. 2. Frances, who married Frank M. Thorne, by which marriage there is one child, Andrea. 3. Alice H. 4. Margaret B. Both Alice H. and Margaret B. Kempton are living at home with their parents.

ARTHUR ELBERT HOYT—A small patch of potatoes which he worked at night, having put in the day in the employ of a neighboring farmer, was the beginning of prosperity for Arthur Elbert Hoyt, who now owns a farm of one hundred and eighty-five acres on Buzzell Road, just off the Fort Fairfield Road, in Northern Maine, and spends his winters in Presque Isle.

Born January 14, 1871, in Fort Fairfield, Maine,

son of Richard Sheppard and Dorcas (Russell) Hoyt, he was one of eight children, and when his father died, all had to join in the effort to keep the family going. Arthur Elbert Hoyt, who was then seventeen years of age, and had completed the courses in the local schools, was even then an experienced farm worker. Out of his savings he advanced one hundred dollars to his mother as his contribution to the family's maintenance, and then, obtaining work as a farm hand, worked his own potato patch at night, and saved every penny. After three years of intensive labor he had accumulated enough money to go into partnership with his cousin, Ray C. Hoyt, in the purchase of a farm of one hundred and twenty-five acres, which they worked together for the next five years. They produced a fine variety of table potato for the local market, besides the usual crops of diversified farming. This property was divided between the partners at the end of the five year period, and Mr. Hoyt has made his home on the tract thus acquired, which he has considerably enlarged. He is a director in the Presque Isle Starch Company, and of the Northern Maine Fair Association. He is a Republican and has been a member of the school board for six years. He is also a member of the Independent Order of Odd Fellows, of the Patrons of Husbandry, and of the Three Link Club. He and his wife have long been active in the work of the Methodist Episcopal church.

Arthur Elbert Hoyt married Mary Elizabeth Richardson, daughter of Charles H. and Alvina Lucinda (O'Brien) Richardson, of Presque Isle. Their children are: 1. Lois, who married Clair Perry, of Weston Spring, Illinois, before which she was a music teacher, having been graduated from the Faelten Music School, Boston; they have one child, Joan. 2. Nina, who married Elmer H. Davis, and they have a son, Elmer H., Jr. 3. Helen, who was graduated from Bates College, and was a teacher until her marriage to Hollie H. Rutland. 4. Dorothy, a graduate of Normal School and Bates College, and taught school until her marriage to Morton Bartlett. 5. Mirriam. 6. Arthur Elbert Hoyt, Jr.

LEWIS STEPHEN DUNCAN—Owner and proprietor of a fertile agricultural tract of three hundred acres abutting on the Houlton Road, rural

delivery route No. 2, Presque Isle, Lewis Stephen
Duncan engages in the growth of both seed and
table potatoes, devoting the greater portion of his
farm to this crop, and marketing his produce in
the market of Presque Isle. He also deals in well
bred cattle, and maintains continuously a herd of
about fifteen head. Lewis Stephen Duncan was
born at Andover, New Brunswick, Dominion of
Canada, February 28, 1899, son of Lewis and
Josephine (Kennedy) Duncan, his father having
been engaged in farming at Andover until he
removed with his family to Maine, where he settled on a farm south of that belonging to Lewis
Jr., on the Houlton Road.

Lewis Stephen Duncan received his education in
the public schools of Presque Isle and on completion of studies joined with his father in work
upon the farm. Meanwhile the family moved
northward to the farm on Houlton Road, and here
both Lewis, Sr., and Josephine (Kennedy) Duncan died. On the death of his father, Lewis Stephen Duncan purchased the shares in the farm bequeathed to other heirs, and has since owned and
conducted it exclusively for himself. He has always taken an active part in affairs in the commercial life of Presque Isle and of the countryside,
where he is accounted among those agriculturists
most advanced in application of scientific methods
to the peculiarities of the soil of the vicinity,
adapting modes best suited to it and applying them
to crops most favored by it. Moreover, Mr. Duncan, though but twenty-eight years of age (1927),
is accounted one of the most progressive of citizens, public-spirited, industrious, substantial, and
a decided asset to the community of the countryside. In political matters he is non-partisan, preferring to vote independently of the major parties,
while favoring certain principles upheld by each
of them; in local political contests he is guided
absolutely by his confidence and judgment of
abilities of candidates, regardless of their party
adherence. He is a member of the Baptist
church.

Lewis Stephen Duncan married Eva Libby,
born at Limestone, Maine, daughter of Frederick
and Mary (Elliott) Libby; and they are the parents of four children: Carleton Lewis, Donaldo
Josephine, Glenda Mary, and Shirley Geraldine.

EUGENE H. DOBLE, M. D.—Specialist in
X-ray work, Eugene H. Doble conducts a medical
practice in Presque Isle, where he has been since
1900, the year in which he finished his professional
school education. In addition to his X-ray work in
the medical field, Dr. Doble has the agency for the
Reo automobile and truck. Having such varied occupations, he naturally is a busy man, but he receives
a great deal of assistance from his wife, Edna C.
(Purvis) Doble, who is an efficient business woman
and helps him in both divisions of his work. Their
son, Howard R. Doble, who has gone through the
public schools and high school in Presque Isle and
has taken a dental course at the University of
Maryland, in Baltimore, where his father studied,
is now a practicing dentist in Baltimore.

Eugene H. Doble was born in Livermore Falls,
Maine, on September 19, 1876, the son of Ronella
Lewis and Lillian (Howard) Doble. His father,
who was a machinist by occupation and was a native
of Maine, is now deceased, as is his mother, who
was a native of Maryland. Eugene H. Doble
attended as a boy the Milo High School, where he
received his early education; and then he studied
medicine at the University of Maryland, in Baltimore, from which he was graduated in the class
of 1900. In his last year at the university, he took
a course in the Maryland General Hospital, where
he acted as an interne while he was still in school.
Then he came to Maine, where he passed the medical board examinations of the State in 1900 and
opened his offices in Presque Isle. During the first
years he maintained a general practice, which he
gave up, however, in 1920, to specialize in office and
X-ray work. His agency for the Reo cars and
trucks, in which his wife gives him valuable assistance, renders his work lucrative and varied. Both
he and Mrs. Doble are substantial and highly respected members of the community. Dr. Doble,
who is keenly interested in political affairs, especially as they affect Presque Isle and vicinity, is
identified with the Democratic party, and is a member of both the Democratic Town Committee and
the Democratic County Committee. He is affiliated
with the American Medical Association and
with the American Radiological Society, and
both he and his wife attend the Congregational
church.

WILLIAM LINTON DUNCAN—Though a native of Scotland, William Linton Duncan has found in this country a land of opportunity, where energy and thrift bring substantial success. He is now (1928) living practically retired, but, with his sons, owns three farms in the town of Washburn, Maine. He lives with the youngest son, Kenneth, on one of the farms located on the West River Road, where, as on the other two farms, located on the Caribou Road, first grade potatoes are grown.

William Duncan, father of Mr. Duncan, was a native of Aberdeenshire, Scotland. With his wife and children he left his native land and came to the New World, settling first in Victoria, New Brunswick. This location proved to be unsatisfactory, and he later came to Washburn, Maine, where opportunity seemed better and prospects brighter. Here he remained to the time of his death. He was well along in years by the time he came to Washburn, but he had five able sons and five daughters, and after coming to the States the sons attended to the work of the farms, of which there were eventually three, one on the West River Road, and two on the Caribou Road. From the beginning the farms were devoted to potato growing and all of the sons are experts in this line of agricultural activity. William Duncan married Elizabeth Linton.

William Linton Duncan, son of William and Elizabeth (Linton) Duncan, was born in Aberdeenshire, Scotland. He received his education in the public schools of Kincardineshire, Scotland, and learned the mason's trade in his native land, but later came to this country with his parents, settling first in Victoria, New Brunswick, Canada. When he was thirty-five years old he removed with his parents from Victoria, New Brunswick, to Washburn, Maine, and here he has since been continuously engaged in farming. As his father was well along in years when the family came to the States, the farming has been done by the sons. William Linton Duncan proved to be a very successful agriculturist and added one farm after another to his possessions until at the present time he owns two farms on the Caribou Road and a farm of seventy acres on the West River Road. He is now (1928) practically retired, but with his sons retains the ownership of the three farms, making his home with the youngest son, Kenneth, on the farm on the West River

Road. Like all Scotchmen, Mr. Duncan is a Presbyterian but he and his wife are attendants now of the Baptist church. Mr. Duncan is interested in local history and has made an interesting souvenir from a piece of wood from the ship "Constitution." He secured the piece of wood from Curtis Wilbur, the Secretary of Navy, and from it made a copy of the original ship "Constitution," which is now in Governor Brewster's office in Augusta, but will be placed in the State Museum when Governor Brewster goes out of office. Politically, Mr. Duncan gives his support to the principles and the candidates of the Republican party, and he is interested in local affairs. Fraternally, he is identified with the Independent Order of Odd Fellows, of Washburn; with Blue Lodge, Free and Accepted Masons, also of Washburn; with the Orangemen and the local Grange.

William Linton Duncan was married to Catherine Coker, who was born in Aberdeenshire, Scotland. Mr. and Mrs. Duncan are the parents of six children: 1. Alexander, who is a farmer operating one of the two farms on the Caribou Road; married Marion Dow. 2. Agnes, wife of John Dow. 3. William, married Lily Cumming. They operate the second farm on the Caribou Road. 4. Florence, wife of Rev. H. A. Clark, a Baptist minister of Gardiner, Maine. 5. Jenny, married Byron H. Smith. 6. Kenneth, who lives with his father on the West River Road farm, which he operates. He married Florence Crouse.

PITT F. COOK—For many years a resident of the town of Presque Isle, Maine, Pitt F. Cook is one of the most successful farmers in that vicinity. He is the owner of one hundred and twenty-five acres of land situated along the Houlton Road and also owns a hundred acre farm at Echo Lake, Maine, on both of which he raises potatoes and general farm produce for sale to local buyers. Mr. Cook is well acquainted with the best farming methods and has been very prosperous in his chosen occupation. He is prominent in Maine Masonic circles, and takes an active interest in civic progress and affairs. He was born on July 4, 1875, at Bridgewater, Maine, the son of Thomas and Fannie (Porterfield) Cook, both of whom are now deceased. His parents were born at Cold Stream, province of New Brunswick, Canada;

were married there, moved to Michigan, and finally came to Bridgewater, Maine, where they bought a farm and remained until their deaths.

Pitt F. Cook attended the local public schools, and when he completed his education, he began work on the farm with his father. When still a young man he came to Presque Isle, and worked for three years on the farm of John C. Seeley, and for five years for Lyman Hayden. At the end of that time he purchased a farm at Westfield, Maine, which he conducted for four years and then sold, buying the farm where he now lives from Orin Weymouth. In addition to raising potatoes and other vegetables Mr. Cook keeps a number of heads of cattle.

Politically, he is a member of the Republican party. He is affiliated fraternally with the Ancient Free and Accepted Masons, in which organization he has taken the degrees of the Blue Lodge, Chapter and Council, at Blaine, Maine. He is also a member of the Presque Isle Chapter of the Grange. He and his family attend the Congregational church.

Pitt F. Cook married Mabel Gartley, who was born in New Brunswick, Canada, the daughter of William Gartley, deceased, and of Eliza (Baird) Gartley, now living at Presque Isle, Maine. Mr. and Mrs. Cook are the parents of two children: 1. Hazel A., who graduated from high school and normal school, was a teacher for one year, then entered the Maine School of Commerce and is now employed at Presque Isle. 2. Merle G., a graduate of the Presque Isle High School in 1928.

DANIEL CHANDLER—After a long and energetic life of continuous activity as a woodsman and then as a farmer, Mr. Daniel Chandler, of Washburn, Maine, is enjoying his home in the village and living on the fruits of a busy early life. He is the son of Daniel and Adeline (Ramsdell) Chandler, both from Kennebec County and came from families of farmers and also owned and operated a farm.

Daniel Chandler, Jr., was born in Presque Isle, Maine, January 14, 1849. He took little education as he was more inclined to work than to study and at an early age became a woodsman and was for years in the Maine woods, where he had much

experience in all the different activities of a woodsman's life, including driving on the stream and other phases of business of lumbering. He followed this life until he was twenty-five years of age, when he became a farmer and for several years owned and operated a farm of four hundred and ten acres at Presque Isle. About forty years ago, he moved to Washburn, where he owned and operated three farms. He continued to operate these farms for twenty years and at the end of that time, he sold off his holdings and came into the village to live. Mr. Chandler is a firm adherent to the Democratic party and an earnest member of the Baptist church.

Daniel Chandler married Elizabeth Beckwith. They have had three children: 1. Myrtle, deceased, was the wife of Herbert Morin. 2. Maude, the wife of Thomas Crawford. 3. Bert, who has been married twice; first to Gerta Gillard; second to Florence Smith.

ERNEST G. BECKWITH—Outstanding in this community as a progressive farmer, Ernest G. Beckwith, of Presque Isle, Maine, has for years been active in the promotion of agriculture. He is the son of James and Mary Ann (Lyons) Beckwith. His father was a native of Maine and his mother a native of New Brunswick. His father was a farmer and his mother's family were farmers also.

Ernest G. Beckwith was born in the little town of Mapleton, Maine, in January, 1862. His father died when he was only one year old and he received only the education offered in the town schools of those days, which was in no way equal to what the average country boy or girl gets today. However, it was in the days when a boy who got even a little schooling soon found out that he could continue to learn by applying himself and this Ernest G. Beckwith did for he was fond of reading and has always taken advantage of every opportunity to inform himself on general topics and is today one of the best informed men in this vicinity. When he was a young man he worked in the woods in the winter and on the farm in the summer. He owns two farms which he operates, one of one hundred acres on the State Extension Road and the other of sixty acres on the back road. When he first owned his land it had not been cleared and he did most of the clearing himself. He erected all the buildings on the farm and has cultivated the land for general farming and for growing potatoes. He raises quite an extensive lot of potatoes, which he sells to the local dealers. In addition to raising and selling his farm products, Mr. Beckwith takes an active part in civic affairs and has served in several of the minor town offices and refused to serve in others. He is an Independent in his politics and interested in bringing about good government in the town affairs and the affairs of the county. He is a member of the Independent Order of Odd Fellows of Presque Isle; Encampment, and Canton; a member of the Three Link Club and the Grange. He and his family attend the Methodist church.

Ernest G. Beckwith has been married twice. His first wife was Ella Ramsdell (deceased), and they had one child, Horace W. His second marriage was to Jennie English. They have six children: 1. Laura (twin) married Vernal Towle. 2. Lucy (twin), is the wife of Donald Kilpatrick. 3. Orin. 4. Maude, who is a school teacher. 5. Byron. 6. Grace, graduated from Normal School and is a teacher.

EDWARD JORDAN BULL—One of the prominent men of the town of Mapleton, Maine, is Edward Jordan Bull. Third selectman for his town he is also the owner of a ninety-acre farm situated along Parsons Road, on which he raises potatoes and other general farm produce for sale to local buyers. Mr. Bull is well acquainted with the best farming methods, and has been very successful in his chosen occupation, handling superior varieties of seed and table potatoes. He is highly esteemed in his community as a public-spirited citizen.

His father, Chipman Bull, was a farmer at Mapleton, and engaged in this work until his death. His mother, who before her marriage was Mahala Jordan, is also deceased.

Edward Jordan Bull was born on May 1, 1886, at Mapleton, Maine. He entered the local public schools and later attended business college at Bangor, Maine. When he completed his education he worked for a number of years as a farm hand, and was also employed in neighboring starch factories. In 1909 he took over the management of a farm, running it on shares, and in 1910 purchased the farm where he now lives, from Daniel Moores, of Presque Isle, and has conducted it since that time. His post office address is Presque Isle, R. D. No. 1, Maine. Politically, Mr. Bull is a member of the Republican party, and he is a member of the Board of Selectmen of the town of Mapleton. He and his family attend the local Adventist church.

Edward J. Bull married Nettie Fox, born in the Province of New Brunswick, Canada, the daughter of Wilmot and Lucy (Baylis) Fox, of that place. Mr. and Mrs. Bull are the parents of eight children: Arden Edward, Alden Stanley, Lucy Winnifred, Wilmot Gordon, Floyd Leland, Merrill Roland, Marshal Robert, and Jasper Deane.

GEORGE J. BROWN—Of all who take a part in the business of farming, conducting their acres as they would a commercial enterprise, George J. Brown holds rank among the most progressive. His farm land comprises one hundred and forty-four acres; it is fertile, and yields substantially under the husbandry of proved and scientific methods. Abutting on the State Road, near the community of Presque Isle, the farm constantly attracts favorable notice from passersby. Here Mr. Brown employs two assistants in the cultivation of crops and care of livestock, and they give the most of their time to the former occupation, engaging in general farming and the growth of table and seed potatoes as specialty. This produce the owner and proprietor disposes of in the local markets; or, if more advantageous prices rule in markets elsewhere, he ships to the more favorable markets. Through diligent application to management Mr. Brown has made of his acres one of the principal farms in the neighborhood, and has ably demonstrated that industry intelligently directed, can and does breed prosperity in the soil.

George J. Brown was born on the State Road farm which he later came to direct, May 17, 1889, son of Woodford and Hannah E. (Sylvester) Brown. Woodford Brown was a native of the province of New Brunswick, Dominion of Canada; his wife Hannah, of Portage Lake, both deceased. George J. Brown attended the grade and high schools of Presque Isle, and on graduation from the latter matriculated in normal school. After a year at the normal he enrolled in the University of Maine, there pursued a general course of study for two terms, and then took charge of a farm belonging to his sister. For several years he conducted this farm, and with good fortune; but, at the request of his father he relinquished the enterprise and returned to the family property to take full charge of it, paying a certain rental therefor. In due time he purchased the farm. As landowner and business man Mr. Brown is well known in the market centers of Aroostook County where he has dealings, and both in these centers and in his own neighborhood of the countryside is highly regarded as a man of character and ability in his many undertakings, a valuable asset of the community in which he lives. Mr. Brown votes independently of the major parties in political questions, and exercises some influence in local elections because of the following he has among those who know him and are prone to agree with him in his judgment of causes and candidates. He is active fraternally as member of Trinity Lodge, Free and Accepted Masons; Caribou Chapter, of Royal Arch Masons; St. Aldemes Comandery, Knights Templar at Houlton; Anah Temple, of the Ancient Arabic Order Nobles of the Mystic Shrine at Bangor; the Independent Order of Odd Fellows, and the Mooseleuk Club. With his family he attends the Episcopal church, and in contributions to charity and other kindred causes of worthy appeal is most ready, giving substantially and in a spirit of sympathy truly humanitarian.

George J. Brown married Bertha E. Ward, native of Presque Isle; and to this union has been born one child, Joyce Justine.

ALBERT O. GOULD—Among the successful business men of Presque Isle, Maine, none is more widely known or more popular than Albert O. Gould, who has been selling farm machinery for many years, and is now a partner in the firm of Gould & Smith.

Born in New Limerick, Maine, April 10, 1873, he was the son of H. H. and Rebecca (Pipes) Gould.

Educated in the schools of Fort Fairfield, after being graduated from the high school he took a special course at the Eastman Business School in Poughkeepsie, New York, and then started in business for himself as a sales agent for machinery. For fifteen years from 1904 he represented the International Harvester Company, and he is now one of the firm of Gould & Smith, representing the International Harvester Company and the Hupmobile automobiles. His partnership with Frank A. Smith (q. v.), began in 1920, and the business has now grown to such proportions as to require a staff of ten people.

Mr. Gould is a member of the Free and Accepted Masons, a Knight Templar, and member of the Ancient Arabic Order Nobles of the Mystic Shrine. He is a member of the Merchants' Association, of the Mooseleuk Club, and of the Unitarian church. He is independent in politics.

Albert O. Gould married Mae Hamor, who was born in Boston, but had lived chiefly in Bar Harbor. Their one child is Evelyn Gould.

———

FRANK A. SMITH—Member of the firm of Gould and Smith of Presque Isle, handling farm machinery, trucks and passenger automobiles, Frank A. Smith was born on September 5, 1891, at Maidstone, Vermont, son of Byron F. and Flora L. (Allen) Smith.

Frank A. Smith received his grade school education in Maidstone, and attended high school at Lancaster, New Hampshire. Here, having specialized in typewriting and stenography, upon graduation he engaged himself in those capacities in a business house, for two years, and at the expiration of this period entered the employ of the International Harvester Company, as bookkeeper, in 1913, and continued with the company for seven years, learning thoroughly the commercial phases of the manufacture and sale of farm machinery. In 1920 he joined in association with Albert O. Gould (q. v.), of Presque Isle, establishing the firm of Gould & Smith. During the years since 1920 the business has expanded, until in 1927, ten hands were employed. The firm deals extensively in International trucks and Hupmobile motor cars. Mr. Smith is personally concerned with the advancement of Presque Isle as a community, and constantly gives of his efforts in that direction. He is independent in political matters, and believes that partisanship should play no part in local and State elections. Widely known in Aroostook County and sincerely respected by his many friends therein, Mr. Smith is a member of the Presque Isle Merchants' Association and the Mooseleuk Club; he is active in Masonry, member of the Blue Lodge, Royal Arch Masons, Royal and Select Masters, Knights Templar, and the Ancient Arabic Order Nobles of the Mystic Shrine. He is a communicant of the Congregational church, and is known for the liberality of his response to charitable appeals sponsored by the church, and for his donations and personal application to relieve the needy in cases not brought to the attention of the church.

Frank A. Smith married Irma C. Richards, born at Boston, Massachusetts; and they are the parents of two children, sons: Frank A., Jr., and Robert M.

FRED LOVELY—The industrious, thorough-going men who supply the population with the necessities of life are among the great contributing factors to the Nation's progress. Such a man is Fred Lovely, of Presque Isle, one of the important potato growers and shippers of the vicinity, having a farm of two hundred and ten acres on the State road from Presque Isle to Easton, and a large storehouse in this town, located on the tracks of the Canadian Pacific Railway. Mr. Lovely was born at Fort Fairfield, May 3, 1867, son of Ransford Lovely of Maine, and Mary E. (Barnes) Lovely of New Brunswick, both of whom are deceased. Ransford Lovely was engaged in the farming trade all his life.

Fred Lovely was educated in the public schools of Fort Fairfield and upon the completion of his formal education, entered the lumber trade. For four years, he was industriously engaged in various branches, working in the woods, sawmills, and in the daring business of logging on the river. Leaving this occupation, he engaged in farming which he has ever since followed successfully, concentrating particularly on the raising of potatoes. In addition to his potato business he owns and operates a large wood lot in the town of Westfield. In politics, Mr. Lovely is a member of the Re-publican party and served one year as assessor, and although petitioned by his fellow-citizens, he refused all further political offices. In his fraternal connections he is a member of the Independent Order of Odd Fellows, Encampment, Canton and Rebekahs, Knights of Pythias and the local Grange. He is an active member of the Methodist church, being a member of the Board of Trustees.

Fred Lovely married (first) Maggie McCray, who died in 1910, daughter of William McCray. Their children are: 1. Orrin H., engaged in the lumber business in the State of Washington. 2. Edgar E., married Gertrude Rouse and they have three children, Margaret, Marie and Helen. 3. Elmer R., married Effie Cleaves and they have one child, Fred. 4. Jessie, educated in Boston, now a dietitian in New York City. 5. Arthur. 6. Lillis, married Theodore Holt. 7. Cora, educated in Presque Isle and State Normal School, and now a teacher. 8. Margaret, a student in the local schools. Mr. Lovely married (second) Zereda Clark, of Presque Isle.

LOUIS A. CYR—In Limestone, Maine, Louis A. Cyr has been sole owner of the thriving general store which he has operated here since 1904. He came to this place to establish the business for Henry Gagnon thirty years ago, later became half owner, and finally, in 1904, became sole owner of the business. He has served as town treasurer for Limestone for seventeen years, and is one of the well-known and active citizens of the place.

Born in the town of Grand Isle, Maine, June 18, 1875, Louis A. Cyr is a son of Alexis C. and Julienne (Sirois) Cyr, both natives of Maine, the first mentioned engaged in farming. Mr. Cyr attended the local public schools and the Normal School of Grand Isle, and then became a student in the University of New Brunswick. For two years he was engaged in teaching, and then he made a change, accepting a position as clerk in the general store of Mr. Gagnon, at Van Buren, Maine. Four years later he came to Limestone to establish a general store for Mr. Gagnon in Limestone, and of this enterprise he was manager for Mr. Gagnon for a period of four years. At the end of that time he purchased a half interest in the business, and in

November, 1904, he purchased the remaining half-interest and became sole owner of the business. Mr. Cyr came to Limestone to establish the business for Mr. Gagnon June 10, 1897, thirty years ago, and in less than eight years he was its owner. The patronage of this enterprise has grown to proportions which require the services of three clerks, and Mr. Cyr is well known in this locality as an able and resourceful business man and as an active and public-spirited citizen. He is one of the progressive and modern men who classes himself as an independent voter, considering personal fitness for office as of more importance than party affiliations, and he has for many years been active in the affairs of Limestone, serving as a member of the Board of Selectmen for a period of three years, and as town treasurer for seventeen years, and giving to the duties of each office the same careful and efficient attention which he gives to his personal business affairs. He is a member of the Knights of Columbus, and his religious membership is with the Roman Catholic church.

Louis A. Cyr married Laura Franck, of Frenchville, Maine, daughter of Joseph and Hortense (Saucier) Franck, the first mentioned of whom is a blacksmith by trade. Mr. and Mrs. Cyr have nine children: Cecile Mary, Esther M., Louis E., Emile J., Lauretta R., Leo G., Sylvio T., Annette E., and Lucille E.

HERBERT W. KITCHEN—Prominent in the civil and financial affairs of the State is Herbert W. Kitchen, who is now serving his third term as member of the State Legislature, and, as a director of the Presque Isle National Bank, is actively interested in everything pertaining to the prosperity and progress of this town. Mr. Kitchen, who has always been engaged in general farming, is president and director of the Northern Maine Fair Association, and in this capacity is a great influence in rural affairs. Mr. Kitchen was born in Carleton County, New Brunswick, October 11, 1878, son of William and Mary H. (Estey) Kitchen, who moved here, locating on his present farm in 1892. They are now deceased and are buried here. William Kitchen was engaged in farming all his life.

Herbert W. Kitchen received his early educa-

tion in the local public schools, but being a member of a large family in which there were five girls and four boys, two of whom are deceased, he was obliged to work long and hard on the farm. He realized the advantages of education but further studies had to be deferred and it was not until after his twenty-first birthday that he was enabled to enter Shaw's Business College for a course of study. Combining the advantages of his business education with his work, Mr. Kitchen has made a conspicuous success of agriculture, specializing in the raising of potatoes, which he sells to local buyers. His large farm of one hundred and seventy-five acres on Caribou Road is a model of its kind and is a visible proof of his energy and industry. Mr. Kitchen has served as selectman of the town, and for fifteen years has been director of the bank. He is also president of the Johnston Cemetery Association. In politics he follows the principles of the Republican party and his fine qualities have always appealed to the voters of the community who have elected him for the third term as a member of the Legislature. In fraternal connections he is a member of Trinity Lodge, Free and Accepted Masons, and of the Chapter and Council; member of the local Grange and of the Mooseleuk Club. In religion, Mr. Kitchen is an active member of the Congregational church.

Herbert W. Kitchen married Annie Sprague Greenlaw, daughter of Samuel C. and Mary E. (Sprague) Greenlaw, and they have one daughter, Alice M., a graduate of Presque Isle High School and of Bryant and Stratton's Business College.

HERBERT L. EMERSON—A varied career has been that of Herbert L. Emerson, chief of police of Fort Fairfield, Maine. Mr. Emerson has been a successful traveling salesman, a professional baseball player, and a worker in the woolen mills, but since 1921 he has been most successful as a chief of police, first in Pittsfield, Maine, and since August 1, 1927, here in Fort Fairfield. So well was the work of Mr. Emerson appreciated in Pittsfield that his resignation was accepted under protest, and he has the assurance that his job there is his whenever he may choose to come back. Here in Fort Fairfield he is rendering equally efficient service and there is little prospect of his going back to Pittsfield if the people of this town have their say in the matter.

Herbert L. Emerson was born in Etna, Maine, July 18, 1882, son of George H. and Anna (Lawrence) Emerson, both natives of Maine, the former of whom was in railroad employ to the time of his death, and the last mentioned of whom lives in Hartland, Somerset County, Maine. Mr. Emerson received his education in the public schools of his birthplace, graduating from Etna High School with the class of 1898. For some time after graduation from high school he was engaged as a professional baseball player during the summers and worked in the woolen mills during the winter season. Later he became a traveling salesman and for years represented various concerns, selling flour for David Stott, of Detroit, Michigan, and meats for a Boston concern. Later, he sold meats on the road as a retail distributor, but after a time he gave this up for a position as clerk in a grocery store. In 1921 he made another change in the line of his activity, becoming chief of the police department of Pittsfield, Maine, and here he continued for a period of five years. His ability in this field attracted the attention of the residents of Fort Fairfield, and he was urgently requested to come to this town and serve in the same capacity. He finally decided to accept the offer tendered, and handed in his resignation in Pittsfield, but here objection arose. The people of Pittsfield did not wish to lose the efficient head of their police department, and said so, emphatically. But Mr. Emerson had made his decision, and insisted upon the finality of his choice and his resignation was finally duly accepted. The job at Pittsfield is waiting for him when he cares to go back, but there are at present no indications that such a change will take place. Fraternally, Mr. Emerson is identified with the Blue Lodge, Free and Accepted Masons; and with the Independent Order of Odd Fellows; also a member of the Encampment. His religious affiliation and that of his family is with the Baptist church.

Herbert L. Emerson is married to Alberta Johnston, and they have one child, Carl Francis.

FREEMAN T. KEIRSTEAD—Conducting his farm as a business, under the firm style of F. T. Keirstead & Sons, Freeman T. Keirstead owns and operates in association with his sons, Wallace T. and Howard G., two hundred and sixty acres of the most fertile land in Aroostook County on the State road between Presque Isle and Caribou. F. T. Keirstead & Sons is one of the largest firms specializing in the growing of potatoes in the county, and also engages in general agriculture, marketing produce of all kinds suited to the soil, in the towns of Caribou and Presque Isle. In each of these communities and to a great degree throughout Aroostook County, Freeman T. Keirstead is well known and sincerely respected, and admired for his success as commercial agriculturist. He is interested in the public and social affairs of both communities, and in these affairs is an active participant.

Freeman T. Keirstead was born of an agricultural family, in the province of New Brunswick, Dominion of Canada, September 16, 1869, son of Abram G. and Jane (Fowlie) Keirstead, and one of a family of five children. In 1892, when Freeman Keirstead was aged twenty-three years, after he had completed his early education in the common schools of the place of his birth, the family came to the United States where, near Presque Isle, Freeman Keirstead worked for ten years as lumberman and farm hand, having previously, in Canada, served six years as lumberman. In 1902 he purchased a farm on the West Caribou Road, which he conducted with success for seven years. In 1909, he bought a half interest in a farm owned by C. E. Hussey, located where the F. T. Keirstead & Sons firm now (1928) lies, and in association with Mr. Hussey continued to do business for thirteen years. In 1922 they divided their holdings, and Mr. Keirstead soon purchased additional lands, bringing his own holding up to a total of two hundred and sixty acres. He is accounted one of the most enterprising farmers and capable business men in the Presque Isle and Caribou areas, efficiently combining modern scientific methods of agriculture with crops to which the land takes most kindly. The annual output of potatoes is considerable. Mr. Keirstead is a member of the Republican party and is well known in political circles of the county. He is a member of the Modern Woodmen of America and of the Ku Klux Klan, and in the activities of the hooded order, which are largely political, is prominently identified. As communicant of the Baptist church he contributes liberally to the charitable and other causes sponsored.

Freeman T. Keirstead married Mabel Day, native of Caribou, daughter of Lewis and Mary Ann (Sharp) Day, both of whom are deceased, her father having been engaged in agriculture. Mrs. Keirstead, before her marriage, was a trained nurse, graduate of the Maine Eye and Ear Infirmary, at Portland. She was a nurse for seven years, and since marriage has been prominent in the social affairs of the neighborhood, and notably, with her husband, in the activities of the Baptist church. Mr. and Mrs. Keirstead are the parents of five children: 1. Wallace T., associated with his father in the agricultural firm of F. T. Keirstead & Sons, graduate of the University of Portland Business College. 2. Howard G., associated with his father in the agricultural firm, graduate of the University of Portland Business College. 3. Forrest D., student in the Presque Isle High School. 4. Marjorie J. 5. Paul.

W. ROSS KEIRSTEAD—Owner of one hundred and twenty acres of the best agricultural land on the State road between Presque Isle and Caribou, Aroostook County, W. Ross Keirstead, brother of Freeman T. Keirstead, a sketch of whom precedes this, also a well-known farmer of this community, engages in general agriculture, and markets his produce in Caribou and Presque Isle, where he is prominently identified in political, civic and social affairs. W. Ross Keirstead was born in the province of New Brunswick, Dominion of Canada, September 15, 1881, son of Abram G. and Jane (Fowlie) Keirstead. Abram Keirstead was, during his life, actively engaged as farmer, first in New Brunswick and later, starting in 1892, in the United States, Aroostook County, Maine, having removed to this vicinity when W. Ross Keirstead was eleven years of age. W. Ross Keirstead received his early education in the place of his birth, then also attended the schools at Presque Isle. He was one of five children.

Like his father, and his brother Freeman T., who is his senior by twelve years, W. Ross Keirstead began his career on a farm, and, also like them, has found such a career worthy of lifelong pursuit. First he worked for his father on the

farm in summer time, and in winter engaged as lumberman in the woods, and at odd times as hand in the sawmills hereabout. He became proprietor and owner of a farm in 1911, on Parkhurst Road, Aroostook County, then, disposing of that property, bought his present (1927) holding on the State road between Presque Isle and Caribou, from Claude DeWitt in 1920. As proprietor of this fertile tract Mr. Keirstead has grown prosperous. He employs the most modern of agricultural methods, applying them to those crops most suited to the land he owns and, as his yields are large and of a general character, he is a familiar figure in the business life of Presque Isle and Caribou, where he disposes of the produce. He is a Republican and possessed of considerable influence in political matters in both towns, as well as in the rural neighborhood; and is active in fraternal affairs, as member of the Blue Lodge of the Free and Accepted Masons, at Presque Isle, Royal Arch Masons, the Knights of the Maccabees, and the Mooseleuk Club. With his family he attends the United Baptist Church and contributes generously to charity.

W. Ross Keirstead married Lura Day, native of Caribou, daughter of Lewis and Mary Ann (Sharp) Day, both of whom are deceased, her father having been engaged in agriculture. Mrs. Lura (Day) Keirstead is a sister of Mabel (Day) Keirstead, wife of Freeman T. Keirstead. Mr. and Mrs. W. Ross Keirstead are the parents of two children: Madolyn Elizabeth and Pauline Lois.

ALBERT HOBART DAMON, M. D.—Physician of Limestone, Aroostook County, since the fall of 1902, Dr. Albert Hobart Damon was born in Washington County, Maine, on October 23, 1871, son of Jason Franklin and Elizabeth (Hobart) Damon, his father having been a native of Charlotte, Maine, and his mother of Edmunds, Maine, both deceased.

Jason Franklin Damon was for the greater number of his years a farmer, but his son, Albert Hobart, evinced slight interest in agriculture. Following his early education in the public schools of Charlotte he entered Hebron Academy, whence he graduated in 1892, matriculating in Dartmouth College, where he pursued pre-medical courses for a year. He graduated from medical college with the degree of Doctor of Medicine in 1900, and served for one year as interne in a lying-in hospital in New York City. In 1901 he began practice for himself at Franklin, Hancock County, Maine, then removed to Limestone, prosperous town of approximately two thousand inhabitants. Here Dr. Damon has built up an extensive practice of a general character in both town and country, and before the automobile came into widespread usage used to spend the most of his time in a buggy drawn by a spirited horse on extended country calls. He has attained a large reputation for his obstetrical work, and is relied upon by many of the better known families of the community for work of this nature, and in general medicine serves an ever growing clientele. Dr. Damon is a Republican, loyal to the party's principles of government, and possessed of a considerable voice in political matters of Limestone and this part of Aroostook County. For a number of years he was a member of the school board, and before the schools were unionized was superintendent of schools. He is president of the Limestone Board of Trade, city physician and chief of the fire department. From this it is apparent, then, how diverse are his interests in the public good. Constantly he is allied with enterprises for the progress of the community. Fraternally also he is most active, with membership in the Limestone Blue Lodge of the Free and Accepted Masons, Caribou Chapter of the Royal Arch Masons, and the Houlton Commandery of Knights Templar. He is Past Master of Limestone Lodge and Past District Deputy Grand Master. When the United States entered the World War Dr. Damon offered his skill as doctor of medicine to his country's cause, as surgeon of the 6th Battalion of the 131st Brigade, and was stationed at Camp Upton, active duty (not overseas) from August, 1918, until March, 1919. He is now (1928) adjutant of the 322d Medical Regiment of the 97th Division, comprising the States of Maine, New Hampshire and Vermont. Dr. Damon attends the Methodist church, and contributes generously to all charitable and kindred worthy appeals whether or not they are sponsored by the church.

Albert Hobart Damon married Ellen Willey, daughter of Burt and Lilla (Hovey) Willey.

Maine—2—14

Mrs. Damon is active in affairs of the Methodist church.

EDWARD L. CLEVELAND—One of the most prominent residents of Aroostook County passed away with the death of Edward L. Cleveland, a man who did much for his native State by making it famous throughout the country as a producer of the highest grade of seed potatoes. In 1878 Mr. Cleveland originated the company which is now known by his name and in a very short time drew to Houlton a business which appreciably added to the wealth and prosperity of the community.

Mr. Cleveland was born in West Camden, Aroostook County, August 19, 1855. After his preliminary education in the public and high schools of that community he took a course in the Dirigo Business College. As stated, he came to Houlton in 1878 and there originated the E. L. Cleveland Company, which speedily became famous throughout the country for its high quality of seed potatoes. For the distribution of his product, Mr. Cleveland had branch houses throughout the county, his seed farms being located in Houlton. In his later years Mr. Cleveland devoted much attention to dealing in investment securities. Outside of his business, Mr. Cleveland was deeply interested in political, educational, musical and civic matters, and he was ever to the fore in all projects for the advancement and betterment of his community. He was a staunch Republican and was chosen to represent his town in the State Legislature. He was a director of the Bangor & Aroostook Railroad; president of the Houlton Savings Bank; president of the Ricker Classical Institute; served for many years as president of the Anti-tuberculosis Association, and was always prominent in a number of other community organizations. He was affiliated with the Independent Order of Odd Fellows, and his religious associations were with the Congregational church.

In 1877, Mr. Cleveland married Eva L. St. Clair. Mr. and Mrs. Cleveland were the parents of four children, two daughters and two sons, as follows: Mrs. Albert E. Mercier, of Hollywood, California; Mrs. Harold Mariott, of West Newton, Massachusetts; Arthur S. Cleveland, and Leigh P. Cleveland, both residents of Houlton.

Mr. Cleveland died in Hollywood, California, February 22, 1928, at the home of his daughter, Mrs. Albert Mercier, following a very brief illness. The news of his death was received with much sincere sorrow by the residents of Houlton, all of whom realized that with Mr. Cleveland had passed one of those who had done much to advance the community, both materially and spiritually.

WESTON NERIAH HARDY—Among the families of old settlers in the State of Maine, is that of Hardy which has been known here for a great many years. It is in a direct line from the earliest of the family that Weston Neriah Hardy, who was for so long known as one of the successful farmers of Presque Isle, was descended. He was the son of Henry P. and Sarah D. (Nichols) Hardy, who lived in the early days in Etna, Maine, coming here in 1880.

Weston Neriah Hardy was born at Etna, Penobscot County, Maine, on September 30, 1847. His family moved to Presque Isle when Mr. Hardy was about thirty-three years of age and purchased what was then known as the old Nason farm, and has since been known as the Hardy homestead and is now run by Ralph W. Hardy, son of Weston N. Hardy. The choice of this particular piece of land was most fortunate for the land is beautifully situated for making a successful farm. It is high and fertile and near to the village of Presque Isle, giving it advantages in many ways as well as having the advantage of being particularly adapted to profitable cultivation. The Hardy family have always typified the Maine characteristics of thrift and industry and in Weston N. Hardy were always found and exemplified those sturdy virtues of his family, the habits of industry and frugality and thoroughly good management of their affairs. He was always a prosperous man, wasting nothing and after years of hard work he was able to enjoy an affluence which was his well-earned reward of prudence. He not only set an example worthy of being followed by his own immediate family, but by all citizens in business, in his interest in public affairs, in his careful judgment and lack of haste in making a

decision or giving an opinion. He was kindly and of a neighborly disposition with the highest regard for principles of honor and integrity. He was distinctly a farmer, never attempting any other kind of business and conducting his farm in a most exemplary manner and applying himself diligently to that branch of agriculture which he had selected as a specialty, potato raising. In this line he was especially successful. In 1917, he retired from active farming, and turning the management of his place over to his son, Ralph W. Hardy, he moved into Presque Isle, where he built for himself a handsome and comfortable modern home situated on Dudley Street. He lived here until the time of his death on April 26, 1923. He was a staunch Republican in political views and always keenly interested in the welfare of the party, although he would never accept an office. He was an active member of the Grange and interested in all subjects taken up by the organization; a member of the Independent Order of Odd Fellows, and a regular attendant of the Baptist church. While Mr. Hardy was one of a family of five children, he is survived by only one sister, Coris, who is the widow of Alonzo Plummer.

In 1866, Weston Neriah Hardy married Lula K. Turney, a native of Presque Isle, daughter of Francis Winslow and Jennie (Watt) Turney. Mr. Turney was a farmer and a lumber dealer and he and his wife were the parents of six children, five of whom, including Mrs. Hardy, are now living. Mr. and Mrs. Hardy had three children: 1. Ralph W. 2. Madeline. 3. Lois, who is a graduate of Presque Isle High School and after one year at Wheaton College took a business course at Mrs. Gilman's Business College at Bangor, Maine. The family attend the Baptist church.

ROGER T. HALL—As a partner in the H. O. Perry and Son Agency, which handles general insurance, Roger T. Hall, who is one of the younger business men of Fort Fairfield, has shown himself to be an unusually talented man and a desirable citizen. Although he has been connected with this agency only a small number of years, Mr. Hall holds the responsible position of office manager, and fulfills his duties in a creditable manner. Since the reorganization of this company, it has a broker in Van Buren, one in Caribou, one in Mars Hill, and one in Fort Fairfield, and employs four additional girls in its offices.

Mr. Hall was born in East Mount Vernon, Kennebec County, Maine, on January 14, 1898, a son of John and Annie (Cottle) Hall, the former of whom is deceased and the latter living. The father's occupation was that of carpenter. As a boy, Roger T. Hall attended the public schools and the high school at Hallowell, having been graduated from the high school in the class of 1917. In that year he enlisted for service in the military forces of the United States in the World War; he entered the service in Middlebury, Vermont, and was chosen to do topographical work in the infantry. When the war was ended, he was discharged from the service, and proceeded to continue his education. He became a student at Middlebury College, in Middlebury, Vermont, from which institution he was graduated in the class of 1922. In that year he came to Fort Fairfield. Upon the death of C. W. Perry, of the H. O. Perry and Son Agency, in this town, the company was reorganized and Mr. Hall became a partner in the business, as well as the office manager in Fort Fairfield. In this position he has displayed unusual ability and has become one of the real leaders in the business life of the community. He is active in the work of several organizations and fraternal societies, being a member of the Free and Accepted Masons, in which order he has been admitted to the Blue Lodge; the Independent Order of Odd Fellows; and the American Legion. He and his family attend the Congregational church.

Mr. Hall married Maxine Perry, a daughter of C. W. Perry, and they are the parents of one child, a daughter, Hilda.

SILAS O. HANSON—Having trained himself thoroughly in the study of agriculture and farming problems, Silas O. Hanson is now doing an important work in Maine as superintendent of the Aroostook Farm, Maine Agricultural and Experiment Station, with his headquarters in Presque Isle, Maine. He has filled this position successfully since May 1, 1927, having been recommended for it by the officials of a similar station in Min-

nesota, the State of his birth, and in which he received both his elementary and professional education.

He was born on February 27, 1897, in Minnesota, the son of Hans and Myria (Lien) Hanson, and was educated in the Morris, Minnesota, Agricultural School. Then he became attached to the experimental station in St. Paul, Minnesota, where he remained for seven years. For three years he was at Morris, Minnesota, then for seven years in St. Paul, which town he left to accept his present position as superintendent of the Aroostook Farm, for which he was recommended by the Minnesota station. All indications are that Mr. Hanson's plans foretell an excellent future for the institution which he superintends as well as for himself personally. Already he has shown an active interest in the affairs of his adopted community, especially in political and fraternal matters. His political affiliation is with the Republican party. He is a member of the Free and Accepted Masons. Both he and his family attend the Congregational church.

Silas O. Hanson married Marjorie Wheeler, who was born in Minneapolis, Minnesota, daughter of William C. and Margaret (Robb) Wheeler, the father deceased. Mr. and Mrs. Hanson are the parents of two sons: Melvin and Harold.

WILLIAM B. McLAUGHLIN—For many years William B. McLaughlin has been prominent in the life of Limestone, Maine. He is the owner of two farms, both located near Limestone on the Fort Fairfield State road, one, the Brookdale farm where he lives, seventy-five acres in extent, the other of one hundred and forty-five acres, which is operated by his son. The Brookdale farm, which he purchased in 1893, is ideally located and is one of the finest farms in the vicinity. The buildings, which were mostly built by Mr. McLaughlin himself, are in splendid condition, and the old farm house, situated on a hillside and thoroughly remodelled and refinished, is noticeable for long distances. The soil is very fertile and here Mr. McLaughlin raises the better grade of potatoes and other general farm produce. In addition he is a director of the Limestone Trust Company, and is highly esteemed in his community as a public-spirited citizen.

He was born on August 22, 1866, at Limestone, the son of Bernard McLaughlin, who was born at Fort Fairfield and lived all his life in Aroostook County, and of Susan (Mulhern) McLaughlin, who was born in Ireland, but came to the United States as a child. The family is an old one in the county, Bernard McLaughlin, Mr. McLaughlin's grandfather, having been one of the earliest settlers in the section. He came there about 1847, received a tract of land from the government and cleared it with the aid of his sons, who followed him in his occupation of farmer. This was long before roads were built in the section.

William B. McLaughlin attended the public schools of his birthplace and when he completed his education he began work in the neighboring woodland and on local farms, continuing this work for twelve years. In the fall of 1893 he purchased the Brookdale farm, and he has lived there since that time, greatly improving the property. Later he acquired another farm of one hundred and forty-five acres, which is now operated by his son. Mr. McLaughlin is well acquainted with the best farming methods and has been very successful in his chosen occupation. Politically he is an independent voter, and he is a member of the Grange. He is a director of the Limestone Trust Company. He and his family attend the Roman Catholic church.

He married Maude Martin, who was born at Saint Anne, in the province of New Brunswick, Canada, the daughter of Vetal and Anastasia (Martin) Martin. These two families are unrelated. Mr. and Mrs. McLaughlin are the parents of six children: 1. Bernard, who was graduated from the local high school and completed a business course at Portland. 2. Martin, who married Margaret Greenough. 3. Stella, who attended the local high school, and the Mount Marissa School at Waterville. 4. Irene, who was married to Alfred Green, and they are the parents of one child, Joan. 5. Laura, who attended high school and spent one year in St. Joseph's Academy at Portland, and who has just entered the Madigan Hospital to become a nurse. 6. Annie, who was graduated from high school and attended Saint Joseph's Academy at Portland.

GEORGE JEROME McLAUGHLIN—One of the finest farms in the Limestone section of Maine is owned by George Jerome McLaughlin. One hundred and fifty acres in extent it is situated along the Fort Fairfield State road, where Mr. McLaughlin owns a second farm of some seventy-five acres. On both of these properties he raises potatoes of superior grade and other general farm produce. He has been very successful in this occupation, meeting and solving all problems of farming methods which have arisen. He was also a founder and is now a director of the Limestone Trust Company, and is otherwise active in the life of his community.

The McLaughlin family was established in Aroostook County when Bernard McLaughlin secured a tract of land from the government in 1847, and cleared it with the aid of his sons. He was one of the earliest settlers in the vicinity where he remained until his death.

George Jerome McLaughlin was born at Limestone on April 6, 1873, the son of George McLaughlin, who was a farmer, and of Maggie (Ludgate) McLaughlin. He attended the local public schools, and when he completed his education, he began work on his father's farm where he remained until he was twenty-three years old. From that time on he worked on several other farms in the neighborhood, and finally, in 1902, he purchased the farm where he now lives, which he has operated since that time. Some time later he acquired his smaller farm along the same road, which he also devotes to the raising of potatoes and other vegetables and fruit. Politically, Mr. McLaughlin supports the principles and candidates of the Republican party. He is affiliated fraternally with the Modern Woodmen of America. He and his family attend the local Roman Catholic church.

On April 24, 1907, he married Susie Dorsey, who was born at Fort Fairfield, the daughter of John S. and Elizabeth (Underwood) Dorsey. Her father was born in Maine, while her mother was born in the province of New Brunswick, Canada, and they were the parents of five children, four of whom are now living: Mrs. McLaughlin, Mrs. Annie Conant, Romeo, and Edward. Mr. and Mrs. McLaughlin are the parents of two children: 1. Eva Elizabeth, a graduate of the local high school, who entered St. Vincent's College in New York State in 1927. 2. Bessie Levina, a student in high school.

OLIVER W. HEMPHILL—A harness maker by trade, having learned this trade many years ago in Presque Isle, Oliver W. Hemphill is now the proprietor of Hemphill's leather store, which handles harness, trunks, bags, and all types of leather goods. He originally learned this work with S. H. Hemphill, but later carried on the work alone. He has been employed in many different kinds of occupations, not only in the harness and leather trade, but by railroads and lumber companies. Mr. Hemphill takes an active interest in the public affairs of his community, in which he is regarded with respect and esteem by his friends and with confidence and trust by those with whom he transacts business.

He was born in New Brunswick, Canada, on May 16, 1878, the son of William and Janie (Fleming) Hemphill, both natives of New Brunswick, where the mother still lives, although the father is deceased. Oliver W. Hemphill was educated in the public schools of New Brunswick; then was a farmer until twenty-one years of age, when he came to Presque Isle, Maine, where he learned the harness making trade and opened a shop in Easton, which he continued to operate for two and one-half years. Then he established a store in Presque Isle, which he maintained for two years until his health forced him to sell and obtain outdoor work. Thereupon he worked for two years on a farm; was employed later for two years by the A. V. Railroad Company; then was for two years with the St. John's Valley Railroad, owned by the same company; was inspector of ties for the Canadian Pacific Railroad; then did clerical work for the Scott Lumber Company; and finally became reëngaged in the harness business. In February, 1925, he moved into his present quarters in Presque Isle. Although Mr. Hemphill is one of the town's busiest men, he takes time to participate freely in the fraternal life of his community, being a member of the Independent Order of Odd Fellows, in which he is affiliated with both the Encampment and Canton; and a member of the Rebekahs.

Oliver W. Hemphill married Mrs. Lillian Morris, the widow of Moses Morris, who by her first marriage had two children: Douglas and Alma Morris. The Hemphill family attends the Methodist church, and is especially active in the work of this congregation.

REV. FREDERICK W. FOSTER—Like the apostles of old, Rev. Frederick W. Foster supports himself and his family as a layman and preaches as a voluntary service to his God and to his fellow man. He owns and operates a two hundred and forty acre farm at Fort Fairfield, Maine, located on the State highway between Fort Fairfield and Houlton, and is also an evangelist of the Methodist church. He is the author of a three volume work entitled "The Bible in Sermon," and in all three lines of activity, farmer, preacher, author, has achieved success.

Rev. Frederick W. Foster was born in Broomfield, Carleton County, New Brunswick, in November, 1871, son of James and Jane (Carvell) Foster, both natives of New Brunswick, who came to the States when Frederick W. Foster was a boy and settled in Fort Fairfield, Maine, where they have since lived and where the father is engaged in farming. The grandfather was a veteran of the Revolutionary War. Mr. Foster attended the public schools of New Brunswick and of Fort Fairfield, and then went to work on the farm, but from boyhood he was a close student of the Bible, and as time passed he felt called to preach the Gospel. Being a man of practical ability, he continued with his farming, but entered the ministry as a Methodist Evangelist, thus making it possible to continue his work as a farmer during the summer seasons and to preach during the winter. Even as Paul of old worked hard at his tent-making during the days, thus earning his living and making himself independent of the financial support of those whom he served, so Rev. Frederick W. Foster has for the past twenty-two years been the owner and operator of the big two hundred and forty acre farm on the State highway, known as the old Wingate Haines farm. He is a skilled agriculturist and has never been afraid of work, and from his farm he draws inspiration and material for his sermons, even as his Master drew upon everything about him for illustrative material and themes for his teaching. The healthful out-of-door work, the close touch with the every-day work of the world gives him an advantage over the isolated minister and enables him to bring his message forcibly to his hearers, as well as to deal sympathetically and understandingly with those whom he serves. In addition to his preaching and his farming activities, Rev. Foster is the author of a three volume work, which has been well received, entitled "The Bible in Sermon," published by the Nazarene Publishing Company, at Kansas City. Politically, he supports the principles and the candidates of the Republican party.

Rev. Frederick W. Foster married Belle Plummer, who was born in Waterville, Carleton County, New Brunswick, daughter of George Frederick and Corenia (Kimball) Plummer, farmers, both of whom were born in New Brunswick and have always lived there. Rev. and Mrs. Foster are the parents of two children: 1. Fenton P., who was educated in the public schools of Fort Fairfield, including the high school, in the University of Indiana, and in Bryant and Stratton's Business College. He is married to Nellie Nixon, and they have one child, Gerald, who lives with his father. 2. Carvell D., educated in Fort Fairfield public schools, including the high school, and in Bryant and Stratton's Business College; married Annie Hockinnaugh, and they have two children, Winston Frederick and Isabel Phyllis.

HAROLD K. GRAVES—A man who has played an important part in the business life of Maine despite the fact that he is still comparatively young is Harold K. Graves, who has spent the greater part of his time in Presque Isle, his native town, and has acquired in this and neighboring communities a host of friends among the farmers and business leaders. He is now with the Gould Electric Company and the Maine and New Brunswick Electrical Power Company in the capacity of commercial manager for the entire Maine and New Brunswick property group of the Central Public Service Corporation.

Mr. Graves was born at Presque Isle, Maine, on July 27, 1895, son of Richard and Bessie (Fraser) Graves, both living, and received his early education in the public schools of this town. He finished his work in the Presque Isle High School, from which he was graduated in the class of 1913. He then went to the University of Maine, remained there for one year, and decided to begin his career as a business man. He first took a position with the Stebbins Lumber Company, which placed him in charge of its retail trade. At the end of a three-year period with this company, he went into the hardware business of Sidney Graves who, although he bore the same name, was unrelated by blood to Harold K. Graves, and with this establishment served as clerk in the store, a position that he held until the incorporation of the business in 1919. Upon that occasion, Harold K. Graves was made manager, and continued to hold this office until July 1, 1928, when the business of the Graves Hardware Company was liquidated and the premises were sublet. It was at that time that he made his present connection with the electrical business as commercial manager in the Maine and New Brunswick territory for the Central Public Service Corporation. The steady rise of Mr. Graves in the business life of Presque Isle and Maine speaks well for his abilities, and his experience, extensive for one of his age, has placed him in a splendid position for further successful achievement in the years to come.

Aside from his own private business activities, Mr. Graves takes a prominent part in political and social affairs in his community. He is an independent Republican in his political views, and also is a member of the Free and Accepted Masons, in which order he is affiliated with the Blue Lodge. His religious connection is with the Congregational church.

In Presque Isle, Maine, on September 12, 1917, Harold K. Graves married Ruth E. Stevens, daughter of D. A. and Della (Hoyt) Stevens. By this marriage there have been three children: 1. Sidney K., born January 17, 1923. 2. Robert A., born June 18, 1925. 3. Christine, born September 18, 1926.

G. H. CARY—Having begun his life in business as a machinist, G. H. Cary later came to Presque Isle and entered into the coal business established here by his late father, E. S. Cary. G. H. Cary is the son of Emery S. and Frances A.

(Duncan) Cary. His father was a native of the State of Maine, but his mother was born in New Brunswick.

G. H. Cary was born at Presque Isle, Maine, on April 4, 1881, and was educated by going through all the grades of the public schools including the high school. After his school days were over, he went into New Hampshire where he learned the trade of a machinist and for eighteen years remained in New Hampshire following the trade in which he had made himself proficient. After that time he decided to return to his native town and so came back to Presque Isle where he found a place in his father's coal business. As time went on, he became a partner in the business, which was known as E. S. Cary and Company, and since the death of his father in 1918, he has been the sole owner. He is interested in all the activities of the Masonic order in which he has taken many degrees and attained to membership in the Ancient Arabic Order Nobles of the Mystic Shrine, and he is also a Knight Templar. He is a member of the Mooseleuk Club and an ardent Republican. He attends the Congregational church.

G. H. Cary married, June 6, 1906, Jennie May Morse, who was born in Manchester, New Hampshire, the daughter of Daniel and Ellen (Wilson) Morse. They have two children: Frances, and Ralph, who graduated from the Presque Isle High School and is now in the drug business.

ALFRED LOOMIS SAWYER, M. D., a leading physician of Fort Fairfield, Maine, has a large practice, but finds time also to take an active interest in public affairs and to hold public office. His father was a physician before him and practiced also in Fort Fairfield, so that there is an hereditary element both in his skill and experience and also in the good will that is extended towards him in the community.

Alfred Loomis Sawyer was born at Lisbon Falls, Maine, December 23, 1881, son of Alfred Dow and Mabel (Spear) Sawyer, the father a physician practicing at Fort Fairfield and other places, both parents born in Maine. Alfred L. Sawyer was educated in the schools of Fort Fairfield, both grammar and high school, and then went to Bowdoin, from which he graduated in

1904. He graduated from the Medical School of Maine in 1907 and then started to practice in Fort Fairfield as assistant to his father, and they worked thus together until the father died, after having practiced in Fort Fairfield from 1883. Since his father's death Dr. Sawyer has continued his father's practice while also adding a considerable practice of his own. Dr. Sawyer is an Independent in politics, though he leans to the Democrats. He has been a member of the school board three years. He belongs to the Blue Lodge, Free and Accepted Masons, of Fort Fairfield; Caribou Chapter, Royal Arch Masons; Presque Isle Council, Royal and Select Masters; the Commandery, Chickamauga, Tennessee, and Anah Temple, Ancient Arabic Order Nobles of the Mystic Shrine, of Bangor, Maine, of which he is a charter member. He belongs also to the county, State and American Medical associations.

Dr. Alfred L. Sawyer married Eva Mills, born at Fredericton, New Brunswick, daughter of Abraham and Christie (Morrison) Mills, who later came to this country and resided at St. Francis, Maine. There have been three children to the marriage: Tom Mills, and Alfred Loomis and Herbert Spear, twins. The family attends the Baptist church.

GUY J. DUREPO—With the assistance of his wife, who is an accomplished business woman, Guy J. Durepo, of Washburn, Maine, established a furniture store and undertaking business in 1913, and in both lines has become widely known and respected throughout Aroostook County.

Born in Limestone, Maine, May 1, 1884, Mr. Durepo was the son of John B. and Sarah (Currier) Durepo, both now deceased, and spent his boyhood on their farm. His father, who was of French origin, combined farming with starch manufacturing, and at one time had two factories in Limestone. Guy J. Durepo's first important position was with the Aroostook Valley Railroad Company, where he was time-keeper and paymaster for three years, and also purchased supplies for the road. He resigned to found his present business. Both Mr. and Mrs. Durepo passed the examination, June 29, 1928, of the Board of Embalming Examiners and have their certificates. They are now (1928) opening a modern undertaking establishment at Limestone.

Mr. Durepo is chief of the fire department of the Washburn Volunteer Fire Department, and through his untiring efforts and personal financial assistance in the way of a large cash donation the Washburn Fire Department now has a new American-La France 500-gallon pumper auto truck. He is interested in Republican politics. He is a member of the Free and Accepted Masons, the Rotary Club, and the Chamber of Commerce. He has lately developed an addition to his business by importing granite memorials from Vermont.

Guy J. Durepo married Annie E. Duncan, daughter of David L. and Catherine (Chapman) Duncan, both of Scotch descent. They are members of the Methodist Episcopal church.

ORRIN J. BISHOP—Among the better known of public-spirited citizens of Presque Isle, Aroostook County, is Orrin J. Bishop, dealer in horses, who was born at Fort Fairfield, July 22, 1883, son of Asa A. and Patience (Barnes) Bishop, both natives of Fort Fairfield. Asa Bishop is now (1927) living, having devoted the greater number of years of his active career to agriculture; he is widely known in Fort Fairfield neighborhood and greatly liked by his many friends. His wife, Patience (Barnes) Bishop, is deceased.

Orrin J. Bishop received his early education in the public schools and completed high school at Fort Fairfield. He went to work without loss of time, with his father on the farm, and within the space of a few years became engaged in the shipment of potatoes, and the purchase and transport of horses from the West to the Eastern coast. In 1923 Mr. Bishop gave his time exclusively to horse dealing, finding this occupation very profitable when carried on in an extensive manner. During the years of 1926 and 1927, or the two fiscal years ending on July 1 of those years, he brought forty-eight carloads of horses to the East. The majority of these were purchased in the West and Middle West, though a number came from odd sources scattered along the railroad rights of way, in small groups. Mr. Bishop is well acquainted among horse dealers of the principal western markets, and by them is notified

when specially highly bred animals are to be had. Moreover, he is so well known as a dealer in fine animals at Presque Isle and vicinity thereabout that he is constantly entrusted with orders for future delivery. Upon receipt of such an order he gets in touch with his western connections, and the consignment required is shipped forward at once, if expediency is requested, or held over until a carload of animals is made up for transport. Mr. Bishop also deals in harness at Presque Isle, as well as in other supplies, and finds that the popularity of automobiles and tractors has failed to eliminate the demands of Maine farmers for horses. He is a member of the Democratic party, the Blue Lodge of the Free and Accepted Masons, and the Mooseleuk Club. He attends the Congregational church and is a contributor to all charitable causes meriting support.

Orrin J. Bishop married (first) Eva Sharp, of Presque Isle, and following her death married (second) Grace Chandler. Orrin J. Bishop and his wife Grace are the parents of two children, Mary and James.

LOREN FRANK CARTER, M. D.—Among other natural advantages possessed by the State of Maine is that of climate, the air of the northern regions being especially pure and invigorating, and well suited to the treatment of tuberculosis. On October 7, 1920, the Northern Maine Sanitorium for Tuberculosis was complete and ready for the reception of its first patient, and Dr. Loren Frank Carter, newly appointed superintendent was there to receive him. Dr. Carter has been there ever since, and has brought the institution to a high degree of efficiency.

Born on January 3, 1892, son of Frank L. and Phoebe (Spencer) Carter, of Bradley, Maine, where his father was a farmer, Loren Frank Carter attended the public schools there, was graduated from the Old Town High School, and then spent a year in Colby, preparatory to matriculation at Bowdoin College Medical School, where he received his degree of Doctor of Medicine in 1917. The following year he was an interne in the Eastern Maine General Hospital at Bangor, and joined the Medical Corps for service in the World War, was commissioned first lieutenant, and saw actual service for ten months. After being discharged from the army, he engaged in private practice for nine months in Winterport, Maine, when he was appointed assistant superintendent at the Central Maine Sanitorium, and held that post until his appointment at Presque Isle. Dr. Carter is a member of the Free and Accepted Masons, of the Rotary Club, of the State and county medical societies, and of the American Medical Association. He attends the Congregational church.

Dr. Carter married, June 8, 1918, Jean Mackenzie, who was born in Rexton, New Brunswick, Canada.

WILLIAM R. YERXA—His friends and patrons everywhere have reason to be well satisfied with the excellent annual results of the potato farming of William D. Yerxa, member of the widely known firm of Moore and Yerxa, of Houlton, farmers and potato growers and dealers, since he has put into practice his acknowledged abilities in his specialty and his honest methods of dealing with all to whom his increasing business is known, in Maine or elsewhere. He is one of the most practical and thoroughgoing men in his line in this section of the State, and is highly esteemed in his business and social life.

William R. Yerxa was born July 13, 1866, at Fredericton, New Brunswick, son of William L. and Jennie T. (Douglas) Yerxa, both natives and residents of that province. He received his education in the schools of his boyhood and, coming to Boston, Massachusetts, worked there for twenty-five years. Removing to Houlton afterwards, he was in the employ of the American Express Company five years, and of the Canadian and Pacific Railroad twelve years. It was then that he started in the trucking business, and having bought a farm, gave up the trucking for the farming line, then becoming associated with A. E. Moore in the present firm of Moore and Yerxa, potato dealers and farmers. This firm jointly owns several farming properties, including a year-round dairy farm on the Foxcroft Road, and a lumber mill on the Canadian and Pacific Railroad, having in their employ twenty-five men. Politically, Mr. Yerxa is associated with the interests of the Republican party; he is a charter member of the Benevolent and Protective Order of Elks; and with his family he attends the Presbyterian church.

William R. Yerxa married Henrietta Pennington. They have four children: 1. Clarence, who attended the Houlton public schools, and was graduated at Bowdoin College, and Eastman Business College, Poughkeepsie, New York, in accountancy. 2. Helen, married Russell Cahill, attorney-at-law, at Springfield, Massachusetts. 3. Ruth. 4. George, attended Houlton public schools and is now a student in Eastman Business College.

INDEX

TO VOLUME IV ONLY

INDEX